COMPLETE COLLEGE FINANCING GUIDE

Second Edition

by

MARGUERITE J. DENNIS

DEAN OF ENROLLMENT AND RETENTION MANAGEMENT

SUFFOLK UNIVERSITY

BOSTON, MASSACHUSETTS

BARRON'S

All inquiries should be addressed to:
Barron's Educational Series, Inc.
250 Wireless Boulevard
Hauppauge, NY 11788

International Standard Book No. 0-8120-4950-0

Library of Congress Catalog No. 91-42484

Library of Congress Cataloging-in-Publication Data

Dennis, Marguerite J., 1946–
    Barron's complete college financing guide / by
Marguerite J. Dennis.
        p.   cm.
    Rev. ed. of: Dollars for scholars. c 1989.
    ISBN 0-8120-4950-0
    1. Student aid—United States—Handbooks, manuals, etc.
    2. Student loan funds—United States—Handbooks, manuals,
etc. I. Dennis, Marguerite, J., 1946–   Dollars for scholars.
II. Title. III. Title: Complete college financing guide.
LB2337.4.D455   1992
378.3'0973—dc20   91-42484
                                           CIP

PRINTED IN THE UNITED STATES OF AMERICA
2345 100 987654321

TABLE OF CONTENTS

INTRODUCTION

As a nation we spend more on higher education than most other countries. Postsecondary education, in particular, is a major American industry. In a recent year over $148 billion—approximately 7% of the nation's gross national product—was spent on higher education.

Moreover, a greater proportion of students pursue postsecondary education in the United States than in any other industrialized country. Currently more than 14 million students study at over 8,000 institutions of higher learning throughout the country. According to the U.S. Bureau of Labor Statistics, in 1989 six out of ten high school graduates enrolled in college. This represents the highest college entrance rate ever for high school graduates.

About 6 million undergraduate students received some form of financial assistance. The average amount of Title IV money awarded was approximately $3200. Students enrolled in private schools received an average of $4100.

Despite these statistics, an increasing number of Americans believe that, whereas a college education is important for their children's future, escalating college costs will soon make a college education unaffordable for all except the wealthy. Many families have unrealistic expectations about the cost of higher education, and some high school students have either ruled out college or are uncertain about continuing their education beyond high school. In a recent Gallup poll commissioned by the Council for the Advancement and Support of Education, nearly 25% of the high school students surveyed were unaware of the availability of financial aid to finance a college education. The most frequently mentioned reason for not attending college was lack of money.

Many parents believe that they cannot afford to send their children to college and that funds from other sources are not available to them. Both parents and students have limited knowledge about financial aid programs, and believe that it is difficult, if not impossible, to get accurate information about the financial assistance process. Parents also feel that saving for their child's education reduces whatever slim chance they may have had of obtaining financial aid. Also, many families believe that applying for financial aid is a waste of time because aid is not available for "people like us." And many families do not consider employment and loans as financial aid.

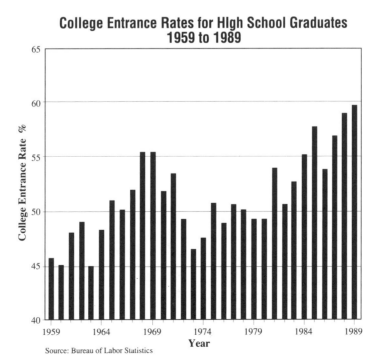

College Entrance Rates for High School Graduates 1959 to 1989

Source: Bureau of Labor Statistics

College Costs

A college education is fast becoming a major consumer purchase, second only to buying a house. Over the past 10 years, college costs have escalated. The cost of tuition at a private college or university increased 50% and tuition costs at public institutions rose 31%. Last year the average total cost of education, including tuition, room and board, and miscellaneous expenses, for 1 year at a public college was $7000. The average annual cost at a private college or university was $14,000. The cost of attending some Ivy League colleges can be more than $20,000 a year. For the average American, stretching the family budget to accommodate such costs is unrealistic. However, to believe that a college education is unaffordable is also unrealistic.

Although college costs continue to increase between 5 and 10% each year, there are many institutions of higher learning that are within the economic reach of most Americans. Last year tuition and fees (not including room and board) at 4-year public institutions averaged $1800 and 2-year public colleges averaged $884. Only 4% of all college students attend schools with tuition costs exceeding $10,000, and only 50% of those students pay the full cost of attendance. The majority of students enrolled in colleges and universities last year paid less than $3000 in tuition costs. The diversity of American higher education presents several options to students and their parents.

Student Financial Aid

Approximately 60% of all students enrolled in higher education receive some type of financial assistance from federal, state, or school sources. Federal aid remains the largest source of financial aid. However, last year cumulative awards from state governments totaled over $2 billion in grant assistance. Nearly 2 million college students received some financial assistance from their state governments. Funding from institutional sources has also substantially increased in the last 10 years. Last year about 30% of all aided undergraduate students received financial assistance from their colleges or universities. And the total amount of financial aid awarded to students from all sources exceeded $28 billion. In short, financial aid from sources other than parents pays for about 60% of the bills of financial aid recipients.

It is important to view college costs in their proper perspective. There are many excellent low cost schools, and funds are available from federal, state, school, corporate, and other sources to help finance an education at most colleges. The federal and state governments can provide assistance, information, and funding. Ultimately, however, each student must design and implement his or her own college financing plan. It is important for parents and students to realize that the job of financing a college education rests primarily with them.

Students should seek information as early as possible about all of the available funding sources. Sometimes the information that is given to high school students is inaccurate, out of date, or confusing. As a result, understanding the process becomes difficult. The number of different financial aid programs, the demands of the application process, and changes in regulations and in eligibility criteria further complicate the process. Students and their parents will need help in understanding the types of aid that are available and the procedures to apply for financial assistance. Help is available from college financial aid officers and from federal, state, and school financial aid publications.

This book will guide you in identifying the sources of financial funding that you and your family may need in order for you to attend a college or university and the ways to apply for these funds. Student financial assistance and student financial planning are discussed. The financial aid application process is outlined along with the major federal aid programs. The financial aid delivery process is presented, and the consequences of unmanageable student debt are discussed. This book attempts to simplify what may appear to be a complicated and confusing process—applying for financial aid and successfully receiving financial assistance.

The process of awarding financial aid to students has changed in recent years, but these changes do not necessarily signal an end to receiving financial aid. They may alter the composition of financial resources and will require earlier and better planning on the part of families. There is some combination of funding that will work for each student.

Is College Worth the Investment?

The fact remains that attending a college or university is expensive and it is likely that the cost will continue to increase in the future. So is college really worth the investment of time and money? The answer is an unequivocal yes. First, many economists predict that most jobs, by the year 2000, will require a college degree. Second, labor reports indicate that workers with college degrees have lower rates of unemployment than do high school graduates. Third, degree holders can expect to earn over $600,000 more during their working years than can their high school counterparts. In 1989, the median pay for all males working full-time was $27,331, but male college graduates earned on average $40,164. The rate of return to investment in college has been estimated to be almost 29%. On the other hand, the median income for men with only high school diplomas declined 16% during the last 10 years, and demographers predict that the economic gap between the college-educated employee and the high-school-educated worker will continue to widen in the future.

Is college worth the investment of time and money? You be the judge.

1 KEY PLAYERS IN THE COLLEGE FINANCING GAME

While most parents believe that it is their responsibility to finance their children's education, most families have not adequately saved for college, have little knowledge about the college financing process, and know even less about the variety of colleges and universities available. Usually families wait until their children are juniors or seniors in high school to begin assembling their college financing strategy. And it isn't until the student is accepted and a decision is made to enroll at a specific school that a family knows what their college expenses will be. Consider the following: letters of admission are usually mailed in March; financial aid notices are generally sent in April; by May 1 students are expected to notify all schools of their decision either to enroll or to decline acceptance; and school begins in August. If a family has not adequately prepared, there isn't a lot of time to get their college financing house in order.

In the past families have often relied on the federal government, through the school's financial aid director, to tell them how their child's education would be financed. This strategy neither is wise nor is recommended. The federal government does not have the money it once did to finance higher education. Loans have replaced grants as the federal government's chief funding source, and changes in the way financial need is determined makes it impracticable to wait until a student is ready to enter college to begin planning how the family will finance his or her education.

There are nine key players in the college financing game, each with a specific role:

1. Parents
2. Students
3. The Federal Government
4. State Governments
5. Colleges and Universities
6. The Financial Aid Director
7. Financial Experts—Certified Financial Planner, Accountant, Banker
8. Private Organizations and Foundations
9. The Library

Let's examine the role of each of the nine key players.

Parents The primary responsibility for financing a child's education rests with the parents. Most families believe that, despite high costs, a college education is still a worthwhile investment. Yet most families do not have a financial strategy for meeting future college bills, nor have they developed a regular savings program. Some financial experts suggest that, as soon as a child is born, the parents should begin investigating college financing options and should put aside some money each week or each month for their child's future tuition needs. Whatever the strategy and whatever the family income, parents should not wait until a school's financial aid award letter arrives in the mail to initiate a college financing plan. Such a passive approach to college financing is a luxury few parents can afford.

Students Except for the parents, students have the greatest responsibility in financing their college education. Students should plan to save some money during their high school years and to work during their college years to reduce the financial burden on their parents and to lower their loan debt. In fact, research indicates that students who work part-time do not suffer academically and are more likely to stay in college.

The Federal Government Although in recent years the federal government has changed its higher education funding philosophy, it still provides over 70% of all of the financial aid awarded to college students.

State Governments Most states are very generous to students. All states have some need-based financial assistance programs, and many also offer some type of merit scholarship or grant programs. Parents and students should find out what state sources are available and what they must do to qualify for these funds.

Colleges and Universities Most schools offer generous scholarship, grant, and loan programs to their students. Many schools also offer flexible payment plans and financing options. Each school has its own philosophy about awarding financial aid, and the student should find out what it is before enrolling. Does the school meet full need? Does the school meet a portion of need? Does the college offer institutional money to families who do not qualify for federal or state aid? Does the school meet full need with grants and loans? What is the average indebtedness of graduating students? Is the same type of funding available after the first year? These are some of the questions you should ask before enrolling in any college or university.

The Financial Aid Director A key player in the college financing game is the school's financial aid director or counselor. Unfortunately most families do not use this resource until the child has been accepted and decides to enroll at a particular school. Many schools offer financial aid workshops which allow a family to receive personalized attention and help in filling out the necessary financial aid forms. Some financial aid offices can provide families, at the time of application, with an estimate of what their financial aid award is likely to be. This kind of assistance allows a family to decide whether they can afford a particular school and, if so, what kind of aid is available to meet their financial need at that college or university.

Financial Experts—Certified Financial Planner, Accountant, Banker These financial experts can offer information and counseling to parents on the best way to finance their child's college education through investments and savings programs. Certified financial planners can tell parents how to shift income, how to increase their resources, and how to time investments to meet future tuition bills. Some financial planners charge only a fee for their services; others sell financial products (investments) as part of their program. The following list of organizations can assist interested parents

with information on how to select a certified financial planner:

Certified Financial Planner

International Board of Standards and Practices for
    Certified Financial Planners, Inc.
5445 DTC Parkway
Englewood, Colorado 80111
(303) 850-0333

Chartered Financial Analyst

Institute of Chartered Financial Analysts
P.O. Box 3668
Charlottesville, Virginia 22903
(804) 977-6600

Chartered Financial Consultant

American College
270 Bryn Mawr Avenue
Bryn Mawr, Pennsylvania 19010
(215) 526-1000

Private Organizations and Foundations Many private organizations and foundations provide financial assistance to students. Some awards are based on need; others, on merit. Some are awarded to students enrolled in a particular major. Some organizations make awards to students from a specific region or high school. Families should begin as soon as possible to locate sources that may be able to provide some financial assistance.

The Library There are several books and magazines dealing with the subject of student financial aid. Instead of buying these sources, the student can visit the local library, which will have many financial aid publications, and begin his or her own college financing investigation.

2 HOW TO APPLY FOR FINANCIAL AID

This chapter will assist you in understanding the financial aid delivery process and your role in applying for and receiving aid. Applying for financial aid can be a confusing process. Many parents are not adequately informed and have unrealistic notions regarding how much money they will need to finance their child's education. The federal government and state governments spend millions of dollars on informational materials. However, many students who receive financial aid materials find the information confusing. Some data are incorrect, out of date, or difficult to understand. It is essential that students and their families learn of the availability of student aid programs and understand the methods of applying for and securing that aid.

Important Facts to Know

1. No matter what your family income, apply for financial aid. If you are denied financial assistance one year, apply the following year.

2. Apply early. You may be eligible for funding but may be denied aid if the money runs out. Check the deadlines set by your college or university.

3. Males must register for the draft to receive financial aid. Check with your local post office for further information and application forms.

4. Don't leave anything blank on the financial aid application you send to the service agency, your school application for financial aid, or your loan application form.

5. Don't forget to sign the application form you submit to the service agency. Also sign all school application forms and loan forms.

6. Always keep a copy of all of your applications and forms.

7. Don't cross out or write in the margins of your application and loan forms. If you hand in neat, clearly written applications, less time will be required to process your form.

8. Fill in your federal financial aid applications with a No. 2 pencil. Don't use a ballpoint pen.

9. Don't forget to include the correct processing fee with your application.

10. Only original application forms will be accepted. Don't mail photocopies.

11. Mail your completed financial aid application to the service agency, not to the college. Mail your completed school financial aid application to the office of financial aid.

Important Terms to Know

Acknowledgment Report   A report sent to the student after the need analysis form has been received by one of the processing agencies.

American College Testing Program (ACT)   A service agency that analyzes family need and family contribution.

Application for Federal and State Student Aid (AFSSA)   A free financial aid application form, accepted by the state of Illinois, which determines an applicant's financial aid eligibility.

Application for Federal Student Aid (AFSA)   A need analysis form used to apply for a Pell Grant and other federal aid programs.

College Scholarship Service (CSS)   A service agency that analyzes family need and family contribution.

Family Financial Statement (FFS)   An application form used to determine a family's financial contribution and financial need. The American College Testing Program processes this form and sends the results to colleges and universities. This form may be used to apply for a Pell Grant, a state award, a Stafford Student Loan, and other types of financial aid.

Financial Aid Form (FAF)   An application form used to determine a family's financial contribution and financial need. The College Scholarship Service of the College Board processes this form and sends the results to colleges and universities. This form may be used to apply for a Pell Grant, a state award, a Stafford Student Loan, and other types of financial aid.

Graduate and Professional School Financial Application Service (GAPSFAS)   A financial aid application form used to determine contribution and financial aid eligibility for graduate and professional students.

Information Request Form   The form that a student receives when the application for a Pell Grant has been rejected. Additional or corrected information is requested from the applicant.

Information Review Form   A form sent to Pell Grant applicants. It summarizes information submitted on the applicant's need analysis form. The financial aid applicant should review this summary for accuracy.

Multiple Data Entry System   A system that allows financial aid applicants to apply for a Pell Grant, federal aid, state aid, and aid from a college or university. Several agencies have contracts with the Department of Education to process information submitted by financial aid applicants. These agencies send the data to a central processor, which calculates the Family Contribution and Pell Grant Index. The information is then sent back to the agency, which, in turn, sends the applicant a Student Aid Report. Currently, there are four multiple data entry services:

1. American College Testing Program
2. College Scholarship Service
3. Pennsylvania Higher Education Assistance Agency
4. United Student Aid Funds

Need Analysis Form   The document, completed either by a student alone (independent student) or by a student and his or her family (dependent student), that determines the student's eligibility for financial assistance. Currently, there are six approved need analysis forms:

1. Application for Federal Student Aid (AFSA)
2. Application for Federal and State Student Aid (AFSSA)
3. Family Financial Statement (FFS)
4. Financial Aid Form (FAF)
5. Pennsylvania Higher Education Assistance Agency Form (PHEAA)
6. Singlefile Form

Part B Loans   Loans authorized under Part B of the Higher Education Act: Stafford Student Loans, PLUS loans, and SLS loans.

Payment Voucher   Part 3 of the Student Aid Report. Students must submit this information to their school's financial aid officer so that the Pell Grant amount can be determined by the financial aid officer.

Pell Grant Index   The number on the Student Aid Report indicating eligibility for the Pell Grant Program. This differs from the Family Contribution number, which indicates eligibility for campus-based programs and the Stafford Student Loan Program.

Pennsylvania Higher Education Assistance Agency Form (PHEAA)   A financial aid form used by residents of Pennsylvania who enroll in colleges or universities within the state.

Simplified Needs Test   An application for financial aid for families who have adjusted gross incomes under $15,000 and who have filed IRS Form 1040A or 1040 EZ, or were not required to file income tax forms.

Singlefile Form   The need analysis form processed by United Student Aid Funds, one of the multiple data entry processors.

Student Aid Application for California (SAAC)   A financial aid form used by residents of California who enroll in colleges and universities within the state.

Student Aid Report (SAR)   A student's official notification of Pell Grant eligibility. The SAR is generally received by the student and the school 4–6 weeks after the student submits the application. The Pell Grant Index is the number that determines Pell Grant eligibility. The Family Contribution number determines eligibility for campus-based programs and the Stafford Student Loan Program. The student is required to sign a three-part statement found at the end of Part 1 of the SAR. The Statement of Updated Information certifies that information on the SAR is correct as of the date the form was signed. The Statement of Educational Purpose certifies that the student agrees to use any financial assistance received from the Department of Education only for educational expenses. The student must also confirm that he or she does not owe a refund on any Title IV grant, and is not in default on any Title IV loan. The Statement of Registration Status certifies that required students have registered with the Selective Service.

The SAR of applicants eligible to receive a Pell Grant consists of three parts. The first part, called the Information Summary, notifies applicants of their Pell Grant eligibility and their Pell Grant Index. The second part, the Information Review Form, should be reviewed for errors and any needed corrections made. The student then signs the certification statement on the back of Part 2 and returns only that part. A new SAR will be received within 4–6 weeks. The third part of the SAR, the Payment Voucher, is used by the applicant's college or university to determine the amount of the Pell Grant award. If all of the information on the SAR is correct and the student is eligible to receive a Pell Grant, he or she should send all three parts to the school's financial aid officer.

Receiving only a two-part SAR indicates Pell Grant ineligibility. The first part, the Information Summary, informs the applicant of Pell Grant ineligibility but may indicate eligibility for other types of federal financial aid. The second part, the Information Review Form, should be reviewed for errors because, even if an applicant is denied a Pell Grant, the SAR should be sent to his or her college or university. Most schools cannot award other types of aid without having this form on file.

For information about the Pell Grant Program you may call the Federal Student Aid Information Center between the hours of 9:00 A.M. and 5:30 P.M. (EST) Monday through Friday. Here are two important numbers:

1-800-4 FED AID   If you need assistance filing your SAR or want to know the eligibility requirements for a Pell Grant.

1-301-722-9200   If you want to know whether your application has been processed or if you want a duplicate SAR.

Call 1-301-369-0518 if you are hearing-impaired.

Verification   The process of certifying a certain percentage of financial aid applications for accuracy. Colleges and universities are required by federal law to certify at least 30% of their applicants for all Title IV programs. The verification worksheet, provided by the processing agency or school, requests information on family size, federal income tax returns, and child support. An applicant selected for verification cannot receive any federal student aid until he or she completes the verification worksheets and submits the required IRS and any other requested forms.

Timetable for Applying for Financial Aid—Senior Year of High School

January
1. By January you should have all of the necessary financial aid application forms from your college, university, or proprietary school. Need analysis forms are usually mailed to high schools and to colleges and universities. You may obtain the necessary forms from your high school guidance counselor or college financial aid director.
2. The next step is to gather all of the documents and information you and your parents will need in order to complete the application forms: income tax returns, mortgage information, bank statements, medical and dental bills, business records, statements of veteran's benefits, social security benefits or welfare benefits, farm records, and documents of additional income, such as income from stocks, bonds, or other investments.

3. You should read carefully all of the instructions for completing the institution's financial aid application and the need analysis forms. Be certain you have answered all of the questions accurately and honestly. Don't submit an application with erasures or notations in the margins. Don't forget to sign the application form, and be sure to enclose a check or money order for the processing fee. Request that a copy of the results be sent to your school's financial aid director, the Department of Education, and your state's scholarship agency.

4. You may use any of the following forms to apply for federal aid, including a Pell Grant:

   Application for Federal Student Aid (AFSA)

   United States Department of Education Form

   Application for Pennsylvania State Grant and Federal Student Aid (PHEAA)

   The Pennsylvania Higher Education Assistance Agency's Form

   Singlefile Form

   United Student Aid Funds Form

   The following forms collect additional information used in applying for nonfederal aid programs:

   Family Financial Statement (FFS)

   The American College Testing Program Form

   Financial Aid Form (FAF)

   The College Scholarship Service Form

5. For information on your application, you may contact the service agencies at the following addresses:

   Application for Federal Student Aid
   Federal Student Aid Programs
   c/o AFSA Processor
   Box 6371
   Princeton, New Jersey 08541
   1-301-722-9200

   Application for Pennsylvania State Grant and Federal Student Aid
   c/o Pennsylvania Higher Education Assistance Agency
   P.O. Box 3157
   Harrisburg, Pennsylvania 17105
   1-800-692-7435 (PA residents only)
   1-717-257-2800

   Family Financial Statement
   American College Testing Program
   P.O. Box 4005
   Iowa City, Iowa 52243
   1-319-337-1200

Financial Aid Form
College Scholarship Service
P.O. Box 6306
Princeton, New Jersey 08541-6306
1-609-951-1025

Singlefile Form
United Student Aid Funds
P.O. Box 50827
Indianapolis, Indiana 46250
(317) 841-1630
1-800-448-3530
1-800-772-3537

Spanish Application for Federal Student Aid Programs
Federal Student Aid Programs
P.O. Box 4162
Iowa City, Iowa 52244

APPLY AS SOON AFTER JANUARY 1 AS POSSIBLE.

6. Last year, the processing fees were as follows:

$ 8.75 — One school receives your application

$ 15.50 — Two schools receive your application

$ 22.25 — Three schools receive your application

$ 29.00 — Four schools receive your application

$ 35.75 — Five schools receive your application

$ 42.50 — Six schools receive your application

$ 49.25 — Seven schools receive your application

$ 56.00 — Eight schools receive your application

Note: Processing fees will increase each year. Read carefully to determine the current cost.

February

1. After submitting your financial aid application, you will receive a Confirmation or Acknowledgment Report, which allows you to verify that the information you submitted was correctly processed. Allow 3 weeks for this form to arrive. You will have an opportunity to review the information and make any necessary corrections.

2. Approximately 4–6 weeks after you submit your application for financial aid, you will receive a report from the service agency you selected containing information on your family's expected contribution and your eligibility for financial assistance. Your college or university and your state's scholarship agency will receive a similar report. If you applied for a Pell Grant, you will receive a Student Aid Report (SAR) that indicates your Pell Grant eligibility. If you are eligible to receive a Pell Grant, send a signed copy of your SAR to your college or university. Once you decide on a school, submit all parts of the SAR to the school's office of financial aid. You are able to revise information previously submitted. Be certain that all new information is sent to both the service agency and the Pell Grant processor.

3. You and your parents should discuss the results of the financial aid application with regard to family contribution, student contribution, student employment, and educational costs. Carefully plan your student budget.

4. If you have any questions about your expected family contribution or Pell Grant eligibility, make an appointment to discuss the questions with a financial aid counselor at your school. Also discuss with the financial aid counselor any changes in your family's financial situation.

March–July

1. Most colleges and universities make financial aid decisions during this time. If your application is complete, your chances of receiving your award letter early are greater than if additional information is required. Check on the status of your application and submit any required forms.

2. Your financial aid award letter is the official document from your school indicating the school budget, the expected family contribution, and the amount of financial aid you will receive for the year. This includes awards from the following programs: Pell Grant, Supplemental Educational Opportunity Grant, College Work-Study, Carl D. Perkins Student Loan, Stafford Student Loan, PLUS or SLS loans, institutional aid, outside awards, and state financial aid.

3. The award letter will also indicate how and when your financial aid will be disbursed and will specify any special conditions regarding the aid. If you were awarded a loan, the interest rate, repayment, and cancellation and deferment options will be included. If you were awarded employment as part of your aid package, you will be informed of your rate of pay and the number of hours you will be permitted to work each week, as well as the maximum amount of money you are entitled to earn. In most cases it will be up to you to find a job. Seek the assistance of your school's financial aid officer, who may have a listing of available jobs, or your school's placement officer.

Each school determines how it will award financial aid. Most colleges credit a student's account, and most schools will make cash refunds to students if the monies awarded exceed tuition, fees, and other direct school charges. Remember that awards are divided in half or in thirds, depending on the academic term (semester or quarter system). Be certain you understand your school's refund system and methods of disbursement.

4. You must sign and return a copy of your award letter to your school if you agree to accept the offer of financial aid. If you need additional funds, or have questions about the aid you were awarded, make an appointment to speak with a financial aid counselor at your school. Do not

wait until the time of registration to do this; act immediately to clarify any questions or problems you have. Keep your award letter in a safe place. This letter serves as an official document indicating how much money you will receive to finance your education for the next school year. Bring it with you to registration.

5. Spring is the time to apply for any loan program that has a separate application form, including Stafford Student Loans, PLUS, and SLS loans. Be certain that you have all necessary applications. Because it takes approximately 6–8 weeks for a loan to be processed, and for the loan check to arrive at your school, you should submit your loan forms as soon as possible.

6. If officials of state agencies have received information from your financial aid application, they will use these data to determine your eligibility to receive funding from state sources. State awards are sent to individual colleges and universities and are incorporated into a student's total financial aid award for the year. Check with your state educational agency if you have not been notified.

7. May 1 is the last date for one of the approved processors to receive your application for financial aid for the current academic year.

Information Commonly Requested on Financial Aid Applications

Most applications for financial aid will request the following information:

Name of Applicant

Permanent Mailing Address

Social Security Number

Home Telephone

State of Legal Residence

Citizenship

Marital Status of Applicant

School Code Number

Enrollment Status

Year in College

Course of Study

Expected Date of Graduation

Colleges Previously Attended

Driver's License Number

Dislocated Worker Status of Applicant and Parents

Displaced Homemaker Status of Applicant and Parents

Income Tax Return of Applicant and Parents

Total Number of Income Tax Exemptions of Applicant and Parents

Gross Income and Assets

Income Tax Paid

Earned Income, Tips

Untaxed Income and Benefits, Dividends

Other Income

Social Security Benefits

Workers Compensation Benefits

Welfare Benefits

Child Support Payments

Alimony Payments

Interest Income

Dividend Income

Net Income from Business, Farm, Trusts, Pensions, Rents, Etc.

Gross Liabilities

Gross Deductions

Uninsured Medical and Dental Expenses

Elementary, Junior High School, and High School Tuition for Number of Dependent Children

IRA Accounts

Savings and Checking Account Amounts of Applicant and Parents

Outstanding Loans

Market Value of Home

Outstanding Mortgage

Real Estate Investments

Veterans' Educational Benefits

Savings, Stocks, Bonds, Pension Plans

Date of Birth of Applicant

Veteran Status

Number of Family Members

Number of Family Members in College

Name and Address of Parents

Occupation of Parents

Marital Status of Parents

State of Legal Residence of Parents

Student Loan Default Status of Applicant

Federal Grant Refund Status of Applicant

Stafford Student Loan Information

Names and Codes of Colleges to Receive
Information

You will need the following documents to complete your application:

Federal, State and Local Income Tax Returns

Bank Statements

Mortgage Information

Medical and Dental Bills

Information on Stocks, Bonds, and Other
Investments

Business Records

Farm Records

W-2 Forms

Untaxed Income Records

Remember that financial aid eligibility is based on your previous year's income. Be certain to keep accurate financial records, which will save you time in completing the financial aid application. Also, your application may be selected for verification. It will be much easier to complete that process if your financial records and documents are in order and are readily available.

Most colleges and universities have their own financial aid applications. The following example indicates the type of information usually requested by college officials.

SAMPLE COLLEGE FINANCIAL AID APPLICATION
Checklist

- Financial Aid Form (FAF) must be forwarded from the College Scholarship Service (CSS), Princeton, NJ.

- Signed copy of parents' 1040 (A) (EZ) 1992 Federal Tax Return, due April 15, 1993.

- Signed copy of student's 1040 (A) (EZ) 1992 Federal Tax Return, due April 15, 1993. (NOTE: All students—dependent and independent—must submit a copy of their tax return.)

- Financial Aid Transcript(s) (not academic transcripts) from all previously attended colleges/universities. This transcript is required even though no financial aid was received at the previous school.

- Statement (from the source) detailing total amount of nontaxable income received during 1992, i.e., AFDC, Welfare, Social Security, Veteran's Benefits, Workers Compensation, Child Support, etc.

- Independent Students—If you are filing as an independent student, this office may require other documentation for proof of claim, i.e., rent receipts, copy of parents' tax return, parents' health insurance records, etc.

1. Name _____

   Social Security No. _____

2. Permanent Address _____

   _____

   Mailing Address _____

3. Status: Freshman ____   Sophomore ____   Junior ____   Senior ____

   School enrolled in: ____Liberal Arts & Sciences   ____School of Management

   No. of credits you plan to enroll for: Fall ____

   (12 or more credits is full-time)   Spring ____

4. Please check those types of aid for which you wish to be considered:

   ____Grants/Scholarships

   ____Loans

   ____Work-Study/Employment

5. a) Are you a U.S. citizen? ____Yes   ____No

   b) Are you a permanent resident of the U.S.?

   ____Yes   ____No   If yes, Registration No. _____

   Note: Eligible noncitizens must submit proof of permanent resident status with this application.

   c) * Optional: City and state of legal residence: _____

   _____* Race _____

6. Have you attended any colleges or universities? If yes, please list the years attended. If you attended another university or college, and have not already done so, you must also submit a financial aid transcript even if you received no financial aid.

   _____

   _____

* Certain scholarships have specific criteria, so it is to your benefit to provide this information.

7. Have you ever borrowed under the Perkins Loan/Stafford Student Loan Program?

___Yes   ___No

8. Are you eligible for Tuition Remission Benefits through an employer? ___Yes   ___No

9. Outside employment—List both full- and part-time jobs you plan to hold during summer, and fall/spring semesters. (If married, please also indicate spouse's earnings.)

	Co. Name	Occupation	Number of Hours per Week	Take-Home Pay per Week	Total Pay
Summer	_____	_____	_____	_____	_____
	_____	_____	_____	_____	_____
	_____	_____	_____	_____	_____
Fall/Spring	_____	_____	_____	_____	_____
	_____	_____	_____	_____	_____
	_____	_____	_____	_____	_____

10. Explain any special circumstances, such as illness, age, or unusual family expenses, which may make it difficult for you or your family to contribute to your educational expenses. Where necessary, attach a copy of documentation or proof of your claim.

_____

_____

11. If you are planning to apply for a Stafford Student Loan please complete the following:

Bank Address:_____

_____

DEPENDENT/INDEPENDENT VERIFICATION

STUDENT'S STATUS

12. a) Was the student born before January 1, 1965? ___Yes   ___No

b) Is the student a veteran of the U.S. Armed Forces? ___Yes   ___No

c) Is the student a ward of the court or are both parents dead? ___Yes   ___No

d) Does the student have legal dependents other than a spouse? ___Yes   ___No

If you answered "Yes" to 12a, 12b, 12c, and 12d, please send student's (spouse's) 1992 federal tax return and proceed to question 17.

If you answered "No" to all 12a, 12b, 12c, and 12d, and you are: unmarried and will be an undergraduate student, go to question 13; married or will be a graduate/professional student, go to question 16.

UNMARRIED UNDERGRADUATE STUDENTS

13. Was the student claimed by parents as a U.S. income tax exemption in:

_____ (year)   ___Yes   ___No   _____ (year)   ___Yes   ___No

14. Did the student receive federal student aid during the _____ (year) school year?

___Yes   ___No

15. Were the student's total income and benefits more than $4000 in

_____ (year)   ___ Yes   ___ No

_____ (year)   ___ Yes   ___ No

Please submit copies of parents' and student's _____ (year) and _____ (year) federal tax returns.

MARRIED STUDENTS

16. Will the student be claimed by parents as a U.S. income tax exemption in _____ (year)?

___ Yes   ___ No

Please submit parents' and student's _____ (year) federal tax returns, if not already on file.

17. Did your parents/you or will your parents/you file an income tax return(s) for _____ (year) (IRS Form 1040, 1040A, or 1040EZ)? Check one: ___ Yes   ___ No

18. If your parents/you answered "Yes" to question 17 attach a signed copy of your parents'/your (and spouse's) _____ (year) income tax return (IRS Form 1040, 1040A, 1040EZ). If your parents filed separate tax returns for _____ (year), attach a signed copy of each tax return. REMINDER: If you are applying for fall _____ (year) and spring _____ (year) financial aid consideration (with the exception of Stafford Student Loan or PLUS only applicants) you must submit copies of your parents/your income tax returns by April 15, or you will be considered a late applicant.

- If your parents/you did not keep a copy of the _____ (year) tax return, request a copy from the regional office of the Internal Revenue Service (IRS) or from the person who prepared the return.

- If your parents/you filed a _____ (year) tax return with Puerto Rico or a foreign country, attach a signed copy of that tax return.

19. If your parents/you answered "No" to question 17, list your parents'/your or your spouse's employers and other sources of income received in _____ (year) and the amount of money from each employer and source of income.

List each (year) employer and source of income, and amount received.

_____ $ _____

_____ $ _____

20. List the amount of child support your parent(s) or you received in _____ (year): $_____

21. List the amount of all nontaxable income you and/or your parents received during _____ (year):

$_____. Include benefits such as: ___ Social Security   ___ AFDC
     ___ Workers Compensation

REMINDER: Applicants must submit a letter of statement from the appropriate office (i.e., Social Security, AFDC) listing the total amount of funding received during _____ (year). This documentation must be forwarded by April 15.

22. Write the names and ages of all people who are members of your parents' or your household. Also, write the name, city, and state of the college(s) or other school(s) beyond high school for all those family members who are or will be attending at least half-time and your parents' dependent children. List anyone who lived with you and/or your parents and received more than half their support from you or your parents at the time you completed your application, and will continue to receive support during _____ (year). This information must agree with that reported on the Financial Aid Form (FAF).

If any other family member is attending college, you may be required to provide proof of his/her registration at that school. Note: You must list all members of your household. (Attach separate sheet if necessary.)

Name	Age	College	City & State

23. If the number of household members listed above is different from the number of exemptions claimed on the _____ (year) income tax return, or the number listed on the FAF, please state reasons for this difference.

_____

_____

_____

Statement of Educational Purpose/Registration Compliance

I hereby affirm that any funds received under the Pell Grant, the Supplemental Educational Opportunity Grant, the College Work-Study, the Perkins/Stafford Student Loan, the Supplemental Loans for Students, or the Parent Loans for Undergraduate Students will be used solely for expenses related to the attendance or continued attendance at the institution below. I further understand that I am responsible for repayment of a prorated amount of any portion of payments made which cannot reasonably be attributed to meeting educational expenses related to the attendance at the institution. The amount of such repayment is to be determined on the basis of criteria set forth by the U.S. Secretary of Education.

I affirm that, to the best of my knowledge, I do not owe a repayment on a Pell Grant, a Supplemental Educational Opportunity Grant, or a State Student Incentive Grant previously received for study at any institution. To the best of my knowledge, I am not in default on a Perkins/Stafford Student Loan or a Parent Loan for Undergraduate Students.

_____ I certify that I am registered with Selective Service.

or

_____ I certify that I am NOT required to be registered with Selective Service because:

    _____ I was born before 1960.

    _____ I have not reached my eighteenth birthday.

    _____ I am a female.

    _____ I am in the Armed Service on active duty. (Members of the National Guard and the Reserves are not considered on active duty.)

    _____ I am a permanent member of the Trust Territory of the Pacific Islands or the Northern Mariana Islands.

Signature _____ Date _____

Notice: You will not receive Title IV financial aid unless you complete the statement and, if required, provide proof that you are registered with Selective Service. If you state falsely that you are registered or that you are not required to register, you may be subject to fine, imprisonment, or both.

I also certify that the information contained in this application is true and complete. I will notify the Director of Financial Aid in writing of any change in my family's financial status.

WARNING: If you purposely give false or misleading information on this form, you may get a fine, a prison sentence, or both.

_____ Date_____

Signature   Spouse's Signature

_____ Date_____

Parent's Signature(s)

Deadline: March 1

Some Final Notes on Applying for Financial Aid

1. Apply early. Observe deadlines and dates.

2. Get help in filling out the applications for financial aid. Most colleges and universities have financial aid counselors who can assist you and your family.

3. Don't estimate financial information. Make every effort to provide accurate data.

4. Remember that you have to apply each year for financial aid. The amount may differ from year to year, depending upon your financial circumstances, school allocations, and federal regulations.

5. Since most colleges and universities have their own forms for determining aid from institutional sources, make certain that you file all of the appropriate forms.

6. Be certain to file all of the forms necessary to be considered for state financial assistance programs.

7. Keep copies of all your financial aid applications.

8. Congress is in the process of reauthorizing all of the regulations governing student financial aid. Some of the information stated in this chapter may change. Check with your school's financial aid director for the latest information.

Don't try to "beat" the system. Always be honest and accurate in all of the information you submit. There are penalties for falsifying information.

3 HOW FINANCIAL NEED IS DETERMINED

Financial need is one of the most confusing concepts in the entire financial aid process. However, it is important to understand how financial need is determined. *Need analysis*, the process of determining each student's financial need, is a systematic method of assessing a family's ability to contribute financially to their child's postsecondary education. It is based upon a set of calculations of the parents' and student's income and assets. College and university financial aid personnel determine financial need and financial aid eligibility based upon figures calculated by one of the approved need analysis service agencies. Your college or university financial aid director will tell you which of the need analysis agencies to use.

Important Facts to Know

1. Financial need is the difference between two numbers: (1) the expected family contribution and (2) the total cost of attendance. The *expected family contribution*, which is the total amount to be contributed by the student and parents toward meeting college expenses, is determined by the process of *need analysis*. The need analysis calculation includes the following: adjusted gross income, untaxed income and benefits, federal and state income taxes, medical and dental expenses not covered by insurance, elementary and secondary tuition costs, employment allowance, standard maintenance allowance, home equity, cash, bank account balance, real estate and investment equity, business net worth, asset protection allowance, discretionary net worth, and number of family members enrolled in college at least half-time. The *total cost of attendance* includes tuition and fees, room and board expenses, transportation costs, personal expenses, child care costs, and miscellaneous expenses.

2. Two financial need calculations are computed for each applicant. One determines Pell Grant eligibility; the other, eligibility for campus-based programs and the Stafford Student Loan Program.

Campus-based programs are Supplemental Educational Opportunity Grant, College Work-Study, and the Perkins Loan.

3. The expected family contribution index figure for the Pell Grant is called the Student Aid Index (SAI). The Expected Family Contribution (EFC) is the expected family contribution figure for the campus-based programs and the Stafford Student Loan Program.

4. It is important to know the school's policy with regard to meeting financial need. Some schools have a financial aid policy that meets the full needs of all financial aid recipients. Another school may be able to meet only a certain percentage of an applicant's financial need.

5. The amount of aid you may qualify for can differ from one school to another. One school's total cost of attendance may be higher than another school's expenses, or one school's policy regarding meeting the full needs of all financial aid applicants may differ from another school's policy.

6. Dependent students are required by federal law to contribute a minimum of $700 as freshmen and a minimum of $900 as upperclassmen, or 70% of their after-tax earnings, to meet their college expenses. In addition, students are expected to contribute 35% of their savings and assets each year to pay their school bills.

7. All changes in your financial situation must be reported to your financial aid director as soon as they occur.

Important Terms to Know

Adjusted Gross Income   The income listed on the federal income tax return minus allowable deductions.

Appeal Process   The process of requesting from the school's financial aid director a review of an applicant's financial aid eligibility.

Assets   The items that indicate a family's financial worth. Included in this category are home or business value, savings and checking account funds, money market funds, stocks, bonds, real estate property, trust funds, and mutual funds.

Award Letter   The official document, issued by a college or university's financial aid office, which lists all of the financial aid that has been awarded to a student. The award letter also indicates the family contribution, the cost of attendance, and all of the terms of the aid awarded.

Campus-based Programs   The following are federal programs: Supplemental Education Opportunity Grant Program (SEOG), College Work-Study Program (CWSP), and the Perkins Loan Program. Funds for these programs are awarded by the financial aid director and are based upon the school's allocation of funds.

Congressional Methodology   A need analysis method developed by Congress and used to determine eligibility for campus-based programs and Stafford Student Loans. The formula estimates a family's contribution based upon income and assets.

Cost of Attendance   The total amount it will cost a student to attend a particular school. The expenses considered as part of the cost of attendance under the Pell Grant Program include: tuition and fee charges, room and board costs, books, supplies, transportation costs, child care allowances, handicapped allowance, and personal allowances. The expenses considered as part of the cost of attendance under the campus-based programs and Stafford Student Loan Program include: tuition and fee charges, books, supplies, transportation costs, personal expenses, room and board allowance, dependent care allowance, and handicapped allowance.

Entitlement Program   A financial aid program that is funded so that all applicants who qualify to receive funds are awarded moneys. The Pell Grant Program is an example of an entitlement program.

Exceptional Financial Need   A category that includes those applicants for financial assistance who have the lowest expected family contributions. A recipient of a Perkins Loan, a Health Professions Student Loan, or a Supplemental Educational Opportunity Grant, for example, would be classified as having exceptional financial need.

Expected Family Contribution   The figure determined by the need analysis services using a federally approved formula. The figure is the total amount the student and family are expected to contribute to the student's education. Income, assets, savings, and the net value of all real estate, including home equity, are included in computing expected family contribution.

For awarding campus-based programs and Stafford Student Loans, Congressional Methodology is used to determine the family's contribution. The Pell Grant Methodology is used to determine Pell Grant eligibility.

Financial Aid Director   The designated school official who reviews and processes financial aid applications and determines how financial need will be met by awarding the student some combination of grant, loan, and/or work.

Financial Aid Package   The total amount of financial assistance a student receives as listed in the school's financial aid award letter. Grant, loan, and work programs are included in a student's financial aid package. Financial aid from the college or university, as well as any outside scholarship or loan programs, are also included in the financial aid package.

Financial Aid Transcript   The record of financial aid a student has received. It is part of the student's financial aid file and is updated annually. A student's financial aid transcript is sent to a new school if the student transfers, or if the student attends graduate or professional school and requests financial aid.

Financial Need   The difference between two numbers: (1) the expected family contribution and (2) the total cost of attendance.

Gift Aid   That portion of a student's financial aid award that is a grant or scholarship. It does not have to be repaid and does not require any employment.

Merit-based Aid   Aid that is based on an applicant's scholastic achievements or particular talent. Merit-based assistance does not consider financial need.

Need Analysis   The process that determines a student's eligibility to receive financial aid. The parents' and student's income and assets are analyzed to determine the amount of money the family is expected to contribute to meeting the student's educational expenses. Need analysis computation formulas are approved by Congress and are adjusted annually. Two of the most commonly used undergraduate need analysis forms are the Financial Aid Form (FAF) of the College Scholarship Service (CSS), and the Family Financial Statement (FFS) of the American College Testing Program (ACT). The most commonly used need analysis form for graduate and professional students is the Graduate and Professional School Financial Application Service (GAPSFAS) of the Educational Testing Service (ETS).

Need-based Aid   Financial assistance based on the financial need of the student and family.

Nontaxable Income   Income that is not taxed by federal, state, or local governments, including social security benefits, unemployment income, or welfare benefits.

Professional Judgment   The authority given by the federal government to the school's financial aid director to make adjustments to a student's financial aid eligibility and to treat special circumstances that relate to financial need.

Self-help The amount of money a family is expected to contribute to meeting college costs, including loans and student employment.

Simplified Needs Test Formula A formula that uses a limited number of data elements to calculate a student's expected family contribution. To qualify for a simplified needs test a family's adjusted gross income must be $15,000 or less, and the family members either file IRS Form 1040A or 1040EZ, or are not required to file at all.

Special Condition A situation in which the student's and parents' Pell Grant Index is based on current year income instead of last year's income. There are specific criteria for applying for special condition, and students are advised to seek the advice of their school's financial aid counselor if unusual or extenuating circumstances arise affecting the family's financial situation.

Statement of Educational Purpose/Certification Statement on Refund and Default The statement that a student signs agreeing to use the awarded financial aid only to meet educational costs. This statement also asks the student to certify that he or she does not owe a refund on a Pell Grant, a Supplemental Educational Opportunity Grant, or a State Grant or is not in default on a Perkins Loan or a Stafford Student Loan. Students must also sign a statement indicating they are drug-free.

Statement of Selective Service Registration Document attesting to draft registration. Males who were born on or after January 1, 1960, who are at least 18 years old, and who are citizens or eligible noncitizens, and are not on active duty, are required to register with the Selective Service. This document must be signed before a student can receive federal, need-based aid.

State Student Incentive Grants The federal matching dollars given to states for the purpose of establishing financial aid programs.

Student Aid Index The number on the Student Aid Report (SAR) which includes Pell Grant eligibility or ineligibility.

Taxable Income The income reported on a family's income tax form. It includes income from salaries, tips, and interest and dividends minus allowances and deductions.

Unmet Need The difference between the amount of money a college or university awards a student and the expected family contribution.

How Pell Grant Eligibility Is Determined

Pell Grant eligibility is based upon a formula that is revised and approved each year by Congress. You may obtain a booklet describing the formula by writing to Formula Book, Department K-9, Public Documents Distribution Center, Pueblo, Colorado 81009-0015. Applications for the Pell Grant are available at high school guidance counselors' offices, college and university financial aid offices, and public libraries. Students may submit one of the following forms to be considered for a Pell Grant: the Application for Federal Student Aid, the Financial Aid Form, the Family Financial Statement, the Application for Pennsylvania State Grant and Federal Student Aid, the Student Aid Application for California, or, in Illinois, the Application for Federal Student Aid. For information on the Pell Grant you can call the Information Center at 1-800-4 FED AID.

Pell Grant eligibility takes into account the following factors:

Cost of Attendance

Full- or Part-time Enrollment

Taxes

Unusual Medical Expenses

Employment Expenses

Private Tuition Costs

Number of Family Members in College

The Student Aid Index (SAI), which is the number used to determine Pell Grant eligibility, ranges from 0 to 2000 or higher. The SAI number, produced by one of the analysis services, is based upon the information provided by the family. A score of 0 indicates that the applicant qualifies for the maximum grant amount. A score of 2000 indicates qualification for minimal assistance. If the number exceeds 2000, the applicant does not qualify for any Pell Grant assistance.

Your personal information, including your SAI, will be sent to you in the form of a Student Aid Report (SAR). The SAR is sent to the student approximately 4–6 weeks after the application is submitted to the analysis service. The format of the SAR is as follows: Part 1, Information Summary; Part 2, Information Review Form or Information Request Form; and Part 3, Payment. The analysis service has determined your SAI by using the information you provided on your need analysis form. Once the SAR is received, a copy should be signed and sent to your college financial aid office.

The financial aid officer determines the actual Pell Grant award amount based upon the SAI, the cost of attendance, the time of enrollment (one or two semesters), and the enrollment status (part-time or full-time). The financial aid director uses a Payment Schedule provided by the Department of Education to determine the actual Pell Grant award.

When the adjusted gross income of a dependent student's family is less than $15,000, or the family members are nontax filers, or use the 1040A or 1040EZ income tax forms, the need analysis used is a Simplified

Formula. Under this formula, assets and veteran's educational benefits to the student are excluded. Medical and dental expenses are not allowed as deductions on this form.

The only data elements used in a Simplified Formula are adjusted gross income, state and local taxes, total number of family members, and number of family members in college.

The following are examples of how need is determined for the Pell Grant Program:

1. State and other taxes are subtracted from parental income.

2. The Student Aid Index is evenly divided among all family members attending college.

3. Dependent students who earned more than $3500 will have part of these earnings assessed in the Student Aid Index.

4. Independent students with no dependents other than a spouse will have increased eligibility because of a subtraction for state and other taxes.

5. Independent students with dependents other than a spouse will benefit from the state and other tax subtraction and the division by number in college. The taxation rate on discretionary income for these students is the same as that used for the parents of dependent students.

How Expected Family Contribution Is Determined for Campus-based Programs and the Stafford Student Loan Program

The current formula used to calculate eligibility for all campus-based programs, as well as the Stafford Student Loan program, is called Congressional Methodology. This is the formula used by the analysis services to calculate expected family contribution. The Educational Amendments of 1986 replaced Uniform Methodology with Congressional Methodology as the federally approved method of determining financial need. Congressional Methodology significantly changed the way financial need is calculated. Under this system the base year income, rather than the estimated year income, is used to calculate the expected family contribution for a dependent student. The base year is the prior calendar year. For example, a financial aid application for the 1993–94 academic year would be based upon 1992 income.

Four factors are used to determine parental contribution:

Taxable and Nontaxable Income

Assets—Savings, Investments, Home, Farm, Business

Number of Dependents

Number of Family Members Enrolled in College

Parental income includes the annual earnings of both father and mother, as well as income derived from welfare benefits, pension funds, social security benefits, interest and dividends. Parental expenses include federal, state, and social security taxes, and any adjustments to income. Also included in the category of adjustments to income are medical and dental costs not covered by insurance and elementary and secondary school expenses of other family members. A standard maintenance allowance, based upon family size and the number of family members in college, and an employment allowance for each working parent, is also included as part of parental expenses.

Parental assets include home equity, business or farm equity, and any other real estate equity. A family's cash, savings, and checking account balances, and the value of any other parental investment are also included in this category.

Allowable deductions include an asset protection allowance that is based upon the age of the oldest parent. The asset protection allowance is slightly higher for a one-parent household.

REMEMBER: The current need calculation used by the federal government requires parents to contribute 5.6% of their assets and 47% of income over $16,000. That same formula requires students to contribute 35% of their assets and 70% of their income to meet their educational expenses. If two children are enrolled in college at the same time, the parental contribution is divided by 2.

The following are estimates of average and approximate expected parental contributions. These calculations are based only on income, assets, and number of family members.

Income	Assets	Number in Family	Contribution
$20,000	$80,000	4	$1,425
$60,000	$100,000	5	$12,190

Quite often families stare in disbelief at the amount of money they are expected to contribute. Remember that these amounts are financial estimates of what has been calculated to be a family's ability over a period of time to contribute to the cost of education. The formula used to arrive at expected family contribution is annually adjusted. It was never claimed that this system is foolproof, and it still has flaws and inequities. Maybe it always will. However, the system does allow human compassion and understanding to become part of the equation. If a family does not understand how its expected contribution was calculated, if the amount listed is considered totally unrealistic, or if a family's financial circumstances have changed since the application for financial aid was filed, parents are urged to contact the school's director of financial aid.

The three categories of student figures used in calculating the expected student contribution of a dependent student are income, allowances, and assets. Student income includes the student's annual wages, as well as any dividends, interest, benefits, or untaxed income. Student allowances include federal tax, state tax, and social security tax. Allowances are subtracted from income to leave available income. Seventy percent of available income, or a minimum of $700 for freshmen and $900 for upperclassmen, is included as part of the student's expected contribution. Students are also expected to contribute 35% of their assets each year to meeting their college expenses. Assets include savings, stocks, and bonds.

Summary of Need Analysis

Parental Contribution from Income:	47.0%
Student Contribution from Income:	70.0%
Parental Contribution from Assets:	5.6%
Student Contribution from Assets:	35.0%

Financial Aid Package and Award Letter

The financial aid award letter, issued by each school, lists by program and dollar amount, the amount of funding the financial aid officer awards a student. This amount is based upon the calculations of expected family contribution and total cost of attendance. In addition, the financial aid award letter details the student's expense budget and the expected family contribution. Most award packages include some combination of Pell Grant, Supplemental Educational Opportunity Grant, College Work-Study, Stafford Student Loan, Perkins Loan, school scholarship or loan, outside scholarships or loan, and PLUS or SLS loans. Financial aid recipients can (1) accept the award letter as presented, (2) accept parts of the award package, or (3) appeal for additional funds. The student is required to sign and date the award letter and return a copy to the school's office of financial aid. In addition, students must submit the appropriate loan application forms and sign any required promissory notes.

Most financial aid packages are built around the Pell Grant award. That amount of money serves as the foundation on which the rest of the award package is based. Most financial aid awards attempt to first meet the remaining financial need with grant or scholarship funds from either the state or the school. If need still exists, either a loan or student employment will be added to the aid package. It is the student's responsibility to report all financial assistance received from private organizations or foundations. The amount of outside funding must become part of the student's financial aid award.

Example of Financial Aid Package

Cost of Attendance	$11,000
Expected Family Contribution	$ 3,000
Financial Need	$ 8,000
Stafford Loan	$ 2,000
State Grant	$ 4,000
College Scholarship	$ 2,000
Unmet Need	0

SAMPLE FINANCIAL AID AWARD LETTER

Student ID # _____

Status: _____

Program: _____

Class: _____

Academic Year: _____

Date: _____

Please sign and return the white copy of this award offer by _____ (Date). Replies not received by this date will result in your award being revoked. You must accept (ACC) or reject (REJ) each item offered, indicating your decision by a check mark in the appropriate column.

Type of Financial Aid	First Semester	Second Semester	Total	ACC	REJ
Trustees' Scholarship	$1000.00	$1000.00	$2000.00		
State Grant	2000.00	2000.00	4000.00		
Stafford Student Loan	1000.00	1000.00	2000.00		
TOTAL AID AWARDED	$4000.00	$4000.00	$8000.00		

Total Aid Awarded does not include estimated awards. Pell Grant and State Scholarship values may be estimated, and they will not be actual awards or credited to your account until actual documentation/payment is received from the funding agency.

Comments: _____

Status: signifies the enrollment/attendance status on which this award is made. A change in attendance status will result in a revised award.

ACCEPTANCE/RELINQUISHMENT:

_____ I accept all aid so indicated above. I have read and signed the Educational Affidavit on the reverse side. I understand that this award is not official until copies of current tax returns or other income verification is received and reviewed by the Office of Financial Aid.

_____ I do not accept this award and hereby relinquish these funds.

AWARDS NOT MENTIONED:

_____ I have received $_____ from _____

_____ I have not received any additional awards but will notify the Office of Financial Aid in writing if I do.

Appeal Process

Most schools have an appeal process that allows students to request a review of their financial aid eligibility and award. Each school determines its own regulations for this process, and students should be aware of their school's procedures.

Be specific in requesting additional funds. State clearly the reasons for your appeal, and request a specific amount of money. Type or print your request, and submit any required documents or bills with your letter of appeal. Make an appointment to speak with a financial aid counselor to discuss your situation; most financial aid officers are reasonable in responding to a student's legitimate request for additional funds. Always be honest. How and when you appeal for more money will determine, to some extent, whether your request will be accepted or denied. The school's allocation of funds and the amount of institutional aid are also key factors in the appeal process. A financial aid director cannot give you money the school does not have. Be certain that you understand all of the rules and regulations of the appeal process, and follow directions.

Role of the Financial Aid Officer

The financial aid director at your school is required by federal law to allocate funds to students based upon established laws and regulations. However, the financial aid director has been given some freedom in interpreting rules. This *professional judgment* allows the financial aid director to alter calculations of family contribution and financial need if, in his or her opinion, there is sufficient reason. Seek the advice of this person whenever you have a financial problem. Remember that the financial aid director is there to help you.

Ten Tips on Qualifying for Financial Aid

Is there any way to "beat the system" when you apply for financial aid? Can families rearrange their finances to to make themselves eligible to receive more aid? There are two things to remember before these questions can be answered. First, families should always be honest when applying for financial aid. Second, the federal government can, and often does, change the rules and regulations determining how financial aid is awarded. Today's savvy financial aid strategy may not be applicable next year. Rather than manipulating income and assets to obtain financial aid, families should structure their entire college financing process to maximize their resources to meet the expenses of higher education.

There are, however, certain peculiarities in the current financial aid need analysis system that families should understand when applying for financial aid.

1. The current federal formula expects students to contribute 35% of their assets each year to meet their college costs, but parents need contribute only 5.6% of their assets. If a family has assets of $10,000, it is better to have this financial resource in the parents' name, rather than the child's. Parents would have to contribute 5.6% of $10,000, or $560, under the current need analysis formula. The child, however, would be expected to contribute 35% of $10,000, or $3500, toward meeting school bills.

2. Home equity loans allow parents to borrow against the value of their house to pay for their child's education. Parents can take out a second mortgage of up to $100,000 on their house and establish a line of credit based upon the equity they have built up in the house. The interest on home equity loans, unlike other consumer loans, is tax deductible.

3. Since financial aid is based on the previous tax year, timing is important. Parents should shift income or plan to take profits from investments or real estate holdings so that they are not included as part of the family's income for the year preceding college enrollment.

4. Parents should investigate ways of reducing their income and assets, including investing in retirement accounts and life insurance policies.

5. The first $500 of unearned income of children under the age of 14 is tax-free. The second $500 is taxed at the child's rate, and everything over $1000 is taxed at the parents' rate.

6. When a child reaches the age of 14, parents can transfer money to the child and it will then be taxed at the child's lower rate of 15%.

7. The family contribution is reduced according to the number of family members in college at the same time. If two children are in college, for example, the family's expected contribution is reduced by almost 50% for each child.

8. Parents should be aware that consumer debt is not used in financial need calculations. High Visa or MasterCard bills will not help a family qualify for more financial assistance.

9. Students should remember that they are expected to contribute 70% of all their after-tax earnings, or a minimum of $700. Parents are expected to contribute 47% of all of their earnings over $16,000.

10. Parents may use moneys from PLUS as part of their expected family contribution. Independent students may use moneys from SLS as part of their expected contribution.

Some Final Notes on Need Analysis

1. Don't become confused by all of the forms and calculations of need. Seek the advice of your school's financial aid director if you do not understand how your need was calculated or if you feel the expected contribution is not an accurate reflection of your family's financial situation.

2. Know the financial aid policies of your school before you enroll.

3. Know how need is calculated and what percentage of need is met at your school.

4. Understand what must be done to appeal for additional funds.

5. Always be honest and accurate in all of your actions with regard to financial aid.

6. Congress is in the process of reauthorizing all of the regulations used to determine financial aid eligibility. The rules and regulations stated in this chapter may change. Check with your school's financial aid director for the latest information.

4 EARLY FINANCIAL PLANNING OPTIONS FOR FAMILIES

Many Americans believe that financing their children's education is beyond their ability and that increasing college costs will soon make a higher education unaffordable for all except the wealthy. For most families, financing a college education is a major financial investment. The financial burden of putting a child through college is a reality that all parents face, regardless of income.

Few parents save regularly for future college costs. Fewer high school students save for college while still in high school. Most families do not have additional monthly income to set aside for future college expenses. Other families, who may have limited financial resources to meet this future expense, do not know how best to save or how much to save. Both groups want and need more information on family financial planning for college, financing options, college costs, and financial aid.

Parents should begin planning for their children's education as soon as possible. College costs will continue to increase. Federal, state, and school resources will vary from one year to another. Parents should analyze their finances in light of their children's future educational needs and then plan their budgets, savings, and investments according to a carefully constructed program.

Many sources are available to parents and students to assist in this planning process. Some families rely on the services of an accountant, a banker, a stock broker, or an investment planner to help them determine the best way to meet their children's future educational expenses. There is another group of experts, called *certified financial planners,* that can provide expert financial planning advice. Certified financial planners can give families information on shifting income to meet future college expenses, ways to increase a family's financial resources, and methods whereby a family can increase its monthly cash flow. However, parents should be careful in selecting a certified financial planner and should request information on the person's education and credentials before hiring. Some financial planners charge only a fee for their services. Others sell products (investments) as part of their services. The following list of organizations can assist families with information on how to select a certified financial planner:

Certified Financial Planner

International Board of Standards and Practices for
    Certified Financial Planners, Inc.
5445 DTC Parkway
Englewood, CO 80111
(303) 850-0333

Chartered Financial Analyst

Institute of Chartered Financial Analysts
P.O. Box 3668
Charlottesville, Virginia 22903
(804) 977-6600

Chartered Financial Consultant

American College
270 Bryn Mawr Avenue
Bryn Mawr, Pennsylvania 19010
(215) 526-1000

Another group of experts that can assist families in their financial planning process are financial aid directors. All postsecondary schools have personnel who are responsible for administering federal, state, and school financial aid programs. However, a word of caution is necessary. Although financial aid directors are experts in the area of financial aid, they are not financial planners and cannot provide the same type of information that a certified financial planner can offer. They cannot, for example, recommend stocks or certain other types of investments. For this reason their advice should be sought in conjunction with that of other financial experts. Also, financial aid directors spend a great deal of their time processing financial aid applications and loan forms, and maintaining the records necessary to comply with federal regulations. Often, they do not have a great deal of time to discuss family financial planning. Nonetheless, they are an invaluable source of information, and parents and students should seek their advice.

Financial Planning Suggestions

"Baccalaureate" Bonds These special savings bonds, sold in $1000 units, are tax-exempt municipal bonds that are often sold by state agencies as zero coupon bonds (see page 27). Fourteen states already offer college savings bonds, and others have passed legislation authorizing this type of financial plan. With "baccalaureate" bonds parents know how much cash will be available when a child begins college. Parents should be careful, however, in investing in this type of bond. Some financial experts believe that these bonds are risky because they are tied to inflation and interest rates and that they should be considered only as part of an entire financial portfolio. Other experts suggest that selection should be limited to bonds with an AAA or AA rating. "Baccalaureate" bonds can be purchased only through a broker.

Certificates of Deposit One way for families to meet tuition expenses is to put a sum of money in a certificate of deposit. The amount of the deposit can be as little as $500 or as much as $100,000. Certificates of deposit yield a higher return on the deposit than do savings plans. However, holders of certificates of deposit must keep their money in the bank for a specific period of time; there are severe penalties for early withdrawal. Parents can coordinate the maturity dates of their certificates of deposit to coincide with semester or annual tuition bills. Further information can be obtained from any local banker.

Charitable Remainder Trust This type of trust allows parents to combine a charitable gift with a financing plan for their child. Parents can present a gift to a charitable institution with the provision that a certain amount of the gift be set aside for the child's tuition account. Further information on this type of trust may be obtained from a certified financial planner, banker, or accountant.

Clifford Trust The Tax Reform Act of 1986 substantially altered the benefits of these trusts; however, they can still be used for educational purposes. Clifford Trusts are legal arrangements transferring some type of property from one person to another. The properties are managed by a trustee for the benefit of the beneficiary. Anyone can be named as the beneficiary of the trust, and there may be several beneficiaries. The trust can be funded for the child after his or her fourteenth birthday. Financial experts can provide more information on this type of trust arrangement.

Crummey Trust In this type of trust, parents name their child as the beneficiary. Under the terms of agreement, parents may make annual tax-free gifts of up to $20,000 if they are married, and $10,000 if they are single. Income can remain in this type of trust for an indefinite period of time. Parents should seek the advice of financial experts for more information on this type of trust arrangement.

Custodial Account This type of account is one way that parents can transfer some of their financial assets to their children. The Tax Reform Act of 1986, however, introduced the so-called kiddie tax, which made this type of account less attractive financially than was previously the case. For example, if a child is under the age of 14, the first $500 of income is tax-free and the second $500 is taxed at the child's rate, usually 15%. Anything over that amount is taxed at the parents' rate until the child reaches age l4, when income is again taxed at the child's rate. For further information on this type of investment, parents should seek the advice of their banker, accountant, or certified financial planner.

IRA, Keogh, and 401(K) Retirement Accounts Employees and self-employed persons are eligible to contribute $2000 per year to an Individual Retirement Account (IRA). A nonworking spouse can contribute $2250 per year. This contribution reduces a family's taxable income by the amount of the contribution as long as the employee is not covered by another company profit-sharing plan or pension plan or if the combined adjusted gross income is below $40,000 for a married couple; the income limit is $25,000 for a single person. Keogh plans are similar to Individual Retirement Accounts. Further information can be obtained from the employer, a banker, or an accountant.

Employees who participate in their company's 40l(K) retirement plan can save up to $7000 of their earnings each year. They pay no income tax on the deferred amount. Employees should check with their company's personnel officer or accounting department's director to determine whether they can borrow from their retirement account. If so, this money can be used to pay for college expenses. There is no tax penalty for early withdrawals to pay college bills.

Life Insurance One way for parents to finance their children's education is to borrow against the cash value of a life insurance policy. Some types of policies combine insurance with a tax-deferred account that can be invested in a variety of funds and that allows money to compound; included in this category are single-premium life, convention whole life, flexible-premium, and universal life insurance policies. Premiums on all of these policies earn income. Parents with life insurance have access to their money and can make withdrawals depending upon their financial needs, including borrowing against the value of the policy without paying taxes if the funds are used to pay college expenses. Some financial experts suggest that insurance should be a part of every family's financial plan because it provides financial security in the event of the death of the major wage earner. Costs and returns vary from one company to another, however, and investors should be careful in selecting an insurance company.

Money Market Accounts Money market accounts provide another way for parents to save for their children's college education. Interest rates on these accounts are determined by a bank. Although depositors can expect to earn the best prevailing interest rate on their investment, the rates change on a monthly basis. Usually a minimum deposit of $1000 is required. Depositors can withdraw their money according to their needs. Money market accounts are insured by the FDIC or the FSLIC. A local banker can provide further details.

Money Market Funds   A money market fund is a type of mutual fund; money is invested in various securities. Interest is compounded daily, and monthly dividends are paid to shareholders. The minimum investment amount is usually $500. Funds can be sold on short notice, thereby providing needed access to cash for tuition bills. A stockbroker or financial counselor should be consulted for additional information on money market funds.

Savings Accounts and Gifts   If families do nothing but save a certain amount of money each month to meet future college expenses, a substantial sum will be available by the time the child is ready to enter college, thanks to the magic of compound interest. The key is to begin saving several years before the child will enter college. Parents or grandparents can give as much as $10,000 per year to a child and pay no gift tax if the money is paid directly to the college to cover future tuition costs.

Let's look at savings another way. Let's assume you have two children. One has just entered high school, and the second has just entered the fourth grade. If you save $20 per week for each child, and we assume that you receive a 5.5% return on your savings, at the end of 4 years the first child will have $4655.51 for college expenses and in 8 years the second child will have $10,456.53. That's not a bad return on a relatively simple (and painless) investment.

Stocks, Bonds, Mutual Funds   Many financial experts suggest that families should diversify their financial portfolios. The younger the child, the more permissible it is for parents to take some financial risks. Conversely, the nearer the child is to entering college, the more secure the financial investing should be. A good way for inexperienced investors to put money into the stock market is through the purchase of mutual funds, which are professionally managed and diversified portfolios of common stock. However, mutual funds are subject to federal tax. Parents should consult with a stockbroker or financial planner for advice.

Tax-free Municipal Bonds   The interest earned on this investment is free of federal, state, and local taxes. Families should seek the advice of their stockbroker or financial planner before investing in tax-free municipal bonds.

Tuition Futures Programs and Prepayment Plans
These types of programs, offered by some schools and states, allow families to purchase a fixed, discounted tuition. Typically, the family is charged the current 4-year cost of education at a private school or a state institution, and the family's money is then invested either by the school or by the state, respectively. A family investing in this type of program has the security of knowing how much their child's education will cost, but there are disadvantages to a tuition futures program. It eliminates the student's chance to choose a college. Also, by putting their money into this type of program, parents lose potential higher returns from other investments. A U.S. Department of Education ruling may also make this program less attractive; the department has ruled, in the case of the Michigan Education Trust, that money invested in the trust will be considered a student asset when calculating financial need. By counting the trust money as a student asset, the ruling could limit a student's ability to qualify for federal aid programs. Families should seek the advice of their accountants before investing in these types of programs.

Uniform Gifts to Minors Act   Through this type of financial arrangement, an adult can make gifts to minors. A custodian, generally a parent, is named to manage the trust. Stocks, mutual funds, money, securities, and life insurance policies are the most common forms of investments managed by a custodian. If the child is under the age of 14, the first $500 of income is tax-free; the next $500 is taxed at the child's rate, usually 15%. All taxable income over $1000 is taxed at the parents' rate of income until the child reaches 14 and at the child's rate thereafter. Each parent may also put $10,000 per year into this type of account without any tax penalty. Although this financing option still gives parents a tax break, it is less financially appealing than it was before the Tax Reform Act of 1986. Parents are advised to seek the advice of a financial expert for additional information on this type of financial arrangement.

United States EE Savings Bonds   One of the technical amendments to the new tax laws allows interest from U.S. Savings Bonds purchased after December 31, 1989, to be tax-free if the bonds are held for at least 5 years and the money is used to pay for college tuition and fees. No tax is charged until the bonds are cashed. The tax-exemption option does not apply if the bonds are used to pay for living expenses. Also, tax exemption begins to be phased out when single income reaches $40,000 or joint income exceeds $60,000; it disappears when single income reaches $55,000 or joint income exceeds $90,000. To qualify, the buyer of the bonds must be older than 24 and must purchase the bonds in his or her name. The bonds mature 12 years from the purchase date, and parents may purchase bonds to mature at the time their child will be ready to enter college. Bonds are generally sold at half their face value. There are many types of bonds; for example, municipal bonds are issued by state or local governments.

United States EE bonds carry a variable rate of interest, which is adjusted every 6 months, but they guarantee a minimum rate of return of 6%. Savings bonds provide parents with a financing option that is secure and offers a reasonable rate of return on their investment. Savings bonds may be purchased at banks or credit unions in denominations as little as $50 or as much as $10,000. Parents should seek the advice of their banker or financial planner for more information on this type of investment.

Zero Coupon Bonds Zero coupon bonds, issued at face values of $1000 by the U.S. Treasury or by some corporations, may be purchased through stockbrokers. These bonds may be either tax-free or taxable and pay a fixed sum at maturity. Treasury zeros are guaranteed by the federal government; corporate zeros are not. Investors in zero coupon bonds receive no interest payments until the bonds mature, but interest is taxable every year unless the bond is a municipal bond. The amount received at maturity is a combination of the principal and the interest that has accrued. Zero coupon bonds are sold at a considerable discount from their face values, and the interest is compounded. With zero coupon bonds it is advisable to "lock in" a set interest rate on both principal and interest for the life of the bond or the period for which the purchaser wants to own the bond.

Parents should be cautious about investing in this type of bond, which can be volatile. The bonds offer high yields, but unless the interest rate has been set they are tied to current rates. When interest rates are high, it is possible to realize a good return on the original investment. When interest rates are low, however, the return may not be so profitable. Also, the bonds may be called before they mature; this means that interest stops accumulating. Investors have to keep track of when and if their bonds have been called. Zero coupon bonds cannot be purchased from the U.S. Treasury. Parents should seek the advice of their broker before investing in these bonds.

Treasury zero bonds, often called stripped treasuries, are bonds that have in the past yielded more than U.S. savings bonds. These bonds are exempt from federal, state, and local taxes. The date of maturity should be tied to the child's fourteenth birthday, when income is taxed at the child's lower rate. Parents interested in this type of investment should consult their stockbroker.

Publications Offering Articles on Financial Planning

Business Week
Changing Times
Financial Planning
Forbes
Fortune
Money

Publications Providing Information on Family Financing Options

Alternative Approaches to Tuition Financing National Association of College and University Business Officers

How to Pay for Your Children's College Education Gerald Krefetz

Nearly Free Tuition Alexander A. Bove, Jr.

Planning Now for College Costs: A Guide for Families Coopers and Lybrand

A Ten-Point Program of Awareness

As college costs continue to rise, parents and students must become aware of the basic points involved in financing a college education and assume the primary responsibility for finding the funds necessary to meet college expenses. Consider the following:

1. College costs will continue to rise.

2. Parents can no longer wait until their child is a senior in high school before deciding how they will finance the student's college education.

3. Families must act responsibly. Both parents and students should take an active role in locating the resources necessary to fund college costs.

4. Families should obtain information on a wide range of colleges. There are many low-cost schools offering excellent academic programs.

5. Families should seek information about all of the funding sources available at each school they are considering.

6. In 1980 the federal debt per person was about $4000. In 1992 it was approximately $16,000 per person. It is unlikely that the federal government in the future will substantially increase financial aid allocations to colleges and universities.

7. Professional help is available. Financial planners can formulate college financing strategies and investments. College financial aid counselors can provide valuable assistance and information on the financial aid process.

8. There are legitimate ways of reducing family income and assets in order to qualify for federal and state student financial assistance programs.

9. Families should learn how financial aid is awarded and the financial aid policies of each school they are considering. Financial need will differ from one school to another, depending upon the costs at each school.

10. Most families cannot save or invest enough money to meet all college costs. Most students will have to work while they are in college, and

many will have to borrow to meet some of their expenses.

Some Final Notes on Early Planning

1. Parents should try to save regularly to meet the future educational needs of their children.

2. Students should begin to save for their college education while still in high school.

3. Families should obtain as much information as possible about college costs and financial aid because that information is essential in implementing a successful college financial plan.

4. Parents and students should seek the advice of a financial aid director.

5. Parents should be careful in selecting a financial expert to assist them in their financial planning program.

6. Families should be careful and selective in using a scholarship search service. With a little hard work and investigation, they can often obtain for themselves the same information.

5 ALTERNATIVE FINANCING PROGRAMS

There are many ways to finance your education. Do not become discouraged if, after investigating a few sources, you cannot find the money you need. Dig deeper into the financial aid well to locate the financial assistance you need to attend college. This chapter will help you discover some alternative financing programs.

Important Facts to Know

1. Apply for all *federal, state,* and *institutional* aid before seeking alternative funding sources. Generally this money is less expensive than alternative programs.

2. Be certain that you and your parents understand all of the regulations and eligibility requirements of any alternative funding program *before* you pay any fee or sign any form. You don't want any surprises at a later date.

3. Compare alternative financing programs, and select the one that best meets the financial needs of the family.

4. Inquire as to whether any of the colleges you are considering will subsidize the interest charges on any alternative loan programs. This could save the family a great deal of money over the course of 4 years.

Important Terms to Know

Assets   Anything that you own, including cash, real estate, retirement accounts, trust funds, stocks, bonds, and money market and mutual funds.

Credit   An advance of money or merchandise given in exchange for a promise to repay in the future.

Collateral   The property or income, or some other assets, pledged to obtain a loan.

Commercial Loan   A type of loan, usually extended on a short-term basis, by a bank or lending institution.

Line of Credit   The maximum amount of money a bank will allow a customer to borrow.

Alternative Sources

Academic Management Services   This organization provides families with a monthly deferred billing plan, which allows students and parents to pay all or part of annual tuition costs in ten equal monthly installments without any interest charges. The enrollment fee includes the cost of a Life Benefit Insurance Plan, which guarantees payment of the balance of the budgeted amount in the event of the death of the parent, student, or spouse. Write to Academic Management Services, Inc., 50 Vision Boulevard, East Providence, Rhode Island 02914 for further details on the program, or call 1-800-635-0120 for additional information and application materials.

Bay Banks Education Financing Programs

Bay Banks PEP Loan provides funds from $2000 to $20,000 per year to qualified graduate students enrolled at least half-time in an approved professional or medical program. The interest rate is set at 2% above the prime rate, and recipients have up to 20 years to repay. Call 1-800-332-8374 for further information and application forms.

Bay Banks TERI Loan provides loans from $2000 to $15,000 per year to qualified graduate and undergraduate students. The interest rate is set at 2% above the prime rate and is adjusted monthly. Payments begin 45 days after the funds are issued. Recipients have 15 years to repay. Call 1-800-322-8374 for further information and application forms.

Chase Manhattan Bank Loans

Chase Home Equity Line of Credit lets the family establish a line of credit that can be used to meet tuition costs. No interest is charged until the credit is used. Visit the nearest Chase branch to obtain further details.

Chase TERI provides funds to meet education expenses through a private loan supplement. The interest rate is tied to the prime rate, and repayment may extend for 15 years. Call Chase Customer Service at 1-800-645-8246, Ext. 60, for further information.

Chemical Bank This bank offers a number of college financing programs for families and students. For further information call 1-800-243-6226, Ext. 4911.

Collegeaire This plan takes a family's savings account funds and stretches that amount to pay for educational bills. The family's savings continue to earn interest, but interest is paid only on the actual amount of credit that is used, not on the total credit line. For further information, write Collegeaire, P.O. Box 88370, Atlanta, Georgia 30356 or call (404) 952-2500.

CollegeCredit Loan Program This new loan program of the College Board, the Student Loan Marketing Association, and the Teachers Insurance and Annuity Association/College Retirement Equities Fund allows students at participating colleges and universities to receive Stafford Loans and other federally guaranteed loans. For further information on this program, write to The College Board, 45 Columbus Avenue, New York, New York 10023-6992.

College Prepayment Fund This fund of Ann Arbor, Michigan, is the first national prepaid tuition program. So far the plan is available through 18 colleges in 14 states. As with other prepayment programs, the College Prepayment Fund permits parents to pay for their child's education at current tuition rates. Participating colleges guarantee that the amount that parents prepay will cover their tuition charges by the time the child is ready to enroll. However, this program is different from other prepayment programs because it does not limit college selection to a single state. Families can transfer the money that has accumulated from one participating college to another, and will receive their money back, with interest, if the child decides not to attend any college or not to attend a participating college. The following schools are currently participating in the College Prepayment Fund: California Baptist College, Central Wesleyan College, Columbia Union College, The Defiance College, George Fox College, Grace Bible College, Greenville College, Jacksonville University, Jarvis Christian College, Jordan College, Lane College, Lincoln Memorial University, Rust University, Sioux Falls College, Spring Arbor College, Stillman College, Tiffin University, and the University of Findlay. Contact any of the participating schools for further information.

CollegeSure Certificates of Deposit These CDs, issued by the College Savings Bank of Princeton, offer a private, federally insured, long-term investment plan with a return tied directly to the average cost of a college education. CollegeSure guarantees to cover college costs at maturity, and families are not locked into a particular college. A minimum initial deposit of $1000 is required, and the CDs are insured by the FDIC for up to $100,000. The interest rate is tied to an index based on an annual average basis, and there are penalties for early withdrawal. The fact that the yield is set at 1.5 percentage points below the college inflation rate may make this type of investment less profitable than other savings programs. For more information, contact The College Board at (212) 713-8000.

ConSern Loans Families are provided with loans of up to $15,000 per year with as long as 15 years to repay. The interest rate is adjusted monthly and equals the 3-month commercial paper rate plus 4.1%. Repayment begins 30 days after the money is received. Deferment options are available. This loan is available only at certain schools. For further information and application forms, write to ConSern, 205 Van Buren Street, Suite 200, Herndon, Virginia 22070, or call 1-800-767-5626.

Educational Credit Corporation This privately operated loan program allows families to borrow for education expenses based on their ability to pay, not on financial need. Families may borrow from $2000 to $15,000 per academic year. The interest rate fluctuates and is tied to the prime rate. An automatic credit life insurance plan is part of each loan. Borrowers have up to 15 years to repay the loan. Contact Educational Credit Corporation, Service Center, P.O. Box 1119, Blue Bell, Pennsylvania 19422 for further details and application forms.

EXCEL Loan Program This supplemental loan program is designed to assist students and their parents to meet the costs of higher education. EXCEL offers low-cost education loans to creditworthy families. Annual loan amounts range from $2000 to $20,000 per year. The financial aid director at each school must certify loan eligibility. Interest rates are competitive, and applicants can select either a monthly variable rate loan or a 1-year renewable rate loan. Repayment begins 45 days after the funds are disbursed. The repayment period may extend to 20 years. Call 1-800-634-9308 for further information, or write Nellie Mae, 50 Braintree Hill Park, Suite 300, Braintree, Massachusetts 02184.

Family Choices Plan Developed by TERI, this plan offers families the option of either using current income or borrowing money to meet college expenses. Families choose the amount of money they can contribute monthly, and the rest of the college bill is financed through a TERI loan. Loan approval is based upon creditworthiness, and families have up to 20 years to repay. An annual $45 enrollment fee is charged, and there is an automatic life benefit feature in the program. Families should consult with their school's financial aid officer about this financing plan. For further information and application materials, write to The Education Resources Institute (TERI), 330 Stuart Street, Suite 500, Boston, Massachusetts 02116-5237, or call 1-800-255-TERI.

Family Education Loan Program This program allows families to borrow up to the cost of education minus financial aid. The program is administered through the Massachusetts Education Loan Authority, but Massachusetts residency is not required. Eligibility is based on family income, assets, family size, and the number of family members in college. Home mortgage options are available. Repayment begins within a month after the loan is made, and borrowers have up to 15 years to repay the loan. For further information, write the Massachusetts Education Loan Authority, 176 Federal Street, Boston, Massachusetts 02110, or call 1-800-842-1531.

Fleet National Bank This bank offers several college financing options. The Prepaid Tuition Plan allows families to select from several installment plans that spread college costs over a period of months, so that families are not faced with having to pay one large bill at the beginning of each semester. A fee is charged to participate in the program, but there are no interest or finance charges. The Universal Education Loan allows families to borrow up to $15,000 per year (with a total maximum of $60,000) to meet educational expenses. A variable interest rate is charged, usually 2% over the prime rate. Repayment may extend up to 15 years. Write to Fleet National Bank, P.O. Box 486, Providence, Rhode Island 02901-9972, or AFSA Date Corporation, P.O. Box 22771, Long Beach, California 90801-9803

GradEXCEL These loans are made available to graduate and professional school students and are financed by The New England Education Loan Marketing Corporation (Nellie Mae). A student may borrow up to $7500 a year, or up to $20,000 a year with a creditworthy cosigner. Loan approval is based upon creditworthiness, and borrowers have up to 20 years to repay the loan. A variable interest rate is charged, but it cannot exceed the prime rate plus 2%. For further information and application forms, write to Nellie Mae, Supplemental Loan Programs, 50 Braintree Hill Park, Suite 300, Braintree, Massachusetts 02184, or call 1-800-634-9308 or (617) 849-3447.

GradSHARE Loan Program This loan program provides loans to qualified graduate and professional school students. Eligibility is based upon creditworthiness. A variable rate of interest is charged and is determined on a monthly basis. Contact Nellie Mae at 1-800-634-9308 for further information and application forms.

Home Equity Loans This program allows parents to borrow up to 85% of the equity they have in their home to finance their children's education. Contact your local bank for specific information.

Irving Trust "School-Chex" Plan This financing program allows a student to reserve money for college expenses by writing a check made payable to the student's school. A maximum of $20,000 may be borrowed. Families make monthly payments based on budget allowances. Interest is paid on the unpaid bal-

ance. For further information, write Irving Trust Company, 1 Wall Street, 13 East, New York, New York 10015.

Richard C. Knight Insurance Agency, Inc. This agency administers an FDIC-insured savings plan providing a method of paying for education expenses from monthly income. Low-cost life insurance is included in the plan. The amount allotted for college costs is determined by the family and the student. Payment to the college is made by the Knight Insurance Agency, and the family makes monthly payments to Knight. An Extended Repayment Plan, which allows families to reserve the moneys necessary to meet 4 years of tuition costs, is also available. Write to the Insured Tuition Payment Plan, 855 Boylston Street, Boston, Massachusetts 02116-9854, or call 1-800-225-6783 for further information.

Life Insurance and Pension Funds Loans to meet college costs may be made against private pension funds or life insurance policies. Contact your company's personnel office for specific details.

Lines of Credit Some banks provide lines of credit to creditworthy families, and this money can be used to meet college expenses. Contact your local bank for further information.

Mellon Bank EduCheck This program offers families a $3500–$15,000 line of credit to pay for college expenses. The interest rate is adjusted monthly, and is tied to the 90-day CD rate. Repayment begins 45 days after the money is issued. This financing program is available in Delaware, Maryland, Ohio, Pennsylvania, Virginia, and Washington, D.C. For further information and application materials, write to the Mellon Bank EduCheck Plan, P.O. Box 8888, Wilmington, Delaware 19899, or call 1-800-323-7105.

National Prepaid Tuition Plan Unlike other prepayment programs, this nationwide tuition prepayment program, designed by the HEMAR Education Corporation of America, allows families to transfer moneys prepaid from one college or university to another. Contact your state education office for further information on this program.

Share Loan Program This program makes loans to graduate and undergraduate students. Annual loans range from $2000 to $20,000 per year. A monthly variable interest rate is charged. Borrowers from certain states can secure their loan with a mortgage on their primary residential property. Eligibility includes creditworthiness. For applications and further information, write to Nellie Mae, Credit Department, 50 Braintree Hill Park, Suite 300, Braintree, Massachusetts 02184, or call 1-800-634-9308.

TERI Professional Education Plan (PEP) This private loan program provides assistance to graduate and professional school students. Students may borrow up to $20,000 a year to meet their education expenses. Interest rates are low, and repayment terms are flexible. The program is not need-based. Deferment terms are allowed. Call 1-800-255-TERI for more information.

TERI Supplemental Loan Program This loan financing program allows families to borrow up to $20,000 per year to meet college costs. Loan approval is based upon creditworthiness and cannot exceed 40% of the family's gross income. However, there is no income cap. The interest rate charged is variable, and there are repayment options. Borrowers have up to 20 years to repay the loans. Call 1-800-255-TERI for more information, or write The Education Resources Institute (TERI), 330 Stuart Street, Suite 500, Boston, Massachusetts 02116-5237.

The Tuition Plan, Inc. This program allows families to budget college costs so that they may be paid out of current monthly income. There is also a finance plan that allows parents to borrow money and repay it on a monthly basis. For more information, write The Tuition Plan, Inc., 57 Regional Drive, Concord, New Hampshire 03301, or call 1-800-822-8764.

6 TAX REFORM AND FINANCIAL AID

The 1986 Tax Reform Act initiated sweeping changes in the methods used to calculate tax rates, tax exemptions, and interest deductions. For families with young children or with children already in college, financial planning has changed. No longer can income be shifted as easily as it once was from parents to children to pay for college expenses. Some school administrators believe that the new tax regulations have eliminated some incentives that families previously had to save for their children's education.

As a general rule it is best to save money in the parents' names, not in the child's name. Remember that any investment exceeding $1000 in a child's account will be taxed at the parent's rate until the child reaches the age of 14. A tax break exists only for the first $1000 in unearned income. Children under the age of 14 get a standard deduction of $500 and pay tax at 15% on the remaining $500. If, however, the child's income exceeds $1000, the child will be taxed on the excess at the parents' rate, which is usually 28%. If a child is over the age of 14, the tax rate is 15% for the first $17,850 of income and 28% thereafter.

Changes Mandated by the 1986 Tax Reform Act Affecting Student Financial Aid Programs and Recipients

Clifford Trusts Previously, this type of trust shifted income from a taxpayer in a higher income bracket, usually the parent, to a taxpayer in a low income bracket, usually the child, for a certain period of time. Assets could be set aside for 10 years and then returned to the donor. Under the new regulations, income is now taxed at the donor's rate of income.

Custodial Accounts Income on gifts of more than $1000 from parents to children are now taxed at the parents' rate of income.

Degree Candidates Under the new tax laws, only degree-seeking students are eligible for tax-exempt student financial aid. Nonmatriculating students receiving a fellowship or scholarship must pay taxes on the full amount of the award.

Financial Aid Eligibility For some families, the removal of certain tax credits makes the adjusted gross income higher in the need analysis computation that determines estimated family contribution and financial need. Also, the changes in the tax rate schedules show, in certain cases, a reduced amount of taxes paid by the family. Both can have a negative impact in determining a student's financial need by making the expected family contribution higher than was previously the case. This can result in decreased student eligibility for certain types of financial aid.

Foreign Students Schools are now required to withhold a certain percentage of grants awarded to foreign students.

Graduate Fellowships and Assistantships Colleges and universities are now required to designate what portion of a graduate student's award is for services provided to the school in the form of teaching or research, and what portion of the award is a grant. The compensation portion is taxable income, and institutions must now withhold taxes on the compensation part of the student's award. However, under certain circumstances the stipend may be tax free. If the graduate student is a degree candidate and is conducting research, teaching, or performing other services that meet specific requirements for the degree, and the same kinds of services are required of all candidates for the degree, the stipend may not be taxed. Graduate students who have already paid taxes on their stipends, and who meet this criteria, should file an amended return on Form 1040X.

Low-Income Students Low-income students are usually high grant recipients. However, if these students receive taxable scholarships or grants, they cannot file a 1040A or 1040EZ income tax form because there is no place to report taxable scholarships or grants on those forms. The students are required to file the more complicated 1040 form, which then disqualifies them from using the simplified need analysis test to determine financial need.

Personal Exemptions Students who are eligible to be claimed by their parents as income tax exemptions cannot declare themselves as personal exemptions on their own income tax returns. This regulation applies even if a student is not claimed on the parents' income tax form.

Scholarship and Grant Taxation   Under the new tax laws, scholarships and fellowships are treated as taxable income and are subject to federal income tax. Living expense stipends are also taxed as income.

Student Loans   Student loans are now treated as personal loans, and interest deductibility has been phased out.

Student Tax Liability   There is the potential for increased tax liability for students who receive scholarships, grants, fellowships, or assistantships.

Some Final Notes on Tax Reform and Financial Aid

1. There is a possibility that in the coming years new tax regulations will be written that will have implications for financial aid recipients.

2. Parents with children in college or with young children should seek the advice of their accountant, financial planner, or tax expert to determine the implications of all tax laws on financing their children's education.

3. Parents and students should seek the advice of the financial aid director to determine the effects of new tax regulations on family contribution and student need.

4. The federal government places the responsibility on the student to report all taxable income.

5. Educational loans, including federally subsidized student loans, are not considered income for tax purposes.

6. A college or university employee who is enrolled in graduate courses for which there is no tuition charge is required to pay federal income taxes on the dollar value of the courses. Only if filers can prove that the courses are necessary for them to improve in their current jobs may a deduction be granted.

7. Families enrolled in certain prepaid tuition plans should be aware that, for tax purposes, the funds are considered student assets. In some cases this may reduce a student's eligibility for certain types of financial aid. Also, the Internal Revenue Service recently ruled that the Michigan Education Trust is required to pay annual corporate taxes on its earnings in addition to the deferred taxes that students must pay as they withdraw funds for college. However, it is important to remember that in the years to come IRS regulations may change with regard to prepaid tuition plans. Families should seek the advice of an accountant, banker, or financial aid director in weighing the advantages against the disadvantages of this type of program.

8. Scholarship awards for tuition, fees, books, and equipment are tax-free. Scholarships awarded for room, board, and travel, however, are taxable.

9. While the Tax Reform Act of 1986 did alter previously existing saving mechanisms, it is still possible for parents to make sound investments in their child's education. They should consider Savings Bonds, tax-exempt securities, zero-coupon municipal bonds, and long-term municipal bonds when planning their investment strategy.

7 STUDENT DEBT

There is no doubt that more students are borrowing more money to finance their higher education. It is also true that loans allow some people, who otherwise would have been unable to enroll, to attend college. For these reasons, it is important to put student borrowing into perspective. Of all college students who borrow, the majority meet their loan obligations. However, some students graduate from college owing more money than they can reasonably expect to repay. The purpose of this chapter is to warn students against borrowing too much while in college and to offer suggestions on ways to avoid unmanageable student debt.

The practice of borrowing for college is relatively new. Before 1960, most families paid for their children's education either from savings or from income. All that changed with the advent of the "Great Society" programs. During President Lyndon Johnson's administration, funding for education increased, as did the number and type of student financial aid programs. From 1960 to 1980, more grant assistance was available to students than now. Since 1980, financial aid funding has shifted from grants to loans. Borrowing for college has now become an acceptable way to meet college expenses. Approximately 13,000 banks participate in the Stafford Student Loan Program, and there are guarantee agencies in all 50 states.

Some students treat their education as their parents once treated a home mortgage. They consider college as a consumer item to be financed and paid for with future earnings. However, student loans are not like other consumer loans. The former are based upon financial need; the latter, on creditworthiness. Borrowing for college implies the hope that future earnings will allow repayment of student debt. Unmanageable debt, however, can dramatically shape a person's life for many years after graduation and it can postpone the "good life" for a long time. Some students, unwilling or unable to secure adequate funding for college, will postpone a secondary education or will base their enrollment only upon financial considerations. Other students, heavily indebted from undergraduate school, may decide not to pursue graduate work. Still other students may decide on a choice of major based only upon potential economic return. Finally, borrowers who default on their student loans may find it difficult or impossible in the future to obtain other types of loans. None of these scenarios is recommended. The wise student will borrow prudently and will seek *all* other avenues of financing before turning to loans.

Important Facts to Know

1. Last year the average student debt was about $10,000 from a private school and about $8000 from a public school.

2. Federal student loans have tripled in the last 15 years.

3. Loan volume in the Stafford Student Loan Program increased 185% from 1980 to 1990, and defaults increased 1600%.

4. Since the program began, more than 3 million students have defaulted on Stafford Student Loans.

5. There has been a 200% increase in default costs to the federal government in the past 5 years.

Important Terms to Know

Accrued Interest   Interest on loans that is paid at a later date, usually in installments. Accrued interest may be simple or compound.

Amortization   The gradual reduction of loan debt by monthly payments of principal and interest.

Bankruptcy   The condition of a person who asks to be judged insolvent, and the legal action taken against a person who cannot meet financial obligations.

Cancellation   The amount of a student's loan that is forgiven or is cancelled because of death or disability. Many loans can be called or forgiven by various kinds of service. Check the chapter in Section II on State Financial Assistance Programs for forgiveness options.

Compound Interest   Interest earned on principal plus interest that was earned earlier.

Consolidation   The process whereby loans are combined and all loans are transferred to one lender.

Credit Bureau   The agency that keeps credit history and financial information and reports this information to lenders.

Debt Burden   The portion of a college graduate's earnings that will be needed to repay student loans. Debt burden is usually highest during the first years of employment and decreases as earnings increase.

Default   Failure of the borrower to meet the payments due on student loans. Defaults are recorded on a person's permanent credit record and may prevent the individual from obtaining loans in the future. The Internal Revenue Service may withhold an income tax refund from student loan defaulters.

Deferment   The postponement, for a limited time, of loan and interest payments due from the borrower. Deferments are usually given to graduate school students. Loan counseling should include a list of all deferment categories.

Delinquency   Failure on the part of borrowers to make payments on their student loans when they are due.

Disbursement   The issuing, by a lender, of a student loan check.

Disclosure Statement   A statement of the terms and costs of a loan to the borrower. The lender must include this statement to the borrower either before or at the same time that the loan check is disbursed.

Discretionary Income   The income available to meet living expenses after taxes and loan repayments have been met. Discretionary income can also be used to finance investments and to improve one's standard of living.

Exit Interview   An interview conducted by personnel at colleges and universities. Federal law requires that all students receiving federal loan assistance must participate in an exit interview, during which the terms and obligations of the student's loan are discussed. Refinancing, deferments, and loan consolidation options are also provided. An exit interview must be conducted whenever a student leaves a school.

Forbearance   An arrangement whereby the lender may delay repayment of loans because of financial hardship. This prevents a borrower from falling into default status.

Grace Period   The span of time allowed before repayment of a student loan must begin.

Gross Income   The income a person earns before any taxes or deductions are taken.

Interest   The fee charged to borrow money. Interest charges are added to the principal of the loan. Interest may be simple or compound.

Net Income   The money available from salary or wages after all deductions have been made. Deductions include federal and state taxes, social security payments, health insurance, life insurance, and retirement or other benefits.

Origination Fee   The fee charged by a bank to process a student loan. The amount of the fee is deducted from the dollar amount of the loan.

Principal   The amount of a loan that must be repaid upon maturity and the amount upon which interest will be charged.

Promissory Note   The binding document a student signs before receiving a loan check. The promissory note includes information about the terms and agreement of the loan.

Repayment Schedule   A list of monthly loan payments, outlining principal and interest charges.

Simple Interest   Interest calculated only on the original amount of a loan.

Manageable and Unmanageable Debt

One way to calculate the approximate or manageable amount of debt is to estimate earnings after graduation. The more you earn, the easier it will be for you to meet your monthly loan payments. Generally, 5–15% of gross income is considered manageable to repay student loan bills. For example, a borrower graduates with a Stafford Student Loan of $10,000. This college graduate now earns $20,000 a year. With this debt, the loan bill will be about $133 per month. Women should remember that they will probably earn less than their male colleagues in the same career fields and should keep this in mind when borrowing.

One of the first things a recent college graduate should do is to calculate expenses and available resources and to budget student loan payments as part of monthly costs. To establish a budget, write down your gross monthly salary and then, from that amount, subtract federal, state, and social security taxes. The net amount is the money you have to pay your bills and meet your fixed expenses. Your monthly bills and expenses will depend upon your life-style. YOUR STUDENT LOAN PAYMENT SHOULD NOT BE LEFT TO DISCRETIONARY INCOME. TREAT THIS BILL AS A FIXED EXPENSE. Also, try to save some of your salary each month and to put money aside for emergencies.

Remember that there are no absolutes in student borrowing. Tailor your loans to meet your current and future needs, and use loans as a *last resort* in your college financing plans. Seek *grant*, *scholarship*, and *work* funds before turning to loans. Plan to meet your college expenses creatively.

The following suggestions will help you to avoid borrowing too much money.

Career Planning

What does career planning have to do with student financial planning and debt management? Debt management and financial planning must begin with a discussion of careers and future income potential. Debt can be considered manageable or unmanageable in light of future employment and earnings. High school students can begin planning their careers in a number of ways. The following approaches are suggested.

Soul-search to analyze your interests, abilities, goals, and values. What do you like to do? What are your hobbies and outside interests? What life-style appeals to you? Do you like to travel? Are you better in the arts, humanities, or sciences? This self-analysis should be the beginning of your career search. The next step is careful consideration of career options that are compatible with your interests and abilities. The following publications are helpful in analyzing and comparing careers:

Handbook 1988 - Career Education That Works for America, published by the National Association of Trade and Technical Schools.

Occupational Outlook Handbook, published by The Bureau of Labor Statistics.

What Color Is Your Parachute? by Richard Nelson Bolles.

The Bureau of Labor Statistics publishes the following periodicals highlighting employment and earnings:

Business, Managerial, and Legal Occupations

Clerical and Other Administrative Support Occupations

Communications, Design, and the Performing Arts

Computer and Mathematics-Related Occupations

Dietetics, Nursing, Pharmacy, and Therapy Occupations

Education, Social Science, and Related Occupations

Educational Attainment of Workers

Employment Projections

Engineering and Related Occupations

Geographic Profile of Employment and Unemployment

Monthly Labor Review

Occupational Projections for Training Data

Consult with Guidance Counselors in your high school guidance or career planning office or college admission office. Although the services of these professionals are most often used to process applications for postsecondary education, they can also be helpful in determining career choices. Most offices have publications listing different career options and employment prospects for various career fields. Many schools can also administer a battery of personality tests that can help the high school student determine job suitability. Finally, many guidance counselors can offer professional opinions based on their personal knowledge of the student.

Attend Career Fairs sponsored by high schools where students can obtain the most recent information on a variety of careers. Pertinent literature should be read, and future employment prospects and trends should be carefully considered.

Meet with Specialists to obtain information. You can make an appointment to meet with people currently employed in the career fields you are considering. The benefits and drawbacks can be discussed, and a realistic appraisal of your future career can be made.

Obtain on-the-Job Training in the career fields you are considering. If you cannot obtain employment, volunteer your services. Find out, through your own personal experience, if this is the type of work you wish to pursue. Many companies offer internship programs, providing job-related experiences for young people. Students can locate internships through their high school guidance department, newspaper ads, employment services, professional organizations, personal contacts, or direct applications. For further information on internship programs, write to the National Society for Internships and Experiential Education, 122 St. Mary's Street, Raleigh, North Carolina 27605.

Choosing a career is one of the most important decisions you will ever make. You and your family will be investing time and money to obtain specialized knowledge. It is important that the right choice be made. This is an investment in your future and in *you*.

Selecting a Postsecondary Institution

After deciding on a career, the next step is to locate an appropriate school that offers the specific programs you are seeking. Take the following factors into consideration, establish the importance of each one to you, and then use your own ranking system to facilitate your decision-making process.

Factor	School #1	School #2	School #3
Academic programs	_____	_____	_____
Number of faculty	_____	_____	_____
Number of faculty with higher degrees	_____	_____	_____
Cost	_____	_____	_____
Special programs	_____	_____	_____
Library facilities	_____	_____	_____
Location	_____	_____	_____
Research opportunities	_____	_____	_____
Financial aid policies	_____	_____	_____
Size	_____	_____	_____
Religious affiliation, if any	_____	_____	_____
Student body profile	_____	_____	_____
Athletic opportunities	_____	_____	_____
Extracurricular activities	_____	_____	_____
Housing	_____	_____	_____
Crime rate	_____	_____	_____
Graduation rate	_____	_____	_____
Average student indebtedness	_____	_____	_____
Placement after graduation	_____	_____	_____

Gather Information, Make Comparisons, Investigate Colleges and Universities by writing for the school catalog, the financial aid brochure, and any information on the placement of graduates. After obtaining this information, you and your family can compare the various schools and decide which you wish to investigate. This investigation can include, whenever possible, a visit to the campus and an interview with the admissions officer, financial aid counselor, and placement director. The interview at the admissions office can include questions regarding the academic quality of the programs offered and the student/faculty ratio.

Questions posed to the financial aid administrator can cover the type of financial assistance programs available, application deadlines, the awarding process, the financial aid appeal process, special aid programs, and the average indebtedness of recent graduates. This last statistic is critical because it can show several things: how rich the average student's family is; how expensive the college is; how generous scholarship aid is; and how closely the financial aid office monitors its students' debt burden. If this information is not available at the time of your meeting, ask when it will be made available.

Meet with the placement director and ask what placement services are available. What is the profile of recent graduates? How many graduates are placed through the office? What are the average first-year starting salaries in various career fields? If it is not possible for you to visit all the schools, telephone and obtain answers to your questions about admission, financial aid, and placement.

Analyzing Costs

By the time you are a senior in high school, you should have completed a school search and conducted comparative analysis of postsecondary institutions. The next step is to apply to the schools that meet your academic and financial requirements. A careful analysis of school costs at this time is essential. By now you should know what it will cost you to attend each of the schools you are considering and what resources will be needed to meet these costs.

Prospective students and parents can make the mistake of assuming that payment in full is due upon registration. This mistake may cause them to eliminate a preferred school because it is too expensive, or they may borrow hastily without exploring other college financing options. Breaking down aggregate expenses can show you where you can economize, such as buying second-hand books or living at home and commuting to classes. You can break costs down into the following categories: (1) tuition; (2) books, fees, and miscellaneous expenses; (3) living expenses. Assuming that financial assistance will not meet all of these expenses, let us further assume that some combination of student, family, and school resources will meet the educational costs of attendance. It is the primary responsibility of students and their families to finance their education. Schools have a responsibility to assist families in this process. Careful planning, creative resourcefulness, and hard work are the key ingredients, but one other factor is essential—determination. It is important that families and students approach student financial planning with a positive attitude. Millions of families have done it and continue to do it. So can you!

A Plan for Meeting Educational Costs

Category 1: Tuition Costs

Prior to admission, applicants should know the institution's financial aid policies and understand its financial aid application and awarding process. In addition to federal and state programs administered through the school's financial aid office, private or corporate programs can be investigated. Often local unions, churches, civic organizations, and charitable institutions will sponsor needy students. The objective in exploring the various avenues of financial assistance is to attempt to meet tuition costs through a combination of federal, state, and private sources. No source should be eliminated from consideration. Scholarship assistance should have priority over loan sources. However, you should be prepared to borrow a portion of tuition expenses if necessary.

This early process of financial planning to meet tuition expenses allows you and your family to organize your finances. The search for financial aid funds can follow immediately after the career analysis and school search have been completed and before you enroll in any postsecondary institution. *Remember: careful and early planning is essential if this procedure is to work for you.*

Category 2: Books, Fees, and Miscellaneous Expenses

You can work during the summer months of your high school years to save the money necessary to pay a portion of books, fees, and other expenses. These costs can be estimated. A resourceful person can plan ahead and find employment that will fulfill the objectives of saving for school and obtaining valuable work experience. Carefully calculate what you will need to meet these costs at each school you are considering. Then find a job that will allow you to save to meet this portion of your educational expenses.

Category 3: Living Expenses

Information obtained from the school's financial aid bulletin will assist in estimating living expense costs. A monthly budget should include housing costs, food allowance, transportation, clothing allowance, medical costs, personal needs, and an entertainment allowance. It is important that a monthly record of these expenses be kept. This allows you to calculate expenses and resources, and it teaches one of the principles of sound money management.

The following is a list of typical living expenses. This list can be used to keep track of monthly costs and to project costs for the entire year.

	Month	Year
Housing	___	___
Food	___	___
Utilities	___	___
Telephone	___	___
Clothing	___	___
Laundry/dry cleaning	___	___
Entertainment	___	___
Personal expenses	___	___
Transportation	___	___
Insurance	___	___
Medical expenses	___	___
Child care	___	___
Prior indebtedness	___	___
Other expenses	___	___
TOTAL	___	___

Students should consider educational expenses in light of all available financial resources. Consider the following categories when calculating assets:

Personal savings	___
Student's earnings	___
Spouse's earnings	___
Scholarships	___
Aid from parents or guardian	___
Aid from other relatives	___
Veterans benefits	___
Social security benefits	___
Loans	___
Stocks, bonds	___
Other resources	___
TOTAL	___

One suggested method of meeting living expenses during the academic year is for you and your family to divide these costs. This will allow your parents to include in their monthly budget the money they will send you, and it will allow you to calculate the amount of money you can contribute to meet your monthly living expenses. For example, if the monthly living budget is set at $500, you would be responsible for contributing $250 per month, and your family would provide the other $250. Many schools require that room and board costs be met prior to each semester. If a family's budget does not permit that, the family should discuss the matter with the aid administrator or budget officer. Many schools have deferred payment plans and will accept partial payment for these expenses on a monthly basis. Most schools will accommodate students whenever possible.

If your parents cannot afford to contribute anything to meet living expenses, you should investigate housing alternatives. Many housing offices list low-cost or no-cost housing. Check with the housing officer.

If low-cost housing is not an option at your school, maybe a high-paying job is possible. The average student can work approximately 10–20 hours per week without jeopardizing academic studies. Try to find a job that pays more than the minimum wage. A resourceful student can expect to earn about $200 a month. Over the course of an academic year this represents approximately $2000 that can be used to meet expenses. Seek help from the financial aid administrator's office in locating employment. Most students participate either in the College Work-Study Program (CWSP) or in the school's employment program. Both programs can assist in employment placement.

You can also capitalize on any particular job skills you possess. Can you tutor, paint, or serve as a bartender? Meeting some expenses through employment is useful in keeping debt levels manageable. If you know beforehand that working is an essential part of your financial plan, you will be better prepared to incorporate employment into your academic schedule. Over the course of 4 years, the money you earn can go a long way toward reducing the amount of money you borrow to meet your college costs.

What about the student who, for academic reasons, cannot work while attending classes? Not all students should work. Your financial plan must consider academic success a first priority. Special arrangements can be made for students who cannot work and maintain an acceptable academic grade point average. Consult with your school's financial aid counselor and academic dean to find a solution to the problem. Some schools have scholarship funds set aside for these situations.

The financial planning process you began in high school can follow you through college, and should be continued if you plan to pursue a graduate degree. Do not wait until graduation to begin this same financial planning process for graduate or professional school. Begin early the search for a graduate school. Then carefully review the financial aid policies of the schools being considered and determine the family and student resources needed. Be advised that funding on the graduate and professional school level is not as abundant as it is for undergraduate education. Graduate students borrow at a rate that is twice that of undergraduate students. It is likely that you will have to borrow if you pursue a graduate degree.

The key to successful financial management after graduation depends upon a realistic understanding of financial obligations. The planning you began in high school should never end. It is a process of continuous growth and development.

Let's summarize your planning process from high school through graduate school.

High School Junior
- Begin career investigation.
- Read career-related publications.
- Meet with guidance counselor.
- Speak with job specialists.
- Attend college fairs.
- Analyze family finances and assets.
- Begin postsecondary school investigation.
- Contact the admissions officer, financial aid administrator, and placement director at each school under consideration.
- Get school catalogs.
- Compare and contrast the admission policies, academic programs, financial aid programs, placement opportunities, and average student indebtedness at each school.
- Visit schools.
- Begin search for financial aid.

High School Senior
- Complete school admission applications.
- Determine how costs will be met at selected schools through parent, student, and school resources.
- Complete financial aid forms.
- Investigate low-cost housing, employment opportunities, and deferred payment programs.
- Take Scholastic Aptitude Test and other achievement tests and apply for all possible and pertinent awards.

College Junior
- Determine career choice.
- Meet with job specialists in career field.
- Estimate first-year starting salary.
- Project salary increases.
- Investigate graduate schools.
- Contact the admission officer, financial aid administrator, and placement director at each school.
- Obtain school catalogs and financial aid information.
- Obtain employment profile of graduates.
- Compare academic programs, admission policies, financial aid programs, placement opportunities, and average student debt at each school.

- Estimate family contribution.

- Calculate summer savings and academic year employment.

- Compare graduate school costs with family resources and employment savings to determine estimated financial need.

College Senior

- Complete school admission applications.

- Apply for financial aid.

- Investigate low-cost housing, employment opportunities, and available school aid.

- Investigate scholarship programs.

- Add graduate school debt to undergraduate indebtedness, and compare total debt to projected income.

- Calculate monthly loan payments and contrast that amount with projected monthly income.

Not all college students can totally support themselves. Some can and do. Others, with help from their parents, can manage to meet their educational expenses. Still others do the same with assistance from federal and state financial aid sources. Finally, some students may need to find their own funding sources based on ability, location, or a particular ethnic or religious affiliation. Some combination of resources will work for all students. It is up to you, your family, and the school you attend to identify the combination that will work best for you.

Approach educational costs in a positive and optimistic way. View these costs separately in order to provide a realistic plan for financing your education. Explore opportunities for reducing costs. Be determined. Begin the planning process early.

Loan Counseling

Federal law requires all schools that receive federal funds to provide their student borrowers with loan counseling and debt management information. The following is a suggested list of the type of information your school should make available:

1. Were you advised of the school's financial aid policies before you enrolled? Were you informed of application procedures and deadlines?

2. Were you advised of institutional costs, including tuition, fees, books and supplies, room and board, and any additional costs of specific programs?

3. Were you advised how your financial need is determined? Do you know what resources are counted in determining need?

4. Were you advised of potential student debt and ways to structure that debt to meet your educational and future employment objectives?

5. Were you advised about the effect of excessive debt on your future borrowing ability?

6. Were you advised of alternative financing plans offered by your school?

7. Were you advised of the financial counseling services available at your school?

8. Did you receive assistance with constructing a monthly student budget?

9. Did you receive the names and addresses of all of your lenders?

10. Did you participate in an entrance interview at the time of admission and an exit interview at the time of graduation or withdrawal from school?

11. Were you advised of any special charges added to the cost of your loan (origination fee, insurance fee)?

12. Were you advised of the annual and cumulative amounts that can be borrowed in each loan program?

13. Were you advised of monthly interest payments after graduation?

14. Were you advised of the interest rate and the type of interest (simple or compound) for each of your loans?

15. Were you advised of your repayment schedule, your minimum and maximum repayment period, and when repayments must begin?

16. Were you advised of the consequences of defaulting on your student loans?

17. Were you advised of the impact of excessive debt on your personal and future career goals?

18. Were you given a written record of all of your loans?

19. Were you advised of special consolidation or refinancing options after graduation?

20. Were you advised of deferment and forebearance regulations?

21. Do you know *where* and to *whom* to send your loan payments?

22. Do you know whom to contact if you have difficulty meeting your loan payments?

23. Were you advised about the option to prepay your loans at any time without penalty?

24. Were you advised when your loan was sold, and do you know who the new servicer is?

25. Were regular loan counseling sessions and debt management information made available to you?

Students also have responsibilities when they borrow money during college. The following lists some of these obligations:

1. Did you read and understand all of the terms and agreements of your loans?

2. Did you keep copies and accurate records of all of your loan transactions?

3. Did you notify your lender when you graduated?

4. Did you notify your lender if you withdrew from school or dropped below full-time status?

5. Did you notify your lender if you transferred to another school?

6. Do you understand what *deferment* and *loan consolidation* mean?

7. Do you know that you have an obligation to notify your lender of anything that would affect your ability to repay your loan?

8. Do you have an understanding of manageable and unmanageable student debt?

9. Do you realize you will have to make student repayment a part of your financial life after college?

10. Do you realize that you have a *moral* as well as a legal obligation to repay all of your student loans?

11. Do you know that you must attend an exit interview before you leave school?

Default

Let's now consider those students who default on their student loans. Last year the federal government paid over $2.5 billion to lenders to repay the defaulted student loans of undergraduate, graduate, and professional school borrowers. About $8 billion is still in default. Who are the borrowers who fail to repay their student debts? Although there is no one "typical" defaulter, certain characteristics seem to apply to most of this group.

1. Students who do not complete their postsecondary education, dropping out of college or proprietary school before graduation, have a high default rate. Borrowers who last borrowed as first-year students also have a high default rate.

2. Students who attend vocational/technical schools represent the largest group defaulting on student loans.

3. Students from economically disadvantaged backgrounds seem to have difficulty repaying their student loans. However, defaulters include all income groups and races.

4. Borrowers who received no financial assistance from their families represent another large group of defaulters.

5. The majority of defaulters received inadequate loan counseling and debt management information.

Stafford Student Loan Defaults:
Cost to the Federal Government

1978	$ 207,333,000
1979	222,667,000
1980	239,431,000
1981	254,541,000
1982	288,154,000
1983	531,193,000
1984	712,744,000
1985	1,032,252,000
1986	1,371,122,000
1987	1,278,000,000
1988	1,618,000,000
1989	1,700,000,000
1990	2,400,000,000
1991 (estimated)	3,500,000,000

Source: U.S. Department of Education

What are some of the implications of defaulting on your student loan?

1. Defaulters are reported to local credit bureaus, and a delinquent student loan account may prevent you from obtaining other types of credit, such as credit cards, a home mortgage loan, or a car loan.

2. Defaulters will not be permitted to obtain financial aid from other federal financial assistance programs.

3. Defaulters can be taken to court.

4. Defaulters may have their assets taken from them.

5. Defaulters can lose their federal or state income tax refund. The Family Support Act contains a provision allowing the Internal Revenue Service to withhold tax refunds from student loan defaulters.

6. Defaulters may be charged legal fees for collecting their loan.

7. Defaulters are ineligible for student loan deferments.

8. Defaulters may find that their colleges and universities withhold their transcripts.

9. Defaulters may have difficulty obtaining employment in federal agencies.

10. Defaulters may have difficulty enrolling in graduate school.

Repayment

Let's assume you managed to graduate from school with some debt. What happens now? Repayment of a student loan depends upon the type of loan you have.

For Stafford Student Loans, repayment begins 6 months after you graduate, leave school, or drop below half-time status. The same repayment provision regulates Perkins Loans. Parents who have borrowed under the Parent Loans for Undergraduate Students (PLUS) begin repayment approximately 1 month after the first check was issued. Deferment options are available.

Be certain that you have a repayment schedule for each of your loans. This will tell you the exact amount you must pay each month to meet your student loan obligations. This information should be given to you at the time the loan is made. Do not wait until you graduate to find out what you will be required to pay after graduation. If you plan to continue with your studies, you should know all about deferment eligibil-ity. Also remember that you can prepay your entire loan or any portion of it without any penalty and that under certain conditions your loan may be reduced or cancelled. It is your responsibility to notify your lender of any change in your status or any changes of address. Many lenders will issue you a coupon book, which you will use each month to make your loan payment. If your lender sells your loan to another financial institution, this transaction will not change the amount of money you owe.

Keep accurate records while you are in school. Be certain you know the *source* of each loan, the *amount* you borrowed, and *what* you will owe after gradua-tion. Keep copies of all correspondence.

Here is a list of the most common loans and their repayment provisions:

Loan	Interest Rate	Grace Period after Graduation	Years to Repay
Perkins Loans	5%	6 months	10 years
Stafford Student Loans	8%–10%	6–12 months	10 years
Health Professions Loans	5%	1 year	10 years
HEAL Loans	Variable	9 months	25 years

Now let's look at a sample repayment schedule.

Loan	Amount Borrowed	Total Owed	Monthly Bill
Perkins Loans	$ 10,000.00	$ 12,720.00	$ 106.00
Stafford Student Loans	$ 10,000.00	$ 14,559.60	$ 121.00
PLUS Loans	$ 4,000.00	$ 6,885.60	$ 57.38
Health Professions Loans	$ 1,000.00	$ 1,173.87	$ 18.87
HEAL Loans	$ 10,000.00	$ 21,600.00	$ 120.00 (15-year repayment)

44

STUDENT LOAN RECORD

Program	Academic Year	Lender/Address	Amount Borrowed
Stafford Student Loan	_____	_____	_____
	_____	_____	_____
	_____	_____	_____
	_____	_____	_____
PLUS/SLS Loans	_____	_____	_____
	_____	_____	_____
	_____	_____	_____
	_____	_____	_____
Perkins Loan	_____	_____	_____
	_____	_____	_____
	_____	_____	_____
	_____	_____	_____
Health Professions Student Loan	_____	_____	_____
	_____	_____	_____
	_____	_____	_____
Health Education Assistance Loan	_____	_____	_____
	_____	_____	_____
	_____	_____	_____
	_____	_____	_____
School Loans	_____	_____	_____
	_____	_____	_____
Other Loans	_____	_____	_____
	_____	_____	_____
	_____	_____	_____
	_____	_____	_____

Forbearance

What happens if, for some reason, you cannot meet your monthly loan bills? You have two choices. The first is to slip into default status with serious future implications. The second is to contact your lender and make arrangements to pay *some* portion of your bill. NEVER default on your student loan. *Always* be honest and attempt to make payment arrangements with your lender.

If your financial situation makes it impossible to pay your monthly student loan bill, most lenders will grant forbearance, which will allow you to stop making payments temporarily or reduce the amount of your monthly payments. REMEMBER: the federal government will not pay the interest on your federal student loans during a period of forbearance. Your lender will ask you to sign a Forbearance Agreement that indicates the length of forbearance and the required payments. Forbearance is granted for no more than 6 months at a time.

Deferments

A student loan deferment is a temporary postponement of your loan payments. A deferment may be for 6 months or for many years. During this time the federal government pays the interest on your federal student loans to your lender. You take over those payments once the deferment ends.

You may be granted a deferment if you fall into any of the following categories:

1. Deferments may be granted to students enrolled in eligible undergraduate postsecondary schools.

2. Deferments may be granted to students enrolled full-time in approved graduate or professional schools.

3. Deferments may be granted to borrowers who are attending school at least half-time at an approved institution and have obtained loans under Part B of the Higher Education Act.

4. Deferments may be granted to persons participating in an approved rehabilitation training program.

5. Deferments may be granted to persons who are unemployed after graduation.

6. Deferments may be granted to borrowers who are on active duty in the Armed Forces or the National Oceanic and Atmospheric Corps.

7. Deferments may be granted to students participating in an eligible internship or fellowship program.

8. Deferments may be granted to borrowers who are full-time volunteers in such organizations as the Peace Corps, Vista, Action, or other tax-exempt organizations.

9. Deferments may be granted to pregnant women, or to borrowers caring for a newborn or adopted child, who have been enrolled in an eligible school during the last 6 months.

10. Deferments may be granted to borrowers who are disabled, and to borrowers who cannot work because they are caring for a disabled spouse or dependent.

11. Deferments may be granted to borrowers who are teaching full-time in a public or private elementary or secondary school in a teacher shortage area.

12. Deferments may be granted to borrowers who serve as officers in the Commissioned Corps of the United States Public Health Service.

13. Deferments may be granted to borrowers who borrowed under the Stafford Student Loan program after July 1, 1987, and who are the mothers of preschool children, are reentering the work force after a 5-year absence, and are earning less than $1 over the minimum wage.

14. A parent borrower may be eligible for a deferment if the dependent student meets certain deferment conditions.

Loan Forgiveness

Under certain conditions, your student loans may be rescinded or cancelled. These conditions include:

1. Borrowers agree to teach in a designated shortage area or state rural region.

2. Borrowers agree to practice medicine, dentistry, or other health care specialties in a shortage area.

3. Borrowers are active members of the Army, Army Reserves, and the National Guard.

Be certain you know and understand the eligibility requirements of all available loan forgiveness programs. This information could save you a great deal of money.

Loan Consolidation

One way to manage your loan repayment obligations better is by participating in a loan consolidation program. Loan consolidation is not recommended for every borrower, but for some it is advisable. Loan consolidation allows borrowers to make a single monthly payment and lowers monthly payments by extending the length of repayment. For some borrowers, a lower interest rate for some loans will be charged through consolidation, and the flexible payment plans offered will make repayment easier.

Loan consolidation allows a borrower to combine outstanding loans into a single loan, with an extended repayment period. To be eligible for loan consolidation a borrower must have an outstanding student loan debt of at least $5000 and must be in repayment or in the grace period right before repayment begins. Borrowers may not be more than 90 days delinquent or in default on any of the loans they want to consolidate. Under the terms of consolidation, the length of time you have to repay your loans is extended. The interest rate for the consolidated loan will be the weighted average interest rate of all the loans you are consolidating, but cannot be less than 9%. As you can see, loan consolidation is for certain borrowers only.

The following loans may be consolidated:

Stafford Student Loans

Perkins Student Loans

Parent Loans for Undergraduate Students (PLUS)

Supplemental Loans for Students (SLS)

Health Professions Student Loans

Many financial organizations offer loan consolidation programs. The following is a partial list:

Bank One, Merrillville, NA
1000 E. 80th Place
Merrillville, Indiana 46410
1-219-738-6000

Chase Manhattan Bank
1985 Marcus Avenue
New Hyde Park, New York 10042
1-800-645-8246, California borrowers
1-800-632-3219, New York borrowers
1-800-645-8308, Other borrowers

Manufacturers Hanover Trust
100 Duffy Avenue
Hicksville, New York 11801
1-800-MHT-7722

Nellie Mae, Inc.
50 Braintree Hill Park
Braintree, Massachusetts 02184-9916
1-800-852-0603
1-617-849-7708

Pennsylvania Higher Education Assistance Authority
Network Consolidation Center
P.O. Box 8134
Harrisburg, Pennsylvania 17105-9875
1-800-692-7392

Sallie Mae
P.O. Box 1304
Merrifield, Virginia 22116-1304
1-800-524-9100

Remember that loan consolidation is not for everyone. There are trade-offs attached to the program. Because you are extending the repayment period, you will have lower monthly payments, but you will be paying your loans for a longer period of time. You will pay more interest on your loans in a consolidation

program. Your 5% loan may turn into an 8% loan after your other loans are consolidated. Carefully consider whether loan consolidation will benefit you under your particular set of financial circumstances, and then investigate the programs that are available. Check with your school and lender before entering into any loan consolidation agreement.

Note: Congress is reauthorizing all of the federal higher education assistance programs, including loan programs. Regulations governing forbearance, loan deferments, forgiveness, and consolidation may change. Check with your school's financial aid director for the latest information.

Financial Planning after College

The key to successful financial management after college graduation depends upon a realistic understanding of financial obligations. Student financial planning after graduation should take the following into consideration:

1. Graduate school and the loss of income during those years of study

2. Income projections

3. Discretionary income

4. Spouse's income and the possible loss of that income during childbearing years

5. Life-style

Remember to include the following in your monthly budget expenses:

1. Gross income

2. Net income

3. Rent or home mortgage

4. Utilities

5. Food

6. Transportation costs

7. Automobile expenses

8. Medical and dental expenses

9. Insurance premiums

10. Clothing

11. Entertainment expenses

12. Credit card expenses

13. Student loan repayment

14. Miscellaneous expenses

15. Emergency funds

16. Discretionary income, that is, what is left over after all of your other expenses and fixed costs have been met.

You may have to adjust your life-style or your expected life-style to meet all of your financial obligations. For this reason it is important that you do not borrow more money than you can realistically pay back. Be careful; be savvy. Get help if you need it. Don't wait until you are over your head in debt to try to solve the problem. Student loan borrowing does not have to be a problem, but it is up to you to keep your debt under control. *Don't mortgage your future.*

Some Final Notes on Debt

1. Financial management should be an ongoing process that you began in high school. You can master the basics of student financial planning and prepare yourself to continue the process after graduation. This is a process that never ends and is one of continued growth and development.

2. Under no circumstances should a borrower default on a student loan. Make an arrangement with your lender to pay *some* amount.

3. As of July 1991, any college or university with a default rate exceeding 35% will be eliminated from the Stafford Student Loan Program and from the PLUS and SLS loan programs. If you will need to borrow, be certain that any school you are considering does not fall into this category.

8 FEDERAL PROGRAMS

Last year numerous sources awarded billions of dollars in financial aid to college students. The federal government, the largest source of financial assistance, although not the only one, was responsible for 75%. The following list shows the federal dollars allocated to the major student financial assistance programs:

Pell Grant Program	$ 5,374,282,000
Student Educational Opportunity Grant Program (SEOG)	$ 520,155,000
Stafford Student Loan Program	$ 5,381,422,000
Carl D. Perkins Loan Program	$ 156,144,000
College Work-Study Program (CWSP)	$ 594,689,000

Allocations for other federal programs were as follows:

State Student Incentive Grant Program	$ 63,531,000
Paul Douglas Teacher Scholarship Program	$ 14,639,000
Income Contingent Loan (ICL) Program	$ 4,880,000
Byrd Merit Fellowship Program	$ 9,300,000
McAuliffe Fellowship Program	$ 2,000,000

Important Facts to Know

1. The federal government, in recent years, has increased the amount of loan money, but decreased grant funds.

2. The federal government provides to students information from various sources. *The Student Guide: Five Federal Financial Aid Programs* lists all of the federal financial aid programs and gives eligibility requirements for each program. It is available to students and parents free of charge. For a copy of this booklet, write to The Federal Student Aid Information Center, P.O. Box 84, Washington, D.C. 20044, or call 1-800-433-3243.

3. Students should remember that eligibility for federal aid programs may change from year to year and that these changes can increase or decrease correspondingly the amount of money a student receives. Always check with your school's financial aid director to learn of any new regulations. These could change the amount of money your parents must contribute, the amount of money you will borrow, and the number of hours you may have to work.

4. Recently the Omnibus Drug Bill was passed, which allows federal judges to deny federal student aid to persons convicted of drug offenses. Federal student assistance can be denied for up to 5 years.

Important Terms to Know

Ability to Benefit   This regulation applies to students who do not have a high school diploma, or its equivalent, or a General Education Development certificate (GED). A test, approved by the Department of Education, is administered independently to this category of student to assess the individual's ability to benefit from further education.

Anti-drug Abuse Act Certification   To receive a Pell Grant, financial aid applicants must sign a statement certifying that they will not make, use, possess, or distribute drugs during the period covered by the Pell Grant. The Drug Act requires all colleges and universities receiving federal funds to have drug prevention programs and to publicize these programs, as well as the penalties for using illegal drugs.

Campus-based Programs   The federally financed financial aid programs administered by financial aid administrators at colleges and universities are as follows: Perkins Loan, College Work-Study, and the Supplemental Educational Opportunity Grant.

Citizenship   To receive federal financial aid funds, students must be citizens of the United States, permanent residents, or qualified noncitizens.

Congressional Methodology   This is the method used to determine a family's ability to pay college costs, and the method used to determine need for campus-based programs and the Stafford Student Loan Program.

Dependent Student This is a student who is dependent on his or her parents for financial support and is declared as a dependent on the family's federal income tax form.

Dislocated Worker This is a person who has been officially classified as dislocated by a state agency. Often dislocated workers are unemployed because of plant or business closings. Farmers who were once self-employed but are now unemployed because of drought or other natural disasters also fall into this category. Dislocated workers usually qualify for most financial assistance programs. Local state employment agencies and college financial aid offices can provide additional information on eligibility requirements.

Displaced Homemaker This is a person, usually a woman, who has not worked outside the home for at least 5 years. The category also includes people who have received public assistance income or who are currently receiving assistance for dependent children, as well as persons who are classified as underemployed (working part-time). Displaced homemakers may qualify for federal financial aid programs. The financial aid director at the nearest college or university should be consulted for further information on eligibility.

Exceptional Financial Need This is the criterion used to determine eligibility for SEOG, HPSL, and the Perkins Loan Program. Only applicants with the lowest expected family contribution are eligible to receive funding from these federal programs.

Full-time Student Generally, students taking 12 or more credit-hours per semester are classified as full-time. Most state financial assistance programs are available only to full-time students.

Half-time Student To receive a Pell Grant, a Stafford Student Loan, SEOG, Parent Loans for Undergraduate Students, or Supplemental Loans for Students, a student must be classified as at least half-time by the college or university. This classification is determined in the following ways:

Semester, Quarter, or Trimester—The student must attend school for 6 semester or quarter hours per term.

Credit-Hour System—The student must register for 12 semester or 18 quarter hours per school term.

Clock-Hour System—The student must enroll for 12 hours per week.

Independent Student For classification as an independent student, at least one of the following criteria must be met:

Student was born before January 1, 1965, and is at least 24 years old.

Student is enrolled as a graduate or professional student.

Student has legal dependents other than a spouse.

Student is a ward or orphan of the court.

Student is a veteran of the Armed Forces.

Student is married and is not declared as a tax deduction for the calendar year of the award year.

Student is a single undergraduate with no dependents who was not claimed on the parents' income tax returns for two years preceding the award year.

Student has an annual income of at least $4000.

Student has been classified as independent by the school's financial aid director after considering extenuating circumstances and exercising professional judgment.

Parental Leave Deferment Loan payments can be postponed for up to 6 months if the borrower is pregnant or is taking care of a newborn or newly adopted baby. The borrower must be unemployed and not enrolled in school. It is necessary to apply for this deferment within 6 months of leaving school or dropping below half-time status.

Part B Loans This name is used for the Stafford, SLS, and PLUS loan programs.

Pell Grant Index This is the number that appears on the Student Aid Report (SAR) indicating Pell Grant eligibility. This index is calculated using a standard formula and is based on the information reported when a student applies for federal student aid.

Professional Judgment This is the authority given to the school's financial aid director to make adjustments to a student's eligibility for federal financial aid programs and to treat special circumstances that relate to a student's or family's financial situation.

Satisfactory Academic Progress This is a school's written policy of what it considers academic achievement and progress. Generally, students must maintain at least a C average by the end of each academic year or meet the school's other academic requirements for graduation. A one-time waiver can be obtained upon review. Students enrolled in programs shorter than 2 years should check with their schools for clarification of the policy regarding satisfactory academic progress. All students must meet the criteria established by their schools in order to receive federal financial aid.

Self-help Aid This type of financial assistance usually refers to loans or employment.

Special Conditions These are specific circumstances that would alter a student's eligibility for a Pell Grant. Examples of special conditions include death, separation, or divorce; loss of nontaxable income such as social security benefits, welfare payments, or unemployment benefits; or loss of a full-time job.

Statement of Educational Purpose and Certification Statement on Refunds and Default This statement must be signed by a student in order to receive federal funds. The form states that the student agrees to use the financial aid funds only to meet educational costs and that the student has not defaulted on any Title IV loan and does not owe a refund on any Title IV grant.

Statement of Registration Status This statement must be signed by students required to register with the Selective Service. Males born on or after January 1, 1960, who are at least 18 years old and are citizens or eligible noncitizens are required to register. Members of the Armed Forces currently on active duty are not required to sign this statement. A Statement of Registration Status must be on file in order for a student to receive federal student aid.

Statement of Updated Information This statement certifies that certain items of the Student Aid Report were correct at the time the SAR was submitted to a student's college or university. Information that changes after submission of the SAR must be corrected, or a student will not be eligible to receive federal student aid.

Verification The process of verifying information submitted on applications for financial assistance is required by federal regulations. All colleges and universities participating in Title IV programs must verify 30% of all financial aid applications. The U.S. Department of Education selects a certain number of Pell Grant recipients to be verified by their college or university's financial aid administrator. If you are selected for verification, you will be required to submit income and tax information, social security benefit reports, child support statements, and data regarding size of household, capital gains, asset verification, pensions, annuities, and unemployment compensation. Or the verification process may request proof of independence or proof of citizenship. Financial discrepancies totaling more than $200 will require reprocessing.

General Eligibility Requirements for Federal Financial Assistance Programs

In general, for a student to receive funding from federal sources, the following criteria must be met:

- Applicant must have financial need.
- Applicant must have a high school diploma or a general equivalency diploma, or must meet the federal criteria for demonstrating ability to benefit from the desired educational program. Legislation requires postsecondary institutions to give high school dropouts and other students who enter college without earning a high school diploma an independently administered examination to determine their ability to benefit from higher educa-

tion. This regulation applies only to students applying for federal financial assistance.

- Applicant must be enrolled at least half-time as a regular student in an eligible program that leads to a degree or certificate to receive a Pell Grant, Stafford Student Loan, or PLUS or SLS loan.
- Applicant must be a citizen or eligible noncitizen. Eligible United States nationals include natives of American Samoa or Swain's Island. United States permanent residents with I-551 or I-551C status are also eligible to receive federal financial assistance. A student with I-94 status (Arrival-Departure Record) indicating one of the following categories may also be eligible for financial aid: Refugee, Asylum Granted, Indefinite Parole, Humanitarian Parole, Cuban-Haitian Entrant, and Status Pending. A student with a Temporary Resident Card (I-688) is also eligible to apply for financial aid, as are students who have deportation cases pending before Congress.
- Applicant must be making satisfactory academic progress toward a degree or certificate.
- Applicant must sign a Statement of Educational Purpose and a Certification Statement on Refunds and Default.
- Applicant must sign an Anti-drug Abuse Act Certification.
- Applicant must sign a Statement of Updated Information.
- Applicant must sign a Statement of Registration Status.
- Applicant must file student aid application by May 1.
- Applicant must present credible identification before a cash refund from Title IV funds can be dispersed.

Pell Grant Program

The Pell Grant Program is the largest federal need-based program. Last year over 3 million students were awarded more than $5 billion in Pell Grants. The amount of the award varies according to financial need as determined by the U.S. Department of Education through a standard needs analysis formula. Awards range from a low of $200 to a high of $2400, or 60% of the student's college costs, whichever is less.

Eligibility

To receive a Pell Grant, students must meet the following criteria:

1. Recipients must have financial need.
2. Recipients must be enrolled or accepted for enrollment in an approved school, either in an

undergraduate degree or certificate program, and must have a high school diploma or the equivalent.

3. Recipients must be enrolled at least half-time. (Less than half-time may be accepted if funding permits.)

4. Recipients must maintain satisfactory academic progress as determined by the school.

5. Recipients must not owe a refund on any grant or be in default on any loan.

6. Recipients must be U.S. citizens or eligible noncitizens.

7. Male recipients between the ages of 18 and 26 years must meet the requirements of the Selective Service.

8. Recipients must file a Statement of Educational Purpose, stating that all Title IV funds will be used only for educational expenses.

9. Recipients must sign an Anti-drug Abuse Act Certification.

Application Process

The needs analysis system used to calculate financial need is called the Pell Grant Methodology. The formula assigns each applicant a Pell Grant Index (PGI), which determines his or her Pell Grant eligibility. The Student Aid Report (SAR) contains the information submitted on the application for federal student aid. This report, sent to the student approximately 4–8 weeks after it is received by the Pell Grant processor, contains numbers indicating the student's eligibility for a Pell Grant.

Carefully review Part 2 of the SAR, which indicates the information used to determine your Pell Grant eligibility or ineligibility, and contact the processor immediately if an error was made in calculation. If the application is approved, the returned form will have three parts. Part 3 is the payment voucher used by your school. If the request for a Pell Grant is denied, the returned form will have two parts. REMEMBER: eligibility is determined by financial need, college costs, the length of the program, and the student's status (part-time or full-time).

If all of the information on the SAR is correct, sign the form and send a copy of Part 1 to the office of financial aid for each school you are considering. Later, after deciding on one school, you should send all three parts of the SAR to that school's financial aid office. The financial aid counselors will use the SAR to calculate your exact Pell Grant award.

Students should apply after January 1 preceding the academic year of attendance. The application for a Pell Grant must be received by the approved federal Pell Grant processor no later than May 1 of the academic year of enrollment. Students must submit to their school's financial aid office a copy of their Student Aid Report by June 30 or the last day of enrollment. Apply early. Get the necessary forms in as quickly as possible.

Application Forms

The following forms may be used when applying for a Pell Grant:

Application for Federal and State Student Aid (AFSSA)

Application for Federal Student Aid (AFSA)

Family Financial Statement (FFS)—American College Testing Program

Financial Aid Form (FAF)—College Scholarship Service

Pennsylvania Higher Education Assistance Agency's Application for State Grant and Pell Grant (PHEAA)

Student Aid Application for California

United Student Aid Funds Singlefile Form

Note: Processing fees will increase each year.

Sources of Information

You will find the following phone numbers useful in obtaining Pell Grant information:

To ask any questions about Pell Grants, call 1-800-4 FED AID.

To find out whether your application has been processed or to obtain a duplicate copy of your SAR, call 1-301-722-9200.

The number for hearing-impaired callers is 1-301-369-0518.

Some Final Notes on Pell Grants

1. Funding for this program will change from year to year, based on congressional approval and availability of funds. Do not assume that your Pell Grant will be the same each year.

2. Students who transfer to other schools will have to request an official copy of their SAR for the new school. Students who change their student status from part-time to full-time enrollment may change their Pell Grant eligibility or amount of award.

3. If new or changing circumstances affect the family financial resources, and these changes, in turn, affect Pell Grant eligibility, students should file a Special Condition Application. Examples of special conditions are loss of nontaxable income, loss of employment, separation, divorce, and death.

4. Any change in financial circumstances should be discussed with the school's director of financial aid, who may be able to make adjustments that would qualify you for Pell Grant eligibility.

5. Graduate students and professional students are not eligible for Pell Grants.

6. Even if the SAR indicates Pell Grant ineligibility, students should still send a copy to their school's office of financial aid. The Family Contribution number, listed on the SAR, may be used in reviewing eligibility for other federal financial assistance programs.

7. Federal law requires that a certain percentage of financial aid applications are checked each year for information accuracy. The process is called *verification*. If your application is selected, you will be asked to verify your income, federal income tax paid, size of household, untaxed income and benefits, and the number of members in the family who are enrolled at least half-time in a program of postsecondary education. Your school's financial aid director will request certain documents from you and your parents; income tax returns and W-2 forms are most frequently requested. As soon as the required information is received and verified, you will receive the awarded financial aid. Students who do not submit the necessary documents will not receive federal financial assistance. If the financial information listed on the application for federal student aid does not match the data submitted in the verification process, the student will be required to return any overpayment. Always be honest in applying for financial aid. There are penalties if falsified documents or information is submitted.

Supplemental Educational Opportunity Grant (SEOG) Program

Like the Pell Grant Program, the Supplemental Educational Opportunity Grant (SEOG) Program provides moneys to undergraduate students with exceptional financial need. The amount of the award ranges from $100 to $4000, depending upon the student's need and the school's allocation from the federal government. Each participating postsecondary school receives an annual amount of SEOG funds, and the director of financial aid awards the grants to eligible students. Awards vary from year to year. Students are advised to apply early for this program and to observe carefully the deadlines for application established by their school.

Eligibility

To receive a Supplemental Educational Opportunity Grant, students must meet the following criteria:

1. Recipients must be eligible for a Pell Grant.

2. Recipients must have exceptional financial need.

3. Recipients must be enrolled or accepted for enrollment in an approved school.

4. Recipients must be enrolled or accepted for enrollment in a degree or certificate program.

5. Recipients must be citizens or eligible non-citizens.

6. Recipients must not be in default on any loan or owe a refund on any grant.

7. Recipients must maintain satisfactory academic progress as determined by the school.

8. Male recipients must meet the requirements of the Selective Service.

9. Recipients must sign a Statement of Educational Purpose stating that all Title IV funds will be used only for educational expenses.

Application Process

Students cannot apply separately or directly for this program. The school's director of financial aid determines which students will receive Supplemental Educational Opportunity Grants.

Some Final Notes on Supplemental Educational Opportunity Grants

1. Both part-time and full-time students are eligible for this program.

2. Graduate and professional students are not eligible for this program.

3. Students must be eligible to receive Pell Grants in order to qualify for SEOG.

4. Because the Supplemental Educational Opportunity Grant Program receives an annual allocation from the federal government, the amount of the grant may change from one year to the next, depending on the amount of money the school receives.

Stafford Student Loan Program

The Stafford Student Loan Program is a federally subsidized, low-interest loan program. Approximately 5000 schools throughout the United States participate in this largest federal loan program. Undergraduate as well as graduate and professional students are eligible to participate, and Stafford Student Loans are available also to eligible students in approved vocational, business, technical, and trade schools. Students who are enrolled or accepted for enrollment in teacher certification programs on at least a half-time basis are eligible to receive funding under the Stafford Student Loan Program.

There is no annual allocation from Congress for Stafford Student Loans. Any student who meets the criteria for a Stafford Student Loan will receive one. Last year over 3 million students borrowed from this loan program. Eligibility is determined by the school's director of financial aid after reviewing the financial information of the student and parents. Guidelines for the awarding of Stafford Student Loans are established in a list of awarding regulations called the *Congressional Methodology*. Parental and student income, assets, and the number of members in the family are all taken into consideration by the financial aid director in awarding Stafford Student Loans.

Undergraduate first- and second-year students may borrow up to $2625 per academic year; third- and fourth-year students, up to $4000 per year. Students needing a fifth year of school to complete their undergraduate program may also apply for a Stafford Student Loan. The total amount that an undergraduate can borrow through the Stafford Student Loan Program is $17,250. Graduate and professional school students may borrow up to $7500 per academic year, for a total of $54,750, including the amount borrowed as an undergraduate student.

Stafford Student Loans are made to students by banks, credit unions, or savings and loan associations. The loans are insured by a guarantee agency and are reinsured by the federal government. The government pays the interest on the loan while the student is in school and also pays the lenders a special fee that is tied to the interest rate on U.S. Treasury bills.

Eligibility

To receive a Stafford Student Loan, students must meet the following criteria:

1. Recipients must have financial need.

2. Recipients must be enrolled or accepted for enrollment in a certificate or a degree program.

3. Recipients must be enrolled or accepted for enrollment in an approved school.

4. Recipients must be U.S. citizens or eligible non-citizens.

5. Recipients must be enrolled at least half-time.

6. Recipients must not be in default on any loan or owe a refund on any grant.

7. Recipients must maintain satisfactory academic progress as determined by the school.

8. Recipients must have their Pell Grant eligibility determined.

9. Male recipients must meet the requirements of the Selective Service.

10. Recipients must sign a Statement of Educational Purpose stating that all Title IV funds will be used to meet educational expenses.

Application Process

The procedure for obtaining a Stafford Student Loan is as follows:

1. The student obtains a loan application and a form for any other required federal test of financial need from his or her school or lender.

Undergraduate students must first apply for a Pell Grant before they can be considered for a Stafford Student Loan.

2. The student completes the application form. On some applications it is also possible to complete the promissory note at the time of application.

3. After completing Section I of the application, the student takes the form to the school's financial aid office. The financial aid director determines eligibility and completes Section II of the application.

4. The financial aid director sends the completed application to the lender. The form is reviewed and the lender completes its portion of the form. The loan application is then sent to the guarantee agency.

5. The guarantee agency reviews the loan application for eligibility. The lender is then informed whether or not the loan will be guaranteed by the guarantee agency.

6. If the lender receives a guarantee for the loan application, a promissory note and/or a loan disclosure statement is prepared and sent to the student by the lender. A statement of rights and responsibilities is also forwarded to the student.

7. After the signed promissory note is received from the student, the lender issues a check.

8. An origination fee of 5% is deducted from each loan disbursement. The lender may also charge an insurance premium of up to 3% of the loan principal.

Repayment

Students pay no interest on this loan while they are in school and have a grace period of 6–12 months after graduation before they must begin to repay their Stafford Student Loan. During the first 4 years of repayment, an interest rate of 8% is charged. The interest rate rises to 10% beginning in the fifth year of repayment. Borrowers have up to 10 years to repay their Stafford Student Loan. The minimum monthly payment is $50, and the minimum annual payment is $600.

Deferments

In certain situations, repayment of Stafford Student Loans may be postponed or deferred. The following is a list of these situations:

1. Student is enrolled full-time or half-time at an approved school.

2. Student is enrolled full-time at an institution of higher learning operated by the federal government.

3. Student is enrolled in an eligible graduate fellowship program or a rehabilitation training program for the disabled. The deferment is granted for the time the student remains enrolled.

4. Student is enrolled in an approved graduate or professional school. The deferment is granted for the time the student remains enrolled.

5. Borrower is on active duty in the U.S. Armed Forces or serves as an officer in the Commissioned Corps of the United States Public Health Service. A deferment may be granted for up to 3 years.

6. Borrower serves in the Peace Corps or ACTION Programs. A deferment may be granted for up to 3 years.

7. Borrower serves as a full-time volunteer for a tax-exempt organization. A deferment may be granted for up to 3 years.

8. Borrower is unemployed. A deferment may be granted for up to 2 years.

9. Borrower is enrolled in an internship or residency program required by a licensing agency before beginning professional practice or service. A deferment up to 2 years may be granted.

10. Borrower is temporarily totally disabled or cannot work because of caring for a disabled spouse or other dependent. A deferment may be granted for up to 3 years.

11. Borrower is working for the National Oceanic and Atmospheric Administration Corps. A deferment may be granted for up to 3 years.

12. Borrower is a full-time teacher in a public or private elementary school in a designated teacher shortage area. A deferment may be granted for up to 3 years.

13. Borrower is the mother of preschool-age children and is working or returning to work at a salary that is no more than $1 over the federal minimum wage. A deferment may be granted for up to 1 year.

14. Borrower is on parental leave, caring for a newborn or adopted child. A deferment may be granted for up to 6 months.

Cancellation

Stafford Student Loans can be cancelled or forgiven for the following reasons:

1. The borrower dies or becomes totally and permanently disabled.

2. The borrower becomes bankrupt.

3. Borrowers who serve as enlisted personnel in the U.S. Army, the Army Reserves, or the Army National Guard may have a portion of their loan repaid by the Department of Defense.

Sources of Information

For further information on the Stafford Student Loan Program, contact the following guarantee agencies:

ALABAMA
Alabama Commission on Higher Education
1 Court Square, Suite 221
Montgomery, Alabama 36197-0001
(205) 269-2700

ALASKA
Alaska Commission on Postsecondary Education
400 Willoughby Avenue
Pouch FB
Juneau, Alaska 99811
(901) 465-2962

ARIZONA
Arizona Educational Loan Program
2600 N. Central Avenue, Suite 621
Phoenix, Arizona 85004
1-800-352-3033 (in-state)
(602) 252-5793

ARKANSAS
Student Loan Guarantee Foundation of Arkansas
219 S. Victory
Little Rock, Arkansas 72201
(501) 372-1491

CALIFORNIA
California Student Aid Commission
P.O. Box 945625
Sacramento, California 94245
(916) 322-0435

COLORADO
Colorado Student Loan Program
999 18th Street, #425
Denver, Colorado 80202
(303) 294-5050

CONNECTICUT
Connecticut Student Loan Foundation
P.O. Box 1009
Rocky Hill, Connecticut 06067
(203) 257-4001

DELAWARE
Delaware Postsecondary Education Committee
Carvel State Office Building
820 N. French Street, Fourth Floor
Wilmington, Delaware 19801
(302) 571-3240

DISTRICT OF COLUMBIA
Higher Education Loan Program
1023 15th Street, N.W., Suite 100
Washington, D.C. 20005
(202) 289-4500

FLORIDA
Office of Student Financial Assistance
Department of Education
Knott Building
Tallahassee, Florida 32399
(904) 488-4095

GEORGIA
Georgia Student Finance Commission
2082 E. Exchange Place, Suite 200
Tucker, Georgia 30084
(404) 493-5472

HAWAII
Hawaii Education Loan Program
P.O. Box 22187
Honolulu, Hawaii 96822
(808) 536-3731

IDAHO
Student Loan Fund Processing Center
P.O. Box 730
Fruitland, Idaho 83619
(208) 452-4058

ILLINOIS
Illinois State Scholarship Commission
106 Wilmot Road
Deerfield, Illinois 60015
(708) 948-8550

INDIANA
State Student Assistance Commission of Indiana
964 N. Pennsylvania Street
Indianapolis, Indiana 46204
(317) 232-2366

IOWA
Iowa College Aid Commission
201 Jewett Building
Ninth and Grand
Des Moines, Iowa 50309
(515) 281-4890

KANSAS
Higher Education Assistance Foundation
6800 College Boulevard, Suite 600
Overland Park, Kansas 66211
(913) 345-1300

KENTUCKY
Kentucky Higher Education Assistance Authority
1050 U.S. 127 South, Suite 102
West Frankfort, Kentucky 40601
(502) 564-7990

LOUISIANA
Governor's Special Commission on Education and
    Services
P.O. Box 91202
Baton Rouge, Louisiana 70821-9202
(504) 922-1011

MAINE
Maine Educational Assistance Division
Division of Higher Education Services
State House Station 119
Augusta, Maine 04333
(207) 289-2183

MARYLAND
Maryland Higher Education Loan Corporation
2100 Guilford Avenue, Room 305
Baltimore, Maryland 21218
(301) 333-6555

MASSACHUSETTS
Massachusetts Higher Education Assistance
    Corporation
Berkeley Place
330 Stuart Street
Boston, Massachusetts 02116
(617) 426-9796

MICHIGAN
Michigan Higher Education Assistance Authority
Box 30047
Lansing, Michigan 48909
(517) 373-0760

MINNESOTA
Higher Education Assistance Foundation
85 E. Seventh Place
St. Paul, Minnesota 55101
(612) 227-7661

MISSISSIPPI
Mississippi Guarantee Student Loan Agency
3825 Ridgewood
Jackson, Mississippi 39211-6453
(601) 982-6663

MISSOURI
Coordinating Board for Higher Education
P.O. Box 1438
Jefferson City, Missouri 65102
(314) 751-3940

MONTANA
Montana Guaranteed Student Loan Program
33 S. Last Chance Gulch
Helena, Montana 59620
(406) 444-6594

NEBRASKA
Higher Education Assistance Foundation
Cornhusker Bank Building
11th and Cornhusker Highway, Suite 304
Lincoln, Nebraska 68521
(402) 476-9129

NEVADA
Nevada State Department of Education
400 W. King Street/Capitol Complex
Carson City, Nevada 89710
(702) 885-5914

NEW HAMPSHIRE
New Hampshire Higher Education Assistance
    Foundation
P.O. Box 877
Concord, New Hampshire 03302
(603) 225-6612

NEW JERSEY
New Jersey Higher Education Assistance Authority
C.N. 00543
Trenton, New Jersey 08625
(609) 588-3200

NEW MEXICO
New Mexico Educational Assistance Foundation
P.O. Box 27020
Albuquerque, New Mexico 87125
(505) 345-3371

NEW YORK
New York State Higher Education Services
    Corporation
99 Washington Avenue
Albany, New York 12255
(518) 473-1575

NORTH CAROLINA
North Carolina State Education Assistance Authority
P.O. Box 2688
Chapel Hill, North Carolina 27515-2688
(919) 549-8614

NORTH DAKOTA
Bank of North Dakota
Student Loan Department
Box No. 5509
Bismarck, North Dakota 58502
(701) 224-5656

OHIO
Ohio Student Loan Commission
P.O. Box 16610
Columbus, Ohio 43266-0610
(614) 644-6627

OKLAHOMA
Oklahoma State Regents for Higher Education
550 Education Building
State Capitol Complex
Oklahoma City, Oklahoma 73105
(405) 521-8262

OREGON
Oregon State Scholarship Commission
1445 Willamette Street, No. 9
Eugene, Oregon 97401
1-800-452-8807
(503) 346-3200

PENNSYLVANIA
Pennsylvania Higher Education Assistance Agency
660 Boas Street
Harrisburg, Pennsylvania 17102
1-800-692-7392
(717) 257-2860

RHODE ISLAND
Rhode Island Higher Education Assistance Authority
560 Jefferson Boulevard
Warwick, Rhode Island 02886
(401) 277-2050

SOUTH CAROLINA
South Carolina Student Loan Corporation
Interstate Center, Suite 210
P.O. Box 21487
Columbia, South Carolina 29221
(803) 798-0916

SOUTH DAKOTA
Education Assistance Corporation
115 First Avenue, S.W.
Aberdeen, South Dakota 57401
(605) 225-6423

TENNESSEE
Tennessee Student Assistance Corporation
404 James Robertson Parkway
Nashville, Tennessee 37243-0820
(615) 741-1346

TEXAS
Texas Guaranteed Student Loan Corporation
P.O. Box 15996
Austin, Texas 78761
(512) 835-1900

UTAH
Utah Higher Education Assistance Authority
P.O. Box 45202
Salt Lake City, Utah 84145-0202
(801) 538-5240

VERMONT
Vermont Student Assistance Corporation
Champlain Mill
P.O. Box 2000
Winooski, Vermont 05404
1-800-642-3177
(802) 655-9602

VIRGINIA
State Education Assistance Authority
6 N. Sixth Street, Suite 300
Richmond, Virginia 23219
(804) 786-2035

WASHINGTON
Washington Student Loan Guarantee Association
500 Colman Building
811 First Avenue
Seattle, Washington 98104
(206) 625-1030

WEST VIRGINIA
Higher Education Assistance Foundation
P.O. Box 591
Charleston, West Virginia 25322
(304) 345-7211

WISCONSIN
Wisconsin Higher Education Corporation
2401 International Lane
Madison, Wisconsin 53704
(608) 246-1800

WYOMING
Higher Education Assistance Foundation
American National Bank Building
1912 Capitol Avenue, Suite 320
Cheyenne, Wyoming 82001
(307) 635-3259

AMERICAN SAMOA
Pacific Islands Educational Loan Program
United Student Aid Funds, Inc.
1314 S. King Street, Suite 962
Honolulu, Hawaii 96814
(808) 536-3731

NORTHERN MARIANA ISLANDS, FEDERATED STATES OF MICRONESIA, MARSHALL ISLANDS, REPUBLIC OF PALAU
Pacific Islands Educational Loan Program
United Student Aid Funds, Inc.
1314 S. King Street, Suite 962
Honolulu, Hawaii 96814
(808) 536-3731

GUAM
Pacific Islands Educational Loan Program
United Student Aid Funds, Inc.
1314 S. King Street, Suite 962
Honolulu, Hawaii 96814
(808) 536-3731

PUERTO RICO
Higher Educational Assistance Corporation
P.O. Box 42001
Minillas Station
San Juan, Puerto Rico 00940
(809) 723-6000

VIRGIN ISLANDS
Board of Education
P.O. Box 11900
St. Thomas, Virgin Islands 00801
(809) 774-4546

Some Final Notes on Stafford Student Loans

1. Students should apply as soon as possible for a Stafford Student Loan. It often takes up to 2 months for a student to receive a check after the application is filed.

2. Borrowers should know the name, address, and phone number of the lender and guarantee agency.

3. Some lenders offer students who do not meet the criteria for a federally subsidized loan an unsubsidized Stafford Student Loan. This means that instead of the federal government paying the interest costs while the student is in school, the student is required to pay the interest. However, the same low rate of interest is charged.

4. Because of the high default rates for some schools, the regulations governing the Stafford Student Loan Program may change. Students should check with their school's financial aid director for the latest information on the program.

Carl D. Perkins Loan Program

Perkins Loans are federal low-interest loans made to eligible undergraduate, graduate, and professional school students. The awards are based upon need and are awarded by the school's director of financial aid in accordance with an annual allocation of funds. The interest rate charged on Perkins Loans is 5%, and is deferred until 9 months after graduation and 6 months after every deferment. Eligible students may receive up to $4500 for the first 2 years of study and up to $9000 for the second 2 years of undergraduate school. Graduate and professional school students may receive up to $18,000, including Perkins Loans received as undergraduate students.

Eligibility

To receive a Perkins Loan, students must meet the following criteria:

1. Recipients must have financial need.

2. Recipients must be enrolled or accepted for enrollment at an approved school.

3. Recipients must be enrolled or accepted for enrollment in a degree or certificate program.

4. Recipients must be U.S. citizens or eligible noncitizens.

5. Recipients must maintain satisfactory academic progress as determined by the school.

6. Recipients must not be in default on any loan or owe a refund on any grant.

7. Recipients must sign a Statement of Educational Purpose stating that all Title IV funds will be used only for educational purposes.

8. Male recipients must meet the requirements of the Selective Service.

Application Process

Students cannot apply separately or directly for Perkins Loans. Awards are made by the school's director of financial aid and are based upon the student's financial need and the amount of money available to the college to lend. Each school determines its own deadline for applying for this loan. The amount available for lending will vary from year to year based on the federal allocation to the school. Colleges and universities generally credit a student's account with the amount of the awarded loan after the student signs a promissory note that outlines the terms of the loan and the repayment obligations.

Repayment

1. Borrowers must pay a minimum of $30 per month or $360 per year.

2. Repayment begins 9 months after graduation and 6 months after each deferment. Borrowers have 10 years to repay their loans.

Deferments

A deferment is an extension, granted by the federal government to students with federal loans, which extends the period of time before a student must begin repaying the loan. Deferments are not automatic; borrowers must apply to their school to get approval. Deferments are granted for Perkins Loans in the following situations:

1. Borrower is a member of the Armed Forces, ACTION, Peace Corps, Public Health Service, or National Oceanic and Atmospheric Administration Corps. Deferments of up to 3 years may be granted.

2. Borrower is enrolled in an internship or residency program. Deferment status will last for the duration of enrollment in the program, or up to 2 years.

3. Borrower is disabled or is caring for a disabled spouse. Deferments of up to 3 years may be granted.

4. Borrower is unemployed. The length of the deferment will vary and is at the school's discretion.

5. Borrower is the mother of preschool children and is working in a job paying no more than $1 over the minimum wage. Deferments of up to 1 year may be granted.

6. Borrower is on parental leave. Deferments of up to 6 months may be granted.

7. Borrower is encountering a period of hardship as determined by the school.

Cancellation

In some cases, Perkins Loans will be partially cancelled or forgiven by the federal government. The following are examples of reasons for loan cancellation:

1. Borrower teaches handicapped children on a full-time basis. Part of the loan will be cancelled for each year of teaching.

2. Borrower is teaching full-time in an elementary or secondary school that serves low-income students. Fifteen percent of the loan will be cancelled for each of the first 2 years; 20% for the third year; 20% for the fourth year; and 30% in the fifth year.

3. Borrower is employed full-time in a Head Start Program. Fifteen percent of the loan will be cancelled for each year of employment.

4. Borrower is serving in the Peace Corps or Vista. Part of the loan is cancelled for each year of service, up to a total maximum of 70%.

5. Borrower dies or becomes permanently disabled.

6. Borrower is a serviceperson stationed in an area of hostility. A maximum of 50% may be cancelled.

7. Borrower becomes bankrupt.

College Work Study Program (CWSP)

The College Work-Study Program (CWSP) is a federal employment program for graduate and undergraduate students that is administered by individual schools. It provides jobs to qualified students both on-campus and off-campus. Often the jobs are career-related and provide an opportunity for students to learn about their prospective careers. It is an excellent way for students to meet some of their college expenses and reduce their student debt. Studies prove that students who work between 10 and 20 hours a week often do better academically in school than students who do not work. The amount a student is allowed to earn may vary from year to year depending

on the school's federal allocation. However, the amount of the award cannot exceed a student's financial need as determined by one of the approved need analysis systems. Students employed in the CWSP will be paid at least the current minimum wage.

Eligibility

To participate in the College Work-Study Program, students must meet the following criteria:

1. Recipients must have financial need.

2. Recipients must be enrolled or accepted for enrollment in an approved school.

3. Recipients must be enrolled or accepted for enrollment in a degree or certificate program.

4. Recipients must be U.S. citizens or eligible non-citizens.

5. Recipients must maintain satisfactory academic progress as determined by their school.

6. Recipients must sign a Statement of Educational Purpose stating they will use all Title IV funds to meet educational expenses.

7. Male recipients must meet Selective Service requirements.

8. Recipients must not be in default on any loan or owe a refund on any grant.

9. Recipients must be enrolled at least half-time.

Application Process

Each school has its own application process, deadlines, and method of placement. Request specific information from the director of financial aid or the CWSP coordinator.

Some Final Notes on the College Work-Study Program

1. This program is available to undergraduate and graduate students.

2. The amount you earn may vary from year to year depending on your academic schedule, your need, and the school's allocation from the federal government. Most students earn between $1000 and $2000 per academic year.

3. CWSP employment is a popular program. Apply early. Discuss options with your director of financial aid or work-study coordinator.

4. You should not work if your academic program will be compromised as a result. Remember that you are in school first to learn. Discuss any academic difficulties you have with your academic advisor and financial aid director.

Robert C. Byrd Honors Scholarship Program

This federal program awards outstanding high school students with $1500 scholarships on the basis of merit. The awards are based upon high school grades, test scores, and high school academic awards. Personal references are also taken into consideration for awarding the scholarship. The $1500 awards are granted for only 1 year and are not renewable. Interested students should contact their high school guidance counselors or college financial aid directors for further information and application materials.

Paul Douglas Teacher Scholarship Program

The Paul Douglas Teacher Scholarship Program provides scholarship assistance to outstanding high school seniors who plan to pursue a career in teaching. The program offers scholarships up to $5000 per year for 4 years. The amount of the award is based upon financial need. Under the terms of agreement, for each year the award was received a student agrees to teach 2 years in a public or private elementary or secondary school anywhere in the United States. If the student does not meet the program's specific conditions, the scholarship becomes a loan and must be repaid at a 10% interest rate.

Eligibility

To receive a Paul Douglas Teacher Scholarship, students must meet the following criteria:

1. Recipients must be U.S. citizens or permanent residents.

2. Recipients must be enrolled as full-time students.

3. Recipients must have graduated from high school in the top 10% of their class, or be ranked in the upper 10% of students taking the SAT or ACT examinations.

4. Recipients must be enrolled or accepted for enrollment in a certified teacher training program.

5. Recipients must submit an essay stating the reasons for selecting a teaching career.

Application Process

Applications may be obtained from high school guidance counselors and college financial aid directors, or by writing to Department of Education, 400 Maryland Avenue, S.W., Washington, D.C. 20202.

Some Final Notes on the Paul Douglas Teacher Scholarship Program

1. The scholarships are competitive and are awarded to academically outstanding students.

2. The scholarship program is available only to undergraduate students enrolled on a full-time basis. Part-time students, and graduate and professional students, are not eligible for this program.

3. Recipients must maintain satisfactory academic progress as determined by their school in order to continue to receive funds under this program.

4. Recipients who agree to teach in a state-designated shortage area may have their teaching obligation reduced by 50%.

Income Contingent Loan (ICL) Program

The Income Contingent Loan (ICL) Program is a new federal loan program, authorized by the Higher Education Amendments of 1986. Although regulated by the federal government, the ICL is unlike other federal loan programs. There are no interest subsidies, and the interest rate is set at 3% above the U.S. Treasury bill rate.

The ICL Program allows students to borrow up to $4000 during the first 2 years of study and $5000 after the second year, up to a total of $50,000. Repayment begins 90 days after a borrower ends at least half-time student status. Borrowers have up to 30 years to repay this loan. Repayment provisions are flexible, are tied to income, and may not exceed 15% of a borrower's adjusted gross income.

Eligibility

Students must meet the same eligibility standards as for other aid programs.

Application Process

The ICL is available only at selected colleges and universities. Check with your school's director of financial aid for further details and application procedures.

Some Final Notes on the Income Contingent Loan Program

1. This is a relatively new loan program. There is some doubt that the program will continue if the early pilot project results prove unfavorable.

2. This is an *expensive* loan. Treat an ICL as a loan of last resort. REMEMBER: the next 30 years of your life could be affected.

3. Only a small number of schools have applied to participate in the ICL Program. Check with your director of financial aid to determine whether your college or university is eligible to make awards under the program.

Parent Loans for Undergraduate Students (PLUS) and Supplemental Loans for Students (SLS)

PLUS loans are made to parents regardless of income and are generally utilized by families who do not qualify for other federal loan programs. SLS loans are made to independent undergraduate students and graduate and professional school students who are ineligible to receive other types of federal financial aid. Under both loan programs, eligible borrowers may obtain $4000 a year to meet educational expenses. The total amount that can be borrowed may not exceed $20,000. These loans can be used to offset expected family contributions. The interest rate is variable but cannot exceed 12%. Repayment begins 2 months after the loan is made but can be deferred.

Eligibility

To qualify for a PLUS or SLS loan, students must meet the following criteria:

1. Recipients must be enrolled or accepted for enrollment in a degree or certificate program.

2. Recipients must be enrolled or accepted for enrollment in an approved school.

3. Recipients may be enrolled in undergraduate, vocational, trade and technical schools, business schools, or graduate and professional schools. Students who are enrolled or accepted for enrollment at least half-time in a teacher certification program are eligible to receive aid under the PLUS and SLS programs.

4. Recipients must be U.S. citizens or eligible non-citizens.

5. Male recipients must meet the requirements of the Selective Service.

6. Recipients must be enrolled at least half-time.

7. Recipients must maintain satisfactory academic progress as defined by the school.

8. Recipients must not be in default on any loan or owe a refund on any grant.

9. Recipients must sign a Statement of Educational Purpose stating that all Title IV funds will be used to meet educational expenses.

10. Recipients of SLS loans must first have their eligibility for a Pell Grant and Stafford Student Loan determined. SLS eligibility is limited to the cost of attendance minus other financial aid received, including a Stafford Student Loan.

11. Dependent undergraduate students are eligible to borrow under the SLS program if the financial aid director determines that exceptional circumstances would preclude the student's parents from borrowing under the PLUS program.

Application Process

The procedure for obtaining a PLUS or SLS loan is as follows:

1. Borrower should obtain an application form from the appropriate lender or college or university financial aid office.

2. For PLUS loans, the parent completes Section IA of the application form, and the student completes Section IB and returns the form to the school's financial aid office.

3. For SLS loans, the student completes Section IA and Section IB and returns the form to the school's financial aid office.

4. The financial aid director completes Section II and sends the application to the appropriate lender.

5. Lenders may require a credit check before approving the loan. However, there is no needs test.

6. After the loan is guaranteed, the application and promissory note are returned to the lender.

7. The lender will send a check directly to the parents. If you are a student borrower, the check will be sent to your school. A student borrower may have the check made payable to him or her and the school.

8. First-year undergraduate students enrolled in a program of less than a full academic year have different annual borrowing limits for SLS loans. For students enrolled in a program that is at least two-thirds of an academic year but less than a full academic year, $2500 is the limit. For students enrolled in a program that is less than two-thirds but is at least one-third of an academic year, $1500 is the limit.

9. Before a student can receive a SLS loan, the college or university must determine eligibility for a Stafford Loan and for a Pell Grant. If a student is eligible to receive aid from either of these two sources, the amount of the SLS loan may be affected. A student may not borrow more than the cost of education minus other financial aid.

10. A lender may charge an insurance premium of up to 3% of the loan principal. This premium is deducted from each loan disbursement. There is no origination fee for these loans.

Repayment

Repayment of the principal and interest begins within 60 days after the loan is made. Interest accrues as soon as the loan is made. Borrowers may defer the interest while in school, but this makes the loans more expensive. Lenders can capitalize the interest as much as four times a year. The minimum annual repayment is $600, and the repayment period extends up to 10 years. Although there are no origination or service charges, an insurance fee of up to 3% is charged. Both of these loans are made by banks, savings and loan associations, credit unions, and states. State guarantee agencies can provide information on available lenders for PLUS and SLS loans.

Deferments

Deferments may be granted in certain situations.

1. Borrowers who are enrolled at least half-time in an approved postsecondary school are eligible for a PLUS and SLS deferment for the length of time they remain enrolled.

2. Borrowers who are studying at a school operated by the federal government are eligible for a PLUS and SLS deferment while they remain enrolled as full-time students.

3. Borrowers who are enrolled in eligible graduate fellowship programs or in rehabilitation programs for the disabled are eligible for a PLUS and SLS deferment while they remain enrolled as full-time students.

4. Borrowers who serve in the Peace Corps or ACTION programs, or other tax-exempt organizations, are eligible to receive a deferment of up to 3 years for SLS loans. There is no deferment in this category for PLUS borrowers.

5. Borrowers who serve on active duty in the Armed Forces or in the Commissioned Corps of the United States Public Health Service are eligible to receive a deferment of up to 3 years for SLS loans. There is no deferment in this category for PLUS borrowers.

6. Borrowers who serve on active duty in the National Oceanic and Atmospheric Administration Corps are eligible to receive a deferment of up to 3 years for an SLS loan. There is no deferment in this category for PLUS borrowers.

7. Borrowers who are unemployed may receive a deferment of up to 2 years for PLUS and SLS loans.

8. Borrowers who are temporarily totally disabled, or who cannot work because of caring for a temporarily totally disabled spouse or other dependent, are eligible to receive a deferment of up to 3 years for PLUS and SLS loans.

9. Borrowers who are full-time teachers in a public or private primary or secondary school that has been designated as a teacher shortage area are eligible to receive a deferment of up to 3 years for SLS loans. There is no deferment in this category for PLUS loans.

10. Borrowers who are enrolled in approved internship programs are eligible to receive a deferment of up to 2 years for SLS loans. There is no deferment in this category for PLUS loans.

11. Borrowers who are on parental leave are eligible to receive a deferment of up to 6 months for SLS loans. There is no deferment in this category for PLUS loans.

12. Borrowers who are the mothers of preschool children and who are going to work or returning to work at a salary no more than $1.00 over the minimum wage are eligible to receive a deferment of up to 1 year for SLS loans. There is no deferment in this category for PLUS borrowers.

Cancellation

PLUS and SLS loans can be cancelled for the following reasons:

1. Borrower dies or becomes totally and permanently disabled.

2. Borrower becomes bankrupt.

3. Borrowers who serve as enlisted personnel in the U.S. Army, the Army Reserves, or the Army National Guard may have a portion of their loan repaid by the Department of Defense.

Some Final Notes about Obtaining Federal Financial Aid

1. It is important to remember that, no matter what your income, you should file for federal financial aid every year. Most schools will not consider you for their own financial assistance programs if you do not have a federally approved financial aid application on file. Also, your financial circumstances may change during the year. If a financial aid application is on file, it will be much easier for the financial aid counselor to consider your request for assistance.

2. ·The Congressional Scholarship for Math, Science, and Engineering Act authorizes federal funding for students pursuing careers in math and science. The new programs provide financial assistance to freshmen who agree to study science, mathematics, or engineering; to junior and senior students who agree to pursue one of these three fields in graduate school; and to junior and senior students who agree to teach in elementary or secondary school for two years for each year of aid they receive. Check with your school's financial aid counselor for further information.

3. The Student Right-To-Know and Campus Security Act requires colleges and universities to make available the following statistics: the graduation rates of all students and of student athletes, the job placement rates of all students and of student athletes, campus security policies, and campus crimes.

4. The National and Community Service Act of 1990 authorizes colleges and universities to develop community service projects. No more than 50 students would be selected at each participating institution, and financial assistance would

not exceed the cost of tuition and fees. Check with your school's financial aid officer for further information.

5. A word to the wise: Federal regulations frequently change the eligibility requirements and also the way in which federal financial aid is awarded. Remember that you must reapply each year for aid. Even though you receive aid one year, there is no guarantee that you will receive it the next year. Also, the amount of your award may change from one year to another. Apply early—as soon after January 1 as possible—especially for the Pell Grant Program. Check with your school's financial aid counselor as to the regulations to follow to receive aid from the school. Be aware of any changes in federal rules.

Meet all of the deadlines. Good luck!

SUMMARY OF ELIGIBILITY FOR FEDERAL STUDENT AID PROGRAMS

Eligibility Requirements: ⬇	Pell Grants	Stafford Loans (Formerly Guaranteed Student Loans [GSL])	Supplemental Educational Opportunity Grants (SEOG)	College Work-Study (CWS)	Perkins Loans
Undergraduate	Yes	Yes	Yes	Yes	Yes
Graduate	No	Yes	No	Yes	Yes
At least half-time	Yes*	Yes	Yes*	Yes*	Yes*
Must pay back	No	Yes	No	No	Yes
Must be a U.S. citizen or eligible noncitizen	Yes	Yes	Yes	Yes	Yes
Must be registered with the Selective Service (if required)	Yes	Yes	Yes	Yes	Yes
Must have financial need	Yes	Yes	Yes	Yes	Yes
Must attend a participating school	Yes	Yes	Yes	Yes	Yes
Must be working toward a degree or certificate	Yes	Yes**	Yes	Yes	Yes
Must be making satisfactory academic progress	Yes	Yes	Yes	Yes	Yes
Must not be in default or owe a refund on a Federal grant or educational loan	Yes	Yes	Yes	Yes	Yes
Having a Bachelor's degree makes applicant ineligible	Yes	No	Yes	No	No
Conviction of drug distribution or possession may make student ineligible	Yes	Yes	Yes	Yes	Yes

*   In some cases, students going to school less than half-time may be eligible.
** In some cases, students don't have to be in a degree or certificate program.

SOURCE: U.S. Department of Education

LOAN PROGRAMS COMPARISON CHART

	STAFFORD LOAN (formerly GSL)	SLS	PLUS	PERKINS
LOAN DESCRIPTION	• Low interest, federally subsidized loan	• Federally guaranteed, Educational Loan Program for independent students	• Federally guaranteed, Educational Loan Program for dependent students	• Low interest, federally subsidized loan
ELIGIBLE BORROWERS	• U.S. Citizen or Eligible Noncitizen (I-151 or I-551) • Student who is enrolled or has been accepted for enrollment as at least half-time • Student who is maintaining satisfactory academic progress • Student who is not in default on any student loans nor obligated to refund any grants	• U.S. Citizen or Eligible Noncitizen (I-151 or I-551) • Student who is enrolled or has been accepted for enrollment as at least half-time • Student who is maintaining satisfactory academic progress • Student who is not in default on any student loans nor obligated to refund any grants	• U.S. Citizen or Eligible Noncitizen (I-151 or I-551) • Student who is enrolled or has been accepted for enrollment as at least half-time • Student who is maintaining satisfactory academic progress • Student and parent who are not in default on any student loans nor obligated to refund any grants • Borrower must be student's mother, father, legal guardian, or adoptive parent	• U.S. Citizen or Eligible Noncitizen (I-151 or I-551) • Student who is enrolled or has been accepted for enrollment as at least half-time • Student who is maintaining satisfactory academic progress • Student who is not in default on any student loans nor obligated to refund any grants
SIGNERS OF APPLICATION	• Borrower/Student • School • Lender	• Borrower/Student • School • Lender	• Borrower • School • Student • Lender	• Borrower/Student
ANNUAL LOAN LIMITS	•$2625 Freshman & Sophomore • $4000 Junior, Senior, & 5th Year • $7500 Graduate • Borrowers required to demonstrate financial need	• $4000 • May not exceed the student's estimated cost of attendance less the estimated financial aid award	• $4000 per dependent student • May not exceed the student's estimated cost of attendance less the estimated financial aid award	• Up to $4500 for the first two years of undergraduate study up to $9000 for the second two years of undergraduate study • Graduate and Professional school students may receive up to $18,000 including Perkins Loans received as undergraduates
CUMULATIVE LOAN LIMITS	• $17,250 Undergraduate •$ 54,750 Total	• $20,000 Total	• $20,000 Total per dependent student	• $9000 Undergraduate • $18,000 Total
INTEREST RATE	• 7%, 8%, 9% Prior Borrowers • 8%–10% New Borrowers (Increase to 10% after four years of payment)	• 10.45% Variable Rate (7/1/88 – 6/30/89)	• 10.45% Variable Rate (7/1/88 – 6/30/89)	• 5%
FEES	• Administrative Fee of 1% • Origination Fee of 5%	• Administrative Fee of 1%	• Administrative Fee of 1%	• No fees
CHECK ISSUED	• 30 days prior to start of school • Check co-payable to borrower and school • Two installments may be necessary	• 30 days prior to start of school • Check co-payable to borrower and school • Two installments may be necessary	• 30 days prior to start of school • Check payable to borrower	• No check issued • Promissory note signed by student
REPAYMENT BEGINS	• 8% & 9%: Six-month Grace Period • 7%: Nine-month Grace Period	• Sixty days after disbursement unless principal deferred	• Sixty days after disbursement unless principal deferred	• Six months after graduation and six months after each deferment
MINIMUM MONTHLY PAYMENT	• $50.00	• $50.00	•$50.00	• $30.00
LENGTH OF PAYMENT	• 120 Months (Maximum)	• 120 Months (Maximum)	• 120 Months (Maximum)	• 120 Months

PRINTED WITH THE PERMISSION OF THE VERMONT STUDENT ASSISTANCE CORPORATION

9 STATE PROGRAMS

While state spending on student aid exceeded $40 billion last year, that was about $80 million less than the previous year. However, states do provide residents with many financial assistance programs.

The educated and savvy student assumes the responsibility for obtaining as *much* information as *early* as possible about state financial aid programs. The state resources listed in this chapter will assist you in this process. When writing or calling your state educational agency, be certain to request the following information appropriate to your situation:

TUITION FUTURES AND PREPAYMENT PROGRAMS

STATE SCHOLARSHIP AND GRANT PROGRAMS

STATE LOAN PROGRAMS

STATE EMPLOYMENT PROGRAMS

SPECIAL FINANCIAL AID PROGRAMS

FINANCIAL ASSISTANCE FOR MINORITY STUDENTS

FINANCIAL AID FOR GRADUATE STUDENTS

FINANCIAL ASSISTANCE FOR HANDICAPPED STUDENTS

FINANCIAL AID PROGRAMS FOR INTERNATIONAL STUDENTS

Be persistent. Be patient. Be inquisitive. Don't give up.

Important Facts to Know

1. All state educational agencies provide need-based financial assistance, and many state agencies award merit-based scholarship assistance.

2. Over three-fifths of all states have created some kind of guaranteed tuition plan or educational savings program for their state residents. The following states offer prepaid tuition plans, allowing parents to pay a certain sum of money, years in advance, for their children's education, or tuition savings plans, usually in the form of tax-exempt bonds or zero coupon bonds: Alabama, Arkansas, Colorado, Connecticut, Delaware, Georgia, Hawaii, Illinois, Indiana, Iowa, Kentucky, Louisiana, Maine, Maryland, Michigan, Minnesota, Missouri, New Hampshire, New Jersey, New York, North Carolina, North Dakota, Ohio, Oklahoma, Oregon, Pennsylvania, Rhode Island, Tennessee, Texas, Virginia, Washington, West Virginia, Wisconsin, and Wyoming. In addition, Louisiana, Florida, Texas, and Ohio have adopted the "Taylor Plan," which guarantees that the state will pay the tuition costs of eligible moderate- and low-income students who meet the academic qualifications to attend college.

3. The following states offer work-study programs: California, Colorado, Connecticut, Florida, Iowa, Indiana, Kansas, Louisiana, Massachusetts, Michigan, Minnesota, Nevada, New Mexico, North Carolina, Pennsylvania, Rhode Island, South Carolina, Texas, Vermont, and Washington.

4. The following states offer loan-forgiveness programs for specific professions such as education or health-related careers: Alabama, Arkansas, California, Connecticut, Delaware, Florida, Georgia, Hawaii, Illinois, Indiana, Iowa, Kentucky, Louisiana, Maryland, Massachusetts, Mississippi, Missouri, New Jersey, New Mexico, New York, North Carolina, Ohio, Oklahoma, Oregon, Pennsylvania, South Carolina, Tennessee, Texas, Utah, Vermont, Virginia, Washington, West Virginia, and Wisconsin.

5. The following states offer tuition-equalization programs, which allow participants to reduce the difference in cost between public and private colleges: Alabama, Florida, Georgia, North Carolina, Ohio, and Virginia.

6. Fourteen states participate in the Western Undergraduate Exchange Program administered by the Western Interstate Commission for Higher Education (WICHE). This program allows students to participate in tuition reciprocity agreements. The states in the WICHE program are Alaska, Arizona, Colorado, Hawaii, Idaho, Montana, Nevada, New Mexico, North Dakota, Oregon, South Dakota, Utah, Washington, and Wyoming.

7. The following states provide financial assistance to students attending private colleges and universities within the state: Connecticut, Iowa, Kansas, Kentucky, Maryland, Michigan, South Carolina, South Dakota, Texas, and Wisconsin.

8. The following states offer special state loan programs to assist students in meeting their financial obligations: Alaska, Colorado, Connecticut, Delaware, District of Columbia, Hawaii, Indiana, Maryland, Massachusetts, Minnesota, Nevada, New Hampshire, New York, Pennsylvania, South Carolina, Texas, Vermont, and West Virginia.

9. The following states offer merit-based scholarships or state student incentive grants: Alabama, Alaska, Arizona, Arkansas, California, Colorado, Connecticut, Delaware, Florida, Georgia, Hawaii, Idaho, Illinois, Indiana, Iowa, Kansas, Kentucky, Louisiana, Maine, Maryland, Massachusetts, Michigan, Minnesota, Mississippi, Missouri, Montana, Nevada, New Hampshire, New Jersey, New Mexico, New York, North Carolina, North Dakota, Ohio, Oklahoma, Oregon, Pennsylvania, Rhode Island, South Carolina, South Dakota, Tennessee, Texas, Utah, Vermont, Virginia, Washington, West Virginia, and Wyoming.

10. The following states have adopted guaranteed free-tuition plans to qualified and needy students: Arkansas, Florida, Indiana, Louisiana, Maryland, New Mexico, and Texas. (These programs are based upon the ones developed in New York by Eugene Lang, founder of the I Have a Dream Foundation, and Patrick Taylor, the businessman behind the "Taylor Kids" Program in Louisiana.)

Following is a list, for each state, of all state scholarship and loan agencies and the state student assistance programs offered. Please remember the deadline dates often change, as does the amount of money awarded and the regulations governing awarding.

Alabama

Average tuition and fees:
 Public 4-year institutions—$1522
 Public 2-year institutions—$ 622
 Private 4-year institutions—$5484
 Private 2-year institutions—$3703

State spending on student aid:
 Need-based—$4,353,000; 4783 awards
 Merit-based—$6,637,000; 7446 awards
 Other—$4,891,000

Scholarship, Grant, and Loan Information

Alabama Commission on Higher Education
Suite 221, One Court Square
Montgomery, Alabama 36197-0001
(205) 269-2700

Special State Programs

Alabama Student Assistance Program provides financial assistance to state residents at participating colleges and universities within Alabama. Students apply through their participating schools.

Alabama Student Grant Program provides financial aid to state residents enrolled as undergraduate students in state independent, nonprofit colleges and universities. Awards are made to both full-time and half-time students. See your school's financial aid director for further information.

Alabama Nursing Scholarship Program provides financial aid to state residents who agree to practice nursing for at least one year in Alabama and who are enrolled in eligible nursing programs. Contact your school's financial aid office for application forms and further details.

Alabama Medical Scholarship and Loan Program provides financial assistance to students enrolled in accredited medical programs. For application forms and information, write to the Alabama Board of Medical Scholarship Awards, University Station, 1600 Eighth Avenue South, Birmingham, Alabama 35294.

Alabama Dental Scholarship Awards provide scholarships to students enrolled in accredited dental schools. For application forms and information, write to the Alabama Board of Dental Scholarship Awards, University Station, 1600 Eighth Avenue South, Birmingham, Alabama 35294.

State of Alabama Chiropractic Scholarship Program provides scholarship assistance to state residents who are enrolled in accredited chiropractic colleges and who have financial need. For application forms and further information, write to the Alabama State Chiropractic Association, 134 High Street, Montgomery, Alabama 36104.

Emergency Secondary Education Scholarship Program is designed to attract students into the teaching profession in mathematics, science, computer education, and any other subjects designated by state officials as critical areas. Graduates may have their loans cancelled or forgiven for teaching in state public schools. Contact the Alabama Commission on Higher Education for further information.

Alabama National Guard Educational Assistance Program provides financial assistance to Alabama National Guard members who are state residents and are enrolled for degree study at accredited post-secondary institutions. Contact your local unit for further details.

Alabama GI Dependent Educational Benefit Program provides tuition, fees, and book assistance to the children and wives of eligible Alabama veterans. For application forms, contact the Alabama State Department of Veterans Affairs, P.O. Box 1509, Montgomery, Alabama 36102.

Two-Year College Academic Scholarship Program makes awards to students enrolled at public 2-year postsecondary educational institutions in Alabama. The awards may not exceed the cost of in-state tuition and books. For further information, contact the financial aid office at any public 2-year school in Alabama.

Junior and Community College Athletic Scholarship Program makes awards to students enrolled at public junior and community colleges in Alabama. The awards are based upon athletic ability, not financial need. Contact the coach, athletic director, or financial aid officer at any public junior or community college in Alabama.

Junior and Community College Performing Arts Scholarship Program makes awards to students enrolled in public junior and community colleges in Alabama. The awards are based upon talent demonstrated through auditions, not financial need. Contact the director of financial aid at any public junior or community college in Alabama.

Alabama Scholarships for Dependents of Blind Parents provide financial assistance for children from families in which the head of the family is blind. The award may not exceed the cost of tuition or fees at an Alabama college or university. For further information and application materials, write to the State of Alabama Department of Education, Administrative and Financial Services Division, Gordon Persons Building, 50 North Ripley, Montgomery, Alabama 36130.

Wallace-Folsom Prepaid College Tuition Program is a contract that guarantees 4 years of fully paid undergraduate tuition at any public junior college, college, or university in Alabama. An amount equal to the average cost of Alabama tuition will be provided for students who attend private or out-of-state institutions. Families may obtain further information on this program by contacting the State Treasurer's Office, 204 Alabama State House, Montgomery, Alabama 36130.

Police Officer's and Firefighter's Survivor's Educational Assistance Program awards grants to the eligible dependents of Alabama police officers and firefighters killed in the line of duty. Only students enrolled in undergraduate programs of study in public institutions in Alabama are eligible to apply for this program. For further information and application materials, write to the Alabama Commission on Higher Education, Suite 221, One Court Square, Montgomery, Alabama 36197-0001.

Alaska

Average tuition and fees:
    Public 4-year institutions—$1280
    Public 2-year institutions—N/A
    Private 4-year institutions—$5078
    Private 2-year institutions—N/A

State spending on student aid:
    Need-based—$464,000; 307 awards
    Merit-based—$2,111,000

Scholarship, Grant, and Loan Information

Alaska Commission on Postsecondary Education
400 Willoughby Avenue
Box FP
Juneau, Alaska 99811
(907) 465-2854

Special State Programs

Alaska Student Loan Program is available to graduate, undergraduate, and vocational students. Students must be in good academic standing to receive this loan. The interest rate charged is 8%. Loan forgiveness options are available. Contact the Division of Student Financial Aid, Alaska Commission on Postsecondary Education, Box FP, 400 Willoughby Avenue, Juneau, Alaska 99811, or call (907) 465-2962 for more information.

Teacher Scholarship Loan Program provides financial assistance to high school graduates who are planning to pursue teaching careers in rural elementary and secondary schools in Alaska. To be eligible, students must be enrolled in a teacher education program. Loan forgiveness options are available. Contact the Alaska Commission on Postsecondary Education for more information.

The Family Education Loan Program serves as an alternative to the Alaska Student Loan program and provides low-interest loans to students. Contact the Alaska Commission on Postsecondary Education for further information.

Jean Kline Memorial Scholarship Program provides scholarship assistance to women enrolled in the University of Alaska Southeast in a B.B.A., M.B.A., or M.P.A. program. Financial need and academic excellence are used in awarding this scholarship. For applications, contact the Financial Aid Office of the University of Alaska Southeast, Whitehead Building, 11120 Glacier Highway, Juneau, Alaska 99801.

Mike Miller Endowed Scholarship Program provides scholarship assistance to University of Alaska Southeast students who are enrolled in a communications program. Awards are based upon need and academic excellence. For applications, contact the Financial Aid Office of the University of Alaska Southeast, Whitehead Building, 11120 Glacier Highway, Juneau, Alaska 99801.

A. W. "Winn" Brindle Memorial Scholarship Program provides financial aid to full-time undergraduate or graduate students who are enrolled in approved programs in fisheries, fishery science, fishery management, seafood processing and food technology. Recipients are selected by the Student0 Financial Aid Committee of the Alaska Commission on Postsecondary Education. Call (907) 465-2854 for further information.

Alaska State Educational Incentive Grant Program provides grants to eligible students enrolled in their first year of undergraduate studies at both in-state and out-of-state colleges and universities. Applicants must be residents of Alaska for at least 2 years prior to application. For further information and application materials, contact the Assistant Director for Programs, Alaska Commission on Postsecondary Education.

Michael Murphy Memorial Scholarship Loan Funds provide financial assistance to eligible state residents. Funds of up to $1000 per year are awarded to both undergraduate and graduate full-time students. To be eligible, a student must be pursuing a degree in law, law enforcement, or some other related field. For further information and application materials, write to Alaska State Troopers, Michael Murphy Scholarship Fund, 2760 Sherwood Lane, Juneau, Alaska 99801.

Robert C. Thomas Memorial Scholarship Loan Fund makes loans to students enrolled in accredited colleges and universities who are pursuing a career in education, public administration, or some other related field. For further information and application materials, write to the Department of Education, Box F, Juneau, Alaska 99811.

Arizona

Average tuition and fees:
Public 4-year institutions—$1362
Public 2-year institutions—$519
Private 4-year institutions—$4127
Private 2-year institutions—$11,007

State spending on student aid:
Need-based—$3,427,000; 5000 awards
Merit-based—None

Scholarship and Grant Information

Arizona Commission for Postsecondary Education
3030 N. Central Avenue, Suite 1407
Phoenix, Arizona 85012
(602) 255-3109

Loan Information

Arizona Educational Loan Program
1400 E. Southern Avenue, Suite 200
Tempe, Arizona 85282
1-800-352-3033
(602) 831-9988

Special State Programs

Arizona State Student Incentive Grant Program provides funds to needy students who attend participating postsecondary educational institutions in Arizona. Awards are made to both undergraduate and graduate students. Recipients must be state residents and have financial need. Financial aid officers at participating schools can provide further details.

Bureau of Indian Affairs Grant Program provides annual grants to Native American students. The amount of the award varies and is need-based. Contact your school's financial aid office for further information.

WICHE Student Exchange Program helps state residents obtain access to professional education not available in Arizona but made available at participating institutions in other western states at a reduced tuition rate. Contact your financial aid director for further information.

Arkansas

Average tuition and fees:
Public 4-year institutions—$1376
Public 2-year institutions—$644
Private 4-year institutions—$3175
Private 2-year institutions—$6102

State spending on student aid:
Need-based—$4,137,000; l0,307 awards
Merit-based—$790,000; 388 awards
Other—$180,000

Scholarship and Grant Information

Arkansas Department of Higher Education
1220 W. Third Street
Little Rock, Arkansas 72201-1904
(501) 324-9300

Loan Information

Student Loan Guarantee Foundation of Arkansas
219 S. Victory
Little Rock, Arkansas 72201-1884
(501) 372-1491

Special State Programs

Arkansas Student Assistance Grant Program provides grants to assist financially needy undergraduate students. For information and applications, contact the Arkansas Department of Higher Education.

Emergency Secondary Education Loan Program assists students who are pursuing a course of study leading to secondary teacher certification in foreign language, music, mathematics, chemistry, physics, biology, physical science, general science, or art. The loan may be forgiven at a rate of 20% per year for each year the recipient teaches full-time in a teacher shortage area in a public or private secondary school in Arkansas. For further information and application forms, contact the Arkansas Department of Higher Education.

Governor's Scholars Program provides $2000 merit grants each year to 100 academically superior high school graduates. Recipients must be state residents enrolled or accepted for enrollment as full-time undergraduate students at an approved postsecondary institution. The scholarship is renewable if academic criteria are fulfilled. Further information and application forms may be obtained from the Arkansas Department of Higher Education.

California

Average tuition and fees:
   Public 4-year institutions—$1123
   Public 2-year institutions—$112
   Private 4-year institutions—$9489
   Private 2-year institutions—$7664

State spending on student aid:
   Need-based—$164,797,000; 76,968 awards
   Merit-based—None

Scholarship and Grant Information

California Student Aid Commission
P.O. Box 51084
Sacramento, California 94245-0845
(916) 445-0880

Loan Information

California Student Aid Commission
1515 S Street
Sacramento, California 94245-0845
(916) 323-0435

Special State Programs

Cal Grant A Program assists low- and middle-income students meet their educational expenses. Recipients are selected on the basis of grade point average and financial need. Students must be enrolled at least half-time to be eligible for this program. Contact the California Student Aid Commission for further information.

Cal Grant B Program provides financial assistance to very low-income students. Most of the recipients of this grant are enrolled in public community colleges. The amount of the award varies but generally provides a living allowance and sometimes tuition and fee financial assistance. Contact the California Student Aid Commission for additional information.

Cal Grant C Program helps vocational school students with tuition and training costs. Recipients must be enrolled at a community college, independent college, or vocational school. Three-year hospital-based nursing students are also eligible for this program. Contact the California State Aid Commission for further details.

State Work-Study Program offers eligible college and university students the opportunity to earn money to meet some of their expenses. Students may be placed with public institutions or nonprofit or profit-making enterprises. Contact your campus financial aid office for more information.

Assumption Program for Loans of Education (APLE) assists students enrolled in teacher preparation courses at participating postsecondary institutions. Participants must commit themselves to 3 consecutive years of teaching in California public schools. Loan forgiveness provisions are available. For applications, contact any California college or university offering an approved program.

Graduate Fellowship Program provides financial assistance to students pursuing recognized advanced or professional degrees. Applicants are ranked according to undergraduate grades, test scores, and disadvantaged background. The filing deadline is March 2. Contact the Graduate Fellowship Program, California Student Aid Commission, for further information.

Educational Opportunity Programs (EOP) and Extended Opportunity Programs and Services (EOPS) provide grant assistance and counseling services to disadvantaged students. To be eligible for these programs, recipients must be classified as disadvantaged according to state criteria, and must be enrolled at least half-time at one of the California state universities, or full-time at a community college. The campus EOP/EOPS office can provide further information.

Board of Governors Grant Program (BOGG) provides financial aid to students who are receiving AFDC aid or who have qualified for Pell Grant assistance or Cal Grant aid. Dependents of deceased or disabled veterans may also qualify for this program. For more information, contact the financial aid office at your local community college.

Aid to Families with Dependent Children (AFDC) provides financial assistance to families with a deceased parent, unemployed parents, or parents with physical or mental disabilities. Contact your local county welfare department for more information.

Aid for American Indians provides financial aid to California Native Americans. Recipients must prove they are members of a federally recognized California tribe. For applications for grants and vocational assistance, contact regional offices of the U.S. Bureau of Indian Affairs, or write the Bureau's Office of Indian Education, 2800 Cottage Way, Sacramento, California 98525.

Disabled Students Program provides financial assistance to students with severe disabilities. All public schools and colleges and many independent schools provide services to disabled students. For more information, contact the disabled students office at your school or college or the community or national organizations serving your particular disability.

Veterans Benefits provide financial assistance to the dependent children and spouses of deceased or disabled veterans. For more information, contact the local office of the U.S. Veterans Administration, or call the California Department of Veterans Affairs at (916) 445-2334.

Colorado

Average tuition and fees:
Public 4-year institutions—$1830
Public 2-year institutions—$792
Private 4-year institutions—$9188
Private 2-year institutions—$8036

State spending on student aid:
Need-based—$12,087,000; 15,280 awards
Merit-based—$10,911,000; 12,821 awards
Other—$1,281,000

Scholarship and Grant Information

Colorado Commission on Higher Education
1300 Broadway, Second Floor
Denver, Colorado 80203
(303) 866-2723

Loan Information

Colorado Guaranteed Student Loan Program
11990 Grant, Suite 500
North Glenn, Colorado 80233
(303) 450-9333

Special State Programs

Colorado Student Grant Program provides grant assistance to undergraduate students with documented financial need. Recipients must be state residents and enrolled in an eligible postsecondary program in Colorado. Contact the Colorado Commission on Higher Education for further details.

Colorado Diversity Grant Program provides financial assistance to underrepresented groups. Recipients must be state residents and enrolled in an eligible postsecondary institution in Colorado. Contact the Colorado Commission on Higher Education for more information.

Colorado Student Incentive Grant Program (CSIG) provides grants to undergraduate students with substantial financial need. Funding is provided from federal and state sources. Contact the Colorado Commission on Higher Education for further information.

Colorado Work-Study Program provides part-time employment to help students meet their college expenses. Contact your school's financial aid office for further information.

Undergraduate Merit Program makes awards available to students with superior academic ability. Contact the Colorado Commission on Higher Education for further details.

Colorado Graduate Grant Program provides grant assistance to graduate students with financial need. Contact your school's financial aid director for more information on this program.

Colorado Graduate Fellowship Program provides merit-based awards for graduate students. Contact your school's financial aid office for more information and application forms.

National Guard Tuition Assistance Program pays a maximum of 75% of in-state tuition for National Guard personnel enrolled in public institutions. Contact local guard units for applications.

Law Enforcement/POW/MIA Dependents Tuition Assistance pays the tuition for dependents of Colorado law enforcement officers, fire or National Guard personnel killed or disabled in the line of duty, and prisoners of war or service personnel listed as missing in action. For applications, contact the Colorado Commission on Higher Education.

Colorado Nursing Scholarships are available to students who are enrolled in nursing education programs and who agree to practice in Colorado. For further information, write to the Colorado Commission on Higher Education.

Connecticut

Average tuition and fees:

Public 4-year institutions—$2017
Public 2-year institutions—$915
Private 4-year institutions—$11,268
Private 2-year institutions—$7906

State spending on student aid:
Need-based—$20,803,000; 15,500 awards
Merit-based—$200,000; 20 awards
Other—$15,164,000

Scholarship and Grant Information

Connecticut Department of Higher Education
61 Woodland Station
Hartford, Connecticut 06105-2391
(203) 566-2618

Loan Information

Connecticut Student Loan Foundation
25 Pratt Street
Hartford, Connecticut 06103
(203) 547-1510

Special State Programs

State Scholastic Achievement Grant Program provides grants to state residents who graduated in the top one-third of their high school class or scored at least 1100 on the SAT examination or 27 on the ACT test. The awards are need-based and must be used at a Connecticut college or in states with reciprocity agreements with Connecticut. The application deadline is February 15. Contact your high school guidance office for applications.

Connecticut Independent College Student Grant Program provides grants to state residents with financial need. Recipients must attend a Connecticut independent college. Contact your college financial aid office for application materials.

Connecticut Aid for Public College Students provides financial assistance to state residents attending a Connecticut public college. Recipients must have financial need. The amount of the award varies but can equal up to the amount of unmet financial need. Apply at your college financial aid office.

Tuition Aid for Needy Students Program provides assistance up to the amount of unmet need to qualified students. Recipients must attend a Connecticut public college and must demonstrate financial need. Contact your college financial aid office for further information and application forms.

Tuition Waiver for Veterans Program provides financial assistance, equal to tuition only, to state residents who are veterans enrolled in college. The children of Vietnam veterans declared MIA/POW, who are attending a Connecticut public college, are also eligible for this program. For applications, contact your college financial aid offices.

Connecticut Nursing Scholarship Program provides financial assistance to state residents enrolled full-time in a 3-year hospital school of nursing in Connecticut or in a 2- or 4-year nursing program in a Connecticut college. The awards are based upon academic merit and financial need. Contact officials at participating colleges and hospital schools of nursing.

Delaware

Average tuition and fees:
   Public 4-year institutions—$2768
   Public 2-year institutions—$882
   Private 4-year institutions—$5388

State spending on student aid:
   Need-based—$1,462,000; 1734 awards
   Merit-based—$197,000; 188 awards
   Other—$189,000

Scholarship, Grant, and Loan Information

Delaware Postsecondary Education Commission
Carvel State Office Building
820 French Street, Fourth Floor
Wilmington, Delaware 19801
Loan Information—(302) 571-6055
Grant Information—(302) 571-3240

Special State Programs

Delaware Postsecondary Scholarship Fund provides financial assistance to state residents with financial need. Students are eligible if they attend a public or private institution in the state or an accredited nonprofit college in Pennsylvania or Maryland. Contact your school guidance counselor or college financial aid director for more information.

Diamond State Scholarship Program provides scholarship assistance to eligible high school graduates who are state residents. Awards are based upon the students' rank in high school and SAT scores. Contact your high school guidance counselor for further information.

Delaware Nursing Incentive Scholarship Loan Program provides financial assistance to students enrolled in nursing programs. Recipients are required to repay each year of support with 1 year of nursing assistance at a state-operated hospital or clinic. Contact the Delaware Postsecondary Education Commission for further information and application forms.

Professional and Graduate Financial Assistance Programs are sponsored by the state of Delaware. These programs for graduate and professional school students include Delaware Institute for Medical Education and Research, Delaware Institute for Veterinary Medical Education, Optometric Institutional Aid Program, Delaware Postsecondary Scholarship Fund, and the Delaware Higher Education Loan Program. Contact the Delaware Postsecondary Education Commission for further information.

District of Columbia

Average tuition and fees:
   Public 4-year institutions—$664
   Private 4-year institutions—$9489

Spending on student aid:
   Need-based—$974,000; 829 awards
   Merit-based—None

Scholarship and Grant Information

Office of Postsecondary Education, Research, and
 Assistance
D.C. Department of Human Services
1331 H Street, N.W.
Suite 600
Washington, D.C. 20005
(202) 727-3688

Loan Information

Higher Education Loan Program of Washington, D.C.
1023 15th Street, N.W.
Tenth Floor, Suite 1000
Washington, D.C. 20005
(202) 289-4500

Special State Programs

D.C. Student Incentive Grant Program provides
grant assistance to D.C. residents who are enrolled
or accepted for enrollment in an eligible institution.
Students must be enrolled at least on a half-time
basis and must have financial need. Applications
are processed by the college's financial aid director. Contact the Office of Postsecondary Education,
Research, and Assistance for further details.

CONSERN Loan Program provides financial assistance to families who may not be eligible for federal student loan programs or who need more financial aid than was awarded. CONSERN loans may
be used only at certain schools located in the
District of Columbia. For further information and
application materials, contact the CONSERN Loan
Program at (202) 265-1313.

Florida

Average tuition and fees:
 Public 4-year institutions—N/A
 Public 2-year institutions—$729
 Private 4-year institutions—$7153
 Private 2-year institutions—$5519

State spending on student aid:
 Need-based—$27,132,000; 25,116 awards
 Merit-based—$41,928,000; 26,767 awards

Scholarship, Grant, and Loan Information

Florida Department of Education
Office of Student Financial Assistance
The Florida Education Center, Suite 1334
Tallahassee, Florida 32399-0400
Loan Information—(904) 488-8093
Grant Information—(904) 488-6181

Special State Programs

**Florida Student Assistance Grant Program
(FSAG)** awards grants to full-time undergraduate
students with financial need. Recipients must be
residents of Florida for 2 years and must be
enrolled at an eligible Florida school. For application forms, contact your high school guidance
office or college financial aid office.

Florida Tuition Voucher Program (FTV) awards up
to $2000 per year to full-time undergraduate stu-
dents who are enrolled at an independent Florida
college or university. The program is not based on
need. For applications, contact the financial aid
office of the institution you plan to attend.

Florida Undergraduate Scholars' Fund awards
$2500 per academic year to public and private high
school seniors with outstanding academic achievement who will attend an eligible Florida school.
For applications, contact your high school principal
or guidance officer.

Florida Graduate Scholars' Fund awards scholarships of $10,000 per year to full-time graduate stu-
dents in the areas of high technology and industry.
For applications, contact the financial aid office or
the office of graduate admissions at participating
schools.

**Public School Work Experience Program
(PSWEP)** provides needy undergraduate students
with employment as teacher aides or science laboratory assistants in a public elementary or secondary school. The amount of the award varies. For
applications, contact the financial aid office at the
institution you plan to attend.

**College Career Work Experience Program
(CCWEP)** provides undergraduate students with
off-campus employment. The amount of the award
varies according to financial need. For applications,
contact your college financial aid office.

**"Chappie" James Most Promising Teacher
Scholarship Loan Program** provides scholarships
for public high school seniors who plan careers in
teaching. Loan forgiveness options are also provided. The application deadline is March 1. For applications, contact your high school principal or guidance counselor.

Teacher Scholarship Loan Program provides finan-
cial assistance to students who plan careers in
teaching. Loan forgiveness options are available.
For applications, contact the Office of Student
Financial Assistance of the Florida Department of
Education.

Masters' Fellowship Loan Program for Teachers
provides financial assistance to graduate students
who agree to teach in a critical teacher shortage
area. For applications, contact the financial aid
office or the Dean of the School of Education at
participating schools.

**Critical Teacher Shortage Tuition Reimbursement
Program** encourages Florida teachers to become
certified in, or gain a graduate degree in, a critical
teacher shortage area. For applications, contact the
Office of Student Financial Assistance of the
Florida Department of Education.

Student Loan Forgiveness Program provides loan forgiveness for 4 years for teachers with undergraduate degrees and up to 2 years for teachers with graduate degrees. For applications, contact the Office of Student Financial Assistance.

Student Regents Scholarship Program awards scholarships to students who serve as student members of the Board of Regents. For applications, contact the Office of Student Financial Assistance.

Virgil Hawkins Fellowship provides fellowships to minority students attending Florida State University or the University of Florida. For applications, contact the Florida State University or the University of Florida Law Schools.

José Marti Scholarship Challenge Grant Fund provides need-based scholarships for Hispanic students. Recipients must be U.S. citizens or permanent residents, and Florida residents for 2 years. For applications, contact the Office of Financial Assistance.

Challenger Astronauts Memorial Scholarship Program provides scholarship assistance to students who plan to pursue careers in the liberal arts or teaching. Recipients must be enrolled at a state university or community college. For applications, contact your high school principal or guidance counselor.

Scholarships for Children of Deceased or Disabled Veterans provide scholarship assistance equal to the cost of tuition and fees for eligible dependents of veterans. For applications, contact the financial aid office of the school you plan to attend.

Seminole/Miccosukee Indian Scholarship Program provides scholarship assistance for qualified Native Americans who are enrolled full-time or part-time at eligible Florida institutions. The program is available to both undergraduate and graduate students. The application deadline is September 1. Contact the Office of Student Financial Assistance for further information.

Florida Student Tuition Scholarship Grant Fund provides financial assistance to eligible high school graduates. Under this fund program, the state pays tuition at any public community college or vocational-technical school. For further information, contact the Florida Department of Education.

Georgia

Average tuition and fees:
Public 4-year institutions—$1631
Public 2-year institutions—$825
Private 4-year institutions—$7076
Private 2-year institutions—$3194

State spending on student aid:
Need-based—$5,174,000; 14,141 awards
Merit-based—$16,316,000; 17,298 awards
Other—$1,568,000

Scholarship, Grant, and Loan Information

Board of Regents
University System of Georgia
244 Washington Street, S.W.
Atlanta, Georgia 30334
Loan Information—(404) 493-5468
Grant Information—(404) 493-5444

Special State Programs

Student Incentive Grant Program makes awards available to state residents enrolled or accepted for enrollment as full-time undergraduate students at an approved school. The application deadline is June 1. Interested students should complete the Georgia version of the FAF or FFS form and request that the Student Incentive Grant Program receive a copy of the results.

Georgia Tuition Equalization Grant Program provides grants, administered by the Georgia Student Finance Authority, for state residents who are attending approved schools. Interested students should complete the Georgia Student Grant Application and submit it to the financial aid office of the college or university they plan to attend.

Law Enforcement Personnel Dependents Grant Program makes grant awards to the children of Georgia law enforcement officers, firemen, and prison guards who have been permanently disabled or killed in the line of duty. Applications should be filed by August. Interested students should complete the Georgia Student Grant Application, and request the forms necessary to document their eligibility.

State Direct Student Loan Program makes loans, with loan forgiveness options, to Georgia students enrolled in approved fields of study in which personnel shortages exist in the state. This program is also available to members of the Georgia National Guard. Interested students should complete the Georgia needs analysis form and designate the school that is to receive a copy of the results.

State-Sponsored Loan Program makes loans available to Georgia students who are ineligible for the maximum State Direct Student Loan. For more information on this loan program, contact the Board of Regents.

Governor's Scholarship Program recognizes graduating Georgia high school seniors of exceptional academic accomplishments who plan to attend an eligible college or university located in Georgia. To be eligible for this program, a student must be selected by the Georgia Department of Education as a Georgia Scholar and must be enrolled or accepted for enrollment as a full-time student. The award is equal to the amount of tuition, up to a maximum of $1540 per academic year. Georgia Scholars will automatically receive an application for this program. For more information, contact the Board of Regents.

Regents Scholarship Program provides scholarship assistance to state residents with superior ability and financial need. Recipients must be enrolled or accepted for enrollment as full-time students in a school of the University System of Georgia. Graduate students may also apply for this program. Contact your college financial aid director for further information.

Charles McDaniel Teacher Scholarship Program makes scholarship awards to junior and senior college students who are pursuing teaching careers at a public college or university in Georgia. The amount of the award varies. For further information, contact the Board of Regents.

Regents Opportunity Grant for Graduate and Professional Students provides grant assistance to graduate and professional students who are economically disadvantaged and who are enrolled full-time in approved graduate programs. Contact your college financial aid director for further information and application forms.

Medical Scholarship Program provides service scholarship assistance to state residents who have been accepted at an accredited medical college. Scholarship awards are based on financial need. Completed applications must be received by May 15. Awards are repayable by practicing medicine in an approved Georgia community 1 year for each year of aid received. Contact the State Medical Education Board at (404) 656-2226 for further information.

Osteopathic Medical Loan Program provides loans to residents of Georgia who have been accepted at an accredited school of Osteopathic Medicine. Awards are based on financial need and are repayable by practicing primary care in a medically underserved area in Georgia, 1 year for each year of aid received. Contact the Board of Regents for more information.

Hawaii

Average tuition and fees:
    Public 4-year institutions—$1293
    Public 2-year institutions—$410
    Private 4-year institutions—$4008

State spending on student aid:
    Need-based—$611,000; 700 awards
    Merit-based—None

Scholarship and Grant Information

State Postsecondary Education Commission
209 Bachman Hall
University of Hawaii
2444 Dole Street
Honolulu, Hawaii 96822
(808) 948-8213

Loan Information.

Hawaii Education Loan Program
P.O. Box 22187
Honolulu, Hawaii 96822-0187
(808) 536-3731

There is a $3.00 charge to receive information on state financial assistance programs.

Special State Programs

Hawaii Student Incentive Grant Program provides tuition grants to full-time undergraduate students who are state residents. Recipients must have financial need and must be eligible to receive a Pell Grant. Contact your high school guidance counselor or college financial aid director for further information.

Regents Scholarships for Academic Excellence award scholarships to 20 incoming students who are state residents. The awards are renewable. For application forms, contact any University of Hawaii financial aid office.

Presidential Achievement Scholarship Program awards scholarships to ten college juniors who are state residents and enrolled at the Manoa, Hilo, or West Oahu campus of the University of Hawaii. The awards are renewable. For application forms, contact any University of Hawaii financial aid office.

State Higher Education Loan Program (SHEL) provides loans to financially needy undergraduate and graduate students who are state residents. Maximum and aggregate amounts are the same as for the Perkins Loan Program. Repayment begins 9 months after a student ceases to attend school. For further information, contact the Hawaii Education Loan Program.

Idaho

Average tuition and fees:
    Public 4-year institutions—$1119
    Public 2-year institutions—$779
    Private 4-year institutions—$6669
    Private 2-year institutions—$1400

State spending on student aid:
    Need-based—$485,000; 800 awards
    Merit-based—$245,000; 98 awards

Scholarship and Grant Information

Office of State Board of Education of Idaho
650 W. State Street, Room 307
Boise, Idaho 83720
(208) 334-2270

Loan Information

Student Loan Fund of Idaho, Inc.
Processing Center
P.O. Box 730
Fruitland, Idaho 83619
(208) 452-4058

Special State Programs

State of Idaho Scholarship Program provides financial assistance to graduating high school seniors who plan to attend an Idaho college or university. Recipients must be state residents and maintain satisfactory academic progress. Contact your high school guidance counselor for further information.

Idaho Governor's Scholarship Program provides scholarships to outstanding Idaho high school graduates who attend eligible Idaho public or private colleges and universities. Recipients must rank in the top 10% of their graduating class and score in the top 5% of ACT participants nationwide. Contact your high school guidance counselor for more information.

Paul L. Fowler Memorial Scholarship Program awards scholarships on the basis of class rank and ACT scores. Recipients must be state residents and must enroll as full-time students in an institution of higher learning. Contact the Office of State Board of Education of Idaho for further information.

Education Incentive Fee Waiver Program provides financial assistance to state residents who graduated from a secondary school in Idaho and who plan a career in teaching. Recipients must rank in the upper 15% of their graduating high school class. Contact the Office of State Board of Education of Idaho for further information.

Illinois

Average tuition and fees:
    Public 4-year institutions—$2370
    Public 2-year institutions—$871
    Private 4-year institutions—$8281
    Private 2-year institutions—$5505

State spending on student aid:
    Need-based—$180,650,000; 112,000 awards
    Merit-based—$18,285,000; 20,842 awards
    Other—$4,148,000

Scholarship, Grant, and Loan Information

Illinois State Scholarship Commission
106 Wilmot Road
Deerfield, Illinois 60015
(708) 948-8550

Special State Programs

Monetary Award Program (MAP) provides grants to needy students. To be eligible, students must be state residents and must be enrolled at least half-time in an approved school. The amount of the award is based upon financial need. Contact your high school guidance counselor or college financial aid director for further information and application materials.

Illinois Merit Recognition Scholarship Program provides a one-time grant to state residents who rank in the top 5% of their high school class. Students must enroll in an approved Illinois school at least on a part-time basis to be considered for this program. Contact your high school guidance counselor for further information.

National Guard/Naval Militia Grant provides tuition reimbursement for graduate or undergraduate study to members of the Illinois National Guard or Illinois Naval Militia. For applications, contact local units or college financial offices.

Illinois Veterans Grant pays tuition and certain fee costs at all Illinois state colleges, universities, and community colleges. To be eligible, students must be state residents with at least 1 year of active duty in the Armed Forces. For applications and additional information, contact the Illinois Department of Veterans Affairs, college financial aid offices, and the Client Services Division of the Illinois State Scholarship Commission.

Police, Fire Personnel, and Correctional Workers Grants provide grant assistance to the spouses and children of police, fire personnel, and correctional officers killed in the line of duty. For applications and further information, contact the Client Services Division of the Illinois State Scholarship Commission.

Illinois Opportunity Programs, currently being developed by the Illinois Student Assistance Commission, are aimed to assist middle-income families to finance their children's postsecondary education. One program is a college savings and investment plan, and the other is a nonsubsidized Stafford Loan Program. For further information on these programs, write to the Illinois State Scholarship Commission, Attention: Client Relations, Elementary Parent Information, 106 Wilmot Road, Deerfield, Illinois 60015, or call (708) 948-8550.

Indiana

Average tuition and fees:
Public 4-year institutions—$1975
Public 2-year institutions—$1374
Private 4-year institutions—$8267
Private 2-year institutions—$7412

State spending on student aid:
Need-based—$46,488,000; 34,500 awards
Merit-based—$966,000; 808 awards

Scholarship, Grant, and Loan Information

State Student Assistance Commission of Indiana
964 N. Pennsylvania, First Floor
Indianapolis, Indiana 46204
Loan Information—(317) 232-2366
Grant Information—(317) 232-2350

Special State Programs

Minority Teacher Scholarship Program provides annual scholarships to black and Hispanic state residents. Recipients must be enrolled in a teacher certification program and agree to teach after graduation in an accredited Indiana elementary or secondary school. For applications, contact the college financial aid office.

State of Indiana and Lily Endowment Grants award need-based grants. To be eligible, students must be state residents and attending or planning to attend an approved Indiana institution of higher learning. Contact your high school counselor for further details.

State Work-Study Program provides work opportunities, administered by the State Student Assistance Commission of Indiana, to eligible students. Wages and hours are determined by the employer. Contact the State Student Assistance Commission for further information.

Iowa

Average tuition and fees:
Public 4-year institutions—$1823
Public 2-year institutions—$1225
Private 4-year institutions—$7945
Private 2-year institutions—$6423

State spending on student aid:
Need-based—$37,748,000; 22,442 awards
Merit-based—$904,000; 1308 awards
Other—$1,517,000

Scholarship, Grant, and Loan Information

Iowa College Aid Commission
201 Jewett Building
Ninth and Grand Avenue
Des Moines, Iowa 50309
Loan Information—(515) 281-4890
Grant Information—(515)281-3501

Special State Programs

State of Iowa Scholarships provide scholarship assistance to high school seniors who rank in the upper 15% of their high school class. Interested high school students should complete the State of Iowa Scholarship application form in September or October of their senior year. Contact your high school guidance counselor for further information.

Iowa Tuition Grants provide need-based grants to eligible students. Recipients must be state residents and enrolled or planning to enroll in an undergraduate program at an eligible school. To be considered for this program, interested students should file an FAF or FFS form. Contact your high school guidance counselor or college financial aid director for further information.

Iowa Vocational/Technical Tuition Grants provide grants to state residents who plan to attend an Iowa community college and pursue a vocational/technical course. Interested students should file an FAF or FFS form. Contact your local community college for additional information.

Iowa Guaranteed Loan Payment Program provides forgiveness loans to college graduates with a major in mathematics or science. In exchange for teaching sciences or advanced mathematics at an approved secondary school, the state of Iowa will repay a portion of Stafford Loans. For applications, contact the Iowa College Aid Commission and college financial aid offices.

Iowa Work-Study Program provides part-time employment to help students attending Iowa schools meet their college expenses. Contact your college financial aid director for further information.

Veterans Programs provides financial assistance for the children of deceased or disabled veterans. Contact the Department of Veterans Affairs, Camp Dodge, Iowa, for more information.

Occupational Therapy Loan Repayment Program reimburses the student loan payments of occupational therapists who are Iowa residents employed within the state. Contact the Iowa College Aid Commission for further details.

Kansas

Average tuition and fees:
Public 4-year institutions—$1467
Public 2-year institutions—$711
Private 4-year institutions—$460
Private 2-year institutions—$3962

State spending on student aid:
Need-based—$6,585,000; 4492 awards
Merit-based—$31,000; 78 awards
Other—$50,000

Scholarship and Grant Information

Kansas Board of Regents
Capitol Tower, Suite 609
400 S.W. Eighth
Topeka, Kansas 66603-3911
(913) 296-3517

Loan Information

Kansas Higher Education Assistance Foundation
6800 College Boulevard, Suite 600
Overland Park, Kansas 66211-1532
(913) 345-1300

Special State Programs

State Scholarship Program recognizes outstanding high school seniors. Recipients must enroll as full-time students in any eligible Kansas college, university, or postsecondary institution and must maintain a grade point average of 3.3. The awards are also based on need. Contact your high school guidance counselor for further details.

Tuition Grant Program provides grants to state residents who attend eligible private Kansas colleges. Eligibility is based upon financial need. Interested students should complete the Family Financial Statement, and send the results to the Kansas Board of Regents.

Kansas Career Work-Study Program is a work program that provides off-campus employment for eligible students. The amount of the award varies and is based upon financial need. For further information, contact the financial aid director of your college or university.

Vocational Education Scholarship Program provides a one-time scholarship to students interested in pursuing a career in vocational education. Students interested in this grant must register to take a competitive examination. For further information and application materials, contact any postsecondary institution offering vocational educational programs.

Kansas Honors Program is a need-based financial assistance program for students enrolled in a gifted or honors program at Kansas colleges and universities. For further information, contact the college official responsible for the honors program at your school.

Kansas Minority Scholarship Program is a need-based scholarship program for minority students. Applicants must meet the program's academic requirements, and must be enrolled or plan to enroll full-time at a Kansas 2-year or 4-year public or private college or university. For further information and application materials, write to the Kansas Board of Regents.

Kansas Nursing Scholarship Program is a scholarship program for full-time students enrolled in nursing programs at Kansas postsecondary schools.

For further information and application materials, write to the Kansas Board of Regents.

Kansas Teacher Scholarship is a state-funded scholarship loan program designed to encourage teaching careers at both the elementary and the secondary school level. Applicants must be state residents and must be enrolled or plan to enroll in a full-time teacher education program. For further information and application materials, contact the Kansas Board of Regents.

Kansas Osteopathic Scholarship Program is a scholarship loan program designed to attract osteopathic physicians to medically underserved areas in Kansas. Applicants must be state residents who are enrolled or accepted for enrollment at an accredited osteopathic school. For further information and application materials, contact the Kansas Board of Regents.

James B. Pearson Fellowship program provides financial assistance to state residents for graduate study abroad. Applicants must be state residents for at least 5 years and plan to pursue a program of study relating to foreign affairs. For further information, contact the Kansas Board of Regents.

Kansas Rhodes Scholarship provides financial assistance to state residents designated as Rhodes scholars for further graduate study. Applicants must be enrolled or accepted for enrollment in a graduate program at a state university. For further information and application materials, contact the Kansas Board of Regents.

Dental Assistance Program provides tuition assistance to Kansas dental students enrolled at the University of Missouri-Kansas City School of Dentistry. For further information, contact the Kansas Board of Regents.

Optometry Scholarship Program provides tuition assistance that pays the difference between resident and nonresident tuition for Kansas students who enroll in eligible out-of-state institutions. Candidates must be enrolled or plan to enroll full-time at approved optometry schools and must agree to return to Kansas to practice 1 year for each year assistance is received. For further information, contact the Kansas Board of Regents.

Kentucky

Average tuition and fees:
  Public 4-year institutions—$1316
  Public 2-year institutions—$693
  Private 4-year institutions—$4689
  Private 2-year institutions—$4669

State spending on student aid:
  Need-based—$19,393,000; 27,400 awards
  Merit-based—None

Scholarship, Grant, and Loan Information

Kentucky Higher Education Assistance Authority
1050 U.S. 127 South, Suite 102
Frankfort, Kentucky 40601
(502) 564-7990

Special State Programs

State Student Incentive Grant Program (SSIG)
provides financially needy state residents with
need-based grant assistance. A recipient must be
enrolled full-time as an undergraduate student at an
eligible Kentucky school. Interested students
should file a Kentucky Financial Aid Form to be
considered.

Kentucky Tuition Grant Program (KTG)
provides grant assistance to students attending one
of the independent nonprofit colleges. The awards
are need-based. Interested students should file a
Kentucky Financial Aid Form to be considered.

Teacher Scholarship Program provides financial
assistance to attract academically talented students
into the teaching profession. To be eligible, students must rank in the top 10% of their graduating
class and must be accepted for enrollment at a
Kentucky participating institution. Recipients are
required to teach one semester in a Kentucky public
school for each semester of scholarship assistance.
Contact your high school guidance counselor for
further information.

College Access Program (CAP) provides grants to
the state's neediest residents to attend an in-state
public or private school. The total family contribution cannot exceed $2000, and the recipient may
not receive other state or federal funds designated
specifically for tuition. For further information,
contact the Kentucky Higher Education Assistance
Authority.

Kentucky Educational Savings Plan Trust assists
parents, grandparents, or other benefactors to save
in a planned way for the higher education of a child
under the age of 15. The Trust Account can be
opened with as little as $25. Earnings are exempt
from Kentucky income tax. For further information, contact the Kentucky Higher Education
Assistance Authority.

Louisiana

Average tuition and fees:
    Public 4-year institutions—$1768
    Public 2-year institutions—$837
    Private 4-year institutions—$9257
    Private 2-year institutions—$5648

State spending on student aid:
    Need-based—$4,196,000; 4292 awards
    Merit-based—$770,000; 1833 awards

Scholarship, Grant, and Loan Information

Louisiana Student Financial Assistance Commission
P.O. Box 91202
Baton Rouge, Louisiana 70821-9202
(504) 342-9415

Special State Programs

State Student Incentive Grant Program provides
financial assistance to needy state residents.
The awards are based upon financial need. Contact
your school's financial aid director for further
information.

T. H. Harris Scholarship Program provides
scholarships to high school graduates who
plan to enroll in a state college or university.
The awards are merit-based. Recipients are selected
by the Governor's Special Commission on
Education Services. Call 1-800-626-0115 for further information.

High School Rally Scholarship Program provides
scholarships to high school students who are first-
place winners in written examination contests.
Contact the Chairman of the High School Rally
Committee at Louisiana State University at (504)
388-6652 for further information.

Rockefeller Scholarship Program provides financial
assistance to eligible students majoring in forestry,
wildlife, fisheries, or marine science. This program
is available to both undergraduate and graduate students. Contact your school's financial aid director
for further information and application materials.

Maine

Average tuition and fees:
    Public 4-year institutions—$1980
    Public 2-year institutions—$1134
    Private 4-year institutions—$10,425
    Private 2-year institutions—$3787

State spending on student aid:
    Need-based—$5,100,000; 8000 awards
    Merit-based—None

Scholarship, Grant, and Loan Information

Maine Department of Educational and Cultural
    Services
Division of Higher Education Services
State House Station #119
One Western Court
Augusta, Maine 04333
1-800-228-3734
(207) 289-2183

Special State Programs

Maine Student Incentive Scholarship Program
provides state residents who are full-time undergraduate or graduate students with need-based

grant assistance. Interested students should submit a Maine Financial Aid Form by April 30. Contact your school's financial aid director for further details and application forms.

Blain House Scholars Program provides loans to eligible students. The loans, which are competitive and based upon academic merit, carry no interest charges. A total of $6000 may be borrowed. For applications contact any high school guidance office or college financial aid office.

Indian Scholarships award tuition and fee waivers to eligible Native Americans attending a postsecondary institution in the University of Maine system. For application forms, contact the University of Maine's financial aid office.

Tuition Waiver Program for Children of Firefighters and Law Enforcement Officers Killed in the Line of Duty provides tuition waivers for eligible dependents to attend any Maine public postsecondary educational institution. Apply to the Maine Department of Educational and Cultural Services, Division of Higher Education Services.

Veterans Dependents' Educational Benefits provide financial assistance to the spouses or children of veterans killed or permanently disabled as a result of military service. Contact the Bureau of Veterans Services, State House Station 117, Augusta, Maine, for further information and application forms, or call (207) 289-4060 for information.

Maine Education Loans are available to parents and students through the Maine Education Loan Authority. Loans at reduced rates are offered to creditworthy Maine residents and also to out-of-state residents attending Maine institutions. Repayment begins immediately. For further information on Maine loans, call the Maine Educational Loan Authority at (207) 623-2800.

Osteopathic Loan Program is a state-funded program available to Maine residents attending any accredited school of osteopathic medicine. Loans may not exceed $5000 annually, and recipients may have up to 25% of their loan forgiven for each year of practice in behalf of an underserved area or population. For further information on this program, contact the Maine Osteopathic Association at (207) 623-1101.

Postgraduate Health Professions Program secures seats for a limited number of state residents at 7 schools of graduate medicine, 2 schools of dentistry, 2 schools of veterinary medicine, 18 schools of allopathic medicine, and 1 school of optometry. Students must repay an amount of money equal to the difference between nonresident tuition and the tuition charged state contract students. Students may cancel 25% of their debt for each year of practice in behalf of a designated underserved area or population. For further information on this program, contact personnel in your school's financial aid office.

Maryland

Average tuition and fees:
  Public 4-year institutions—$2120
  Public 2-year institutions—$1172
  Private 4-year institutions—$9914
  Private 2-year institutions—$8393

State spending on student aid:
  Need-based—$15,669,000; 19,096 awards
  Merit-based—$5,110,000; 3371 awards
  Other—$135,000

Scholarship and Grant Information

Maryland Higher Education Commission
16 Francis Street
Annapolis, Maryland 21401-1781
(301) 974-5370

Loan Information

Maryland Higher Education Loan Corporation
2100 Guilford Avenue, Room 305
Baltimore, Maryland 21218
(301) 333-6555

Special State Programs

General State Scholarship Program provides scholarship assistance to qualified, full-time undergraduate students and part-time nursing students. The program is need-based and is available only to state residents. Contact your college's financial aid director for application forms and further details.

Senatorial Scholarships provide assistance to qualified undergraduate and graduate students. The awards are need-based and are available only to state residents. Contact your school's financial aid director for further information.

House of Delegates Scholarship Program provides grant assistance to both full-time and part-time undergraduate and graduate students. The program is not based on need. Only state residents are eligible to apply. Awards are made by state delegates within their legislative districts.

Professional Scholarships provide scholarship aid to qualified graduate and undergraduate students. The awards are need-based and are available only to state residents. Contact your school's financial aid director for application forms and further details.

Tolbert Grants provide awards to full-time, non degree-seeking students. The awards are based on need and are available only to state residents. Recipients must be nominated by officials of a private vocational/technical school in Maryland.

Distinguished Scholar Program provides grant assistance to full-time, undergraduate students. The awards are made on the basis of SAT scores and high school rank, not need. Contact your high school guidance counselor for further information.

Teacher Education Distinguished Scholarship Program provides assistance to qualified full-time, undergraduate students. The awards, which are not based on need, are available only to state residents. Recipients must agree to teach 1 year in a Maryland public school for each year they receive the award. Contact the Maryland Higher Education Commission for application forms.

Sharon Christa McAuliffe Memorial Critical Shortage Teacher Education Tuition Assistance Program provides financial assistance to qualified students who are state residents. Recipients must be full-time undergraduate students or public school teachers. The awards are not based upon need. Students must agree to teach in a teacher shortage area 1 1/2 years for every year the award is received. Contact the Maryland Higher Education Commission for further information.

Nursing Grants provide grants of up to $2000 to full-time and part-time graduate students who are enrolled in graduate nursing programs in Maryland. The awards are made only to state residents and are based upon need. Recipients must agree to teach or serve in a shortage area. Contact your school's financial aid director for further information and application forms.

Family Practice Medical Scholarships are awarded to students enrolled in the University of Maryland's School of Medicine. Awards are need-based and available only to state residents. Recipients must be willing to enter general practice medicine and serve for 3 years in Maryland. For application forms, contact the Maryland Higher Education Commission.

Edward Conroy Grants (War Orphans Grants) provide grant assistance to undergraduate and graduate students who lost one or both parents during World War II or the Vietnam conflict. Up to $5000 is available per year. The awards are not based on need. Contact the Maryland Higher Education Commission for further information.

Firemen Reimbursement Program provides assistance to Maryland firemen. The financial assistance covers up to tuition costs at eligible Maryland institutions. The program is available to undergraduate and graduate students and is not need-based. Contact the Maryland Higher Education Commission for further information.

Loan Assistance Repayment Program awards funds to graduates of Maryland institutions who are employed by the state or local government or by a nonprofit institution. The award is available for only 1 year but is renewable. Priority is given to employment fields in which there are critical short-

ages. For further information, contact the Maryland Higher Education Commission at (301) 974-5370.

Physical and Occupational Therapist and Assistants Program provides grants to undergraduate students who are enrolled full-time in a postsecondary institution with an approved program of occupational or physical therapy leading to a license as a physical or occupational therapist. For further information on this loan program, contact the Maryland Higher Education Commission at (301) 974-5370.

Child Care Provider Program makes awards to both full-time and part-time graduate and undergraduate students. Only students enrolled in eligible Maryland institutions with eligible child care programs may apply for this program. There is a service obligation after graduation. For further information on this program, contact the Maryland Higher Education Commission at (301) 974-5370.

Massachusetts

Average tuition and fees:
Public 4-year institutions—$2052
Public 2-year institutions—$1132
Private 4-year institutions—$11,450
Private 2-year institutions—$7186

State spending on student aid:
Need-based—$53,283,000; 39,400 awards
Merit-based—$48,000; 50 awards
Other—$18,636,000

Scholarship and Grant Information

The Board of Regents of Higher Education
Scholarship Office
150 Causeway Street, Room 600
Boston, Massachusetts 02114
(617) 727-9420

Loan Information

Massachusetts Higher Education Assistance
Corporation
Berkeley Place
330 Stuart Street
Boston, Massachusetts 02116
(617) 426-9796

Special State Programs

General Scholarship Program provides scholarship assistance to residents of at least 1 year. Recipients must be enrolled in an approved postsecondary school. The application deadline is May 1. Interested students should file the Massachusetts FAF.

Gilbert Matching Scholarship provides scholarship assistance determined by the school's financial aid director and is awarded to state residents. Contact your college's financial aid director for further details.

Tuition Waiver Program provides tuition waivers for eligible state residents enrolled in a state-supported college or university. The award amounts are determined by the school's financial aid director.

Medical, Dental, or Veterinary Scholarship Program provides scholarship assistance to eligible state residents enrolled at approved graduate schools of medicine, dentistry, or veterinary medicine.

Christa McAuliffe Teacher Incentive Grant Program provides grants to eligible state residents. Recipients must agree to teach full-time after graduation. Contact your school's financial aid director for further information and application forms.

Fire/Police/Corrections Scholarship and War Orphans Scholarship provide scholarship aid. Recipients must be state residents and the children of a deceased fire, police, or corrections officer, or a war veteran whose death was service related. Contact the Massachusetts Scholarship Office for further information and application materials.

Family Education Loan Program allows students or parents to borrow for college expenses. Home mortgage options are available. Borrowers have up to 15 years to repay the loan. Repayment begins 30 days after the loan is disbursed. Call the Massachusetts Educational Financing Authority at 1-800-842-1531 for further information and application forms. The **Graduate Education Loan Program** offers terms similar to those for the Family Education Loan except that borrowers can defer payment of principal and interest while in school. Call (617) 426-9796 for further information.

Michigan

Average tuition and fees:
  Public 4-year institutions—$2484
  Public 2-year institutions—$1047
  Private 4-year institutions—$6520
  Private 2-year institutions—$6400

State spending on student aid:
  Need-based—$73,160,000; 58,500 awards
  Merit-based—None
  Other—$1,718,000

Scholarship and Grant Information

Michigan Department of Education
P.O. Box 3008
Lansing, Michigan 48909
(517) 373-3394

Loan Information

Michigan Department of Education
Guaranteed Student Loan Program
Box 30047
Lansing, Michigan 48909
(517) 373-0760

Special State Programs

Michigan Competitive Scholarship Program provides scholarship assistance to Michigan students attending public and private in-state colleges and universities. Awards are based on ACT scores. Interested students must complete an FAF or FFS form. Contact your school's guidance counselor for further information.

Michigan Tuition Grant Program provides financial need-based assistance to Michigan students attending nonpublic degree-granting in-state colleges and universities. The FAF or FFS is required for consideration for this program. Contact your high school's guidance counselor for further information.

Michigan Education Trust (MET) guarantees payment of in-state tuition and fees. Purchasers sign an agreement with MET for the guarantee of future Michigan college tuition. The family's money is invested by MET, and investment earnings are used to pay the college costs for students enrolled in the program. For further information, call 1-800-MET-4-KID.

Vocational Rehabilitation Programs provide educational benefits to students with physical or mental disabilities that result in a substantial handicap to employment. Call the Michigan Department of Education at (517) 373-3394 for further details.

Veterans Benefits Programs offer state-administered financial assistance to veterans, disabled veterans, and the dependents of disabled or deceased veterans. Contact your county VA office or college VA counselor for specific details and eligibility requirements.

Social Services Program provides tuition and fee awards at Michigan community colleges for students from lower income families who graduate from high school or complete the GED examination before the age of 20. For further information, contact the Tuition Incentive Program, P.O. Box 30037, Lansing, Michigan 48909, or call 1-800-243-2847.

Bureau of Indian Affairs awards educational benefits to students who are members of federally recognized American Indian tribes. For further information, contact the Michigan Agency, Bureau of Indian Affairs, U.S. Department of the Interior, P.O. Box 884, Sault Ste Marie, Michigan 49783, or call (906) 632-6809.

Michigan Commission on Indian Affairs makes awards of free tuition at Michigan public 2-year and 4-year colleges and universities. Recipients must be of at least one-fourth treaty-certifiable North American Indian descent. For further information, contact the Michigan Commission on Indian Affairs, Department of Management and Budget, P.O. Box 30026, Lansing, Michigan 48909, or call (517) 373-0654.

Vocational Education—Single Parent and Home-maker Program provides single parents and homemakers with financial assistance to attend a Michigan community college. For further information, contact your local Michigan community college financial aid office or women's resource center.

Children of Michigan National Guard Personnel Program provides tuition and fees for the children of Michigan National Guard personnel killed or totally disabled as a result of active state service. The awards may be used at Michigan public institutions of higher learning. For further information, contact your local National Guard armory or the Department of Military Affairs, 2500 S. Washington Avenue, Lansing, Michigan 48913, or call 1-800-292-1386.

ACES Tuition Assistance Program provides part-time students with up to 75% of tuition costs for one or two courses each term. Eligibility includes membership in the National Guard. For further information, contact your local National Guard armory or the Department of Military Affairs, 2500 S. Washington Avenue, Lansing, Michigan 48913, or call 1-800-292-1386.

Army National Guard Federal Student Loan Repayment Program provides to members of the National Guard repayment of federal student loans. For further information, contact your local National Guard armory or the Department of Military Affairs, 2500 S. Washington Avenue, Lansing, Michigan 48913, or call 1-800-292-1386.

Wade McCree, Jr. Incentive Scholar Program is a cooperative program, sponsored by the President's Council of Michigan Universities, involving fifteen 4-year public colleges in Michigan. Colleges and universities in the program offer full-tuition scholarships to selected minority students entering high school. The program also provides each student with a faculty mentor who works with the student while he or she attends high school. For further information, contact the Michigan Department of Education, P.O. Box 3008, Lansing, Michigan 48909, or call (517) 373-3394.

Adult Part-time Grant provides grant assistance for needy undergraduate students who have been out of high school for at least 2 years. Recipients must be enrolled on a part-time basis (3 to 11 credits) at an approved public or private degree-granting Michigan college or university. For further information, contact personnel at your school's financial aid office.

Michigan Educational Opportunity Grant Program provides grant assistance to needy undergraduate students who are enrolled at least part-time at a Michigan public college. For further information, contact personnel at your school's financial aid office.

Minnesota

Average tuition and fees:
   Public 4-year institutions—$2063
   Public 2-year institutions—$1499
   Private 4-year institutions—$8776
   Private 2-year institutions—$5181

State spending on student aid:
   Need-based—$76,074,000; 66,527 awards
   Merit-based—None
   Other—$1,720,000

Scholarship and Grant Information

Minnesota Higher Education Coordinating Board
Capitol Square, Suite 400
550 Cedar Street
St. Paul, Minnesota 55101
(612) 296-3974

Loan Information

Minnesota Higher Education Assistance Foundation
85 E. Seventh Street, Suite 500
St. Paul, Minnesota 55101
(612) 227-7661

Special State Programs

State Program awards grants based on financial need. The amount varies but may not exceed 50% of the total cost of education. Recipients must be enrolled at least half-time to be considered for this program. Contact the Minnesota Higher Education Coordinating Board for further information.

State Part-time Grant-in-Aid Program provides grant assistance to part-time students. The grants are based on need, and the amount of the award is determined by the school's financial aid director.

Dislocated Rural Workers Program provides financial assistance to residents of rural Minnesota enrolled in adult farm management programs or programs designed to provide preparation for employment. Unemployed persons, displaced homemakers, and farmers and their spouses with severe financial need are also eligible for this program. The amount of the award varies. Contact your school's financial aid director for further information and application materials.

Minnesota Indian Scholarship Program provides financial aid to eligible Native Americans. Recipients must be state residents and accepted for enrollment at an approved institution. Contact the Scholarship Officer, Indian Education, 1819 Bemidji Avenue, Bemidji, Minnesota 56601 for further information and application forms.

State Work-Study Program provides employment opportunities to eligible state residents enrolled full-time in undergraduate, graduate, or vocational programs. Contact your campus financial aid office for application forms.

Student Educational Loan Fund (SELF) provides loan assistance to both undergraduate and graduate students. The interest rate is variable, and all recipients must be enrolled at least half-time in an eligible school in Minnesota. State residents attending out-of-state schools may also qualify for the loan. Contact the Minnesota Higher Education Coordinating Board for application materials.

Graduated Repayment Income Protection Program (GRIP) provides loan funds to eligible graduate and professional school students. Loan repayments are based upon annual income. Contact your school's financial aid director for further information and application forms or call (612) 227-7661.

Veterans Benefit Programs offer several state-administered financial assistance programs to veterans and their dependents and to the dependents of deceased or disabled veterans. Contact the Minnesota Department of Veterans Affairs at the Federal Building in St. Paul, (612) 726-1454 or your county VA office for further details and application materials.

State Reciprocity Agreements allow state residents to receive tuition waivers according to reciprocity agreements involving the state of Minnesota with several states. Students pay a regional reciprocity rate that varies by type of institution. Contact the Minnesota Higher Education Coordinating Board for further details on these agreements.

Nursing Grant Program awards are based upon financial need and the cost of attendance at nursing school. Recipients must be state residents and enrolled at least half-time as undergraduate students. For further information, contact the Minnesota Higher Education Coordinating Board.

Child Care Grant Program provides financial assistance to state residents with children 12 years of age or younger, or children up to 14 years old who are handicapped. A recipient must be enrolled at least half-time in an undergraduate program, and cannot be receiving assistance under Aid to Families with Dependent Children Program. For further information, contact personnel at your school's financial aid office.

Mississippi

Average tuition and fees:
  Public 4-year institutions—$1858
  Public 2-year institutions—$680
  Private 4-year institutions—$4826
  Private 2-year institutions—$3602

State spending on student aid:
  Need-based—$1,136,000; 2200 awards
  Merit-based—$705,000; 130 awards

Scholarship and Grant Information

Board of Trustees of State Institutions of Higher Learning
P.O. Box 2336
Jackson, Mississippi 39225-2336
(601) 982-6570

Loan Information

Mississippi Guarantee Student Loan Agency
3825 Ridgewood Road
P.O. Box 342
Jackson, Mississippi 39211-6453
(601) 982-6570

Special State Programs

State Student Incentive Program provides state-administered grant assistance to eligible state residents. Each school selects the recipients through its regular financial aid process. Contact your college financial aid director for further information.

Nursing Education Scholarship Grant Program provides scholarships to registered state nurses who apply for an accredited bachelor of science nursing degree or a graduate degree nursing program. Upon completion of the college program, the recipient must work in nursing service or nursing education in Mississippi. Contact the Board of Trustees of State Institutions of Higher Learning for further information.

Nursing Education Scholarship for Study in Baccalaureate Nursing Education Program awards need-based scholarships to state residents studying in a Mississippi school of nursing. Recipients must agree to work in the state after graduation. Contact the Board of Trustees of State Institutions of Higher Learning for more information.

Law Enforcement Officers and Firemen Scholarships provide scholarship assistance to the children of full-time state law enforcement officers and firemen who were fatally injured or totally disabled while performing their official duties. The scholarship may be used only in state-supported colleges and universities in Mississippi. Contact the Board of Trustees of State Institutions of Higher Learning for more information.

Southeast Asia POW/MIA Scholarship Program provides 4-year scholarships at any state-supported institution to children of Vietnam veterans who are missing in action, returned prisoners of war, or deceased prisoners of war. Call (601) 982-6570 for further information.

Medical Education Loan Program makes loans to state residents enrolled in accredited medical and dental schools. A service obligation is part of the loan contract. Contact your school's financial aid director for further details.

Special Medical Education Loan Program
makes loan money available to state residents with
financial need who are enrolled in the University of
Mississippi School of Medicine. Recipients must
be third- or fourth-year students and must rank in
the upper 50% of their class. A service obligation is
part of the loan agreement. Contact your school's
financial aid director for more information.

Public Management Graduate Internship Program provides students pursuing graduate degrees
in public administration, public policy and adminis-
tration, or criminal justice administration with prac-
tical work experience in a state agency. Internships
are for 3 or 4 months, depending on the time of year.
A stipend of $1000 per month is part of the award.
Recipients are selected on the basis of grades and
must be enrolled at Jackson State University,
Mississippi State University, the University of
Mississippi, or the University of Southern Mississippi. For further information, contact the
Program Coordinator, Public Management Graduate
Internship Program, MSU Graduate Education, P.O.
Office Drawer PC, Mississippi State, Mississippi
39762, or call (601) 325-7859 or (601) 325-2711.

William Winter Teacher Scholar Loan Program
offers financial assistance to students enrolled in a
teacher education program leading to a Class A
teaching certificate. Recipients must be enrolled in
an accredited public or private institution in
Mississippi and must agree to repay the scholarship
by teaching a specified subject full-time in
Mississippi. For further information, contact the
Board of Trustees, Institutions of Higher Learning,
Student Financial Aid, 3825 Ridgewood Road,
Jackson, Mississippi 39211-6453, or call (601)
982-6570.

Academic Common Market Program is an interstate agreement among southern states for sharing
academic programs. The waiver of out-of-state
tuition cannot be granted to state residents interested in pursuing degree programs available at institutions of higher learning in Mississippi. For further
information, contact the Board of Trustees of State
Institutions of Higher Learning, Student Financial
Aid, 3825 Ridgewood Road, Jackson, Mississippi
39211-6453, or call (601) 982-6570.

**Graduate and Professional Degree Scholarship
Program** provides financial assistance to students
pursuing graduate or professional degrees in a field
of study not offered at an institution of higher
learning in Mississippi. The amount of assistance is
the difference between the out-of-state tuition and
the in-state tuition charged at the institution where
the student is enrolled. There are no repayment provisions in this program. For further information,
contact the Board of Trustees of State Institutions
of Higher Learning at (601) 982-6570.

Southern Regional Education Board Program
contracts with the Board of Trustees of State
Institutions of Higher Learning and the state of
Mississippi to provide spaces for Mississippi students studying optometry or osteopathic medicine.
Recipients must be legal residents for at least 12
consecutive months before making application. For
further information, contact the Board of Trustees
of State Institutions of Higher Learning at (601)
982-6570.

Missouri

Average tuition and fees:
Public 4-year institutions—$1532
Public 2-year institutions—$815
Private 4-year institutions—$7170
Private 2-year institutions—$5554

State spending on student aid:
Need-based—$11,144,000; 8950 awards
Merit-based—$10,091,000; 4513 awards
Other—$260,000

Scholarship, Grant, and Loan Information

Coordinating Board for Higher Education
P.O. Box 1438
Jefferson City, Missouri 65101
(314) 751-3940

Special State Programs

Missouri Student Grant Program provides need-
based grant assistance to state residents who are
enrolled as full-time undergraduate students at an
approved Missouri school. Students may apply for
this grant by completing a Missouri Family
Financial Statement or a Missouri Financial Aid
Form. Contact your school's guidance counselor
for more information.

Higher Education Academic Scholarship Program
provides scholarship assistance to high school
seniors with superior academic achievement. A
recipient must be a state resident and must be
attending a participating Missouri postsecondary
institution as a full-time undergraduate student.
Call (314) 751-3940 for application materials.

Teacher Education Scholarship Program provides
scholarships to students who plan careers in teaching. Scholarship recipients must agree to teach in a
Missouri public school for 5 years after certification. For applications, write to the Missouri
Department of Elementary and Secondary
Education, P.O. Box 480, Jefferson City, Missouri
65102.

Montana

Average tuition and fees:
Public 4-year institutions—$1535
Public 2-year institutions—$877
Private 4-year institutions—$5034
Private 2-year institutions—$1144

State spending on student aid:
    Need-based—$383,000; 1100 awards
    Merit-based—None

Scholarship, Grant, and Loan Information

Montana Guaranteed Student Loan Program
Montana University System
33 S. Last Chance Gulch
Helena, Montana 59620-3104
(406) 444-6594

Special State Programs

State Student Incentive Grant provides need-based grant assistance to eligible state residents. Contact your school's financial aid director for further details.

Bureau of Indian Affairs Grant and Scholarship Programs offer several state-administered grants and scholarships to eligible state Native Americans. The programs are need-based. Contact your tribal education specialist for more information.

State Work-Study Program provides employment opportunities to state residents who are full-time undergraduate or graduate students. The program is based upon need. Contact your college's financial aid director for more information.

Fee Waiver Program grants waivers to a limited number of undergraduate and graduate students who meet specific requirements. The awards are based on financial need and academic achievement. For further information, contact personnel in the financial aid office of any unit of the Montana University System.

Nebraska

Average tuition and fees:
    Public 4-year institutions—$1519
    Public 2-year institutions—$919
    Private 4-year institutions—$6442
    Private 2-year institutions—$3410

State spending on student aid:
    Need-based—$2,196,000; 3328 awards
    Merit-based—None

Scholarship and Grant Information

Nebraska Coordinating Commission for
    Postsecondary Education
Sixth Floor, State Capitol
P.O. Box 95005
Lincoln, Nebraska 68509
(402) 471-2847

Loan Information

Higher Education Assistance Foundation
Cornhusker Bank Building, Suite 304
11th and Cornhusker Highway
Lincoln, Nebraska 68521
(402) 476-9129

Special State Programs

Edgar J. Boschult Memorial Scholarships Program provides annual scholarships to students enrolled in the Army, Air Force, and Naval Science courses at the University of Nebraska. Recipients are selected by the Executive Committee of the Nebraska American Legion.

Nebraska Mathematics and Science Teacher Tuition Assistance Act provides financial assistance to mathematics and science students who are enrolled in a teacher training program and who agree to teach in a public or private state school after graduation. Contact your school's financial aid director for more information.

Employment Programs provide state-administered employment opportunities through the Job Training Partnership Act. Under this program, economically disadvantaged, unemployed, and underemployed people can receive assistance to enroll in retraining programs. For more information, call (402) 471-2127.

Nebraska Medical Student Loan Program provides loan funds to encourage medical students to establish practices in underserved and rural areas in Nebraska. A service obligation is part of the loan contract. The program is not based on financial need. Call the Nebraska Commission on Rural Health at (402) 471-2337 for further information and application materials.

Bureau of Indian Affairs Grant (BIA) provides financial aid to eligible state Native Americans. The program is need-based. Contact your school's financial aid director or your tribe's education officer for more information.

Nebraska National Guard offers several state-administered financial assistance programs to National Guard members. To apply, contact your commanding officer.

Nevada

Average tuition and fees:
    Public 4-year institutions—$1100
    Public 2-year institutions—$522
    Private 4-year institutions—$5400
    Private 2-year institutions—N/A

State spending on student aid:
    Need-based—$400,000; 400 awards
    Merit-based—None

Scholarship and Grant Information

Student Services
Office of Student Financial Services
University of Nevada/Reno
Room 200 TSSC
Reno, Nevada 89557
(702) 784-4666

Loan Information

NGSLP Nevada State Department of Education
400 West King Street
Capitol Complex
Carson City, Nevada 89710
(702) 885-5914

Special State Programs

Nevada Student Incentive Grant (NSIG) provides assistance to state residents with significant financial need who are enrolled at least half-time at the University of Nevada/Reno. The grant is available to both undergraduate and graduate students. Contact the Office of Student Financial Services at the University of Nevada/Reno, for more information and application materials.

University of Nevada/Reno Freshman Scholarships provides scholarships, based on academic merit to seniors in Nevada high schools. The University of Nevada/Reno also offers other scholarships. Some are based upon academic accomplishment; others are awarded to students pursuing work in a particular college or department. Contact the Office of Student Financial Services at the University of Nevada/Reno for application forms and further information.

In-State Grants-in-Aid award University of Nevada grants to state residents each semester, based upon scholastic achievement, financial need, and the rendering of special services to the university. Contact the Office of Student Financial Services for further information.

Out-of-State Grants-in-Aid award University of Nevada grants each semester to undergraduate students who are not Nevada residents. Recipients of these awards are not required to pay the nonresident tuition charge. A number of these grants are set aside for international students.

Bureau of Indian Affairs Grants (BIA) provide financial assistance to needy state Native Americans. A special counselor is available in the Thompson Student Services Center at the University of Nevada/Reno to assist students in applying for this grant.

Educational Opportunity Program Grants (EOP) make awards to eligible state high school graduates. For application information, contact the Office of Special Programs in the Thompson Student Services Center at the University of Nevada/Reno.

New Hampshire

Average tuition and fees:
  Public 4-year institutions—$2196
  Public 2-year institutions—$1608
  Private 4-year institutions—$10,299
  Private 2-year institutions—$4050

State spending on student aid:
  Need-based—$775,000; 1544 awards
  Merit-based—$10,000; 10 awards
  Other—$694,000

Scholarship and Grant Information

New Hampshire Postsecondary Education
  Commission
Two Industrial Park Drive
Concord, New Hampshire 03301-9681
(603) 271-2555

Loan Information

New Hampshire Higher Education Assistance
  Foundation
P.O. Box 877
Concord, New Hampshire 03302
1-800-235-2577
1-800-525-2577

Special State Programs

New Hampshire Incentive Grant Program (NHIG) provides grant assistance to eligible state residents. Students must be enrolled full-time in private, public, or vocational/technical schools. Scholarships may be applied to schools within the six New England states. Satisfactory academic progress is required. Contact your school's financial aid director for more information.

New Hampshire Nursing Education Grant Program provides grants to students pursuing careers in nursing. The program is based upon need and is available to full-time state residents enrolled in programs leading to a registered or practical nurse's license. Contact the New Hampshire Postsecondary Education Commission for further details.

New Jersey

Average tuition and fees:
  Public 4-year institutions—$2511
  Public 2-year institutions—$1130
  Private 4-year institutions—$9398
  Private 2-year institutions—$6748

State spending on student aid:
  Need-based—$95,834,000; 58,754 awards
  Merit-based—$6,246,000; 5046 awards

Scholarship and Grant Information

Department of Higher Education
Office of Student Assistance
CN 540
Trenton, New Jersey 08625
1-800-962-INFO

Loan Information

New Jersey Higher Education Assistance Authority
CN 543
Trenton, New Jersey 08625
(609) 588-3200

Special State Programs

Tuition Aid Grants (TAG) Program provides grant assistance based upon the student's financial need. Eligible students must be state residents and must be enrolled or planning to enroll in approved schools. Recipients should file a New Jersey FAF to be considered for the program. For applications, contact your high school guidance office or college financial aid office.

Educational Opportunity Fund Grants (EOF) provide financial assistance to students from disadvantaged backgrounds who have exceptional financial need. The grants are renewable. Recipients must file a New Jersey FAF to be considered. For applications, contact your high school guidance office or college financial aid office.

Garden State Scholars Program awards scholarships to high school students with outstanding academic achievement. The awards are based upon SAT scores and high school grades. Applicants must also have financial need and must plan to enroll as full-time undergraduate students. Recipients should file a New Jersey FAF to be considered. For applications, contact your high school guidance office or college financial aid office.

Distinguished Scholars Program awards scholarships to high school seniors with the highest record of academic achievement. The awards are based upon SAT scores and high school grades, and candidates are selected by their high school principal or guidance counselor. Recipients must be state residents. Financial need is not taken into consideration.

Public Tuition Benefit Program pays for the actual cost of tuition up to a maximum of the tuition charged at the New Jersey Institute of Technology. Eligible students must be state residents who are enrolled in a New Jersey institution of higher learning at least half-time and who are the dependents of service personnel or law enforcement officers killed in the line of duty. The application deadline is October 1. For applications, call 1-800-792-8670.

Direct Loan Program provides loans of last resort for eligible students denied a Stafford Student Loan. Contact the New Jersey Higher Education Assistance Authority for further information.

New Mexico

Average tuition and fees:
Public 4-year institutions—$1326
Public 2-year institutions—$496
Private 4-year institutions—$7335
Private 2-year institutions—N/A

State spending on student aid:
Need-based—$7,257,000; 9156 awards
Merit-based—$3,990,000; 2150 awards
Other—$2,177,000

Scholarship and Grant Information

Commission on Higher Education
1068 Cerrillos Road
Santa Fe, New Mexico 87501-4295
(505) 827-8300

Loan Information

New Mexico Educational Assistance Foundation
3900 Osuna NE
P.O. Box 27020
Albuquerque, New Mexico 87125-7020
(505) 345-3371

Special State Programs

New Mexico Student Incentive Grant Program provides grant assistance to needy state residents who are enrolled at least half-time at approved schools. Contact your college's financial aid director for further information.

Student Choice Act provides funds to needy state residents attending eligible independent institutions of higher education in New Mexico: College of Santa Fe, St. John's College in Santa Fe, and the College of the Southwest in Hobbs. Contact the financial aid director in each of these schools for further information and application materials.

New Mexico Work-Study Program provides employment opportunities to needy students. Eligible students must be state residents and be enrolled at least half-time at institutions of higher learning. Contact your financial aid director for further information.

New Mexico Physicians Loan Program provides loan assistance to state residents who are enrolled in accredited schools of medicine in the United States. The recipient must agree to work in a shortage area for at least a year after graduation. Contact the Commission on Higher Education for further information.

New Mexico Osteopathic Student Loan Program provides loan funds to eligible state residents enrolled or accepted for enrollment at an accredited school of osteopathic medicine. The recipient must agree to work in a shortage area after graduation. Contact the Commission on Higher Education for further information.

Three Percent Scholarship Program provides grant assistance to state residents who are enrolled as undergraduate or graduate students at public colleges or universities. At least one-third of the scholarship must be based upon financial need as determined by an approved need analysis system. For further information, contact financial aid personnel of any New Mexico public postsecondary institution.

New Mexico Scholars Program awards scholarships to state residents who graduated in the upper 5% of their high school class or who scored at least 25 on the ACT examination or 1020 on the SAT. Awards cover the cost of tuition, fees, and books and may be awarded for each of the 4 years of college if the recipient maintains academic progress. Eligibility also includes financial need. For more information, contact financial aid personnel in any New Mexico postsecondary institutions.

Professional Student Exchange Program is designed to obtain access at reduced tuition rates on a preferred admission basis for state residents in out-of-state schools. Applicants must be enrolled in graduate or professional programs not offered at in-state colleges. For further information, contact NMWICHE Exchange Programs, Student Services Center, Room 266, University of New Mexico, Albuquerque, New Mexico 87131.

Graduate Fellowship Program is targeted to increase the graduate enrollment of underrepresented groups, particularly minorities and women, in academic fields needed by the state or nation. Students receiving financial assistance under this program must agree to work at least 10 hours per week in an unpaid internship or assistantship. For further information, contact personnel of the financial aid office of your college or university.

New Mexico Nursing Student Loan Program is designed to increase the number of nurses in medically underserved areas. The loan is based upon financial need, and recipients must agree to practice in an underserved area. Students enrolled in an approved nursing education program or working for a master of science degree in nursing are eligible to apply for this loan program. For further information, contact financial aid personnel at your college or university.

New Mexico Physician Student Loan Program is designed to increase the number of physicians in medically underserved areas. Recipients must be enrolled or accepted for enrollment in an approved medical school and must have financial need. Recipients must agree to practice in an underserved area; loans may be forgiven through service. For further information, contact the New Mexico Educational Assistance Foundation.

Minority Doctoral Assistance Program is designed to increase the number of ethnic minorities and women to teach engineering, physics, mathematics, and other academic disciplines. Recipients must have successfully completed undergraduate and master degree programs and must be accepted for enrollment as full-time doctoral students. Recipients must agree to teach at a sponsoring New Mexico institution. For further information, contact personnel at the graduate school office of your college or university.

New York

Average tuition and fees:
Public 4-year institutions—$1460
Public 2-year institutions—$1412
Private 4-year institutions—$9517
Private 2-year institutions—$5544

State spending on student aid:
Need-based—$408,000,000; 330,630 awards
Merit-based—$30,739,000; 65,620 awards
Other—$385,000

Scholarship, Grant, and Loan Information

New York State Higher Education Services
Corporation
99 Washington Avenue
Albany, New York 12255
Loan Information—(518) 473-1574
Grant Information—(518) 474-5642

Special State Programs

Tuition Assistance Program (TAP) provides grant assistance to needy students. The awards are based upon family income and tuition costs. Contact your high school guidance counselor or college financial aid director for further information.

Aid for Part-time Study (APTS) provides financial assistance to eligible students who are enrolled for part-time study in New York State schools. The awards are based upon income and tuition costs. Contact your high school guidance counselor or college financial director for more information.

Educational Opportunity Programs (HEOP, CD, SEEK, EOP) provide financial assistance to eligible students studying in New York State schools. The programs provide counseling, tutorial assistance, and help in meeting living expense costs. The amount of the award depends upon the program. Contact the New York State Higher Education Services Corporation for further information.

Children of Veterans, Police Officers, Firefighters, and Correction Officers provides financial assistance to the children of deceased or disabled veterans, prisoners of war, or servicepersons missing in action. The children of New York State firefighters, police officers, and corrections officers who died as a result of a service-related injury are also eligible for assistance under this program. Contact the New York State Higher Education Services Corporation for further information.

Regents College and Nursing Scholarship awards are based upon special tests taken by senior high school students. High school performance, class rank, and high school grades are also taken into consideration. Contact your high school guidance counselor for more information. This program depends on future funding.

Empire State Scholarships of Excellence are awarded to outstanding high school seniors. High school rank, class grades, and high school performance are some of the eligibility requirements. Contact your high school guidance counselor for further information. This program depends on future funding.

Liberty Scholarships are awarded to low-income students to help them meet college expenses. Write to the New York State Higher Education Services Corporation for further information. This program will continue to be operational only if funding permits.

Supplemental Higher Education Loan Financing (SHELF) provides loans to graduate students. The amount of the award varies and is based upon creditworthiness. Contact your school's financial aid director for further information.

Regents Physician Loan Forgiveness Program provides loans to eligible medical students. Recipients must agree to practice in shortage areas after graduation. Contact the New York State Higher Education Services Corporation for further information.

Regents Professional Opportunity Scholarships are awarded to students in certain professional fields. Priority is given to disadvantaged students. Contact the New York State Higher Education Services Corporation for application materials.

Jacob Javits Fellows Program awards aid to eligible graduate students enrolled in programs in the arts, humanities, and social sciences. The program is based upon academic merit. Contact your college's financial aid director for application materials.

Regents Health Care Opportunity Scholarships are awarded to eligible students enrolled in medical and dental schools. Priority is given to disadvantaged students. Contact the New York State Department of Education for application forms.

New York State Health Service Corps Fellowships provide scholarships to students enrolled in certain health fields. Contact the New York Health Department, Health Service Corps, Corning Tower, Empire State Plaza, Albany, New York 12237 for further information.

Financial Assistance for Disadvantaged Health Professions Students Program provides assistance to eligible students enrolled in schools of medicine, dentistry, and osteopathic medicine. Priority is given to students from disadvantaged backgrounds. Contact your college financial aid director for application forms.

Supplemental Tuition Assistance Program (STAP) provides financial assistance to full-time undergraduate students who are educationally disadvantaged and who require remedial training. The procedures for applying for these awards are the same as for the Tuition Assistance Program (TAP). Each college or university determines eligibility. For further information, contact the financial aid personnel at any state college or university.

Empire State Challenger Scholarship Program provides financial assistance to students enrolled in teacher education programs. For further information, contact the New York State Education Department, State and Federal Scholarship and Fellowship Unit, Cultural Education Center, Room 5C64, Albany, New York 12230.

Empire State Challenger Fellowship Program provides financial assistance to part-time and full-time graduate students enrolled in certain teacher education and school professional programs. For further information, contact the New York State Education Department, State and Federal Scholarship and Fellowship Unit, Cultural Education Center, Room 5C64, Albany, New York 12230.

Comprehensive Employment Program (CEP) assists urban recipients of Aid to Dependent Children with vocational programs of training and job placement. Assistance can include the cost of tuition, books, and daily expenses. For further information, contact the New York State Department of Social Services, Bureau of Employment Programs, 40 N. Pearl Street, 7B, Albany, New York 12243.

State Aid to Native Americans provides financial assistance to members of Indian tribes within New York State who are enrolled at least half-time in a postsecondary institution. For further information, contact the Native American Education Unit, Room 485 EBA, Albany, New York 12234.

North Carolina

Average tuition and fees:
Public 4-year institutions—$1015
Public 2-year institutions—$288
Private 4-year institutions—$7373
Private 2-year institutions—$4880

State spending on student aid:
Need-based—$3,714,000; 2660 awards
Merit-based—$24,566,000; 26,248 awards
Other—$30,145,000

Scholarship, Grant, and Loan Information

North Carolina State Education Assistance Authority
P.O. Box 2688
Chapel Hill, North Carolina 27515-2688
(919) 549-8614

90

Special State Programs

North Carolina Student Incentive Grant (NCSIG) makes grant awards to eligible state residents. Recipients must be enrolled or accepted for enrollment on a full-time basis at a North Carolina postsecondary institution, and are required to teach in a North Carolina public school for 1 year for each year of scholarship assistance they receive. The awards are based upon financial need. Interested students should file an FAF or FFS to be considered.

North Carolina Teaching Fellows Scholarship Program makes awards to qualified students. Applicants are chosen on the basis of high school grades, class rank, SAT scores, and extracurricular activities. The scholarships are available at only select North Carolina postsecondary institutions. For applications, contact your high school guidance counselor.

North Carolina Legislative Tuition Grant Program provides financial assistance to state residents who attend a North Carolina private college or university. Students must be enrolled full-time in an undergraduate program. The amount of the award varies and is not based upon need. For applications, contact the financial aid offices of an eligible private college or university.

North Carolina Student Loan Program for Health, Science, and Mathematics provides assistance to legal residents of the state who are accepted as full-time students in accredited schools and are working toward degrees in mathematics, health sciences, and allied health and clinical psychology. Loan amounts vary. Contact your school's financial aid director for further details.

Prospective Teacher Scholarship Loan Fund makes loan money available to eligible state residents interested in pursuing a career in teaching. Eligibility includes academic performance, grade point average, class rank, and recommendations. Financial need is not part of the selection process. Call the Scholarship-Loan Section of the State Department of Public Instruction at (919) 733-4736 for application materials and further information.

Prospective Vocational Teacher Scholarships are awarded to qualified state residents who are enrolled in accredited North Carolina colleges and who plan to become vocational education teachers. The program is not based upon financial need. Contact your high school guidance counselor for further information and application forms.

State Contractual Scholarship Program (SCSF) provides scholarship assistance to needy state residents who are enrolled full-time or part-time in an approved North Carolina private college or university. The awards are based upon financial need. Recipients are selected by the financial aid director.

Vocational Rehabilitation Program provides assistance to students with mental or physical disabilities. The value of the awards is based upon need and the type of program. Contact the North Carolina Division of Vocational Rehabilitation Services at (919) 733-5920 for further information.

North Carolina National Guard Tuition Assistance Program provides aid to students who are active members of the North Carolina National Guard. Request application forms and information from the Adjutant General at (919) 733-3770.

North Carolina Community Scholarship Program provides scholarships to state residents who are enrolled at least part-time in a community college. Priority is given to students with the greatest financial need and to minority students. Each community college selects recipients for this program. Contact the Department of Community Colleges at (919) 733-7051 for further information.

Doctoral/Law/Veterinary Medicine Program provides awards to eligible black state residents who are enrolled full-time in a doctoral degree program, law school, or accredited veterinary school at certain colleges and universities in North Carolina. The program is administered by the University of North Carolina. Contact your school's financial aid director for more information.

Minority Presence Grant Program allocates funds to the campuses of the University of North Carolina to increase the enrollment of minority students. The grants are available to state residents who are enrolled in eligible institutions at least half-time. The amount of the award depends upon financial need. For applications, contact the financial aid office of an eligible institution.

Board of Governors Medical and Dental Scholarship Programs provide scholarship assistance to state residents who are enrolled in eligible schools of medicine and dentistry. Awards are renewable annually for 4 years. Financial need is part of the selection process. Contact the North Carolina State Education Assistance Authority for further information.

American Indian Student Incentive Legislative Grant Program makes grant awards to eligible state residents who are Native Americans. Students must be enrolled or accepted for enrollment in a degree-granting school and must have financial need. Awards are determined by the director of financial aid. Apply at any constituent institution of the University of North Carolina.

North Dakota

Average tuition and fees:
    Public 4-year institutions—$1604
    Public 2-year institutions—$1286
    Private 4-year institutions—$5149
    Private 2-year institutions—$2100

State spending on student aid:
    Need-based—$1,200,000; 2000 awards
    Merit-based—$292,000; N/A

Scholarship and Grant Information

North Dakota Student Financial Assistance Program
State Capitol, Tenth Floor
Bismarck, North Dakota 58505-0154
(701) 224-4114

Loan Information

Bank of North Dakota Student Loan Department
P.O. Box 5509
Bismarck, North Dakota 58502-5509
(701) 224-5600

Special State Programs

North Dakota Student Financial Assistance Program provides incentives to students to continue their education. Recipients must be state residents and must be enrolled or plan to enroll at least part-time at eligible institutions of higher learning. Contact your high school guidance counselor for further information.

North Dakota Merit Scholar Program provides tuition scholarships to high school seniors who rank in the top 20% of their high school graduating class and in the top 5% of all students who take the ACT. Contact your high school guidance counselor for more information.

North Dakota Nursing Scholarship Loan Program provides funds to qualified state residents, both graduate and undergraduate students, who plan to pursue careers in nursing. Loan cancellation provisions are available if the graduate is later employed as a nurse in North Dakota. The program is based upon financial need. For further information and application materials, contact the North Dakota Nursing Scholarship-Loan Program, 420 N. Fourth Street, Bismark, North Dakota 58505.

Nurse Education Scholarship Loan Program awards financial assistance through the financial aid offices of North Carolina colleges and universities that offer nurse education programs leading to a certificate or degree that allows the recipient to sit for licensure in North Carolina either as a licensed practical nurse or a registered nurse. The awards are based upon financial need and academic merit, and the maximum award cannot exceed $5000. For further information, contact financial aid personnel of state colleges and universities.

Ohio

Average tuition and fees:
    Public 4-year institutions—$2432
    Public 2-year institutions—$1636
    Private 4-year institutions—$8019
    Private 2-year institutions—$5690

State spending on student aid:
    Need-based—$52,770,000; 73,000 awards
    Merit-based—$27,271,000; 44,319 awards

Scholarship and Grant Information

Ohio Board of Regents
Student Assistance Office
3600 State Office Tower
30 E. Broad Street
Columbus, Ohio 43266-0417
(614) 466-7420

Loan Information

Ohio Student Loan Commission
P.O. Box 16610
Columbus, Ohio 43266-0610
(614) 466-3091

Special State Programs

Student Choice Grant Program provides tuition assistance to students attending Ohio nonprofit colleges or universities. Students must be state residents and must be enrolled full-time in an approved institution. The amounts of the award vary. Eligibility is determined by each school. Contact your college's director of financial aid for further information and application materials.

Ohio Academic Scholarship Program awards financial assistance to outstanding high school seniors. Recipients must be state residents and must plan to enroll in an eligible Ohio school. For applications, contact a high school guidance office.

Ohio Instructional Grant Program provides grant assistance to needy state residents who are enrolled in an eligible Ohio or Pennsylvania school. The amounts of the award vary and are based upon financial need. For applications, contact the Student Assistance Office of the Ohio Board of Regents.

Ohio War Orphans Scholarship Program provides financial assistance to the children of deceased or disabled Ohio war veterans. Recipients must be state residents and must be enrolled full-time in an approved undergraduate program. For applications, contact the Ohio Board of Regents or a high school guidance counselor.

Police and Firefighter Tuition Benefits Program provides financial assistance to the children of Ohio police and firefighters who were killed in the line of duty. Contact your school's financial aid director for more information.

Regents Graduate/Professional Fellowship Program
provides financial assistance to university seniors
or baccalaureate degree candidates who will enroll
as full-time graduate students in eligible Ohio graduate or graduate professional schools. For further
information, contact your college or university academic advisor.

Oklahoma

Average tuition and fees:
  Public 4-year institutions—$1309
  Public 2-year institutions—$840
  Private 4-year institutions—$5133
  Private 2-year institutions—$5382

State spending on student aid:
  Need-based—$13,177,000; 16,026 awards
  Merit-based—$3,201,000; 976 awards
  Other—$18,746,000

Scholarship, Grant, and Loan Information

Oklahoma State Regents for Higher Education
500 Education Building
State Capitol Complex
Oklahoma City, Oklahoma 73105-4503
Loan Information—(405) 521-8262
Grant Information—(405) 525-8180

Special State Programs

Oklahoma Tuition and Grant Program awards
grants to state residents who are enrolled at least
part-time as graduate or undergraduate students at
approved schools in Oklahoma. The grants are
based upon financial need. Students should file an
FAF or FFS to be considered for the program.
Contact your college's financial aid director for
application forms and further information.

Future Teachers Scholarship Program awards
scholarships to outstanding state residents who
graduated in the top 15% of their high school class.
Recipients must be interested in pursuing a career
in teaching. For applications, contact the Oklahoma
State Regents for Higher Education.

William P. Willis Scholarship Program provides
financial assistance to low-income, full-time undergraduate students attending schools in the
Oklahoma system of higher education. Call program
officials at (405) 521-2444 for further information.

Chiropractic Education Assistance Program provides financial aid to eligible state residents who
are pursuing the study of chiropractic medicine at
accredited schools. The amount of the award
varies. The deadline for applying is July 1. The
Oklahoma Board of Chiropractic Examiners makes
the award determinations. Contact the office of the
Oklahoma State Regents for Higher Education for
application materials and further information.

Professional Degree Programs provide financial
assistance to eligible state minority students who
are studying medicine, dentistry, law, veterinary
medicine, or optometry. Participants in the program
may receive the grant for the first 2 years of professional study. Applications must be filed by June 1.
Contact the office of the Oklahoma State Regents
for Higher Education for application forms.

Academic Scholars Program provides scholarship
assistance for students who attend the University of
Oklahoma, Oklahoma State University, the
University of Tulsa, or Oral Roberts University. A
recipient must be a National Merit Scholar,
National Achievement Scholar, National Hispanic
Scholar, or Presidential Scholar. Eligibility also
includes being a state resident and a high school
graduate after July 1, 1988; also, recipients must
attend a private college or university. For further
information, contact the Oklahoma State Regents
for Higher Education.

Oregon

Average tuition and fees:
  Public 4-year institutions—$1738
  Public 2-year institutions—$753
  Private 4-year institutions—$8656
  Private 2-year institutions—$5250

State spending on student aid:
  Need-based— $11,748,000; 16,095 awards
  Merit-based—None

Scholarship, Grant, and Loan Information

Oregon State Scholarship Commission
1445 Willamette Street, Suite 9
Eugene, Oregon 97401
1-800-452-8807
Loan Information—(503) 686-3200
Grant Information—(503) 686-4166

Special State Programs

Need Grant Program makes grants available to eligible state residents attending any institution of
higher education in Oregon. Recipients must be
full-time undergraduate students. The awards are
based upon need. Students must complete an FAF
and submit it to the College Scholarship Service.

Cash Award Program provides awards based upon
academic ability and financial need. Recipients
must be state residents and must be enrolled in any
2- or 4-year nonprofit accredited school. Students
enrolled in hospital schools of nursing are also eligible to apply. Students must complete an FAF and
submit it to the College Scholarship Service to be
considered.

Oregon Teacher Corps Program provides state-
funded forgiveness loans to undergraduate and
graduate students. Recipients must agree to teach

for a specified period of time in a public elementary or secondary school in Oregon. Applicants must be state residents who ranked in the top 20% of their graduating class and who currently rank in the top 20% of their college class. Only students pursuing a career in teaching qualify. For applications, contact the Department of Education of your college.

Medical and Dental Student Loan Program provides loans to qualified state residents who are enrolled full-time in the medical and dental program at the Oregon Health Sciences University or in the veterinary program at the Oregon State University. For applications, contact Oregon State University at (503) 737-4411.

Nursing Loan Program provides loans to qualified state residents who are enrolled as full-time nursing students at the Oregon Health Sciences University. For applications, contact the Oregon Health Sciences University at (503) 279-8249.

Oregon Teacher Corps Loan Program provides forgivable loans to prospective teachers. Recipients must rank in the top 20% of their class, must have completed at least 2 years of undergraduate study, and must be enrolled in an approved teacher education program at an Oregon college or university. For further information, contact the Oregon State Scholarship Commission.

The following privately funded award programs are administered by the Oregon State Scholarship Commission:

Alpha Delta Kappa

AFL-CIO

Bowerman Foundation Program

James Carlson Scholarship Program

Peter Connacher Program

KGON Radio Scholarship Program

Jeannette Mowery Scholarship Program

Oregonian Publishing Company

Oregonian Scholarship Program

Valsetz Scholarship Program

Contact the Oregon State Scholarship Commission for further information and application forms.

Pennsylvania

Average tuition and fees:
    Public 4-year institutions—$3210
    Public 2-year institutions—$1419
    Private 4-year institutions—$9430
    Private 2-year institutions—$5497

State spending on student aid:
    Need-based—$145,057,000; 122,654 awards
    Merit-based—$636,000; 274 awards

Scholarship, Grant, and Loan Information

Pennsylvania Higher Education Assistance Agency
660 Boas Street
Harrisburg, Pennsylvania 17102
Loan Information—1-800-692-7392
Grant Information—1-800-692-7435

Special State Programs

State Grant Program provides grant assistance to state residents who are enrolled full-time in an approved academic program of at least 2 years. Both undergraduate and graduate students may apply for this program. The amount of the award varies and is based upon financial need. Contact your high school guidance counselor or financial aid director for further information and application forms.

Scholars in Education Awards (SEA) provide financial assistance to eligible state residents who are pursuing careers in teaching mathematics or science. Recipients must agree to teach mathematics after graduation. Contact the Pennsylvania Higher Education Assistance Agency for more information.

Pennsylvania Family Partnership Loan provides loans to students and parents. The program is designed for families earning more than $30,000 a year. Contact the Pennsylvania Higher Education Assistance Agency for further information and application forms.

Pennsylvania Work-Study Program provides employment opportunities for eligible state residents who are enrolled in Pennsylvania postsecondary institutions. Contact your school's financial aid director for further information.

Grants for Veterans and POW/MIA Dependents provides financial assistance to qualified veterans who are enrolled as full-time undergraduate students. Grants cannot exceed 80% of tuition and fee costs. Dependent children of deceased or disabled veterans and children of prisoners of war and servicepersons missing in action are also eligible to apply for financial aid from this program. The program is based on financial need. For more information, call 1-800-692-7435.

Rhode Island

Average tuition and fees:
    Public 4-year institutions—$2281
    Public 2-year institutions—$1004
    Private 4-year institutions—$10,143
    Private 2-year institutions—N/A

State spending on student aid:
    Need-based—$10,067,000; 9400 awards
    Merit-based—$123,000; 49 awards
    Other—$425,000

Scholarship, Grant, and Loan Information

Rhode Island Higher Education Assistance Authority
560 Jefferson Boulevard
Warwick, Rhode Island 02886
(401) 277-2050
1-800-922-9855

Special State Programs

Rhode Island Higher Education Scholarship Program rewards outstanding high school students. Awards are based upon SAT scores. Contact your high school guidance counselor for more information.

Rhode Island Higher Education Grant Program provides grants to students whose family resources are not sufficient to meet the costs of higher education. Recipients must be state residents and must attend a postsecondary institution on at least a half-time basis. Applicants should complete the Rhode Island FAF form to be considered.

Governor's Academic Scholars Program provides scholarship assistance to outstanding state high school seniors. Recipients must rank in the top 10% of their graduating class and must enroll as full-time undergraduate students in accredited institutions. The scholarship covers the cost of tuition and fees. Contact your school's high school guidance counselor for further information.

The Best and the Brightest Scholarship Program provides scholarship assistance to outstanding high school seniors who plan careers in teaching. Selection is based upon SAT scores, grade point average, letters of recommendation, and an interview. Applications must be submitted to the Rhode Island Higher Education Assistance Authority.

Moneybook provides directory assistance regarding private scholarship sources for both undergraduate and graduate students. For a copy of this publication, call the Employment and Student Services Unit at (401) 277-2050.

South Carolina

Average tuition and fees:
    Public 4-year institutions—$2162
    Public 2-year institutions—$807
    Private 4-year institutions—$5914
    Private 2-year institutions—$4898

State spending on student aid:
    Need-based—$18,079,000; 6805 awards
    Merit-based—None

Scholarship and Grant Information

Higher Education Tuition Grants Agency
Box 12159
Columbia, South Carolina 29211
(803) 734-1200

Loan Information

South Carolina Student Loan Corporation
Interstate Center, Suite 210
P.O. Box 21487
Columbia, South Carolina 29221
(803) 798-0916

Special State Program

South Carolina Tuition Grant Program provides grants to state residents who are accepted for enrollment in eligible private institutions in South Carolina. The awards are based upon financial need. Contact your school's financial aid director for further information and application forms.

South Carolina Teacher Loan Program provides financial assistance to eligible state residents who plan to teach in certain geographic areas or to teach mathematics or science. Awards are available to both undergraduate and graduate students. The amounts of the loans vary, and loans are forgiven under certain conditions. For applications, contact your school's financial aid office.

South Carolina Graduate Incentive Fellowship Program provides financial assistance to qualified state residents who are enrolled in graduate schools. First-year professional minority students are also eligible to apply for this program. For applications, contact your school's financial aid office.

South Carolina National Guard Tuition Assistance Program provides aid to qualified state residents who are active members of the South Carolina National Guard. The awards are not based upon financial need. Call (803) 734-1200 for further information.

Veterans Program provides financial assistance to the children of deceased or disabled veterans. The awards are not based upon financial need, and the amounts of the awards vary. Contact the South Carolina Department of Veterans Affairs for more information.

Children of Deceased or Disabled South Carolina Firemen, Law Officers, and Members of the Civil Air Patrol or Organized Rescue Squad provides financial assistance to qualified students. The awards are not based upon financial need. The amounts of the awards vary. Contact your school's financial aid director for further information and application materials.

South Dakota

Average tuition and fees:
Public 4-year institutions—$1718
Public 2-year institutions—N/A
Private 4-year institutions—$6224
Private 2-year institutions—$2447

State spending on student aid:
Need-based—$468,000; 1550 awards
Merit-based—$90,000; 60 awards

Scholarship and Grant Information

Department of Education and Cultural Affairs
Richard F. Kneip Building
700 Governors Drive
Pierre, South Dakota 57501-2293
(605) 773-3134

Loan Information

Education Assistance Corporation
115 First Avenue, S.W.
Aberdeen, South Dakota 57401
(605) 225-6423

Special State Programs

South Dakota Student Incentive Grant Program
provides grant assistance to eligible state residents
with financial need. Recipients must be enrolled in
an accredited institution on at least a half-time
basis. The amount of the award varies according to
individual financial need. For applications, contact
your school's financial aid office.

South Dakota Tuition Equalization Grant Program
provides grant assistance to eligible state residents
who are enrolled at an accredited South Dakota private school as full-time undergraduate students.
The awards are based upon financial need. For
applications, contact your college's financial aid
office.

National Guard Tuition Assistance Program
provides tuition assistance to state residents who
are members of the South Dakota Army or Air
National Guard. Recipients may be eligible for a
50% tuition reduction or reimbursement. Contact
your local National Guard officials for further
information.

South Dakota Vocational Rehabilitation Program
provides assistance to eligible state residents who
have a physical or mental disability. Counseling
and training services are provided. Contact the
Department of Vocational Rehabilitation, 700 N.
Illinois Street, Pierre, South Dakota 57501, for further information.

BIA Grant Aid provides financial aid to eligible state
residents who are Native Americans. Awards are
based upon financial need. Preference is given to
qualified Indian students who live on or near reservation areas. For application forms, contact a college financial aid office.

**South Dakota Superior Scholar Scholarship Pro-
gram** makes awards to state residents enrolled in a
participating institution who have been identified as
South Dakota National Merit Scholarship semifinalists. Awards are renewable if recipients maintain
at least a 3.0 grade point average.

Tennessee

Average tuition and fees:
Public 4-year institutions—$1406
Public 2-year institutions—$803
Private 4-year institutions—$6530
Private 2-year institutions—$3395

State spending on student aid:
Need-based—$14,156,000; 24,000 awards
Merit-based—$560,000; 149 awards
Other—$3,286,000

Scholarship, Grant, and Loan Information

Tennessee Student Assistance Corporation
404 James Robertson Parkway
Parkway Towers, Suite 1950
Nashville, Tennessee 37243-0820
1-800-342-1663
(615) 741-1346

Special State Programs

Tennessee Academic Scholars Program encourages
academically superior state high school graduates
to attend a college or university in Tennessee.
Recipients must be state residents. For more information, contact the Tennessee Student Assistance
Corporation.

Tennessee Student Assistance Award provides
grant assistance to needy state residents who are
enrolled or accepted for enrollment at an eligible
educational institution in Tennessee. The Pell Grant
formula is used to calculate eligibility. Contact
your school's director of financial aid for more
information.

Tennessee Teacher Loan/Scholarship Program
provides financial assistance, up to the full cost of
tuition, to students who plan careers in teaching.
Priority is given to students planning to teach mathematics or science in a Tennessee public school.
Students planning to teach music or art and certified state teachers are also eligible to apply. The
awards are based upon academic performance.
Recipients must agree to teach for a specified
period of time in a critical shortage area after graduation. For application forms, contact your college
financial aid office or the Tennessee Student
Assistance Corporation.

**Teacher Loan Program for Disadvantaged Areas
of Tennessee** makes awards to students planning
careers in teaching. Recipients must be attending a
Tennessee institution and must agree to teach in a

disadvantaged area for at least 4 years. For further information, contact either your high school guidance officer or college financial aid director.

Minority Teaching Fellows Program makes awards to minority state residents who are planning careers in teaching. Recipients are selected on the basis of grades and must agree to teach in a Tennessee public school. For further information, contact either your high school guidance counselor or college financial aid director.

Texas

Average tuition and fees:
  Public 4-year institutions—$959
  Public 2-year institutions—$455
  Private 4-year institutions—$6047
  Private 2-year institutions—$5112

State spending on student aid:
  Need-based—$27,318,000; 22,651 awards
  Merit-based—None
  Other—$91,050,000

Scholarship and Grant Information

Texas Higher Education Coordinating Board
Texas College and University System
P.O. Box 12788
Austin, Texas 78711
(512) 462-6400

Loan Information

Texas Guaranteed Student Loan Corporation
P.O. Box 15996
Austin, Texas 78761
(512) 835-1900

Special State Programs

State Student Incentive Grant provides grant assistance to eligible state residents attending private and public nonprofit institutions of higher education. For applications, contact your school's financial aid office.

Tuition Equalization Grant helps students attending independent colleges meet costs. Applicants must be state residents and National Merit Scholarship winners and must be enrolled at least half-time in an approved independent college or university. The awards are need-based, and grants vary according to financial need. Contact your school's financial aid director for further information.

Texas Public Educational Grant provides financial aid to needy students enrolled in a public institution participating in the program. Contact your college's director of financial aid for further information and application materials.

State Scholarship Program for Ethnic Recruitment provides financial aid to eligible minority students who have financial need. Contact your institution's

director of financial aid for application forms and more information.

Hinson-Hazlewood College Student Loan Program makes loan funds available to eligible undergraduate, graduate, and professional students. Students must demonstrate financial need to be considered. Loan forgiveness provisions are available. Contact your financial aid director for further information and application forms for this program.

College Access Loan Program provides loans to students who do not qualify for Stafford Student Loans. Contact your institution's financial aid director for further information and application materials.

Future Teacher Loan Program provides financial assistance to encourage students enrolled in teacher certification programs to teach critical shortage subjects in Texas public schools. Eligible students must demonstrate financial need. Loan cancellation provisions are available. For applications, contact your school's financial aid office.

State Rural Medical Education Program provides loans, grants, and scholarships to state residents who are enrolled or accepted for enrollment at an accredited medical school and who plan to practice medicine in a rural area in Texas. To be considered for this program applicants must have financial need. Loan cancellation provisions are available. Write to the Texas Higher Education Coordinating Board for application forms.

Physician Student Loan Repayment Program provides financial aid to eligible students who plan to practice medicine in an underserved area in Texas. Write to the Texas Higher Education Coordinating Board for more information.

Veterans Programs provide veterans and their dependents with tuition and fee exemptions at Texas public schools. Contact your local Veterans Administration Office for further details.

Highest Ranking High School Graduate Program exempts the highest ranking graduate of each accredited high school in Texas from tuition at a public college in Texas for 2 semesters. Contact your high school guidance counselor for further information.

Good Neighbor Scholarship Program exempts certain students from other nations of the American hemisphere from paying tuition and fees at public schools in Texas. Contact the Texas Higher Education Coordinating Board for further information.

Blind and Deaf Program exempts certain blind and deaf students from tuition and fees at public colleges and universities in Texas. Contact your school's director of financial aid for further information.

Children of Disabled Firemen and Peace Officers exempts the children of deceased or disabled firemen, peace officers, custodial employees of the Department of Corrections, or game wardens from all tuition and fees at public colleges and universities in Texas. Contact your school's financial aid director for more information.

Children of Prisoners of War or Persons Missing in Action exempts the dependent children of state residents who are either prisoners of war or missing in action from tuition and fees at public colleges and universities in Texas. Contact your college's financial aid director for further information.

Academic Common Market provides graduate students pursuing degrees in fields of study not offered in Texas with special tuition rates when attending schools outside the state. For more information, contact the Texas Higher Education Coordinating Board.

Texas College Work-Study Program provides part-time employment for students attending public or private institutions in Texas on at least a half-time basis. The amount of the award is based upon financial need. Jobs may be on or off campus and are arranged through the college or university financial aid office.

Utah

Average tuition and fees:
   Public 4-year institutions—$1429
   Public 2-year institutions—$1136
   Private 4-year institutions—$1975
   Private 2-year institutions—$2768

State spending on student aid:
   Need-based—$1,001,000; 2000 awards
   Merit-based—$984,000; 66 awards
   Other—$9,501,000

Scholarship and Grant Information

Utah State Board of Regents
3 Triad Center, Suite 550
355 W. North Temple
Salt Lake City, Utah 84180-1205
(801) 538-5247

Loan Information

Loan Servicing Corporation of Utah
P.O. Box 30802
Salt Lake City, Utah 84130-0802
(801) 363-9151

Special State Program

State Student Incentive Grant Program provides financial assistance to needy state residents. Contact your school's director of financial aid for further information.

Vermont

Average tuition and fees:
   Public 4-year institutions—$3641
   Public 2-year institutions—$2210
   Private 4-year institutions—$10,928
   Private 2-year institutions—$5,979

State spending on student aid:
   Need-based—$10,965,000; 11,005 awards
   Merit-based—None
   Other—$212,000

Scholarship, Grant, and Loan Information

Vermont Student Assistance Corporation
Champlain Mill
P.O. Box 2000
Winooski, Vermont 05404-2601
1-800-642-3177
(802) 655-9602

Special State Programs

Vermont Incentive Grant Program provides grant assistance to needy state residents who are enrolled full-time in an approved institution. Grants are available for undergraduate as well as graduate students. For state residents attending Vermont private institutions, additional funding is available. Contact your high school guidance director for further information and application materials.

Vermont Part-time Student Grant Program provides grant assistance to state residents who are enrolled in an approved academic program for less than 12 credits per semester. The awards vary depending on the number of credit hours and financial need. For applications, contact college financial aid offices.

Vermont Nondegree Student Grant Program provides grant assistance to any state resident enrolled in a nondegree course. The awards are based upon financial need. For applications, contact any Vermont Job Service office or college financial aid office.

Vermont Extra Loans provide loan assistance to students who are enrolled in a Vermont postsecondary school. Vermont residents attending out-of-state schools are also eligible for this loan program. The amount of the EXTRA loan may not exceed cost of attendance. For applications, contact the Vermont Student Assistance Corporation. Call 1-800-642-3177 for further information.

Virginia

Average tuition and fees:
   Public 4-year institutions—$2532
   Public 2-year institutions—$813
   Private 4-year institutions—$7238
   Private 2-year institutions—$4409

State spending on student aid:
  Need-based—$7,400,000; 8304 awards
  Merit-based—$18,114,000; 13, 441 awards

Scholarship and Grant Information

State Education Assistance Authority
Virginia Education Loan Authority
One Franklin Square
411 E. Franklin Street
Richmond, Virginia 23219
1-800-792-LOAN

Loan Information

State Education Assistance Authority
6 N. Sixth Street, Suite 300
Richmond, Virginia 23219
(804) 786-2035

Special State Programs

Virginia College Scholarship Assistance Program (CSAP) provides grant assistance to state residents who are enrolled full-time in an accredited undergraduate program. The awards are based upon financial need. Contact your college's financial aid director for application forms and further information.

Virginia Scholars Program (VSP) provides scholarships to outstanding state high school students who are enrolled full-time in an approved undergraduate program. Graduates of Virginia's public 2-year colleges who transfer to a senior college in Virginia are also eligible to apply for this program. These merit-based scholarships are renewable for 4 years. Students must be nominated by their high school or public college officials; National Merit Scholarship finalists or semifinalists are automatically nominated for the program.

Virginia Tuition Assistance Grant Program (TAG) provides grants to qualified graduate and undergraduate students as well as to professional students. Applicants must be state residents and must be enrolled in an eligible Virginia private college or university. The program is not need-based. The amounts of the awards vary. For an application, contact any private college in Virginia.

Virginia Transfer Grant Program (VTGP) provides full tuition and fees to minority students who are enrolled full-time in a Virginia public college or university. Applicants must be state residents. For further information, contact your college's admission officer or the State Education Assistance Authority.

Virginia Work-Study Program allows graduate and undergraduate students to work and earn money to help finance their education. The amount of the employment award varies and depends upon financial need. To find out more about this program, contact your college's director of financial aid.

Last Dollar Program provides grant assistance to black undergraduate students enrolled for the first time in a state-supported college or university in Virginia. The amount of the award varies and is based upon financial need.

Edvantage Loan Program is designed to provide loan assistance to families who do not qualify for other forms of financial aid. The loans are made through banks, credit unions, and savings and loan associations, and the program is administered by the State Education Assistance Authority. Edvantage loans are credit-based, and a variable interest rate is charged. Repayment begins 60 days after the funds are received; deferment options are available. For further information, contact the State Education Assistance Authority at (804) 371-3554.

Nursing Scholarship Program provides financial assistance to students who agree to practice nursing in the state for 1 month for each $100 of scholarship awarded. For further information, call the Department of Health at (804) 371-4088.

Medical Scholarship Program makes funds available to students at Virginia medical schools who are studying to be primary care physicians. Recipients must agree to practice in an underserved area for 1 year for each year of the scholarship. For further information, contact the Department of Health at (804) 786-4891.

Rural Dental Scholarship Program awards ten scholarships per year to dental students who agree to work in an underserved area for 1 year for every year the scholarship is awarded. You may obtain further information on this program by contacting the Director of Financial Aid of the Medical College of Virginia at (804) 786-9196.

Virginia Teaching Scholarship Program provides scholarship assistance to college junior and senior students to encourage them to pursue careers in teaching. Recipients must agree to teach for 1 year in a public school for each year of scholarship assistance. For further information, contact the Virginia Department of Education at (804) 225-2013.

Law Enforcement Officers Educational Program provides reimbursement for law enforcement officials who are enrolled in college. For further information, contact the Criminal Justice Services Training Division at (804) 786-7801.

Virginia World War Orphan Education Act provides full tuition and fees for the children of veterans killed in action or 100% permanently disabled as a result of war-time injuries. Recipients must attend a public college or university in Virginia. For further information, call the Division of War Veterans Claims at (703) 857-7104.

Soil Scientist Program awards tuition and fee grants to up to four soil scientist students enrolled at Virginia Tech. Recipients must agree to work for 1 year for each year of scholarship awarded. For further information, call personnel at Virginia Polytechnic Institute and State University at (703) 231-9785.

Washington

Average tuition and fees:
Public 4-year institutions—$1710
Public 2-year institutions—$802
Private 4-year institutions—$8096
Private 2-year institutions—$7045

State spending on student aid:
Need-based—$21,146,000; 22,341 awards
Merit-based—$32,000; 32 awards
Other—$862,000

Scholarship and Grant Information

Washington Higher Education Coordinating Board
917 Lakeridge Way
Olympia, Washington 98504
(206) 753-3571

Loan Information

Washington Student Loan Guaranty Association
500 Colman Building
811 First Avenue
Seattle, Washington 98104
(206) 625-1030

Special State Programs

Washington Need Grant Program provides grant assistance to needy state residents who are enrolled in an accredited 2- or 4-year program or one of the five public vocational/technical institutions. The awards are based upon financial need. The amount of the award varies. Contact your school's financial aid director for further information and application forms.

State Work-Study Program provides employment opportunties to qualified state residents who are financially needy. Students must be enrolled at least on a half-time basis to be considered for the program. Contact your college's financial aid director for further information and application forms.

Tuition Waiver Program allows public 2- and 4-year colleges and universities to waive all or part of the tuition and fee costs of needy or disadvantaged students. Recipients of this program must be state residents and must be enrolled in a public Washington State institution. Contact your school's director of financial aid for further information and application forms.

Teacher Incentive Loan Program for Mathematics and Science provides long-term educational loans to students with financial need who plan to teach mathematics or science in a state school. Loan cancellation provisions are included in the program. Eligible students must be state residents and must maintain satisfactory academic progress in all of their courses. Persons with Washington State teaching certificates are also eligible to apply for this program. For applications, contact your school's financial aid office.

Future Teachers' Conditional Scholarship Program encourages outstanding students to enter the teaching profession. Eligible students must be state residents and enrolled in a graduate or undergraduate program. For applications, contact the financial aid office of a participating school or the Washington Higher Education Coordinating Board.

Washington Scholars Program provides financial assistance to senior high school students who are in the top 1% of their class and are nominated by their high school principal. In addition to academic achievement, recipients must demonstrate outstanding leadership and community service. Scholars attending a Washington public college or university will receive a full tuition and fee scholarship. For further information, contact either your high school guidance counselor or high school principal.

Nurses Conditional Scholarship provides financial assistance to nursing students who agree to serve in a designated state shortage area. The program is not based upon financial need. For further information, contact either your high school guidance counselor or college financial aid director.

West Virginia

Average tuition and fees:
Public 4-year institutions—$1591
Public 2-year institutions—$803
Private 4-year institutions—$7197
Private 2-year institutions—$2554

State spending on student aid:
Need-based—$5,550,000; 5632 awards
Merit-based—None
Other—$7,403,000

Scholarship and Grant Information

West Virginia Higher Education Central Office
P.O. Box 4007
Charleston, West Virginia 25364
(304) 347-1231

Loan Information

Higher Education Assistance Foundation
Higher Education Loan Program of West Virginia, Inc.
P.O. Box 591
Charleston, West Virginia 25322
(304) 345-7211

Special State Programs

West Virginia Higher Education Grant Program provides grant assistance to state residents who are enrolled full-time in accredited postsecondary schools. The awards are based upon financial need and vary in amount. Applicants must submit a West Virginia FAF by March 1. Contact your school's director of financial aid for further information and application forms.

Underwood-Smith Teacher Scholarship provides financial assistance to graduate and undergraduate students. The awards are based upon academic merit and are awarded to students in the top 10% of their class. Recipients must agree to teach in West Virginia. For further information, contact your high school guidance counselor or college dean, or call the West Virginia Higher Education Central Office at (304) 347-1231.

Medical Student Loan Program provides financial assistance to state residents who are enrolled at in-state medical schools. Loans are made on the basis of financial need. For further information, contact personnel at any state medical school.

Teddi-Bear Loan Program provides loan assistance to state residents. The loans are based upon a family's creditworthiness. For further information, call the State Treasurer at 1-800-345-2274.

Public Health Trust Program provides financial assistance to graduate students who are state residents and who are enrolled in a health professions program. The awards are based upon financial need. For further information, contact the Office of the Attorney General of West Virginia, State Capitol Complex, Charleston, West Virginia 25305.

Tuition and Fee Waiver Program provides financial aid to students enrolled at public colleges and universities. The awards, based upon need and merit or abilities, cannot exceed the cost of tuition and certain fees. For further information, contact your college or university financial aid officer.

Wisconsin

Average tuition and fees:
Public 4-year institutions—$1861
Public 2-year institutions—$1160
Private 4-year institutions—$7615
Private 2-year institutions—$4001

State spending on student aid:
Need-based—$42,102,000; 52,280 awards
Merit-based—$700,000; 620 awards
Other—$1,955,000

Scholarship and Grant Information

Wisconsin Higher Educational Aids Board
P.O. Box 7885
Madison, Wisconsin 53707-7885
(608) 267-2206

Loan Information

Wisconsin Higher Education Corporation
2401 International Lane
Madison, Wisconsin 53704
(608) 246-1800

Special State Programs

Wisconsin Higher Education Grant (WHEG) Program provides financial assistance for undergraduate students who are state residents and are enrolled at least half-time at the University of Wisconsin or vocational/technical institutions. The awards are based upon financial need. Contact your school's financial aid director for further information and application materials.

Talent Incentive Program (TIP) provides supplemental grant awards to needy students. The awards are available for the first 2 years of postsecondary education. For additional information, contact the Wisconsin Educational Opportunity Program at Suite 104, 223 W. Galena Court, Milwaukee, Wisconsin 53212.

Wisconsin Tuition Grant (WTG) Program provides grant assistance to undergraduate students enrolled in independent, nonprofit institutions in Wisconsin. The awards are based upon financial need. Recipients must be state residents. Contact your college's director of financial aid for further information and application forms.

Wisconsin Handicapped Program provides grant assistance to undergraduate students who are state residents and are legally blind or deaf. The awards are based upon financial need. For applications, write to the Wisconsin Higher Educational Aids Board.

Minority Student Grant Program provides financial assistance to black, Hispanic, and Native American students who are undergraduates enrolled in private, nonprofit institutions of higher learning in Wisconsin. For additional information, contact the financial aid office at an independent college.

Wisconsin Native American Student Grant Program provides financial assistance to Native American students who are enrolled in public, private, or proprietary Wisconsin institutions. Application is made through the needs analysis form and the Board-BIA-Tribal form.

Minnesota-Wisconsin Reciprocity Agreement makes public colleges and universities more accessible to residents of Minnesota and Wisconsin by allowing students from these states to pay a special reciprocity tuition. Contact the Wisconsin Higher Educational Aids Board for further information.

Academic Scholarship Program provides tuition and fee scholarships to Wisconsin's top high school students. Recipients are nominated by their school districts. The total value of the scholarship is approximately $2000, depending upon the institution attended and the funds available. The award is renewable provided that the scholar maintains at least a 3.0 grade point average. For further information, call the Wisconsin Higher Educational Aids Board.

Minority Teacher Loan Program makes forgivable loans to state minority juniors and seniors enrolled in private colleges or universities in Wisconsin and majoring in education. The loans are forgiven when the borrower is employed in an eligible state school district. For further information, contact the Wisconsin Higher Educational Aids Board.

Nursing Student Stipend Loan Program makes forgivable loans to state residents who are enrolled as full-time students in a program leading to an associate degree, diploma, or bachelor's degree in nursing. Only junior and senior students are eligible to apply for this loan. Recipients must agree to serve in a Wisconsin hospital, nursing home, or public agency for 12 months for each $1000 received. For further information, contact personnel at your school's financial aid office.

Interstate Compacts allow Wisconsin residents to attend a Minnesota public college or university on a space-available basis and pay the reciprocity tuition charged by that institution. For further information on all of Wisconsin's reciprocity agreements, contact the Wisconsin Higher Educational Aids Board.

Wyoming

Average tuition and fees:
  Public 4-year institutions—$1003
  Public 2-year institutions—$613
  Private 4-year institutions—N/A
  Private 2-year institutions—$6900

State spending on student aid:
  Need-based—$241,000; 531 awards
  Merit-based—None

Scholarship and Grant Information

Wyoming Community College Commission
122 W. 25th
Herschler Building
Cheyenne, Wyoming 82002
(307) 777-7763

Loan Information

Higher Education Assistance Foundation
American National Bank Building
1912 Capitol Avenue, Suite 320
Cheyenne, Wyoming 82001
(307) 635-3259

Special State Programs

State Student Incentive Grant Program (SSIG) provides grant assistance to financially needy state residents. Awards are available each academic year. Recipients are selected by the school financial aid director and approved by the Wyoming Community College Commission.

Scholarship Loan Fund for Superior Students provides financial assistance to Wyoming high school graduates with high scholastic achievement who plan to teach in Wyoming schools after graduation. Eligibility is based upon ACT scores, high school grades, high school activities, and letters of recommendation. Contact your high school's guidance counselor for further information.

County Commissioners Scholarship Program provides scholarship assistance to students who are state residents and graduates of Wyoming high schools. Application should be made directly to the Board of County Commissioners in the applicant's county of residence. The scholarship may be used at any public institution in Wyoming.

Wyoming High School Honor Scholarship Program awards scholarships to state high school seniors with high scholastic achievement. The scholarship is usually equal to the full tuition and fees at any state community college, as well as at the University of Wyoming. Contact your high school's guidance counselor for further information.

Bureau of Indian Affairs Scholarship and Loan Program provides financial assistance to Native American students who are financially needy. Contact the Bureau of Indian Affairs for further information and application materials or call (307) 777-7763.

Northern Arapahoe and Shoshone Tribal Scholarship Program awards financial assistance to Native Americans who are members of the Arapahoe and Shoshone tribes. For applications, contact the Community Development Office, Wind River Indian Agency, Fort Washakie, Wyoming 82514.

Veterans Readjustment Benefits Program provides financial assistance to state residents who are veterans and to service persons who are currently on active duty. Veterans' benefits may be used at any public institution in Wyoming. For further information, contact the Veterans Administration Center, Cheyenne, Wyoming 82001.

Wyoming National Guard Educational Assistance Program provides financial assistance to state residents who are members of the Wyoming Air or Army National Guard. Eligible applicants are reimbursed for 50% of the amount of resident tuition and fees. Applications require approval of the local unit commander.

War Orphans Education Assistance Act of 1956 provides financial assistance to the children of deceased or permanently disabled veterans and also to the widows or widowers of deceased veterans.

The benefits may be used at any public institution in Wyoming. Contact your school's financial aid director for further information.

Scholarship/Loan Fund for Superior Students provides assistance to state high school graduates with high scholastic merit and leadership qualities who plan to teach in state public schools. Recipients must attend the University of Wyoming or any community college in the state and major in education. The awards are renewable and depend upon academic achievement. For further information, contact the Office of the Dean, University of Wyoming College of Education or call (307) 777-7763 for further information.

President's Honor Scholarship Program awards scholarships to state residents who are high school seniors and who have demonstrated academic achievement and leadership. Nominations are made by each high school's principal; the number of awards depends upon the size of the graduating class. The awards are renewable if the scholar maintains at least a 2.5 grade point average. For further information, contact your high school guidance counselor or high school principal.

Puerto Rico

Scholarship and Grant Information

Consejo de Education Superior
Apartado 23305
Estación Postal U.P.R.
Rio Piedras, Puerto Rico 00931
(809) 758-3350

Loan Information

Higher Education Assistance Corporation
P.O. Box 42001
Minillas Station
San Juan, Puerto Rico 00940-2001
(809) 758-3356

Special State Programs

All economic aid for students is administered through the institutions of higher education in Puerto Rico. Only students attending local colleges or universities are eligible to participate. Contact your school's financial aid director for information on all financial assistance programs.

Virgin Islands

Loan Information

Virgin Islands Board of Education
P.O. Box 11900
St. Thomas, Virgin Islands 00801
(809) 774-4546

Guam

Scholarship and Grant Information

University of Guam
UOG Station
Mangilao, Guam 96913
(617) 734-2921

Loan Information

Pacific Islands Educational Loan Program
United Student Aid Funds, Inc.
1314 S. King Street, Suite 961
Honolulu, Hawaii 96814
(808) 536-3731

Special Programs

Student Incentive Grant Program provides financial assistance to eligible students who attend institutions of higher learning and who have financial need. The program is available to undergraduate and graduate students. Full-time enrollment is required. Contact the Director of Financial Aid at the University of Guam for further information.

Federated States of Micronesia Loan Program makes loan funds available to eligible students who are residents of Kosrae, Pohnpei, Truk, or Yap. For applications, contact the Department of Social Services, Federated States of Micronesia, Kolonia, Pohnpei 96941, or the Student Financial Aid Coordinator at the University of Guam.

Government of Guam Student Financial Assistance Program (SFAP) awards local government student loans, merit awards, and professional/technical awards for graduate studies to University of Guam students.

Student Loans of up to $3000 a year are available for students enrolled at the University of Guam. The awards are based upon financial need. Contact the Director of Financial Aid at the University of Guam for further information.

Merit Awards are based upon academic excellence. Candidates must have the highest academic standing in their high school graduating class and must be residents of Guam. Contact the Director of Financial Aid at the University of Guam for further information.

Professional/Technical Awards pay full tuition and fees for 4 academic years to residents of Guam who have graduated from college with a 2.5 or better grade point average. Preference is given to students in medicine, dentistry, or law. The award has a service obligation requirement after graduation. Contact the Director of Financial Aid at the University of Guam.

Board of Regents' Nursing Scholarship Funds provide financial aid to nursing students at the University of Guam. For more information, contact the Division of Nursing at the University of Guam.

Teacher Training Scholarship Program assists students who are pursuing careers in teaching. Contact the Dean of the College of Education at (617) 734-2566 for further information and application materials.

Western Undergraduate Exchange Program

Most of the 2- and 4-year colleges in 14 western states participate in a tuition reciprocity agreement. Under the terms of agreement, students who leave their home states to attend a college or university at a participating institution in another state will pay resident tuition plus 50%. The plan is a savings for students enrolled in schools where nonresident costs may be double or triple the resident rates. The states included in this agreement are Alaska, Arizona, Colorado, Hawaii, Idaho, Montana, Nevada, New Mexico, North Dakota, Oregon, South Dakota, Utah, Washington, and Wyoming.

The program, operated by the Western Interstate Commission for Higher Education in Boulder, Colorado, is also available to graduate students.

Some Final Notes on State Financial Assistance Programs

1. Find out whether you can take a state grant with you if you enroll in an out-of-state college or university. Many states have reciprocal agreements with other states.

2. Since most state financial aid programs apply only to state residents, check residency and transfer requirements of each program.

10 SCHOOL PROGRAMS

Over 85% of all colleges and universities offer some type of financing program for students and their families. This chapter will outline some of the major school financing programs and will give you specific examples of what schools do to help their students finance their educations.

Important Facts to Know

1. Ask for all financial aid information at the same time you request admission information. It is the wise student-consumer who does this early in the college search process. Compare academic programs as well as financial aid policies.
2. Phone the financial aid office if you have any questions regarding the awarding of aid or the school's packaging philosophy. If possible, visit the campus and make appointments to speak with an admissions and a financial aid counselor.
3. Ask the financial aid counselor specific questions. Find out the number of scholarships and grants awarded each year from school funds. Find out the school's policy on need-based aid and merit scholarships. Inquire about school loan programs or prepayment plans. Pick up application forms and any additional information that may help you in meeting your college costs. Find out whether the aid award is available for 4 years.

Important Terms to Know

Accreditation Recognition that the constituent parts of a college or university are satisfactory and that its courses are recognized and accepted by other collegiate institutions and by an accrediting or professional agency.

College An institution of higher education that gives instruction in liberal arts, in professional fields, or in both. A college can be a division of a university. Typically, in 4 years, the degree earned will be a bachelor's degree.

Exemption A special waiver of tuition and/or fees.

University An institution of higher learning composed of two or more schools or colleges. A university awards graduate degrees in addition to undergraduate or bachelor's degrees.

Waiver An arrangement that the school has with the student permitting either full or partial tuition remission. Waivers are granted for various reasons.

What Families Should Know about Institutional Financial Aid Programs

1. Families should ALWAYS file for federal and state financial aid. Most colleges and universities cannot consider applicants for their own scholarship and loan programs until these applicants are first denied aid from federal and state sources.
2. The amount of a family's expected contribution will be affected by the cost of the college and the school's financial aid policies. It is possible to receive more aid by attending an expensive school.
3. Families should ask about the school's financial aid policies. Is it the school's policy to meet fully the financial needs of all aid recipients? Or does the school meet only a portion of need? Is aid provided after the first year? What is the average indebtedness of recent graduates? The answers will give you a clue about the school's awarding policy. You should want to know whether a school is meeting the full need of all its financial aid applicants with loans and employment, rather than with grants or gifts.
4. Most colleges and universities offer their students money from institutional funds. Some awards are based on financial need; others, on merit. Some schools offer special scholarships or grants to students with particular talents in, for example, music, drama, or journalism. Find out the criteria used by the college and the average amount awarded.
5. Many schools offer applicants estimates of what their financial aid will be at the time of application. This allows a family to estimate how much money they will need from their own resources to finance a student's education at that school.

Examples of School Financing Programs

Academic Scholarships   Most schools offer some form of scholarship assistance based on the student's academic achievements. Eligibility includes high school grades, high school class rank, and ACT or SAT scores. Some schools offer academic scholarships based on financial need. Academic scholarships usually mean a reduction in tuition and fees, although some scholarships cover these costs completely. It is important to know whether these awards are renewable and, if so, what the requirements are for renewal. It is up to you to find out what the school's policy is regarding academic scholarships and what you must do to receive this type of assistance.

Accelerated Programs   An effective way to cut college costs is to reduce the amount of time spent on campus. Many students do this by enrolling in summer school or in the school's accelerated program. Find out whether this option is available at the schools you are considering and what you must do to be eligible for this type of program. Several schools offer combined degree options, which enable a student to obtain an undergraduate and a graduate or professional degree in a reduced number of years. This option is available to students considering careers in medicine, dentistry, and law. Check with the school's admissions counselor for further information and eligibility.

Advanced Placement (AP) Program and College-Level Examination Program (CLEP)   One way to reduce college costs is to take fewer credits. Students should investigate the colleges and universities that give credit for AP and CLEP examinations. Every school determines its own criteria for crediting courses. Check with the school's admissions counselor for school policy on receiving AP and CLEP college credit.

Athletic Scholarships   A student with athletic ability and determination often will be able to obtain a full or partial scholarship. It is up to you to identify the schools that offer athletic scholarships in your sport and to contact the college coach. Find out about admission and financial aid policies for athletes and the criteria used to award athletic scholarships. Seek the advice of your high school coach, and take the offensive. Request information on the number of athletes who graduate from each school you are considering. Remember that, although sports are important and may be the primary reason you select a particular school, there is life after college. Obtaining a good educational experience is just as important as playing big-time college sports. For further information and assistance, write to National Collegiate Athletic Association, P.O. Box 1906, Shawnee Mission, Kansas 66222, or the Association for Intercollegiate Athletics for Women, 1201 16th Street, N.W., Washington, D.C. 20036.

Cooperative Education Program   Some colleges provide students with the opportunity to work while attending school. Check with your admissions officer, or write to the Commission for Cooperative Education, 360 Huntington Avenue, Boston, Masschusetts 02115.

Emergency Loan Programs   Most schools provide loan funds for students to meet emergency or unexpected costs. The loan is usually short-term, with a low interest rate. The program is often administered by the school's financial aid administrator.

Employee Discount Programs   Most institutions offer tuition discounts or full tuition remission for their employees and their dependent children. Generally you must be a full-time employee and must have worked at the college or university for a specific period of time in order to be eligible for this program. Both faculty and staff employees usually qualify.

Gift Certificates   Some schools sell to families gift certificates that can later be used to cover a portion of tuition or credit-hours. There are usually many conditions with this type of financing option. Contact the school's financial aid counselor or admissions director for more information on eligibility and requirements.

Installment and Deferred Payment Plans   Most schools still require that tuition be paid in two annual amounts, at the beginning of each semester. However, for many families, coming up with large amounts of money twice a year is not possible. Some schools, responding to this situation, now offer families the option of paying tuition and fee costs in installments. This type of program is also called a *deferred payment plan*. It allows families to make 8 or 12 payments spread out over the course of a year. Some colleges and universities even offer loan programs to parents to fund their installment payments. This type of program is generally not need-based and is often used by families who do not qualify for federal or state financial assistance. Check with the school's financial aid administrator for further details. If the school offers this type of financing program, obtain an application. Learn about eligibility requirements and what financial data must support your application.

Institutional Loan Programs   Many colleges and universities offer school loan programs for families who do not meet federal or state requirements for financial assistance, or as a supplement to federal and state programs. At some schools parental income levels are considered in awarding these loans. Check with the school's admission or financial aid administrator about the specific program offered. REMEMBER: use this option as a last resort. Explore all federal and state financial assistance programs before applying for a school loan. In most cases the interest rates are higher for school loans than for federal and state loan programs. Check the chapters on federal and state financial assistance programs.

National Merit Scholarship Program   This scholarship is based, not upon need, but rather on a student's adacemic achievement. The National Merit Corporation awards about 6000 scholarships each year to high school students based on test scores, and extracurricular achievements. To qualify for this scholarship, applicants must take the Preliminary Scholastic Aptitude Test/National Merit Scholarship Qualifying Test (PSAT/NMSQT) in the fall of their junior year in high school. Check with your high school guidance counselor for further information.

Room-Work Exchange Programs

Some schools have developed plans to match students' housing needs with the needs of area residents. Such arrangements include free room and board in exchange for household work. This type of program can save a student several thousand dollars in room and board costs. Check with your school's financial aid administrator for details on this type of program.

Special Discount Programs

Many colleges and universities offer discounts to families with more than one child enrolled. Other schools provide discounts to the children of their graduates. Some private schools will match the tuition of state institutions for certain groups of students. Check with all schools you are considering about the availability of these types of programs.

Tuition Futures Programs and Prepayment Plans

This type of program, offered by several schools and some states, allows families to purchase a fixed, discounted tuition amount for future college costs. The family is charged the current 4-year cost of education, and money is invested by the institution or state. This plan provides a certain amount of security to families fearing increased tuition expenses. The Michigan Education Trust (MET) is the best example of the popularity of this type of financing program. Students and parents should check with schools they are considering to determine whether this type of program is available. Families should ask the following questions when considering this financing option:

1. Is there a maximum amount of money that can be contributed?

2. Does the plan cover all college costs, or just tuition expenses?

3. Are there residency requirements?

4. Can anyone in the family contribute to the plan?

Families should be aware that the Internal Revenue Service has ruled that the Michigan Education Trust must pay annual corporate taxes on its earnings, in addition to the deferred taxes that students must pay as gains are withdrawn for tuition. Therefore, a student will owe taxes on the difference between the money invested and the cost of tuition. The tax will be payable over the course of 4 years of college attendance at the student's rate.

Another drawback for this type of program is a ruling by the U.S. Department of Education that a prepayment contract will be treated as a student asset, not as a family asset, in calculating a student's eligibility for federal aid programs. The result may be a decrease in a student's chances of receiving other federal aid.

Tuition Stabilization Plans

These plans are similar to prepayment plans, but the amount paid is generally less than 4 years of tuition. The student and family pay a portion of their educational costs in advance. The advantage of this type of program is that tuition is capped for all subsequent years the student is enrolled at the school. Parents are required to deposit a certain amount of money with the school at the time the student registers for the first time. Check with the admission or financial aid counselor for information and further details at all schools you are considering.

Specific School Programs

The following is a *partial* list of the types of financing programs available at specific schools. This list is intended only to provide you and your family with some examples of creative school financing programs. It is up to you to check *early* with each school you are considering to learn of its specific programs.

Alderson-Broaddus College This school grants tuition waivers to state residents whose primary wage earner is unemployed.

Amherst College Amherst has developed a Parent Loan Program, which makes loans of up to $10,400 available each year to students and their families.

Bard College This school promises to match the tuition of any state school for applicants in the top 10% of their high school class.

Berea College Berea is known for its Labor Program, which began in 1914. Only students with financial need are admitted to the college, and all must work at least 10 hours a week to pay for their room, board, and fees. There is no tuition charge at Berea.

Calvin College Calvin College offers gift certificates to meet tuition expenses.

Chatham College This Pennsylvania school offers grants to displaced steelworkers and their families.

Coe College This college will discount tuition by 25–50% for full-time students 25 years of age or older.

Columbia University Columbia sponsors a loan forgiveness program for its minority graduates who pursue doctoral programs. Harvard, Stanford, and Northwestern also have loan forgiveness programs.

Cornell Cornell is reducing the debts of its students through its "Cornell Tradition" program. Students are employed during the academic year, as well as in the summer months, under a career-related, partially subsidized employment program.

Drury College This school will match any academic achievement scholarship a student receives from an outside source.

Fairleigh Dickinson University   Arrangements have been made at this university to subsidize the interest charges on PLUS loans.

Guilford Technical Community College   Guilford seeks out private company sponsors for its Technical Scholars Program.

Kings College   When two children from the same family attend this school, the family pays the cost of tuition for a single student.

Lehigh University   Students at Lehigh who maintain a certain grade point average can cancel any loans they have received from the university.

Morningside College   Full-time students entering Morningside College will receive a full room and board grant if they rank in the top 40% of their high school graduating class and have SAT scores of at least 1000 or ACT composite scores of at least 24.

Southampton College   Arrangements have been made between this school and two banks to make loans to students with the school paying the interest while the student is enrolled.

Suffolk University   The President's Incentive Loan Program (PIL) allows a student to receive a loan from Suffolk University which converts, at the time of graduation, to a grant if the student maintains the required grade point average. The purpose of this loan program is to assist the university in its retention activities by providing students with an incentive to stay in school. Suffolk also sponsors a low interest loan program to families denied federal and state financial aid.

Union College   Union will pay off-campus employers a partial reimbursement of wages if the employer hires a Union student.

University of Minnesota   This school reserves all nonacademic positions that are 29 hours per week or less for student workers. Students are paid salaries comparable to those of nonstudent workers.

University of Pennsylvania   The school's Penn Plan offers various financing arrangements, including a single-payment plan for prepaying tuition fixed at the freshman year for 4 years, variable-rate prepayment loans for paying fixed tuition, and a revolving line of credit for tuition or for room, board, and other fees. The Penn Plan offers options for students who do not qualify for other assistance, as well as for those already receiving financial aid.

Vanderbilt University   This university has designated a certain amount of money to make loans to students who are not eligible to receive Stafford Student Loans.

The following schools also offer special financing programs:

Blackburn College

Brown University

Carnegie-Mellon University

Catholic University of America

Clarkson University

Colby-Sawyer College

Colgate University

Concordia College

Creighton University

Denison University

De Paul University

Drake University

Drew University

Emory University

Empire State College

Emporia State University

Eureka College

Franklin College

Franklin Pierce College

George Mason University

George Washington University

Gonzaga University

Hartwick College

Hastings College

Holy Family College

Indiana State University

Jacksonville University

Kent State University

Kentucky Wesleyan College

Kenyon College

Lafayette College

La Salle University

Lewis and Clark College

Loyola College

Marquette University

Marymount College of Virginia

Marywood College

Metropolitan State College

Miami University

Molloy College

Mount Holyoke College

Mount Saint Mary College

New York University

Niagara University

Nichols College

Northern Illinois University

Northern Virginia Community College

North Texas State University

Ohio University

Ohio Wesleyan University

Oklahoma State University

Oregon State University

Pace Univresity

Pacific Lutheran University

Polytechnic Institute of New York

Purdue University

Randolph-Macon College

Rice University

Rochester Institute of Technology

St. John's University, Minnesota

St. Louis University

St. Petersburg Junior College

San Francisco State University

Santa Clara University

Smith College

Southern Methodist University

Suffolk University

Sweet Briar College

Syracuse University

Texas College of Osteopathic Medicine

Tufts University

University of Cincinnati

University of the District of Columbia

University of Florida

University of Iowa

University of Mississippi

University of Missouri-Columbia

University of Oregon

University of Pittsburgh

University of South Carolina

University of Tennessee at Knoxville

University of Texas at Dallas

University of Texas Health Science Center

Virginia Commonwealth University

Virginia Polytechnic Institute

Wake Forest University

Walla Walla College

Warner Pacific College

Washburn University

Washington State University

Washington University, St. Louis

Wayne State University

Wesleyan University

West Virginia University

Wittenberg University

Yale University

Some Final Notes on School Financial Assistance Programs

1. Learn about all school financing arrangements before enrolling. Know what options exist and how you can qualify for school financing programs.

2. Remember to seek federal and state funding sources before considering school financing programs. School programs are generally more expensive than federal and state programs.

3. Consult your school's financial aid director for advice on all school financing programs.

11 EMPLOYMENT PROGRAMS

One way to reduce college costs is by working. Several studies indicate that most students who work between 10 and 20 hours a week actually do better academically. It is not unrealistic for a student to expect to earn between $2000 to $4000 per year, including summer employment. If you multiply that sum by the 4 years you will spend in college, it is obvious that you can make a substantial contribution to your school expenses. That's money you will not have to borrow and your parents will not have to find. Decide that you will earn a portion of your college expenses through working and that work will be an integral part of your college financing plan. Also consider that your college employment can be career-related or even lead to a job after graduation.

A word of caution is in order, however, regarding work. Recent federal legislation requires that students contribute a minimum of $700 if they are freshmen and $900 if they are upperclassmen, or 70% of their after-tax earnings, to pay their college bills. This means that a substantial amount of your earnings will be calculated in the need analysis process used to determine expected student contribution. However, you still should consider employment as part of your college financial financing program.

Important Facts to Know

1. Federal, state, institutional, and private work programs are available to college students both on campus and off campus. Investigate *all* sources.

2. Some work arrangements offer free room and board in exchange for household help. Ask your school whether this type of arrangement is available.

3. You should try to find part-time employment that is career-related. You will gain valuable experience and earn money at the same time. That's a good combination.

4. Your school's financial aid director and career counseling and placement officer can help you find the right job. Seek assistance and advice from the counselors in these offices and use the resources they can provide.

Major Employment Programs Available to Students and Parents

Assistantships   These part-time positions are generally awarded to graduate students to assist professors in classroom instruction. The graduate student receives either a reduction in tuition costs or a stipend to help meet living expenses. Eligibility varies from school to school. Some programs are need-based, while others are based only on academic scholarship. Check with your school's financial aid director or with the dean of your school for further information and eligibility requirements.

College Work-Study Program   One of the most popular work programs is the federal College Work-Study Program (CWSP), which provides employment on campus and off campus for students in postsecondary institutions. It is a need-based program and is administered through the school's financial aid office. The federal government pays 50% of the student's wage for private sector jobs and 70% if the student is employed on campus. Jobs are available to undergraduate, vocational/technical, graduate, and professional students. The dollar earning amount allocated to a student may vary from year to year based on funding levels and cannot exceed financial need. Students may not exceed the amount of their allocations as determined by their financial aid directors. College Work-Study funds are awarded along with other financial aid. To be considered for this program, students must be U.S. citizens or permanent residents and must be enrolled or accepted for enrollment at an eligible institution. Students must also maintain satisfactory academic progress. Contact your school's financial aid office or job referral service for specific application procedures. All recipients must have an FAF, FFS, or GAPSFAS on file.

Company-paid Tuition Programs   Many companies offer their employees tuition benefit plans. Some programs restrict enrollment to job-related courses. Check with your personnel officer or education specialist for further information.

Cooperative Education Programs   These employment/study programs allow students to alternate between working full-time and studying full-time. It generally takes 5 years to complete a bachelor's degree if a student participates in this type of program. Although federal government remains the largest employer, many businesses participate in cooperative education programs. These programs are not based on financial need and are available to undergraduate, graduate, and professional students. The most important and attractive feature of employment programs is matching the student's future career plans with relevant employment. For further information, write to the National Commission for Cooperative Education, 360 Huntington Avenue, Boston, Massachusetts 02115. See the list of participating schools at the end of this chapter.

External Degree Programs   Some colleges and universities award credit based on work experience, thereby reducing the amount of time you have to spend earning a specific number of credits necessary for graduation. Check with your college's admission director for further information.

Fellowships   Fellowships provide financial assistance to graduate students to help them continue with their graduate studies. Financial aid is given in exchange for teaching or clerical work. Eligibility varies from school to school. Check with your dean or college financial aid director for further details.

Government Internships and Fellowships   The federal government employs students through its internship and fellowship programs. Opportunities are available at both the high school and the college level. High school students should seek the advice of their guidance counselors about employment opportunities under the Junior Fellowship Program. College students may obtain information about federal internship opportunities from their school's director of financial aid or from the school's director of employment and cooperative education.

Institutional Employment Programs   Many schools have placement offices that help students find employment. All schools have personnel offices that hire students to work on campus. These programs are not need-based. Check with your college's personnel director for more information. Most colleges and universities also offer to their employees a tuition reduction or waiver program. Under this plan, the school employee and his or her children receive either full tuition remission or partial reduction in tuition costs. These programs are not need-based, and are awarded on the basis of college employment. This type of employment program provides an excellent opportunity to attend college at practically no cost.

Private Sector Employment Programs   Many local business people hire students to work in their companies. Check with your school's placement director for a list of off-campus employment opportunities. Try to find a job in your major field of interest; you may be able to turn part-time student work into a full-time job after graduation.

Resident Advisor Program   This program provides financial assistance to students in the form of reduced tuition or board costs in exchange for working in residence halls. Interested students should contact the Dean of Students on their campus for further information and eligibility requirements.

State College Work-Study Programs   Many states provide employment to residents under state-sponsored work-study programs. These employment programs are administered by state organizations and follow most of the federal eligibility requirements. Check with your school's financial aid office or state scholarship commission for further details.

Schools Offering Cooperative Education Programs

Alabama

Alabama State University, Montgomery, Alabama 36101

Alexander City State Junior College, Alexander City, Alabama 35010

Auburn University, Auburn, Alabama 36849-3501

Auburn University at Montgomery, Montgomery, Alabama 36193-0401

Brewer State Junior College, Fayette, Alabama 35555

Huntington College, Montgomery, Alabama 36194-6201

Jacksonville State University, Jacksonville, Alabama 36265

John C. Calhoun State College, Decatur, Alabama 35601

Lurleen B. Wallace State Junior College, Andalusia, Alabama 36420

Samford University, Birmingham, Alabama 35229

Tuskegee University, Tuskegee, Alabama 36088

University of Alabama, Tuscaloosa, Alabama 35487

University of Alabama at Birmingham, Birmingham, Alabama 35294

University of Alabama in Huntsville, Huntsville, Alabama 35899

University of Montevallo, Montevallo, Alabama 35115

University of South Alabama, Mobile, Alabama 36688

Alaska

University of Alaska/Juneau, Juneau, Alaska 99801

Arizona

Arizona Western College, Yuma, Arizona 85364

Cochise College, Sierra Vista, Arizona 85635

Glendale Community College, Glendale, Arizona 85301

Maricopa Tech, Phoenix, Arizona 85034

Mohave Community College, Kingman, Arizona 86401

Northern Arizona University, Flagstaff, Arizona 86011

Northland Pioneer College, Holbrook, Arizona 86025

Pima Community College, Tucson, Arizona 85702

Scottsdale Community College, Scottsdale, Arizona 85253

University of Arizona, Tucson, Arizona 85721

Arkansas

Arkansas College, Batesville, Arkansas 72501

College of the Ozarks, Clarksvile, Arkansas 72830

East Arkansas Community College, Forrest City, Arkansas 72335

Harding University, Searcy, Arkansas 72143

Mississippi County Community College, Blytheville, Arkansas 72315

North Arkansas Community College, Harrison, Arkansas 72601

University of Arkansas at Fayetteville, Fayetteville, Arkansas 72701

Westark Community College, Fort Smith, Arkansas 72913

California

American River College, Sacramento, California 95841

Bakersfield College, Bakersfield, California 93305

California College of Arts and Crafts, Oakland, California 94618

California Polytechnic State University, San Luis Obisbo, California 93407

California State College/Bakersfield, Bakersfield, California 93309

California State Polytechnical University, Pomona, California 91768

California State University/Chico, Chico, California 95929

California State University/Dominguez Hills, Carson, California 90747

California State University/Fresno, Fresno, California 93740

California State University/Hayward, Hayward, California 94542

California State University/Long Beach, Long Beach, California 90840

California State University/Los Angeles, Los Angeles, California 90032

California State University/Northridge, Northridge, California 91330

California State University/Sacramento, Sacramento, California 95819

Canada Community College, Redwood City, California 94061

Chabot College, Hayward, California 94545

Chapman College, Orange, California 92666

College of Marin, Kentfield, California 94904

College of Notre Dame, Belmont, California 94002

College of the Sequoias, Vialia, California 93277

College of the Siskiyous, Weed, California 96094

Columbia College, Columbia, California 95310

Contra Costa College, San Pablo, California 94806

De Anza College, Cupertino, California 95014

Diablo Valley College, Pleasant Hill, California 94523

East Los Angeles College, Monterey Park, California 91754

El Camino College, Torrance, California 90506

Evergreen Valley College, San Jose, California 95135-1598

Foothill College Foothill/DeAnza, Los Altos Hills, California 94022

Fresno City College, Fresno, California 93741

Golden Gate University, San Francisco, California 94105

Grossmont College, El Cajon, California 92020

Humboldt State University, Arcata, California 95521

Kings River Community College, Reedley, California 93654

Laney College, Oakland, California 94607

Long Beach City College, Long Beach, California 90808

Los Angeles City College, Los Angeles, California 90029

Los Angeles Pierce College, Woodland Hills, California 91371

Los Angeles Trade Tech College, Los Angeles, California 90015

Los Angeles Valley College, Van Nuys, California 91401

Los Medanos College, Pittsburg, California 94565

Merced College, Merced, California 95348

Merritt College, Oakland, California 94619

Monterey Peninsula College, Monterey, California 93940

Ohlone College, Fremont, California 94539-0390

Palomar College, San Marcos, California 92069

Riverside City College, Riverside, California 92506

Sacramento City College, Sacramento, California 95822

San Bernardino Valley College, San Bernardino, California 92410

San Diego State University, San Diego, California 92182-0418

San Jose State University, San Jose, California 95192

College of San Mateo, San Mateo, California 94402

Santa Ana College, Santa Ana, California 92706

Santa Clara University, Santa Clara, California 95053

Santa Rosa Junior College, Santa Rosa, California 95404

Skyline College, San Bruno, California 94066

Solano Community College, Suison City, California 94510

Southwestern College, Chula Vista, California 92010

University of California/Berkeley, Berkeley, California 94720

University of California/Riverside, Riverside, California 92521

University of the Pacific, Stockton, California 95211

University of Southern California, Los Angeles, California 90089-1455

Victor Valley College, Victorville, California 92392-0099

West Los Angeles College, Culver City, California 90230

Colorado

Aims Community College, Greeley, Colorado 80632

Arapahoe Community College, Littleton, Colorado 80120

Colorado School of Mines, Golden, Colorado 80401

Colorado State University, Fort Collins, Colorado 80523

Colorado Technical College, Colorado Springs, Colorado 80907

Fort Lewis College, Durango, Colorado 81301

Front Range Community College, Westminster, Colorado 80030

Lamar Community College, Lamar, Colorado 81052

Mesa College, Grand Junction, Colorado 81501

Metropolitan State College, Denver, Colorado 80204

Northeastern Junior College, Sterling, Colorado 80751

Pikes Peak Community College, Colorado Springs, Colorado 80906

Red Rocks Community College, Golden, Colorado 80401

University of Colorado/Boulder, Boulder, Colorado 80309

University of Colorado at Denver, Denver, Colorado 80202

University of Denver, Denver, Colorado 80208

Connecticut

Central Connecticut State University, New Britain, Connecticut 06050

Hartford College for Women, Hartford, Connecticut 06105

Housatonic Regional Community College, Bridgeport, Connecticut 06608

Mattatuck Community College, Waterbury, Connecticut 06067

Sacred Heart University, Bridgeport, Connecticut 06606

Southern Connecticut State University, New Haven, Connecticut 06515

University of Bridgeport, Bridgeport, Connecticut 06601

University of Connecticut, Storrs, Connecticut 06268

University of Hartford, West Hartford, Connecticut 06117

University of New Haven, West Haven, Connecticut 06516

Western Connecticut State University, Danbury, Connecticut 06810

Delaware

Brandywine College of Widener University, Wilmington, Delaware 19803

Delaware Technical and Community College/Southern Campus, Georgetown, Delaware 19947

Goldey Beacom College, Wilmington, Delaware 19808

University of Delaware, Newark, Delaware 19711

Wesley College, Dover, Delaware 19901

District of Columbia

American University, Washington, D.C. 20016

Gallaudet University, Washington, D.C. 20002

George Washington University, Washington, D.C. 20052

Strayer College, Washington, D.C. 20005

University of the District of Columbia, Washington, D.C. 20008

Florida

Bethune-Cookman College, Daytona Beach, Florida 32015

Brevard Community College, Cocoa, Florida 32922

Broward Community College/Central Campus, Davie, Florida 33314

Central Florida Community College, Ocala, Florida 32670

Daytona Beach Community College, Daytona Beach, Florida 32015

Embry-Riddle Aeronautical University, Daytona Beach, Florida 32014

Florida Atlantic University, Boca Raton, Florida 33431

Florida Institute of Technology, Melbourne, Florida 32901

Florida International University, Miami, Florida 33199

Florida Memorial College, Miami, Florida 33054

Florida State University, Tallahassee, Florida 32306

Fort Lauderdale College, Fort Lauderdale, Florida 33301

Gulf Coast Community College, Panama City, Florida 32401

Lake Sumter Community College, Leesburg, Florida 32748

Manatee Community College, Bradenton, Florida 35506

Miami-Dade Community College, Miami, Florida 33176

Nova University, Inc., Fort Lauderdale, Florida 33314

Okaloosa-Walton Junior College, Niceville, Florida 32578

Pinellas Vocational Technical Institute, Clearwater, Florida 33520

Saint Thomas University, Miami, Florida 33054

Santa Fe Community College, Gainesville, Florida 32601

Seminole Community College, Sanford, Florida 32771

University of Central Florida, Orlando, Florida 32816

University of Florida, Gainesville, Florida 32611

University of Miami/College of Engineering, Coral Gables, Florida 33124

University of North Florida, Jacksonville, Florida 32216

University of South Florida, Tampa, Florida 33620

University of West Florida, Pensacola, Florida 32514

Valencia Community College, Orlando, Florida 32802

Georgia

Albany Junior College, Albany, Georgia 31707

Albany State College, Albany, Georgia 31705

Atlanta University, Atlanta, Georgia 30314-4391

Augusta College, Augusta, Georgia 30910

Berry College, Mt. Berry, Georgia 30149

Devry Institute of Technology, Decatur, Georgia 30030

Georgia College, Milledgeville, Georgia 31061

Georgia Institute of Technology, Atlanta, Georgia 30332

Georgia Southern College, Statesboro, Georgia 30460

Georgia Southwestern College, Americus, Georgia 31709

Georgia State University, Atlanta, Georgia 30303

Kennesaw College, Marietta, Georgia 30061

Middle Georgia College, Cochran, Georgia 31014

Morehouse College, Atlanta, Georgia 30314

Paine College, Augusta, Georgia 30910

Savannah State College, Savannah, Georgia 31404

Southern Technical Institute, Marietta, Georgia 30060

University of Georgia, Athens, Georgia 30602

Valdosta State College, Valdosta, Georgia 31698

West Georgia College, Carrollton, Georgia 30118

Hawaii

Brigham Young University at Hawaii, Laie, Hawaii 96762

Hawaii Community College/University of Hawaii, Hilo, Hawaii 96720

Hawaii Pacific College, Honolulu, Hawaii 96813

Honolulu Community College, Honolulu, Hawaii 96817

Maui Community College of Hawaii, Kahului, Hawaii 96732

University of Hawaii at Manoa, Honolulu, Hawaii 96822

Idaho

University of Idaho, Moscow, Idaho 83843

Illinois

Bradley University, Peoria, Illinois 61625

Chicago State University/College of Business, Chicago, Illinois 60628

College of Lake Country, Grayslake, Illinois 60030

Columbia College, Chicago, Illinois 60605

Devry Institute of Technology, Chicago, Illinois 60618

Devry Institute of Technology, Lombard, Illinois 60148

Elmhurst College, Elmhurst, Illinois 60126

Frontier Community College, Fairfield, Illinois 62837

Greenville College, Greenville, Illinois 62246

Illinois Institute of Technology, Chicago, Illinois 60616

Illinois State University, Normal, Illinois 61761

Kaskaskia College, Centralia, Illinois 62801

Malcolm X College, Chicago, Illinois 60612

Northeastern Illinois University, Chicago, Illinois 60625

Northern Illinois University, De Kalb, Illinois 60115-2875

Rend Lake College, Ina, Illinois 62846

Robert Morris College, Carthage, Illinois 62321

Sangamon State University, Springfield, Illinois 62708

School of Art Institute of Chicago, Chicago, Illinois 60603

Southern Illinois University/Carbondale, Carbondale, Illinois 62981

Southern Illinois University/Edwardsville, Edwardsville, Illinois 62025

Triton College, River Grove, Illinois 60171

Truman College, Chicago, Illinois 60640

University of Illinois at Chicago, Chicago, Illinois 60680

University of Illinois at Urbana-Champaign, Urbana, Illinois 61801

Wright College, Chicago, Illinois 60631

Indiana

Calumet College, Whiting, Indiana 46394

Indiana Institute of Technology, Fort Wayne, Indiana 46803

Indiana State University, Terre Haute, Indiana 47809

Indiana University, Bloomington, Indiana 47405

Indiana University Southeast, New Albany, Indiana 47150

International Business College, Fort Wayne, Indiana 46804

Marion College, Marion, Indiana 46953

Tri State University, Angola, Indiana 46703

University of Evansville, Evansville, Indiana 47702

University of Southern Indiana, Evansville, Indiana 47712

Valparaiso University, Valparaiso, Indiana 46383

Iowa

Clarke College, Dubuque, Iowa 52001

Clinton Community College, Clinton, Iowa 52732

Des Moines Area Community College, Ankeny, Iowa 04750

Drake University, Des Moines, Iowa 50311

Ellsworth Community College, Iowa Falls, Iowa 50126

Indian Hills Community College, Ottumwa, Iowa 52501

Iowa State University, Ames, Iowa 50011

Marycrest College, Davenport, Iowa 52804

Muscatine Community College, Muscatine, Iowa 52761

North Iowa Area Community College, Mason City, Iowa 50401

Northwestern College, Orange City, Iowa 51041

St. Ambrose College, Davenport, Iowa 52803

University of Iowa, Iowa City, Iowa 52242

University of Northern Iowa, Cedar Falls, Iowa 50614

Kansas

Benedictine College, Atchison, Kansas 66002

Bethany College, Lindsborg, Kansas 67456

Bethel College, North Newton, Kansas 67117

Central College, McPherson, Kansas 67460

Cowley County Community College, Arkansas City, Kansas 67005

Donnelly College, Kansas City, Kansas 66102

Emporia State University, Emporia, Kansas 66801

Garden City Community College, Garden City, Kansas 67846

Hesston College, Hesston, Kansas 67062

Johnson County Community College, Overland Park, Kansas 66210

Kansas Newman College, Wichita, Kansas 67213

Kansas State University/College of Engineering, Manhattan, Kansas 66506

Labette Community College, Parsons, Kansas 67357

McPherson College, McPherson, Kansas 67460

Pittsburgh State University, Pittsburgh, Kansas 66762

Wichita State University, Wichita, Kansas 67208

Kentucky

Eastern Kentucky University, Richmond, Kentucky 40475

Henderson Community College, Henderson, Kentucky 42420

Jefferson Community College, Southwest, Louisville, Kentucky 40272

Kentucky State University, Frankfort, Kentucky 40601

Lexington Technical Institute, Lexington, Kentucky 40506

Madisonville Community College, Madisonville, Kentucky 42431

Murray State University, Murray, Kentucky 42071

Northern Kentucky University, Highland Heights, Kentucky 41076

Prestonburg Community College, Prestonburg, Kentucky 41653

Southeast Community College, Cumberland, Kentucky 40823

Thomas More College, Crestview Hills, Kentucky 41017

University of Kentucky, Lexington, Kentucky 40506

University of Kentucky/Hazard Community College, Hazard, Kentucky 41701

University of Kentucky/Paducah City College, Paducah, Kentucky 42001

University of Kentucky/Somerset Community College, Somerset, Kentucky 42501

University of Louisville, Louisville, Kentucky 40292

Western Kentucky University, Bowling Green, Kentucky 42101

Louisiana

Louisiana Technical University, Ruston, Louisiana 71272

Southeastern Louisiana University, Hammond, Louisiana 70402

University of New Orleans, New Orleans, Louisiana 70148

Maine

Andover College, Portland, Maine 04103

College of the Atlantic, Bar Harbor, Maine 04609

Husson College, Bangor, Maine 04401

Unity College, Unity, Maine 04988

University of Maine at Augusta, Augusta, Maine 04330

University of Maine at Fort Kent, Fort Kent, Maine 04743

University of Maine/Machias, Machias, Maine 04654

University of Maine/Orono, Orono, Maine 04469

Maryland

Anne Arundel Community College, Arnold, Maryland 21012

Bowie State College, Bowie, Maryland 20715

Capitol Institute of Technology, Laurel, Maryland 20708

Catonsville Community College, Baltimore, Maryland 21228

Columbia Union College, Takoma Park, Maryland 20912

Coppin State College, Baltimore, Maryland 21216

Dundalk Community College, Baltimore, Maryland 21222

Frederick Community College, Frederick, Maryland 21701

Harford Community College, Bel Air, Maryland 21014

Howard Community College, Columbia, Maryland 21044

Morgan State University, Baltimore, Maryland 21212

Mount Saint Mary's College, Emmitsburg, Maryland 21727

Prince George's Community College, Largo, Maryland 20772

Sojourner Douglass College, Baltimore, Maryland 21205

Towson State University, Baltimore, Maryland 21204

University of Maryland/Baltimore County, Catonsville, Maryland 21228

University of Maryland/College Park, College Park, Maryland 20742

University of Maryland/Eastern Shore, Princess Anne, Maryland 21853

University of Maryland/University College, College Park, Maryland 20742

Massachusetts

Becker Junior College, Worcester, Massachusetts 01609

Boston University, Boston, Massachusetts 02215

Cape Cod Community College, West Barnstable, Massachusetts 02688

Central New England College, Worcester, Massachusetts 01610

Dean Junior College, Franklin, Massachusetts 02038

Gordon College, Wenham, Massachusetts 01984

Holyoke Community College, Holyoke, Massachusetts 01040

Massachusetts Institute of Technology, Cambridge, Massachusetts 02139

Merrimack College, North Andover, Massachusetts 01845

Middlesex Community College, Bedford, Massachusetts 01730

Mount Wachusett Community College, Gardner, Massachusetts 01440

Northeastern University, Boston, Massachusetts 02115

Northern Essex Community College, Haverhill, Massachusetts 01830

North Shore Community College, Beverly, Massachusetts 01915

Quinsigamond Community College, Worcester, Massachusetts 01606

Salem State College, Salem, Massachusetts 01970

Springfield Technical Community College, Springfield, Massachusetts 01105

Suffolk University, Boston, Massachusetts 02108

University of Lowell, Lowell, Massachusetts 01854

University of Massachusetts at Amherst, Amherst, Massachusetts 01003

University of Massachusetts at Boston, Boston, Massachusetts 02125

Wentworth Institute of Technology, Boston, Massachusetts 02115

Worcester Polytechnic Institute, Worcester, Massachusetts 01609

Michigan

Albion College, Albion, Michigan 49224

Alpena Community College, Alpena, Michigan 49707

Baker Junior College, Flint, Michigan 48507

Bay De Noc Community College, Escanaba, Michigan 49829

Central Michigan University, Mt. Pleasant, Michigan 48859

Charles Stewart Mott Community College, Flint, Michigan 48502

Davenport College of Business, Grand Rapids, Michigan 49503

Delta College, University Center, Michigan 48710

Detroit College of Business, Dearborn, Michigan 48126

Eastern Michigan University, Ypsilanti, Michigan 48197

Ferris State College, Big Rapids, Michigan 49307

GMI Engineering and Management Institute, Flint, Michigan 48502-2276

Grand Rapids Junior College, Grand Rapids, Michigan 49503

Grand Valley State College, Allendale, Michigan 49401

Henry Ford Community College, Dearborn, Michigan 48128

Kalamazoo College, Kalamazoo, Michigan 49007

Kalamazoo Valley Community College, Kalamazoo, Michigan 49009

Kellogg Community College, Battle Creek, Michigan 49016

Lake Michigan College, Benton Harbor, Michigan 49022

Lawrence Institute of Technology, Southfield, Michigan 48075

Macomb Community College, Warren, Michigan 48093

Madonna College, Livonia, Michigan 48150

Marygrove College, Detroit, Michigan 48221

Mercy College of Detroit, Detroit, Michigan 48219

Michigan State University/College of Engineering, East Lansing, Michigan 48823

Michigan Technological University, Houghton, Michigan 49931

Muskegon Community College, Muskegon, Michigan 49442

Northwestern Michigan College, Traverse City, Michigan 49684

Oakland Community College, Auburn Hills, Michigan 48057

Oakland University, Rochester, Michigan 48063

Olivet College, Olivet, Michigan 49076

Saginaw Valley State College, University Center, Michigan 48710

St. Clair County Community College, Port Huron, Michigan 48060

Schoolcraft College, Livonia, Michigan 48151

Siena Heights College, Adrian, Michigan 49221

Southwestern Michigan College, Dowagiac, Michigan 49047

Suomi College, Hancock, Michigan 49930

University of Detroit, Detroit, Michigan 48221

University of Michigan/Ann Arbor, Ann Arbor, Michigan 48109-2075

University of Michigan/Dearborn, School of Engineering, Dearborn, Michigan 48128

University of Michigan/Dearborn, School of Management, Dearborn, Michigan 48128

University of Michigan/Flint, Flint, Michigan 48503

Washtenaw Community College, Ann Arbor, Michigan 48106

Wayne County Community College, Detroit, Michigan 48226

Wayne State University, Detroit, Michigan 48101

Western Michigan University/Business School, Kalamazoo, Michigan 49008

Western Michigan University/Engineering School, Kalamazoo, Michigan 49008

Minnesota

Alexandria Vocational Technical Institute, Alexandria, Minnesota 56308

Anoka-Ramsey Community College, Coon Rapids, Minnesota 55433

Augsburg College, Minneapolis, Minnesota 55454

Bemidji State University, Bemidji, Minnesota 56601

Concordia College, Moorhead, Minnesota 56560

Gustavus Adolphus College, St. Peter, Minnesota 56082

Mankato State University, Mankato, Minnesota 56001

Metropolitan State University, St. Paul, Minnesota 55101

Moorhead State University, Moorhead, Minnesota 56560

Normandale Community College, Bloomington, Minnesota 55431

St. Cloud State University, St. Cloud, Minnesota 56302

College of St. Thomas, St. Paul, Minnesota 55105

Southwest State University, Marshall, Minnesota 56258

University of Minnesota/Crookston, Crookston, Minnesota 56716

University of Minnesota/Institute of Technology, Minneapolis, Minnesota 55455

University of Minnesota/Saint Paul, St. Paul, Minnesota 55108

University of Minnesota Technical College, Waseca, Minnesota 56093

Willmar Community College, Willmar, Minnesota 56201

Winona State University, Winona, Minnesota 55987

Worthington Community College, Worthington, Minnesota 56187

Mississippi

Alcorn State University, Lorman, Mississippi 39096-9998

Hinds Junior College, Raymond, Mississippi 39154

Jackson State University, Jackson, Mississippi 39217

Mississippi College, Clinton, Mississippi 39058

Mississippi Gulf Coast Junior College, Perkinston, Mississippi 39573

Mississippi State University, Mississippi State, Mississippi 39762

Northeast Mississippi Junior College, Booneville, Mississippi 38829

Rust College, Holly Springs, Mississippi 38635

Tougaloo College, Tougaloo, Mississippi 39174

University of Mississippi, University, Mississippi 38677

University of Southern Mississippi, Hattiesburg, Mississippi 39401

Utica Junior College, Utica, Mississippi 39175

Missouri

Central Missouri State University, Warrensburg, Missouri 64093

Fontbonne College, St. Louis, Missouri 63105

Lincoln University/Missouri, Jefferson City, Missouri 65101

Lindenwood College, St. Charles, Missouri 63301

Maryville College/St. Louis, St. Louis, Missouri 63141

Missouri Valley College, Marshall, Missouri 65340

Northeast Missouri State University, Kirksville, Missouri 63501

Penn Valley Community College, Kansas City, Missouri 64111

Rockhurst College, Kansas City, Missouri 64110

St. Louis Community College/Florissant Valley, St. Louis, Missouri 63135

Southwest Missouri State University, Springfield, Missouri 65804-0088

University of Missouri/Columbia, Columbia, Missouri 65211

University of Missouri/Rolla, Rolla, Missouri 65401

University of Missouri/St. Louis, St. Louis, Missouri 63121

Washington University/College of Engineering, St. Louis, Missouri 63130

Montana

College of Great Falls, Great Falls, Montana 59405

Montana College of Mineral Science and Technology, Butte, Montana 59701

Montana State University, Bozeman, Montana 59175

Northern Montana College, Havre, Montana 59801

Rocky Mountain College, Billings, Montana 59102

University of Montana, Missoula, Montana 59812

Nebraska

Central Community College, Hastings, Nebraska 68901

Central Community College, Grand Island, Nebraska 68801

Central Community College/Platte Campus, Columbus, Nebraska 68601

Chadron State College, Chadron, Nebraska 69337

Doane College, Crete, Nebraska 68333

Metropolitan Community College, Omaha, Nebraska 68103

Southeast Community College, Lincoln, Nebraska 68520

Southeast Community College/Milford Campus, Milford, Nebraska 68405

Southwest Community College, Milford, Nebraska 68405

University of Nebraska/Lincoln, Lincoln, Nebraska 68588-0495

University of Nebraska/Omaha, Omaha, Nebraska 68182

Nevada

Clark County Community College, North Las Vegas, Nevada 89030

Northern Nevada Community College, Elko, Nevada 89801

New Hampshire

New Hampshire College, Manchester, New Hampshire 03104

University of New Hampshire, Durham, New Hampshire 03824

New Jersey

Atlantic Community College, Mays Landing, New Jersey 08330

Bergen Community College, Paramus, New Jersey 07652

Brookdale Community College, Lincroft, New Jersey 07738

Burlington County College, Pemberton, New Jersey 08068

County College of Morris, Randolph, New Jersey 07869

Georgian Court College, Lakewood, New Jersey 08701

Glassboro State College, Glassboro, New Jersey 08028

Jersey City State College, Jersey City, New Jersey 07305

Kean College of New Jersey, Union, New Jersey 07083

Mercer County Community College, Trenton, New Jersey 08690

Middlesex County College, Edison, New Jersey 08817

Montclair State College, Upper Montclair, New Jersey 07043

New Jersey Institute of Technology, Newark, New Jersey 07102

Ocean County College, Toms River, New Jersey 08753

Passaic County Community College, Paterson, New Jersey 07509

Ramapo College of New Jersey, Mahwah, New Jersey 07430

Rider College, Lawrenceville, New Jersey 08648

Rutgers/Cook College, New Brunswick, New Jersey 08903

Saint Peter's College, Jersey City, New Jersey 07306

Salem Community College, Carneys Point, New Jersey 08069

Seton Hall University, South Orange, New Jersey 07079

Somerset County College, North Branch, New Jersey 08876

Trenton State College, Trenton, New Jersey 08625

New Mexico

College of Santa Fe, Santa Fe, New Mexico 87501

Eastern New Mexico University/Portales, Portales, New Mexico 88130

New Mexico Highlands University, Las Vegas, New Mexico 87701

New Mexico Institute of Mining and Technology, Socorro, New Mexico 87801

New Mexico State University, Las Cruces, New Mexico 88003

San Juan College, Farmington, New Mexico 87401

University of New Mexico, Albuquerque, New Mexico 87131

New York

Borough of Manhattan Community College, New York, New York 10007

Bronx Community College, Bronx, New York 10453

City College of New York, New York, New York 10031

Clarkson College, Potsdam, New York 13676

College of Insurance, New York, New York 10038

Cornell University, Ithaca, New York 14850

CUNY/Herbert H. Lehman College, Bronx, New York 10468

CUNY/Medgar Evers College, Brooklyn, New York 11225

CUNY/York College, Jamaica, New York 11451

Daemen College, Amherst, New York 14226

Genesee Community College, Batavia, New York 14020

Hudson Valley Community College, Troy, New York 12180

Keuka College, Keuka, New York 14478

La Guardia Community College, Long Island City, New York 11101

Long Island University/Brooklyn Campus, Brooklyn, New York 11201

Long Island University/C.W. Post Campus, Greenvale, New York 11548

Long Island University/Southampton Campus, Southampton, New York 11968

Manhattan College, Bronx, New York 10471

Manhattanville College, Purchase, New York 10577

Marist College, Poughkeepsie, New York 12601

Marymount College/Tarrytown, Tarrytown, New York 10591

Monroe Community College, Rochester, New York 14623

Nassau Community College, Garden City, New York 11530

National Technical Institute for the Deaf, Rochester, New York 14623

New York Institute of Technology, Old Westbury, New York 11568

New York University/Center for Foodservice Management, New York, New York 10003

Pace University, New York, New York 10038

Polytechnical Institute of New York, Brooklyn, New York 11201

Pratt Institute, Brooklyn, New York 11205

Rensselaer Polytechnic Institute, Troy, New York 12180-3590

Rochester Institute of Technology, Rochester, New York 14623

Rockland Community College, Suffern, New York 10901

SUNY Agriculture and Technology College/Alfred, Alfred, New York 14802

SUNY/College at Brockport, Brockport, New York 14420

SUNY/College at Buffalo, Buffalo, New York 14222

SUNY/College at Cortland, Cortland, New York 13045

SUNY/College at Fredonia, Fredonia, New York 14063

SUNY/College at New Paltz, New Paltz, New York 12561

SUNY/College at Plattsburgh, Plattsburgh, New York 12901

SUNY/College of Technology at Utica-Rome, Utica, New York 13502

Syracuse University, Syracuse, New York 13210

Tompkins Cortland Community College, Dryden, New York 13053

United States Merchant Marine Academy, Kings Point, New York 11024

Villa Maria College of Buffalo, Buffalo, New York 14225

North Carolina

Beaufort County Community College, Washington, North Carolina 27889

Catawba Valley Technical College, Hickory, North Carolina 28601

Central Piedmont Community College, Charlotte, North Carolina 28235

Cleveland Technical College, Shelby, North Carolina 28150

College of the Albemarle, Elizabeth City, North Carolina 27909

Craven Community College, New Bern, North Carolina 28560

East Carolina University, Greenville, North Carolina 27834

Elizabeth City State University, Elizabeth City, North Carolina 27909

Elon College, Elon, North Carolina 27244

Fayetteville State University, Fayetteville, North Carolina 28301

Fayetteville Technical Institute, Fayetteville, North Carolina 28303

Guilford Technical Community College, Jamestown, North Carolina 27282

Isothermal Community College, Spindale, North Carolina 28160

Lenoir Community College, Kingston, North Carolina 28501

Livingstone College, Salisbury, North Carolina 28144

Meredith College, Raleigh, North Carolina 27611

Mount Olive College, Mount Olive, North Carolina 28365

North Carolina A&T State University, Greensboro, North Carolina 27411

North Carolina State University, Raleigh, North Carolina 27695

North Carolina Wesleyan College, Rocky Mount, North Carolina 27801

Pitt Community College, Greenville, North Carolina 27834

Sampson Technical College, Clinton, North Carolina 28328

Southeastern Community College, Whiteville, North Carolina 28472

Technical College of Alamance, Haw River, North Carolina 27258

University of North Carolina at Charlotte, Charlotte, North Carolina 28223

University of North Carolina at Greensboro, Greensboro, North Carolina 27412-5001

Wake Technical College, Raleigh, North Carolina 27603

Wayne Community College, Goldsboro, North Carolina 27530

Western Carolina University, Cullowhee, North Carolina 28723

Western Piedmont Community College, Morganton, North Carolina 28655

Wilkes Community College, Wilkesboro, North Carolina 28697

Winston-Salem State University, Winston-Salem, North Carolina 27110

North Dakota

Bismarck Junior College, Bismarck, North Dakota 58501

Jamestown College, Jamestown, North Dakota 58401

Mayville State College, Mayville, North Dakota 58257

North Dakota State University/Bottineau, Bottineau, North Dakota 58318

North Dakota State University, Fargo, North Dakota 58102

Valley City State College, Valley City, North Dakota 58072

Ohio

Antioch College, Yellow Springs, Ohio 45387

Baldwin Wallace College, Berea, Ohio 44017

Bowling Green State University, Bowling Green, Ohio 43403

Case Western Reserve University, Cleveland, Ohio 44106

Central State University, Wilberforce, Ohio 45384

Cincinnati Technical College, Cincinnati, Ohio 45223

Clark Technical College, Springfield, Ohio 45501

Cleveland State University, Cleveland, Ohio 44115

College of Mt. St. Joseph, Mt. St. Joseph, Ohio 45051

Cuyahoga Community College, Parma, Ohio 44130

Defiance College, Defiance, Ohio 43512

Dyke College, Cleveland, Ohio 44140

Firelands College, Huron, Ohio 44839

John Carroll University, Cleveland, Ohio 44118

Kent State University/School of Technology, Kent, Ohio 44242

Lakeland Community College, Mentor, Ohio 44060

Marietta College, Marietta, Ohio 45750

Miami University, Oxford, Ohio 45056

Mount Union College, Alliance, Ohio 44601

Notre Dame College, Cleveland, Ohio 44121

Ohio State University, Columbus, Ohio 43210

Ohio University, Athens, Ohio 45701

Sinclair Community College, Dayton, Ohio 45402

Stark Technical College, Canton, Ohio 44720

University of Akron, Akron, Ohio 44325

University of Cincinnati, Cincinnati, Ohio 45221

University of Cincinnati/Applied Sciences, Cincinnati, Ohio 45210

University of Dayton, Dayton, Ohio 45469

Wilberforce University, Wilberforce, Ohio 45384

Wilmington College, Wilmington, Ohio 45177

Wright State University, Dayton, Ohio 45435

Oklahoma

Carl Albert Junior College, Poteau, Oklahoma 74953

Oklahoma Baptist University, Shawnee, Oklahoma 74801

Oklahoma City Community College, Oklahoma City, Oklahoma 73159

Oklahoma State University, Stillwater, Oklahoma 74078

Rogers State College, Claremore, Oklahoma 74017

Tulsa Junior College, Tulsa, Oklahoma 74135

Oregon

Chemeketa Community College, Salem, Oregon 97309

Clackamas Community College, Oregon City, Oregon 97045

Clatsop Community College, Astoria, Oregon 97103

Eastern Oregon State College, La Grande, Oregon 97850

Lane Community College, Eugene, Oregon 97405

Linn Benton Community College, Albany, Oregon 97321

Oregon Institute of Technology, Klamath Falls, Oregon 97601

Oregon State University, Corvallis, Oregon 97331

Portland Community College, Portland, Oregon 97219

Portland State University, Portland, Oregon 97207

Rogue Community College, Grants Pass, Oregon 97526

Southern Oregon State College, Ashland, Oregon 97520

Southwestern Oregon Community College, Coos Bay, Oregon 97420

Pennsylvania

Beaver College, Glenside, Pennsylvania 19038

Bloomsburg University, Bloomsburg, Pennsylvania 17815

Bucks County Community College, Newtown, Pennsylvania 18940

Carnegie Mellon University, Pittsburgh, Pennsylvania 15123

Chestnut Hill College, Philadelphia, Pennsylvania 19118

Cheyney University, Cheyney, Pennsylvania 19319

Community College of Allegheny County, Pittsburgh, Pennsylvania 15212

Community College of Allegheny County/Boyce, Monroeville, Pennsylvania 15146

Community College of Allegheny County/South Campus, West Mifflin, Pennsylvania 15037

Delaware County Community College, Media, Pennsylvania 19063

Delaware Valley College of Science and Agriculture, Doylestown, Pennsylvania 18901

Drexel University, Philadelphia, Pennsylvania 19104-9984

Hahnemann University, Philadelphia, Pennsylvania 19102

Indiana University of Pennsylvania, Indiana, Pennsylvania 15705

King's College, Wilkes-Barre, Pennsylvania 18711

La Salle University, Philadelphia, Pennsylvania 19141

Lehigh University, Bethlehem, Pennsylvania 18015

Lincoln University, Lincoln, Pennsylvania 19352

Lockhaven University, Lockhaven, Pennsylvania 17779

Mercyhurst College, Erie, Pennsylvania 16546

Messiah College, Grantham, Pennsylvania 17027

Millersville University, Millersville, Pennsylvania 17551

Moore College of Art, Philadelphia, Pennsylvania 19103

Peirce Junior College, Philadelphia, Pennsylvania 19102

Pennsylvania Institute of Technology, Media, Pennsylvania 19063

Pennsylvania State University, University Park, Pennsylvania 16802

Philadelphia College of Textiles & Science, Philadelphia, Pennsylvania 19144

Robert Morris College, Pittsburgh, Pennsylvania 15219

St. Joseph's University/Academy of Food Marketing, Philadelphia, Pennsylvania 19131

Saint Vincent College, Latrobe, Pennsylvania 15650

Susquehanna University, Selinsgrove, Pennsylvania 17870

Temple University, Philadelphia, Pennsylvania 19122

Waynesburg College, Waynesburg, Pennsylvania 15370

Westmoreland County Community College, Youngwood, Pennsylvania 15697

Widener College of Widener University, Chester, Pennsylvania 19013-9987

Wilkes College, Wilkes-Barre, Pennsylvania 18766

Williamsport Area Community College, Williamsport, Pennsylvania 17701

Rhode Island

Johnson & Wales College, Providence, Rhode Island 02905

Rhode Island College, Providence, Rhode Island 02908

Roger Williams College, Bristol, Rhode Island 02809

South Carolina

Benedict College, Columbia, South Carolina 29204

Clemson University, Clemson, South Carolina 29631

Coker College, Hartsville, South Carolina 29550

Florence Darlington Technical College, Florence, South Carolina 29501

Furman University, Greenville, South Carolina 29613

Greenville Technical College, Greenville, South Carolina 29606-5616

Lander College, Greenwood, South Carolina 29646

Midlands Technical College, Columbia, South Carolina 29202

Morris College, Sumter, South Carolina 29150

North Greenville College, Tigerville, South Carolina 29688

Piedmont Technical College, Greenwood, South Carolina 29646

South Carolina State College, Orangeburg, South Carolina 29117

Trident Technical College, Charleston, South Carolina 29411

University of South Carolina, Columbia, South Carolina 29208

University of South Carolina at Aiken, Aiken, South Carolina 29801

Winthrop College, Rock Hill, South Carolina 29733

Wofford College, Spartanburg, South Carolina 29301

South Dakota

Huron College, Huron, South Dakota 57350

South Dakota School of Mines & Technology, Rapid City, South Dakota 57701

South Dakota State University, Brookings, South Dakota 57007

Tennessee

Belmont College, Nashville, Tennessee 37203

Chattanooga State Technical Community College, Chattanooga, Tennessee 37406

Cleveland State Community College, Cleveland, Tennessee 37311

Columbia State Community College, Columbia, Tennessee 38401

East Tennessee State University, Johnson City, Tennessee 37614

Fisk University, Nashville, Tennessee 37203

Lemoyne-Owen College, Memphis, Tennessee 38126

Middle Tennessee State University, Murfreesboro, Tennessee 37132

Nashville State Technical Institute, Nashville, Tennessee 37209

Roane State Community College, Harriman, Tennessee 37748

Shelby State Community College, Memphis, Tennessee 38174-0568

Tennessee Technological University, Cookeville, Tennessee 38505

University of Tennessee at Chattanooga, Chattanooga, Tennessee 37403

University of Tennessee at Knoxville, Knoxville, Tennessee 37996-0610

University of Tennessee at Martin, Martin, Tennessee 38238

Texas

Amarillo College, Amarillo, Texas 79178

Bishop College, Dallas, Texas 75241

Brookhaven College, Farmers Branch, Texas 75234

Cedar Valley College/Dallas County, Lancaster, Texas 75134

College of the Mainland, Texas City, Texas 77590

Eastfield College, Mesquite, Texas 75150

East Texas State University, Commerce, Texas 75428

El Centro College, Dallas, Texas 75202

El Paso Community College, El Paso, Texas 79998

Frank Phillips College, Borger, Texas 79007

Galveston College, Galveston, Texas 77550

Houston Community College System, Houston, Texas 77006

Huston-Tillotson College, Austin, Texas 78702

Jarvis Christian College, Hawkins, Texas 75765

Lamar University, Beaumont, Texas 77710

Midland College, Midland, Texas 79701

North Lake College, Irving, Texas 75038

North Texas State University, Denton, Texas 76203

Pan American University, Edinburg, Texas 78539

Prairie View A&M University, Prairie View, Texas 77446

Richland College, Dallas, Texas 75243

St. Edwards University, Austin, Texas 78704

St. Mary's University, San Antonio, Texas 78284

Sam Houston State University, Huntsville, Texas 77341

San Antonio College, San Antonio, Texas 78284

Southern Methodist University/Engineering and Applied Science, Dallas, Texas 75275

South Plains College, Levelland, Texas 79336

Texas A&M University, College Station, Texas 77843

Texas Lutheran College, Seguin, Texas 78155

Texas Southern University, Houston, Texas 77004

Texas State Technical Institute, Waco, Texas 76705

Texas Woman's University, Denton, Texas 76204

University of Houston/Downtown, Houston, Texas 77002

University of Houston/University Park, Houston, Texas 77004

University of Texas at Arlington, Arlington, Texas 76019

University of Texas at Austin, Austin, Texas 78712-1080

Utah

Brigham Young University, Provo, Utah 84602

Dixie College, St. George, Utah 84770

Snow College, Ephraim, Utah 84627

University of Utah, Salt Lake City, Utah 84112

Utah State University, Logan, Utah 84322

Utah Technical College at Provo, Provo, Utah 84603

Utah Technical College at Salt Lake, Salt Lake City, Utah 84131

Weber State College, Ogden, Utah 84403

Westminster College, Salt Lake City, Utah 84105

Vermont

Lyndon State College, Lyndonville, Vermont 05851

Norwich University, Northfield, Vermont 05663

University of Vermont, Burlington, Vermont 05405

Virginia

Blue Ridge Community College, Weyers Cave, Virginia 24486

Central Virginia Community College, Lynchburg, Virginia 24502

George Mason University, Fairfax, Virginia 22030

Germanna Community College, Locust Grove, Virginia 22508

Hampton University, Hampton, Virginia 23668

Lord Fairfax Community College, Middletown, Virginia 22645

New River Community College, Dublin, Virginia 24084

Norfolk State University, Norfolk, Virginia 23504

Northern Virginia Community College/Alexandria, Alexandria, Virginia 22311

Northern Virginia Community College, Annandale, Virginia 22003

Northern Virginia Community College/Loudon Campus, Sterling, Virginia 22170

Northern Virginia Community College, Manassas, Virginia 22110

Northern Virginia Community College, Woodbridge, Virginia 22191

Old Dominion University, Norfolk, Virginia 23508

Patrick Henry Community College, Martinsville, Virginia 24115

Paul D. Camp Community College, Franklin, Virginia 23851

Piedmont Virginia Community College, Charlottesville, Virginia 22903

Thomas Nelson Community College, Hampton, Virginia 23660

Tidewater Community College, Portsmouth, Virginia 23703

Tidewater Community College/Virginia Beach Campus, Virginia Beach, Virginia 23456

University of Virginia Clinch Valley College, Wise, Virginia 24293

Virginia Commonwealth University, Richmond, Virginia 23284

Virginia Polytechnic Institute, Blacksburg, Virginia 24061

Virginia State University, Petersburg, Virginia 23803

Virginia Union University, Richmond, Virginia 23220

Virginia Western Community College, Roanoke, Virginia 24038

Washington

Central Washington University, Ellensburg, Washington 98926

Clark College, Vancouver, Washington 98663

Columbia Basin College, Pasco, Washington 99301

Eastern Washington University, Cheney, Washington 99004

Edmonds Community College, Lynnwood, Washington 98036

Everett Community College, Everett, Washington 98201

Evergreen State College, Olympia, Washington 98505

Fort Steilacoom Community College, Tacoma, Washington 98498

Highline Community College, Midway, Washington 98032-0424

Lower Columbia College, Longview, Washington 98632

Pacific Lutheran University, Tacoma, Washington 98447

Seattle Central Community College, Seattle, Washington 98122

Seattle Pacific University, Seattle, Washington 98119

Skagit Valley College, Mt. Vernon, Washington 98273

South Puget Sound Community College, Olympia, Washington 98502

Spokane Community College, Spokane, Washington 99207-5399

Tacoma Community College, Tacoma, Washington 98465

Walla Walla College, College Place, Washington 99324

Walla Walla Community College, Walla Walla, Washington 99362

University of Puget Sound, Tacoma, Washington 98416

University of Washington, Seattle, Washington 98195

Washington State University, Pullman, Washington 99164

Wenatchee Valley College, Wenatchee, Washington 98801

Whatcom Community College, Bellingham, Washington 98225

West Virginia

Marshall University, Huntington, West Virginia 25701

Parkersburg Community College, Parkersburg, West Virginia 26101

Southern West Virginia Community College, Logan, West Virginia 25601

University of Charleston, Charleston, West Virginia 25304

West Virginia Institute of Technology, Montgomery, West Virginia 25136

West Virginia State College, Institute, West Virginia 25112

West Virginia Wesleyan College, Buckhannon, West Virginia 26201

Wheeling College, Wheeling, West Virginia 26003

Wisconsin

Marquette University/College of Engineering, Milwaukee, Wisconsin 53233

Milwaukee Area Technical College, Milwaukee, Wisconsin 53213

Moraine Park Technical Institute, Fon du Lac, Wisconsin 54935

Mount Senario College, Ladysmith, Wisconsin 54848

Northland College, Ashland, Wisconsin 54806

St. Norbert College, De Pere, Wisconsin 54115

University of Wisconsin/La Crosse, La Crosse, Wisconsin 54601

University of Wisconsin/Madison, Madison, Wisconsin 53706

University of Wisconsin/Milwaukee, Milwaukee, Wisconsin 53201

University of Wisconsin/River Falls, River Falls, Wisconsin 54021

University of Wisconsin/Stevens Point, Stevens Point, Wisconsin 54481

University of Wisconsin/Stout, Menominee, Wisconsin 54751

Waukesha County Technical Institute, Pewaukee, Wisconsin 53072

Wyoming

Western Wyoming College, Rock Springs, Wyoming 82901

Puerto Rico

Inter-American University/College of Arecibo, Puerto Rico 00613

University of Puerto Rico, Mayaguez, Puerto Rico 00708

12 MILITARY AND VETERANS' PROGRAMS

The GI Bill, implemented after World War II, has helped to finance the education of millions of veterans. For some students, financial assistance programs offered by the Armed Services are a way to reduce their college costs. This chapter will examine the numerous scholarship and tuition waiver programs offered by the military to college students and the financial assistance programs offered to veterans and their dependents.

Military Scholarship Programs

Armed Forces Health Professions Scholarship Program
This program, available to qualified health professions students, pays for tuition, fees, and books, and provides a monthly living stipend as well. Recipients must agree to serve for a specified time in one branch of the Armed Forces after graduation. Contact your school's director of financial aid for further information on this program, or write to:

Air Force
Health Professions Recruiting
8855 Annapolis Road
Lanham, Maryland 20706-2924
(301) 436-1569

Army
HQDA (SGPS-PDF)
1900 Half Street, S.W.
Washington, D.C. 20324-2000
(202) 475-0645

Navy and Marines
Naval Medical Command
CODE 544
Washington, D.C. 20372-5120
(202) 653-1318

Reserve Officers Training Corps (ROTC) Scholarship Program
The ROTC Scholarship Program is offered to qualified men and women who are enrolled in either 2-year junior or community colleges or 4-year undergraduate programs. Candidates must be U.S. citizens and between the ages of 17 and 21 when they apply for the scholarship. There are physical requirements for acceptance into the program, and applicants must take either the ACT or SAT. A personal interview is required. The scholarships pay for all tuition expenses, textbooks, laboratory fees, and any other costs associated with the college program as well as provide a monthly living stipend.

Recipients are required to study military science, to participate in summer training sessions, and to maintain satisfactory academic progress as determined by their schools. Upon successful completion of the program and graduation, a recipient is awarded a commission. Scholarship recipients must enlist in the Army, Navy, Air Force, or Marines and must agree to serve for 4 years on active duty and 2 years on reserve status after graduation.

Over 600 colleges and universities participate in this program. Follow these procedures if you are interested in an ROTC scholarship:

1. Decide whether this is a program for you.

2. Find out whether the colleges or universities you are considering have ROTC programs.

3. Speak with the school ROTC representative to obtain specific information, program obligations, and application materials.

Contact the following for additional information:

Air Force
Air Force ROTC Scholarship Program
Recruiting Division
Maxwell Air Force Base
Maxwell, Alabama 36112-6663

Army
Army ROTC Scholarship Program
Box 12703
Philadelphia, Pennsylvania 19134

Marine Corps
Commandant of the Marine Corps
Code MRRO-6, Headquarters
Washington, D.C. 20380-0001

Navy
Navy ROTC Scholarship Program
Information Center
Washington, D.C. 20380-0001
(800) 327-NAVY

Service Academy Scholarships   Service Academy Scholarships are awarded each year to qualified students to attend the U.S. Military Academy, the U.S. Air Force Academy. the U.S. Naval Academy, the U.S. Merchant Marine Academy, and the U.S. Coast Guard Academy. Nominations are usually made by the applicant's U.S. senator or representative. The scholarships are competitive and are based upon a number of factors, including high school grades, SAT or ACT scores, leadership qualities, and athletic ability. Students enrolled in this program receive their undergraduate education at one of the service academies. Recipients pay no tuition or fees, but there is a service commitment after graduation. If you are interested in this type of program, contact your U.S. senator or representative and obtain specific information and application forms. Begin the process very early, especially with regard to securing a nomination from a senator or congressperson. Information may also be obtained by writing to the following:

Air Force
Director of Admissions
U.S. Air Force Academy
Colorado Springs, Colorado 80840-5651
(303) 472-2520

Army
Director of Admissions
U.S. Military Academy
600 Thayer Road
West Point, New York 10996-1797
(914) 938-4041

Coast Guard
Director of Admissions
U.S. Coast Guard Academy
New London, Connecticut 06320
(203) 444-8501

Merchant Marine
Director of Admissions
U.S. Merchant Marine Academy
Kings Point, New York 11024-1699
(516) 773-5391

Navy
Candidate Guidance Office
U.S. Naval Academy-Leahy Hall
Annapolis, Maryland 21402-5000
(301) 267-4361

Financial Assistance Programs for Military Personnel

Each branch of the Armed Services offers numerous programs for both enlisted and officer personnel interested in beginning or continuing their education. Usually, a military base has an education officer who can provide information on specific programs offered at that base both during the period of service and after active duty is completed. Most service programs pay a portion of the cost of college attendance, from 75 to 90% of undergraduate or graduate school tuition.

At the graduate level, commissioned officers are selected to attend a graduate school, at which all of the educational expenses are paid. As an incentive for enlistment, certain branches of the Armed Forces will repay a borrower's student loan. Under the Veterans' Educational Assistance Program, the government will double the monthly education contribution of the serviceperson. The military services offer excellent opportunities to learn new skills and save for higher education at the same time.

Follow these procedures if you are interested in learning more about the educational benefits offered by the Armed Services:

1. Speak with a local recruiting officer. He or she can provide specific information on the educational benefits offered by each branch of the Armed Services.

2. If possible, contact the local military base education officer to obtain more information on specific programs.

3. Determine whether the education benefits offered by the military match your long-term career plans and objectives.

The following programs are examples of the educational benefits offered by the Armed Services:

Air Force

Air Force Aid Society provides educational loan assistance to the children of qualified Air Force personnel. Candidates for the program must be enrolled or accepted for enrollment as full-time students at an approved school. Contact the National Headquarters, Air Force Aid Society, 1735 N. Lynn, Arlington, Virginia 22209 for further information.

Air Force Technical Schools offer career education courses to Air Force personnel. Training opportunities are provided in over 100 occupational specialties. Contact your local recruiter or military base education officer for further details.

The Community College of the Air Force provides the opportunity to earn an associate degree in applied science. Contact your local recruiter or military base education officer for further details.

Operation Bookstrap provides career Air Force personnel with the opportunity to attend regionally accredited colleges and universities while on active duty. Contact the base education officer for further details on this program.

Army

Army College Fund provides a way for Army personnel to finance their college education while still on active duty. Under the plan, army personnel on active duty contribute $100 per month for the first 12 months to their education fund. The Army also contributes to the fund based upon the length of enlistment. Contact your local recruiter or military base education officer for further details.

Army Continuing Education Programs provide numerous educational programs for Army personnel. Through the Army Continuing Education System, a variety of academic and nonacademic educational opportunities are available. The following programs are offered: Basic Skills Education Program, High School Completion Program, English as a Second Language Program, Advanced Skills Education Program, Army Apprenticeship Program, and Defense Activity for Nontraditional Education Support. Contact your local Army recruiter for further information.

Army Emergency Relief Program provides financial assistance to the children of Army personnel who are on active duty status, or who have died or are disabled because of military service. The program awards both scholarships and loans to qualified dependents. Financial need and academic merit are considered in making awards. Contact the Army Emergency Relief Program, 200 Stovall Street, Alexandria, Virginia 22332, for further information and application materials.

Army Nurse Corps enables nursing students interested in careers as Army nurses to participate in Army ROTC while in college. Nursing cadets who meet all of the professional requirements and successfully complete the program are commissioned as second lieutenants upon graduation from college. Contact your local Army recruiter for further information.

Loan Repayment Program offers special financial incentives to regular and reserve Army enlisted persons. Under the program, the Army will repay the Stafford Student Loans and Carl D. Perkins Loans of persons who enlist in areas specified as critical by the Army. Contact your local recruiter or military base education officer for further details.

Servicemembers Opportunity Colleges allows a serviceperson to transfer credits and pursue a program of study regardless of location in a coordinated network of junior colleges, community colleges, and 4-year schools. Flexible course hours and entrance requirements make it possible for Army personnel to continue their education and obtain a college degree. Contact your local recruiter or military base education officer for further details.

Navy

Broadened Opportunity for Officer Selection and Training Program (BOOST) is designed for high school seniors who have good academic grades but not the required College Board test scores for the 4-year Navy ROTC Scholarship Program. Students selected for the BOOST Program attend a training school. After graduation, a student either is granted a 4-year Navy ROTC Scholarship or receives an appointment to the Naval Academy. Contact your local Navy recruiting office for further information.

Dependent's Scholarship Program offers scholarship assistance to the dependent children of Navy, Marine, and Coast Guard personnel. Recipients must be enrolled as full-time students in accredited programs. Write to the Naval Military Personnel Command, Department of the Navy, Washington, D.C. 20370-5121, for additional information.

Navy Federal Credit Union Students Loans offer Stafford Student Loans and Parent Loans for Undergraduate Students (PLUS) to qualified Navy personnel. For information and application forms, contact Navy Federal Credit Union facilities or write to the Navy Federal Credit Union, Security Place, P.O. Box 3350, Merrifield, Virginia 22119-3350.

Navy Relief Society provides loans to the dependent children of qualified regular, reserve, and retired Navy and Marine Corps personnel. Loans are made to both graduate and undergraduate students. Write to the Navy Relief Society, 801 N. Randolph Street, Suite 1228, Arlington, Virginia 22203-1989, for further information.

Second Marine Division Association Memorial Scholarship Fund provides scholarship assistance to the dependent children of Marine personnel who died or became disabled while serving in the Second Marine Division. Write to the Second Marine Division Association, Memorial Scholarship Fund, P.O. Box 734, Wildwood, New Jersey 08260, for further information and application materials.

Supplemental Assistance Program offers interest-free loans and grants to active duty members of the Navy or Marine Corps who are enrolled in the NROTC/ECP/MECEP/EEAP Programs. The awards are based upon need and upon the recommendation of the Commanding Officer. For further information, contact the Navy Relief Society Education Program, 801 N. Randolph Street, Suite 1228, Arlington, Virginia 22203-1989.

Surviving Children of Deceased While on Active Duty (CDAD) provides loans and grants to the unmarried, dependent children of service members deceased while on active duty. For further information and application forms, contact the Navy Relief Society, 801 N. Randolph Street, Suite 1228, Arlington, Virginia 22203-1989.

Marine Corps

Continuing Education Programs are designed to encourage Marine Corps personnel to begin or continue their education. The programs are as follows:

Broadened Opportunity for Officer Selection and Training, Marine Corps Enlisted Commissioning Education Program, Degree Completion Program for Staff Noncommissioned Officers, College Degree Program, and Marine Corps Tuition Assistance Program. The Veterans Education Assistance Program (VEAP) allows enlisted men and women as well as officers to contribute from $25 to $100 per month to an educational fund. When the person enrolls in a postsecondary program, the federal government matches the contribution with $2 for every $1 contributed by the military person. The Tuition Assistance Program pays the serviceperson up to 75% for undergraduate courses and 90% for job-related courses. Contact your local recruiter or military base education officer for further details.

Marine Corps Scholarship Foundation provides scholarship assistance to the dependent children of active service Marines, as well as to the children of discharged and reserve status Marines. The awards are based upon financial need, and the amounts of the scholarship vary. Contact the Marine Corps Scholarship Foundation, P.O. Box 3008, Princeton, New Jersey 08540-3008, for further information on this program.

Oppenheimer Scholarship to Culver Military Academy is available to the sons of regular or reserve Marines with 5 years of active duty service and to the sons of deceased Marines. The scholarship, which pays all tuition costs, may be used only at Culver Military Academy, and candidates must meet all of the admission criteria. For further information, write to the Oppenheimer Scholarship Program, Office of Admission, Culver Military Academy, Winter School, Culver, Indiana 46511.

Educational benefits are also available for persons in the Selected Reserves. Eligibility requirements include a service commitment for at least 6 years and a high school diploma; also, the applicant must not already have a bachelor's degree. Education benefits are payable for up to 36 months.

Financial Assistance Programs for Veterans

Montgomery GI Bill This federal program provides financial assistance to all military personnel who joined one of the Armed Services after June 30, 1985. Under the terms of the program, the government contributes to the serviceperson's education fund $275 a month after 2 years of service and $350 a month after 3 years of service. For some military persons their college fund can exceed $10,000. For further information, contact your local recruiter, base education officer, or local Veterans Administration Office.

Veterans Administration Vocational Rehabilitation and Counseling Service The Veterans Administra-

tion provides counseling services and financial assistance to veterans who were disabled during active service and were honorably discharged. Financial aid can cover the cost of tuition, books, and fees. Contact the Veterans Administration Office in your state for specific details.

Veterans' Educational Assistance Program (VEAP) This federal program provides financial assistance to all military personnel who joined one of the Armed Services between January 1, 1977, and July 1, 1985. Under the terms of the program, the serviceperson contributes $25 to $100 monthly to an education fund, and the government doubles the contribution at a rate of $2 for every $1. For further information, contact your local recruiter, military base education officer, or local Veterans Administration.

Financial Assistance Programs for the Dependents of Veterans

Air Force Sergeants Association Scholarship Program This program provides scholarship assistance to the dependent children of veterans who served in the Air Force, Air National Guard, and Air Force Reserves. The awards are based upon academic merit and financial need. Write to the Air Force Sergeants Scholarship Program, P.O. Box 50, Temple Hills, Maryland 20748-0050.

American Legion Auxiliary National President's Scholarship Program The National Organization of the American Legion Auxiliary awards scholarships each year to the children of veterans. Contact the local unit of the American Legion Auxiliary for further information.

AMVETS National Memorial Scholarship Program This program provides scholarships for dependent children of veterans. Four-year scholarships are awarded to high school seniors who are entering a 4-year college or university; Junior college scholarships, to high school seniors who are entering a 2-year course of study. Continuing scholarships are offered to students completing a 2-year course of study and planning to continue their education. Recipients must be U.S. citizens. The awards are based upon financial need and academic merit. For application forms, write to AMVETS National Service Headquarters, 4647 Forbes Boulevard, Lanham, Maryland 20706-9961.

Daughters of the Cincinnati Scholarship Program This program provides scholarship assistance to the children of Regular Army, Navy, Air Force, Marine Corps, or Coast Guard commissioned officers. For further information and application forms, write to the Daughters of the Cincinnati Scholarship Program, Scholarship Administrator, 122 E. 58th Street, New York, New York 10022.

Disabled American Veterans Scholarship Program This program provides scholarship assistance to the children of disabled veterans whose disabilities are service-related. Awards are based upon academic merit and financial need. For further information on eligibility, write to the Scholarship Program, Disabled American Veterans, P.O. Box 14301, Cincinnati, Ohio 45250-0301.

Federal Benefits Veterans Administration Dependents Education Assistance Act Federal law provides financial assistance to the dependent children and spouses of veterans who have died or who are totally disabled as a result of service-related injuries, as well as to the spouses and children of living veterans. Survivors of deceased veterans, spouses of living veterans, and children between the ages of 18 and 26 are eligible for benefits. For application forms, contact any Veterans Administration office, or the American embassy in a foreign country. For further information, write to the Division of Student Services and Veterans Programs, 400 Maryland Avenue, S.W., Room 4010, Washington, D.C. 20202.

Knights of Columbus Educational Trust Fund The Knights of Columbus Supreme Council offers financial assistance to the children of veterans who were killed in action or permanently disabled as a result of military service. For further information, write to the Director of Scholarship Aid, Knights of Columbus, P.O. Box 1670, New Haven, Connecticut 06507.

Noncommissioned Officers Association Scholarship Foundation This organization awards renewable scholarships to the children of noncommissioned officers who are members of the association. For further information, write to the NCOA Scholarship Foundation, P.O. Box 33610, San Antonio, Texas 78265.

Retired Officers Association Scholarship Loan Program This organization awards financial assistance to the children of active duty or retired members of the uniformed services. Awards are made for up to 5 years of full-time undergraduate study at accredited colleges or technical schools. For applications, write to the Administrator, TROA Scholarship Loan Program, 201 North Washington Street, Alexandria, Virginia 22314-2529.

The following is a list of state programs for veterans and military personnel and the regional Veterans Administration Centers that can provide information on all programs for veterans for their dependents:

Alabama

1425 S. 21st Street
Suite 108
Birmingham, Alabama 35205
(205) 933-0500

110 Marine Street
Mobile, Alabama 36604
(205) 694-4194

474 S. Court Street
Montgomery, Alabama 36104
(205) 262-7781

State Programs

Alabama GI and Dependents Educational Benefit
Program

Alabama National Guard Educational Assistance
Program

Alaska

4201 Tudor Centre Drive
Suite 115
Anchorage, Alaska 99508
(907) 271-3063

235 E. Eighth Avenue
Anchorage, Alaska 99501
(907) 279-6116

712 10th Avenue
Fairbanks, Alaska 99701
(907) 456-4208

905 Cook Street
P.O. Box 1883
Kenai, Alaska 99611
(907) 283-5205

1075 Check Street
Suite 111
Wasilia, Alaska 99687
(907) 376-4308

State Programs

Dependents of POWs and MIAs Benefits Program

Arizona

807 N. Third Street
Phoenix, Arizona 85004
(602) 261-4769

3225 N. Central Avenue
Phoenix, Arizona 85012
(602) 263-5411

637 Hillside Avenue
Suite A
Prescott, Arizona 86301
(602) 778-3469

727 N. Swan
Tucson, Arizona 85711
(602) 323-3271

Arkansas

1311 W. Second Street
Little Rock, Arkansas 72201
(501) 378-6395

132

P.O. Box 1280
Little Rock, Arkansas 72215
(501) 370-3800

State Programs

Benefits for Dependents of POWs and MIAs Program

California

859 S. Harbor Boulevard
Anaheim, California 92805
(714) 776-0161

1899 Clayton Road
Suite 140
Concord, California 94520
(415) 680-4526

157 E. Valley Parkway
Escondido, California 92025
(619) 747-7305

305 "V" Street
Eureka, California 95501
(707) 444-8271

1340 Van Ness Avenue
Fresno, California 93721
(209) 487-5660

251 W. 85th Place
Los Angeles, California 90003
(213) 753-1391

2000 Westwood Boulevard
Los Angeles, California 90025
(213) 475-9509

11000 Wilshire Boulevard
Los Angeles, California 90024
(213) 879-1303

455 Reservation Road
Suite E
Marina, California 93933
(408) 384-1660

709 W. Beverly Boulevard
Montebello, California 90640
(213) 728-9966

287 17th Street
Oakland, California 94612
(415) 763-3904

4954 Arlington Avenue
Suite A
Riverside, California 92504
(714) 359-8967

1111 Howe Avenue
Suite 390
Sacramento, California 95828
(916) 978-5477

2900 Sixth Avenue
San Diego, California 92103
(619) 294-2040

2022 Camino Del Rio North
San Diego, California 92108
(714) 297-8220

25 Van Ness Avenue
San Francisco, California 94102
(415) 431-6021

211 Main Street
San Francisco, California 94105
(415) 495-8900

967 West Hedding
San Jose, California 95126
(408) 249-1643

32 W. 25th Avenue
#202
San Mateo, California 94403
(415) 570-5918

1300 Santa Barbara Street
Santa Barbara, California 93101
(805) 564-2345

16126 Lassen
Sepulveda, California 91343
(818) 892-9227

313 N. Mountain Avenue
Upland, California 91786
(714) 982-0146

State Programs

Children and Unremarried Widows of Veterans
    Benefits Program

Children of Veterans Benefits Program

Colorado

207 Canyon Boulevard
Suite 201A
Boulder, Colorado 80302
(303) 440-7306

411 S. Tejon
Suite G
Colorado Springs, Colorado 80903
(303) 471-9992

1820 Gilpin Street
Denver, Colorado 80218
(303) 861-9281

44 Union Boulevard
Denver, Colorado 80225
(303) 980-1300

State Programs

Colorado Veterans Tuition Assistance Program

Dependents of POWs and MIAs Benefits Program

Connecticut

370 Market Street
Hartford, Connecticut 06120
(203) 240-3543

450 Main Street
Hartford, Connecticut 06103
(203) 278-3230

562 Whalley Avenue
New Haven, Connecticut 06511
(203) 773-2232/6

16 Franklin Street
Room 109
Norwich, Connecticut 06360
(203) 887-1755

State Programs

Aid to Dependents of Deceased/Disabled MIA
Veterans Program

Children of Veterans Benefits Program

Veterans Tuition Waiver Program

Delaware

VA Medical Center Building 2
1601 Kirkwood Highway
Wilmington, Delaware 19805
(302) 994-2878

State Programs

Educational Benefits for Children of Deceased
Military Program

District of Columbia

737½ Eighth Street, S.E.
Washington, D.C. 20003
(202) 745-8400

941 N. Capitol Street, N.E.
Washington, D.C. 20421
(202) 872-1151

State Programs

Children of Veterans Scholarship Program

Florida

400 E. Prospect Road
Fort Lauderdale, Florida 33334
(305) 563-2992/3

255 Liberty Street
Jacksonville, Florida 32202
(904) 791-3621

311 W. Monroe Street
Jacksonville, Florida 32202
(904) 356-1581

2311 10th Avenue, North #13
Lake Worth, Florida 33461
(305) 585-1766

412 N.E. 39th Street
Miami, Florida 33137
(305) 573-8830

Federal Office Building, Room 100
Miami, Florida 33130
(305) 358-0669

5001 S. Orange Avenue
Suite A
Orlando, Florida 32809
(305) 648-6151

15 W. Strong Street
Suite 100 C
Pensacola, Florida 32501
(904) 479-6665

1800 Siesta Drive
Sarasota, Florida 33579
(813) 952-9406

235 31st Street, North
St. Petersburg, Florida 33713
(813) 327-3355

144 First Avenue, South
St. Petersburg, Florida 33731
(813) 898-2121

249 E. Sixth Avenue
Tallahassee, Florida, 32303
(904) 681-7172

1507 W. Slight Avenue
Tampa, Florida 33604
(813) 228-2621

State Programs

Children of Deceased or Disabled Veterans Education
Scholarship Program

Georgia

922 W. Peachtree Street
Atlanta, Georgia 30309
(404) 347-7264

8110 White Bluff Road
Savannah, Georgia 31406
(912) 927-7360

State Programs

Georgia Military Scholarship Program

Hawaii

1370 Kapiolani Boulevard
Suite 201
Honolulu, Hawaii 96814
(808) 541-1764

300 Ala Moana Boulevard
Honolulu, Hawaii 96850
(808) 541-1560

State Programs

Hawaii Veterans Memorial Fund Program

National Guard and Reserve Tuition Waiver Program

Vietnam Veterans Tuition Waiver Program

Idaho

103 W. State Street
Boise, Idaho 83702
(208) 232-0316

550 W. Fort Street, Box 044
Boise, Idaho 83724
(208) 334-1010

1975 S. Fifth Street
Pocatello, Idaho 83201
(208) 232-0316

State Programs

Children of POWs and MIAs Benefits Program

Illinois

547 W. Roosevelt Road
Chicago, Illinois 60607
(312) 829-4400/1

1607 W. Howard Street
#200
Chicago, Illinois 60626
(312) 764-6595

536 S. Clark Street
Chicago, Illinois 60680
(312) 663-5510

1600 Halsted Street
Chicago Heights, Illinois 60411
(312) 754-0340

1269 N. 89th Street
East St. Louis, Illinois 62203
(618) 397-6602

1529 Sixth Avenue #6
Moline, Illinois 61265
(309) 762-6954

155 S. Oak Park Avenue
Oak Park, Illinois 60302
(312) 383-3255/6

605 N.E. Monroe Street
Peoria, Illinois 61603
(309) 761-7300

624 S. Fourth Street
Springfield, Illinois 62702
(217) 492-4955

State Programs

Benefits for Children of Deceased or Disabled
Veterans Program

Benefits for Children of Veterans Program

Illinois National Guard and Naval Militia Members
Scholarship Program

Illinois National Guard "Split-Training" Program

Illinois Scholarships for Veterans Program

MIA/POW Scholarship Program

Indiana

101 N. Kentucky Avenue
Evansville, Indiana 47711
(812) 425-0311

528 W. Berry Street
Fort Wayne, Indiana 46802
(219) 423-9456

2236 W. Ridge Road
Gary, Indiana 46408
(219) 887-0048

811 Massachusetts Avenue
Indianapolis, Indiana 46204
(317) 269-2838

575 N. Pennsylvania Avenue
Indianapolis, Indiana 46204
(317) 269-5566

State Programs

Benefits for Children of POWs or MIAs Program

Benefits for Children of Veterans Program

Iowa

3619 Sixth Avenue
Des Moines, Iowa 50313
(515) 384-4929

210 Walnut Street
Des Moines, Iowa 50309
(515) 284-0219

706 Jackson
Sioux City, Iowa 51101
(712) 233-2300

State Programs

War Orphans Educational Aid Program

Kansas

413 S. Pattie
Wichita, Kansas 67211
(316) 265-3260

901 George Washington Boulevard
Wichita, Kansas 67211
(316) 264-9123

State Programs

Children of Deceased Veterans and of POWs and
MIAs Benefits Program

Kentucky

1117 Limestone Road
Lexington, Kentucky 40503
(606) 276-5269

736 S. First Street
Louisville, Kentucky 40202
(502) 589-1981

600 Federal Place
Louisville, Kentucky 40202
(502) 584-2231

State Programs

Dependents of Permanently Disabled National
Guardsmen, War Veterans, POWs, or MIAs
Benefits Program

Dependents, Widows, or Widowers of Service
Personnel or National Guardsmen Killed While
in Service or Deceased as a Result of Service-
Connected Disability Benefits Program

Louisiana

2103 Old Minden Road
Bossier City, Lousiana 71112
(318) 742-2733

1529 N. Claiborne Avenue
New Orleans, Louisiana 70116
(504) 943-8386

701 Loyola Avenue
New Orleans, Louisiana 70113
(504) 561-0121

510 E. Stoner Avenue
Shreveport, Louisiana 71130
(318) 424-8442

State Programs

Veterans Affairs Scholarship Program

Maine

352 Harlow Street
Bangor, Maine 04401
(207) 947-3391/2

175 Lancaster Street
Room 213
Portland, Maine 04101
(207) 775-6391

VA Medical and Regional Office Center
Togus, Maine 04330
(207) 623-8000

State Programs

State Scholarships for Spouses and War Orphans of
Veterans Program

Maryland

777 Washington Boulevard
Baltimore, Maryland 21230
(301) 539-0171

31 Hopkins Plaza
Baltimore, Maryland 21201
(301) 685-5454

7 Elkton Commercial Plaza
S. Bridge Street
Elkton, Maryland 21921
(301) 398-0171

1015 Spring Street
Suite 101
Silver Spring, Maryland 20910
(202) 745-8411

State Programs

MIA/POW Veterans Grants Program

Massachusetts

800 N. Main Street
Avon, Massachusetts 02322
(508) 580-2730

480 Tremont Street
Boston, Massachusetts 02116
(617) 451-0171

Government Center
Boston, Massachusetts 02203
(617) 227-4600

71 Washington Street
Brighton, Massachusetts 02135
(617) 782-1013

73 E. Merrimack Street
Lowell, Massachusetts 01852
(508) 453-1151

181 Hillman Street
Room 110
New Bedford, Massachusetts 02740
(508) 999-6920

1200 Main Street
Springfield, Massachusetts 01103
(413) 785-5343

8 Worcester Street
West Boylston, Massachusetts 01583
(508) 835-2709

State Programs

Financial Aid for Vietnam Veterans Program

Veterans' Children Benefits Program

Michigan

477 Michigan Avenue
Detroit, Michigan 48226
(313) 964-5110

1940 Eastern Avenue, S.E.
Grand Rapids, Michigan 49507
(616) 243-0385

1766 Fort Street
Lincoln Park, Michigan 48146
(313) 381-1370

20820 Greenfield Road
Oakpark, Michigan 48237
(313) 967-0040/1

State Programs

Children of Veterans Scholarship Program

Minnesota

405 E. Superior Street
Duluth, Minnesota 55802
(218) 722-8654

2480 University Avenue
St. Paul, Minnesota 55114
(612) 644-4022

Federal Building, Fort Snelling
St. Paul, Minnesota 55111
(612) 726-1454

State Programs

Educational Assistance for Veterans Program

Veterans Dependents Student Assistance Program

War Orphans Educational Assistance Program

Mississippi

121 W. Jackson Street
Biloxi, Mississippi 39530
(601) 435-5414

158 E. Pascagoula Street
Jackson, Mississippi 39201
(601) 353-4912

100 W. Capitol Street
Jackson, Mississippi 39269
(601) 965-4873

State Programs

Vietnam POW/MIA Dependents Program

Missouri

3931 Main Street
Kansas City, Missouri 64111
(816) 753-1866

601 E. 12th Street
Kansas City, Missouri 64106

2345 Pine Street
St. Louis, Missouri 63103
(314) 231-1260

1520 Market Street
St. Louis, Missouri 63103
(314) 342-1171

Montana

415 N. 33rd Street
Billings, Montana 59101
(406) 657-6071

VA Medical and Regional Office Center
Fort Harrison, Montana 59636
(406) 442-6839

929 S.W. Higgins Street
Missoula, Montana 59803
(406) 721-4918/9

State Programs

Dependents of POWs and MIAs Benefits Program

Honorable Discharged Veterans Fee Waiver Program

War Orphans Benefits Program

Nebraska

920 L Street
Lincoln, Nebraska 68508
(402) 476-9736

100 Centennial Mall, North
Lincoln, Nebraska 68508
(402) 471-5001

5123 Leavenworth Street
Omaha, Nebraska 68106
(402) 553-2068

State Programs

Vietnam Veterans Educational Benefits Program

Nevada

704 S. Sixth Street
Las Vegas, Nevada 90101
(702) 388-6368

1155 W. Fourth Street
Suite 101
Reno, Nevada 89503
(702) 323-1294

1201 Terminal Way
Reno, Nevada 89520
(702) 329-9244

State Programs

Military Personnel Scholarship Program

New Hampshire

103 Liberty Street
Manchester, New Hampshire 03104
(603) 668-7060

275 Chestnut Street
Manchester, New Hampshire 03101
(603) 666-7785

State Programs

Children of POWs and MIAs Benefits Program

Scholarships for Orphans of Veterans Program

New Jersey

626 Newark Avenue
Jersey City, New Jersey 07306
(201) 656-6986

327 Central Avenue
Linwood, New Jersey 08221
(609) 927-8387

75 Halsey Street
Newark, New Jersey 07102
(201) 622-6940

20 Washington Place
Newark, New Jersey 07102
(201) 645-2150

318 E. State Street
Trenton, New Jersey 08608
(609) 989-2260/1

State Programs

MIA/POW Program

Vietnam Veterans Tuition Aid Program

New Mexico

4603 Fourth Street, N.W.
Albuquerque, New Mexico 87107
(505) 345-8366/9976

500 Gold Avenue, S.W.
Albuquerque, New Mexico 87102
(505) 766-3361

211 W. Mesa
Gallup, New Mexico 87301
(505) 722-3821/2

1996 St. Michael's Drive
Warner Plaza, Suite 5
Santa Fe, New Mexico 87501
(505) 988-6562

State Programs

Benefits for Children of Deceased Members of New Mexico National Guard Program

Benefits for Veterans Children Program

New York

875 Central Avenue
Albany, New York 12206
(518) 438-2508

Clinton Avenue and N. Pearl Street
Albany, New York 12207
(800) 442-5882

116 W. Main Street
Babylon, New York 11702
(516) 661-3930

226 E. Fordham Road
Rooms 216, 217
Bronx, New York 10458
(212) 367-3500/1

165 Cadman Plaza, East
Brooklyn, New York 11201
(718) 330-2825/6

351 Linwood Avenue
Buffalo, New York 14209
(716) 882-0505

111 W. Huron Street
Buffalo, New York 14202
(716) 846-5191

45-20 83rd Street
Elmhurst, New York 11373
(718) 446-8233/4

166 W. 75th Street
New York, New York 10023
(212) 944-2917

252 Seventh Avenue at 24th Street
New York, New York 10001
(212) 620-6901

294 S. Plymouth Avenue
Rochester, New York 14608
(716) 263-5710

100 State Street
Rochester, New York 14614
(716) 232-5290

210 N. Townsend Street
Syracuse, New York 13203
(315) 423-5690

100 S. Clinton Street
Syracuse, New York 13260
(315) 476-5544

200 Hamilton Avenue
White Plains Mall
White Plains, New York 10601
(914) 684-0570

State Programs

Regents Grants for Children of Deceased or Disabled
  Veterans Program

Vietnam Veteran Tuition Program

North Carolina

223 S. Brevard Street
Suite 103
Charlotte, North Carolina 28202
(704) 333-6107

4 Market Square
Fayetteville, North Carolina 28301
(919) 323-4908

2009 Elm-Eugene Street
Greensboro, North Carolina 27406
(919) 333-5366

150 Arlington Blvd.
Suite B
Greenville, North Carolina 27834
(919) 355-7920

251 N. Main Street
Winston-Salem, North Carolina 27155
(919) 748-1800

State Programs

North Carolina National Guard Tuition Assistance
  Program

North Carolina Scholarships for Children of Veterans
  Program

North Dakota

1322 Gateway Drive
Fargo, North Dakota 59103
(701) 237-0942

655 First Avenue, North
Fargo, North Dakota 58102
(701) 293-3656

108 E. Burdick Expressway
Minot, North Dakota 58701
(701) 852-0177

State Programs

Benefits for Children of Veterans Program

Loans to Veterans Program

Ohio

550 Main Street
Cincinnati, Ohio 45202
(513) 579-0505

30 E. Hollister Street
Cincinnati, Ohio 44118
(513) 569-7140

2134 Lee Road
Cleveland, Ohio 44118
(216) 932-8471

11511 Lorain Avenue
Cleveland, Ohio 44411
(216) 671-8530

1240 E. Ninth Street
Cleveland, Ohio 44199
(216) 621-5050

1054 E. Broad Street
Columbus, Ohio 43205
(614) 253-3500

200 N. High Street
Columbus, Ohio 43215
(614) 224-8872

519 Hunter Avenue
Dayton, Ohio 45404
(513) 461-9150/1

State Programs

Ohio National Guard Tuition Grants Program War

Orphans Scholarship Program

Oklahoma

125 S. Main Street
Muskogee, Oklahoma 74401
(918) 687-2500

3033 N. Walnut
Suite 101W
Oklahoma City, Oklahoma 73105
(405) 270-5184

200 N.W. Fifth Street
Oklahoma City, Oklahoma 73102
(405) 235-2641

1855 E. 15th Street
Tulsa, Oklahoma 74104
(918) 581-7105

Oregon

1966 Garden Avenue
Eugene, Oregon 97403
(503) 687-6918

615 N.W. Fifth Street
Grants Pass, Oregon 95726
(503) 479-6912

2450 S.E. Belmont
Portland, Oregon 97214
(503) 231-1586

2009 State Street
Salem, Oregon 97301
(503) 362-9911

Pennsylvania

G. Daniel Baldwin Building
1000 State Street
Suites 1 and 2
Erie, Pennsylvania 16501
(814) 453-7955

1007 N. Front Street
Harrisburg, Pennsylvania 17102
(717) 782-3954

5000 Walnut Street
McKeesport, Pennsylvania 15132
(412) 678-7704

1026 Arch Street
Philadelphia, Pennsylvania 19107
(215) 627-4670

5601 N. Broad Street
Room 204
Philadelphia, Pennsylvania 19141
(215) 924-4670

954 Pennsylvania Avenue
Pittsburgh, Pennsylvania 15222
(412) 765-1193

1000 Liberty Avenue
Pittsburgh, Pennsylvania 15222
(412) 281-4233

959 Wyoming Avenue
Scranton, Pennsylvania 18509
(717) 344-2676

19-27 N. Main Street
Wilkes-Barre, Pennsylvania 18701
(717) 824-4636

State Programs

Children of Veterans Scholarship Program

Veterans State Grant Program

State Grant for Dependents of POWs or MIAs
  Program

Puerto Rico

52 Gonzalo Marin Street
Arecibo, Puerto Rico 00612
(809) 879-4510

35 Mayor Street
Ponce, Puerto Rico 00731
(809) 840-4078

Suite LC 8A and LC 9
Condomino Med.
Center Plaza
La Riviera
Rio Piedras, Puerto Rico 00928
(809) 783-8794

GPO Box 4867
San Juan, Puerto Rico 00936
(809) 753-4141

Rhode Island

172 Pine Street
Pawtucket, Rhode Island 02860
(401) 728-9501

380 Westminister Mall
Providence, Rhode Island 02903
(401) 273-4910

South Carolina

1313 Elmwood Avenue
Columbia, South Carolina 29201
(803) 765-9944

1801 Assembly Street
Columbia, South Carolina 29201
(803) 765-5861

904 Pendleton Street
Greenville, South Carolina 29601
(803) 271-2711

3366 Rivers Avenue
North Charleston, South Carolina 29405
(803) 747-8387

State Programs

Benefits for Children of Veterans Program

South Dakota

610 Kansas City Street
Rapid City, South Dakota 57701
(605) 348-0077

115 North Dakota Street
Sioux Falls, South Dakota 57102
(605) 332-0856

2501 W. 22nd Street
Sioux Falls, South Dakota 57117
(605) 336-3496

State Programs

Benefits for Veterans of Armed Services Program

Dependents of POWs and MIAs Benefits Program

National Guard Tuition Program

Tennessee

2 Northgate Park
Suite 108
Chattanooga, Tennessee 37415
(615) 875-5114

703 S. Rogan Street
Johnson City, Tennessee 37601
(615) 928-8387

1515 E. Magnolia Avenue
Suite 201
Knoxville, Tennessee 37917
(615) 971-5866

1 N. Third Street
Memphis, Tennessee 38103
(901) 521-3506

110 Ninth Avenue, South
Nashville, Tennessee 37203
(615) 736-5251

State Programs

Benefits for Children of Veterans Program

Texas

2900 W. Tenth Street
Amarillo, Texas 79106
(806) 376-2127

3401 Manor Road
Suite 102
Austin, Texas 78723
(512) 476/0607/8

3134 Reid Drive
Corpus Christi, Texas 78404
(512) 888-3101

5415 Maple Avenue
Suite 114
Dallas, Texas 75235
(214) 634-7024

1100 Commerce Street
Dallas, Texas 75242
(214) 824-5440

2121 Wyoming Street
El Paso, Texas 79903
(915) 542-2851/2/3

1305 W. Magnolia
Suite B
Fort Worth, Texas 76104
(817) 921-3733

8100 Washington Avenue
Suite 120
Houston, Texas 77007
(713) 880-8387

4905A San Jacinto Street
Houston, Texas 77004
(713) 522-5354

2515 Murworth Drive
Houston, Texas 77054
(713) 664-4664

717 Corpus Christi
Laredo, Texas 78040
(512) 723-4680

3208 34th Street
Lubbock, Texas 79410
(806) 743-7551

1205 Texas Avenue
Lubbock, Texas 79401
(806) 743-7219

1130 Pecan
Suite G
McAllen, Texas 78501
(512) 631-2147

3404 W. Illinois
Suite 1
Midland, Texas 79703
(915) 697-8222

107 Lexington Avenue
San Antonio, Texas 78205
(512) 299-4025

1916 Fredericksburg Road
San Antonio, Texas 78201
(512) 229-4120

307 Dwyer Avenue
San Antonio, Texas 78285
(512) 226-7661

1400 N. Valley Mills Drive
Waco, Texas 76799
(817) 772-3060

State Programs

Benefits for Children of POWs and MIAs Program

Benefits for Veterans and Dependents Program

Tuition Scholarships for Armed Forces Members
Stationed in Texas

Utah

750 N. 200 West
Suite 105
Provo, Utah 84601
(801) 377-1117

1354 E. 3300, South
Salt Lake City, Utah 84106
(801) 584-1294

125 S. State Street
Salt Lake City, Utah 84147
(801) 524-5960

Vermont

359 Dorset Street
South Burlington, Vermont 05401
(802) 862-1806

Building #2
Gilman Office Center
Holiday Inn Drive
White River Junction, Vermont 05001
(802) 295-2908

VA Medical and Regional Office Center
White River Junction, Vermont 05001
(802) 295-2582

Virgin Islands

United Shopping Plaza
Suite 4 Christiansted
St. Croix, U.S. Virgin Islands 00820
(809) 778-5553

Havensight Mall
St. Thomas, U.S. Virgin Islands 00801
(809) 774-6674

Virginia

7450½ Tidewater Drive
Norfolk, Virginia 23505
(804) 587-1338

Box 83
1030 W. Franklin Street
Richmond, Virginia 23220
(804) 353-8958

320 Mountain Avenue, S.W.
Roanoke, Virginia 24014
(703) 342-9726

210 Franklin Road, S.W.
Roanoke, Virginia 24011
(703) 982-6440

7024 Spring Garden Drive
Brookfield Plaza
Springfield, Virginia 22150
(703) 866-0924

State Programs

Veterans Children Scholarship Program

Washington

1322 E. Pike Street
Seattle, Washington 98122
(206) 442-2706

915 Second Avenue
Seattle, Washington 98174
(206) 624-7200

N. 1611 Division Street
Spokane, Washington 99203
(509) 327-0274

4801 Pacific Avenue
Tacoma, Washington 98408
(206) 473-0731/2

West Virginia

1591 Washington Street, East
Charleston, West Virginia 25301
(304) 343-3825

1014 Sixth Avenue
Huntington, West Virginia 25701
(304) 523-8387

218 W. King Street
Martinsburg, West Virginia 25401
(304) 263-6776

1191 Pineview Drive
Morgantown, West Virginia 26505
(304) 291-4001/2

State Programs

War Orphans Education Program

Wisconsin

147 S. Butler Street
Madison, Wisconsin 53703
(608) 264-5342/3

3400 Wisconsin Avenue
Milwaukee, Wisconsin 53208
(414) 344-5504

5000 W. National Avenue
Milwaukee, Wisconsin 53295
(414) 383-8680

State Programs

Vietnam War Orphans Educational Grant Program

Wisconsin National Guard Tuition Grant Program

Wisconsin Veterans Educational Loan Program

Wisconsin Veterans Full-time Study Grant Program

Wisconsin Veterans Part-time Study Grant Program

Wyoming

641 E. Second Street
Casper, Wyoming 82601
(307) 235-8010

3130 Henderson Drive
Cheyenne, Wyoming 82001
(307) 778-2660

2360 E. Pershing Boulevard
Cheyenne, Wyoming 82001
(307) 778-7396

State Programs

Benefits for Children of POWs and MIAs Program

Wyoming National Guard Educational Assistance
   Program

Publications

Many excellent publications provide information on programs offered by the Armed Services and Veterans Administration. The following should be used to obtain further information:

Army ROTC Scholarship Program Army ROTC Department of Military Science, 73 Harmon Gym, University of California, Berkeley, Berkeley, California 94720. Free.

Federal Benefits for Veterans and Dependents Veterans Administration, Government Printing Office, Washington, D.C. 20402.

Financial Aid for Veterans, Military Personnel, and Their Dependents Reference Service Press, 1100 Industrial Road, Suite 9, San Carlos, California 94070.

How the Military Will Help You Pay for College Don M. Betterton, P.O. Box 2123, Princeton, New Jersey 08543-2123.

Need a Lift? The American Legion, P.O. Box 1055, Indianapolis, Indiana 46206.

Scholarship Pamphlet for USN-USM-USCG Dependent Children Naval Military Personnel Command, NMPC-121D, Navy Department, Washington, D.C. 20370-5121. Free.

Note: For publications not identified as free, there is a charge. Write to the publisher for the cost of any publication in which you are interested.

Some Final Notes on Military and Veterans Programs

1. Many educational benefits are offered by the military. Consider all options in calculating your long-term career and educational objectives.

2. The chapter on State Programs provides specific state programs for military personnel, veterans, and dependents.

3. Recently Congress created a cabinet department for veterans affairs and passed legislation to raise disability benefits and establish a new federal court where veterans can appeal denials of benefits. This Department of Veterans Affairs may alter some of the regulations currently followed in administering programs for veterans. For further information, contact your local Veterans Administration office.

4. The military offers a series of examinations that can help servicepersons to receive credit for life experiences. Ask for information on DANTES (Defense Activity for Nontraditional Educational Support). DANTES also offers correspondence courses and certificate programs that range from the high school level through postgraduate study.

5. Servicemembers Opportunity Colleges is a network of colleges and universities that, recognizing the special needs of military personnel, provide flexible programs for servicepersons. For example, participating institutions will schedule classes around off-duty hours. Flexible transfer policies and residency requirements are other accommodating features of Servicemembers Opportunity Colleges. For further information, contact your base education officer.

6. Reservists called to active duty during the Gulf War should check with their National Guard Units for information on their educational benefits.

13 PROGRAMS FOR MINORITY STUDENTS

Undergraduate minority students may apply for the five federal financial assistance programs. Minority graduate and professional school students are eligible to apply for all financial assistance programs offered specifically for graduate and professional students. In addition to these programs, many states have specific funding programs for minority students, as do many colleges and universities. Minority students needing financial aid to attend school may also seek assistance from private foundations, organizations, and churches.

A Partial List of Financial Assistance Programs for Minority Students Enrolled in Undergraduate and Graduate Programs

American Fund for Dental Health   This organization provides scholarships to qualified black, Native American, Mexican American, and Puerto Rican dental students. Recipients must be U.S. citizens. The scholarships, based upon academic merit, demonstrated financial need, and commitment to dentistry, may be renewed for a second year. For further information, write the American Fund for Dental Health, 211 E. Chicago Avenue, Suite 820, Chicago, Illinois 60611, or call (312) 787-6270.

American Indian Scholarships, Inc.   This scholarship program assists Native American students who are enrolled in graduate programs. The amount of the award is based upon unmet need. For further information write to American Indian Scholarships, Inc., 4520 Montgomery Boulevard, N.E., Albuquerque, New Mexico 87109.

American Institute of Certified Public Accountants This organization provides scholarships to undergraduate minority accounting majors. To be eligible for the scholarship, minority students must be citizens of the United States and must be enrolled in an undergraduate accounting program. For further information, write to the Manager, Minority Recruitment, American Institute of Certified Public Accountants, 1211 Avenue of the Americas, New York, New York 10036-3775. Application deadlines are July 1 and December 1.

American Political Science Association   This organization provides fellowships to black, Latino, and Chicano students who are accepted for enrollment in graduate programs in political science. Contact the American Political Science Association, 1527 New Hampshire Avenue, N.W., Washington, D.C. 20036, for further information.

American Psychological Association Minority Fellowship Program   This organization provides fellowship assistance to U.S. citizens and permanent residents who are black, Hispanic, or Native American, or who are of Japanese, Chinese, Korean, Filipino, Samoan, or Guamanian extraction. Recipients must demonstrate a commitment to a career in mental health, research, or service for ethnic and minority groups. Students enrolled in graduate programs leading to doctoral degrees in psychology are eligible to apply. The criteria for selection include academic ability and motivation. For further information, write to the American Psychological Association Minority Fellowship Program, 1200 17th Street, N.W., Washington, D.C. 20036.

American Sociological Association   This organization sponsors a fellowship program for minority students pursuing doctoral degrees in sociology. For further information and application forms, write to the Minority Fellowship Program, American Sociological Association, 1722 N Street, N.W., Washington, D.C. 20036-2981.

Association of University Programs in Health Administration   This organization offers internship programs to qualified black, Native American, Asian American, Mexican American, and Puerto Rican students. Recipients must be either second- or third-year undergraduate students. Academic ability is considered in awarding the internship. For further information, write to the Association of University Programs in Health Administration, 1911 N. Fort Myer Drive, Arlington, Virginia 22209.

Bureau of Indian Affairs Higher Education Grant Program This program provides financial aid to eligible Native American students. The awards are based upon financial need. For further information, write to the Bureau of Indian Affairs Higher Education Grant Program, Bureau of Indian Affairs, 18th and C Streets, N.W., Washington, D.C. 20245.

California State University Loan Forgiveness Program This program provides financial assistance to minority students pursuing doctoral degrees. Students selected for the program are eligible to receive loans of up to $10,000 per year for a maximum of 3 years. Recipients must agree to teach for 5 years at one of the state universities. Loans are forgiven at the rate of 20% a year for up to 5 years as long as the borrower teaches in a California state university. Contact the California Student Aid Commission, P.O. Box 942845, Sacramento, California 94245-0845, for further information.

Congressional Hispanic Caucus This organization provides fellowships to qualified Hispanic students to work with members of Congress. The fellowships are for one academic term. For further information on this program, contact the Congressional Hispanic Caucus, 504 C Street, N.E., Washington, D.C. 20002.

Consortium for Graduate Study in Management Fellowships for Minorities This organization provides financial assistance to qualified black, Chicano, American Indian, Cuban, or Puerto Rican students. The purpose of the program is to encourage minorities to pursue careers in business. The scholarships cover tuition expenses and provide a living stipend. For further information and application forms, write to the Consortium for Graduate Study in Management, 200 S. Hanley Road, St. Louis, Missouri 03100.

Council for Opportunity in Graduate Management Education This organization provides fellowship support to qualified minority students for the purpose of promoting minorities into managerial positions in organizations. The fellowships can be used only at certain graduate schools. For further information, write to COGME Fellowship Program, General Plaza, 675 Massachusetts Avenue, Cambridge, Massachusetts 02139.

Florida Atlantic University This public university offers free tuition to every black freshman it admits. Admission to the university requires a 3.0 grade point average from high school and an average SAT score of 1000. Out-of-state students may apply for the program, but preference is given to state residents. For further information, call (305) 393-3530.

Ford Foundation The National Research Council awards Ford Foundation postdoctoral fellowships to qualified minority students. Recipients are selected from scientists, engineers, and scholars in the humanities who are U.S. citizens and members of a minority group and who are preparing for or are already engaged in college or university teaching. For application materials, write to the Fellowship Office, GR 420AQ, National Research Council, 2101 Constitution Avenue, Washington, D.C. 20418.

General Electric Foundation This organization provides funding for black, Hispanic, and Native American students who are enrolled in a 2-year or community college and who plan to transfer to a 4-year institution and major in engineering or business administration. Certain students at historically black colleges may also be eligible for this program. To be considered for the scholarship, candidates must be completing their second year of college, have a grade point average of at least 3.0, and be nominated by an official of their school. Financial need is also taken into account. Awards are renewable. Nominations should be made by November 15. For further information, write to the College Scholarship Service, The College Board, 45 Columbus Avenue, New York, New York 10023-6992, or call (212) 713-8000.

General Motors Scholarship Program The GM Corporation provides scholarship assistance to qualified minority undergraduate students through several colleges and universities throughout the United States. For more information, write to the General Motors Scholarship Program, c/o General Motors Corporation, 8-163 General Motors Building, Detroit, Michigan 48202.

Graduate Engineering for Minorities The National Consortium for Graduate Degrees for Minorities in Engineering, Inc., awards fellowships to black, American Indian, Mexican American, and Puerto Rican students to encourage advanced study in engineering. Students may apply beginning in their junior year in college. Participants receive fellowships as well as funds to cover tuition and fee charges. For application materials, write to the Executive Director, National Consortium for Graduate Degrees for Minorities in Engineering, P.O. Box 537, Notre Dame, Indiana 46556.

Indian Education and Psychology Fellowship Program This program, supported by the U.S. Department of Education, provides scholarship assistance to American Indian or Alaskan Native students who are enrolled in accredited undergraduate or graduate school programs in education, psychology, or related fields. Contact the U.S. Department of Education, Indian Education and Psychology Fellowship Program, 400 Maryland Avenue, S.W., Washington, D.C. 20202, for additional information.

Indian Fellowship Program This program provides fellowships to Native American students enrolled in undergraduate and graduate degree programs in business administration, engineering, education, law, medicine, and related fields. The awards are based upon financial need. For further information, write to The Indian Fellowship Program, Office of Indian Education Programs, 1849 C Street, N.W., MS-Room 3525, Washington, D.C. 20242.

Indian Health Employees Scholarship Fund Inc.

This organization provides scholarship assistance to American Indian students. Priority is given to students enrolled in health-related programs. The awards are based upon financial need and availability of funds. Write to the Executive Secretary, Indian Health Employees Scholarship Fund, Federal Building, Room 309, Aberdeen, South Dakota 57401, for additional information and application forms.

Indian Health Scholarship

This program is based upon the National Health Service Corps and pays the tuition and fees for Native American, Alaskan Native, and Aleut students at schools of health disciplines not included in the National Health Service Corps Scholarship Program. For each year of support, recipients must agree to serve for 1 year in the Indian Health Service or in a health manpower shortage area. For further information, write to the Indian Health Service, IHSSP/Twinbrook Plaza, Suite 100, Rockville, Maryland 20857.

International Business Machines Fellowship Program

IBM offers fellowships to minority students beginning graduate programs in physics, chemistry, electrical engineering, mathematics, computer or information science, mechanical engineering, and materials science. The fellowships can be used only at selected universities. For further information, write to the James J. Watson Research Center, P.O. Box 218, Yorktown Heights, New York 10598.

Johnson and Johnson Leadership Awards for Minority Students

This program awards funds to minority students with outstanding leadership qualities who are interested in careers in business management. The 2-year award may be used at selected graduate schools of management. For more information, write to the Assistant Director, Educational Services, United Negro College Fund, 500 E. 62nd Street, New York, New York 10021.

Law School Scholarship Fund

Sponsored by the Mexican American Legal Defense and Education Fund, this program provides financial assistance to needy Hispanic law school students. Only full-time students are eligible to apply. For further information, write to the Mexican American Legal Defense and Education Fund, 634 S. Spring Street, 11th Floor, Los Angeles, California 90014.

League of United Latin American Citizens

This organization makes awards of up to $1000 to qualified Hispanic students who have financial need. For further information, write to the LULAC National Scholarship Fund, National Educational Service Centers, 400 First Street, N.W., Washington, D.C. 20001.

National Achievement Scholarship Program

This program provides grant assistance to outstanding black high school students. Over 600 scholarships, based on the results of the Preliminary Scholastic Aptitude Test/National Merit Scholarship Qualifying Test (PSAT/NMSQT), are awarded each year. The amounts of the scholarship vary. For further information, write to the National Achievement Scholarship Program, One Rotary Center, 1560 Sherman Avenue, Evanston, Illinois 60201.

National Action Council for Minorities in Engineering

This organization provides financial assistance to qualified undergraduate minority students for the purpose of increasing the number of minority engineers. The major funding is directed through incentive grants, which are administered by selected engineering schools. For more information, write to the National Action Council for Minorities in Engineering, 3 W. 35th Street, New York, New York 10001.

National Hispanic Scholarship Fund

This organization provides financial assistance to qualified Hispanic students. Recipients are selected on the basis of academic merit, financial need, and personal qualities. For more information, write to the National Hispanic Scholarship Fund, P.O. Box 728, Novato, California 94948.

National Institute of General Medical Sciences

The National Institutes of Health awards predoctoral fellowships to minority students pursuing degrees in the biomedical sciences. An annual stipend is part of the fellowship award. For further information, write to the National Institutes of Health, Bethesda, Maryland 20205, or call (301) 496-7941.

National Medical Fellowships

This program provides financial assistance to medical minority students with demonstrated financial need. Awards are made only to students enrolled in the first 2 years of medical school. Application forms may be obtained from National Medical Fellowships, Inc., 254 W. 31st Street, New York, New York 10001.

National Merit Scholarship Program

This program provides scholarship assistance to qualified black students. Applicants must be enrolled or accepted for enrollment at accredited schools. Write to the National Merit Scholarship Corporation, One Rotary Center, 1560 Sherman Avenue, Evanston, Illinois 60201, for additional information and application forms.

National Science Foundation

This organization provides 3-year graduate fellowships to qualified minority students who are pursuing careers in science and engineering. An applicant must be a U.S. citizen and a member of one of the following ethnic groups: American Indian, black, Hispanic, Native American, or Native Pacific Islander. Fellowships are awarded for study and research in the sciences or in engineering leading to a master's or doctoral degree. For application materials, contact the Fellowship Office, National Research Council, 1800 G Street, N.W., Washington, D.C. 20550.

National Society of Professional Engineers This organization provides scholarship assistance to minority students who are enrolled in engineering programs. Applicants must graduate in the top 25% of their high school class. Contact the National Society of Professional Engineers, 11 Dupont Circle, Suite 200, Washington, D.C. 20036.

Native American Seminary Scholarships Seminary scholarships are awarded to Native Americans, Aleuts, or Eskimos who are U.S. citizens and members of the Presbyterian church. Further information may be obtained from the Church Vocations/Committee on Higher Education, 100 Witherspoon Street, Louisville, Kentucky 40202-1396.

Office of Postsecondary Education The Department of Education offers financial assistance to minority graduate students who are enrolled full-time in programs leading to degrees in public administration. For further information and a list of participating schools, write to the Office of Postsecondary Education, Graduate Programs Branch, U.S. Department of Education, Washington, D.C. 20202.

Jackie Robinson Foundation This organization awards scholarships to minority high school seniors with high academic standing and leadership qualities. The awards may be used only at a 4-year college or university. Applications may be obtained from the Jackie Robinson Scholarship Foundation, 80-90 Eighth Avenue, New York, New York 10011.

United Methodist Church The Board of Higher Education and Ministry awards scholarships to qualified undergraduate and graduate minority students. Applicants must be U.S. citizens or permanent residents; must be Hispanic, Asian, or Native American; and must be active members of the Methodist church. The United Methodist church also sponsors several scholarship and loan programs for graduate students. A church-sponsored loan program is available to undergraduate as well as graduate students. For additional information, write to the United Methodist Church, Board of Higher Education and Ministry, Box 871, Nashville, Tennessee 37202.

United Negro College Fund This organization awards over 1000 scholarships a year to students attending United Negro College Fund Schools. The awards are based upon financial need and academic merit. The scholarships may be renewed for 3 years. An applicant must file a Financial Aid Form (FAF) or a Family Financial Statement (FFS) in order to be considered for the scholarship. For further information, write to the United Negro College Fund, Inc., Educational Services Department, 500 E. 62nd Street, New York, New York 10021. The following is a list of United Negro College Fund member institutions:

Atlanta University
Atlanta, Georgia 30314

Barber-Scotia College
Concord, New Hampshire 28025

Benedict College
Columbia, South Carolina 29204

Bennett College
Greensboro, North Carolina 27420

Bethune-Cookman College
Daytona Beach, Florida 32015

Claflin College
Orangeburg, South Carolina 29115

Clark College
Atlanta, Georgia 30314

Dillard University
New Orleans, Louisiana 70122

Edward Waters College
Jacksonville, Florida 32209

Fisk University
Nashville, Tennessee 37208

Florida-Memorial College
Miami, Florida 33054

Huston-Tillotson College
Austin, Texas 78702

Interdenominational Theological Center
Atlanta, Georgia 30314

Jarvis Christian College
Hawkins, Texas 75765

Johnson C. Smith University
Charlotte, North Carolina 28208

Knoxville College
Knoxville, Tennessee 37921

Lane College
Jackson, Tennessee 38301

LeMoyne-Owen College
Memphis, Tennessee 38126

Livingstone College
Salisbury, North Carolina 28144

Miles College
Birmingham, Alabama 35208

Morehouse College
Atlanta, Georgia 30314

Morris Brown College
Atlanta, Georgia 30314

Morris College
Sumter, South Carolina 29150

Oakwood College
Huntsville, Alabama 35896

Paine College
Augusta, Georgia 30901

Paul Quinn College
Waco, Texas 76704

Philander Smith College
Little Rock, Arkansas 72203

Rust College
Holly Springs, Mississippi 38635

Saint Augustine's College
Raleigh, North Carolina 27611

Saint Paul's College
Lawrenceville, Virginia 23868

Shaw University
Raleigh, North Carolina 27611

Spelman College
Atlanta, Georgia 30314

Stillman College
Tuscaloosa, Alabama 35401

Talladega College
Talladega, Alabama 35160

Texas College
Tyler, Texas 75701

Tougaloo College
Tougaloo, Mississippi 39174

Tuskegee University
Tuskegee Institute, Alabama 36088

Virginia Union University
Richmond, Virginia 23220

Voorhees College
Denmark, South Carolina 29042

Wilberforce University
Wilberforce, Ohio 45384

Wiley College
Marshall, Texas 75670

Xavier University of Louisana
New Orleans, Louisiana 70125

Earl Warren Legal Training Program, Inc.   This program provides financial assistance to black students entering law school. For further information, write to the NAACP Legal Defense and Education Fund, 99 Hudson Street, Suite 1600, New York, New York 10013.

Roy Wilkins Scholarship Program   This program provides scholarship assistance to financially needy minority students. Write to the NAACP Youth and College Division, 186 Remsen Street, Brooklyn, NewYork 11201, for additional information and application materials.

Organizations That Provide Information on Financial Assistance Programs for Minority Students

American Fund for Dental Health
211 E. Chicago, Suite 1630
Chicago, Illinois 60611

Bureau of Indian Affairs
18th and C Streets, N.W.
Washington, D.C. 20245

Graduate Management Admission Council
1299 Ocean Avenue
Santa Monica, California 90401

Indian Health Service
Parklawn Building, Room 6-12
5600 Fishers Lane
Rockville, Maryland 20857

National Hispanic Scholarship Fund
P.O. Box 748
San Francisco, California 94101

National Medical Association
1012 Tenth Street, N.W.
Washington, D.C. 20001

National Research Council
2101 Constitution Avenue, N.W.
Washington, D.C. 20418

Jackie Robinson Foundation
80-90 Eighth Avenue
New York, New York 10011

United Negro College Fund
500 E. 62nd Street
New York, New York 10021

United States Department of Education
Indian Fellowship Program
400 Maryland Avenue, S.W.
Room 2177
Washington, D.C. 20202

Publications That Provide Information on Financial Assistance Programs for Minority Students

Directory of Financial Aid for Minorities Reference Service Press, 1100 Industrial Road, San Carlos, California 94070.

Directory of Special Programs for Minority Students Garrett Park Press, P.O. Box 190, Garrett Park, Maryland 20896.

Financial Aid for Minority Students in Allied Health Garrett Park Press, P.O. Box 190, Garrett Park, Maryland 20896.

Financial Aid for Minority Students in Business Garrett Park Press, P.O. Box 190, Garrett Park, Maryland 20896.

Financial Aid for Minority Students in Education Garrett Park Press, P.O. Box 190, Garrett Park, Maryland 20896.

Financial Aid for Minority Students in Engineering Garrett Park Press, P.O. Box 190, Garrett Park, Maryland 20896.

Financial Aid for Minority Students in Law Garrett Park Press, P.O. Box 190, Garrett Park, Maryland 20896.

Financial Aid for Minority Students in Mass Communication and Journalism Garrett Park Press, P.O. Box 190, Garrett Park, Maryland 20896.

Financial Aid for Minority Students in Medicine Garrett Park Press, P.O. Box 190, Garrett Park, Maryland 20896.

Financial Aid for Minority Students in Science Garrett Park Press, P.O. Box 190, Garrett Park, Maryland 20896.

Higher Education Opportunities for Minorities and Women: Annotated Selections, 1989 Superintendent of Documents, U.S. Government Printing Office, Washington, D.C. 20402.

Hispanic Financial Resource Handbook The Ohio State University, Hispanic Student Programs, 347 Ohio Union, 1739 N. High Street, Columbus, Ohio 43210.

Minority Organizations: A National Directory Garrett Park Press, P.O. Box 190, Garrett Park, Maryland 20896.

Minority Student Opportunities in U.S. Medical Schools Association of American Medical Colleges, Office of Minority Affairs, Division of Student Programs, One Dupont Circle, Washington, D.C. 20036.

Some Final Notes on Minority Financial Assistance Programs

1. Many organizations provide financial assistance to minority students, who should seek the advice of high school counselors and college financial aid officers in locating sources of funds.

2. Financial assistance is available to minority students on both the undergraduate and the graduate and professional school level.

3. There are many church-sponsored minority programs, and students should seek the advice of their church officials when attempting to locate these funding sources.

14 PROGRAMS FOR WOMEN

Federal Financial Assistance

Since 1970, the enrollment of women in programs of higher education has increased significantly. Many women are returning to the classroom after raising their children. Such women constitute the largest group classified as *nontraditional* students; included in this category are independent, part-time, and older women students. Legislation now makes some federal financial assistance programs available to part-time and nontraditional students, including Pell Grants, Supplemental Educational Opportunity Grants (SEOG), Carl D. Perkins Loans, and the College Work-Study Program (CWSP). Under the new definition of independent student—expanded to include any student with legal dependents—more women students will qualify for financial assistance than previously.

A new category of student, the *displaced homemaker*, also is eligible to apply for all federal student financial aid programs. A displaced homemaker is defined as someone who (1) has not worked in the labor force for 5 years or more, but during those years has worked in the home providing unpaid services for family members; (2) has depended on the income of another family member but is no longer receiving that income, or has been receiving public assistance because of dependent children in the home; or (3) is unemployed or underemployed and is having trouble obtaining or upgrading employment.

Students who are pregnant or are caring for a newborn or adopted child will be able to defer payments on their student loans for up to 6 months. Women who have preschool children, who are entering the work force for the first time or are reentering the work force, and who earn less than $1 above the minimum wage are eligible for loan deferrals of up to 12 months.

In addition to federal, state, and institutional financial assistance programs available to women students, there are many financial aid programs funded specifically for women. Women needing financial assistance should seek the advice of their school's financial aid director.

Other Sources of Financial Aid for Women

The Women's Equity Action League's publication, *Better Late Than Never,* is an excellent financial resource guide for women seeking funding for higher education or for retraining opportunities. The following financial assistance programs are listed in this publication:

American Assembly of Collegiate Schools of Business
This organization provides financial assistance to women who are first-year doctoral business students and are interested in careers in business. For further information, write to the American Association of Collegiate Schools of Business, 605 Old Ballas Road, Suite 220, St. Louis, Missouri 63141-7077.

American Association of University Women Educational Foundation
This organization sponsors a number of financial assistance programs. The fellowship awards support to women completing degrees in graduate school, medical school, dental and veterinary school, law school, and business school. Postdoctoral and dissertation fellowships are also available. For further information and application materials, write to the American Association of University Women Educational Foundation, 1111 16th Street, N.W., Washington, D.C. 20036 or call (202) 872-1430.

American Business Women's Association
This organization offers both loan and scholarship assistance to qualified women students. An applicant must be a U.S. citizen enrolled in an accredited college, university, or vocational school. The amount of the award varies depending upon financial need. Recipients must be sponsored by a local chapter of the organization. Write to the American Business Women's Association, National Headquarters, 9100 Ward Parkway, P.O. Box 8728, Kansas City, Missouri 64114, or call (816) 361-6621.

American Council of Independent Laboratories, Inc.
This organization provides scholarship assistance to junior and senior women students who are majoring in biology or chemistry. For further information, write

to Scholarship Chairperson, American Council of Independent Laboratories, Inc., 2001 Pine Drive, Lancaster, Pennsylvania 17601.

American Medical Women's Association Medical Education Loan Program

This program provides financial assistance to first-, second-, or third-year women medical students. Recipients must be U.S. citizens and members of the American Medical Women's Association. For further information, write to the American Medical Women's Association Medical Education Loan Program, 801 N. Fairfax Street, Suite 400, Alexandria, Virginia 22314.

American Society of Women Accountants

This organization awards scholarships to junior and senior women students who are majoring in accounting. For further information, write to the Scholarship Committee, American Society of Women Accountants, 134 Cliff Avenue, Winthrop, Massachusetts 02152.

Association of American Women Dentists

This organization provides financial assistance to qualified women dental students interested in conducting research. Contact your dental school dean, or write to the American Association of Women Dentists, 211 E. Chicago Avenue, Chicago, Illinois 60611.

Association for Women in Science

This organization provides financial assistance to predoctoral women students in the physical and social sciences. The Luise Meyer-Schutzmeister Memorial Award is given to women pursuing doctorates in physics. For applications, contact the Association for Women in Science, 2401 Virginia Avenue, N.W., Suite 303, Washington, D.C. 20037.

The Verda White Barnes Memorial Scholarship Fund

This fund provides scholarships to qualified women who are pursuing degrees in political science at Idaho State University. Applicants must be Idaho residents and must be enrolled full-time as undergraduate or graduate students. Awards are based upon financial need, academic merit, and feminist views. For further information and application forms, write to the Chair, University Scholarship Committee, P.O. Box 8123, Idaho State University, Pocatello, Idaho 83209-0009.

Mary Ingraham Bunting Institute

This institute, directed by Radcliffe College, is one of the largest centers awarding postdoctoral fellowships to women. Awards are made to candidates pursuing independent study in academic or professional fields. For further information, write to The Mary Ingraham Bunting Institute of Radcliffe College, 34 Concord Avenue, Cambridge, Massachusetts 02138.

Business and Professional Women's Foundation

This organization provides various scholarship and loan programs for women enrolled in health professions schools, engineering, and graduate business schools. Applicants must be at least 25 years old, U.S. citizens, and enrolled at least half-time at an approved school. The amounts of the award vary and are based upon financial need. The organization sponsors the following financial aid programs: New York Life Foundation Scholarship for Women in Health Careers, Loan Fund for Women in Engineering Studies, Loan Fund for Graduate Business Studies, Sally Butler Memorial Fund for Latina Research, Lena Lake Forrest Fellowship Program, Clairol Loving Care Scholarship Program, and the Avon Foundation Scholarship Program for Careers in Sales. For further information, write to the Business and Professional Women's Foundation, 2012 Massachusetts Avenue, N.W., Washington, D.C. 20036, or call (202) 293-1200.

Business and Professional Women's Foundation Loan Fund for Women in Engineering

This fund assists women in their final 2 years of any accredited undergraduate or graduate engineering program. Applicants must be U.S. citizens and demonstrate financial need. For further information, write to the Business and Professional Women's Foundation, 2012 Massachusetts Avenue, N.W., Washington, D.C. 20036.

Business and Professional Women's Sears Roebuck Loan Fund for Women in Graduate Business Studies

This fund provides loan assistance to women in graduate business programs. Applicants must be U.S. citizens, have financial need, and be enrolled in a graduate business school accredited by the American Assembly of Collegiate Schools of Business. For further information, write to the Business and Professional Women's Foundation, 2012 Massachusetts Avenue, N.W., Washington, D.C. 20036.

California State University Loan Forgiveness

This program provides financial assistance to women pursuing doctoral degrees. Recipients must agree to teach for 5 years at one of the state universities. Loans are forgiven at the rate of 20% a year for up to 5 years as long as the borrower teaches in one of the California state universities. Contact the California Student Aid Commission, P.O. Box 942845, Sacramento, California 94245-0845, for further information.

Citizens' Scholarship Foundation of America, Inc.

This organization selects recipients for scholarships funded by corporations, foundations, associations, and other organizations. The requirements vary according to the program. There is a $2 charge for the list of available scholarships. Contact the Citizens' Scholarship Foundation of America, Inc., 1505 Riverview Road, P.O. Box 297, Minneapolis, Minnesota 56082, for further information.

Ada Comstock Scholars Program

This program provides financial assistance to qualified women undergraduates at Smith College. Applicants should complete 1 year of college before applying to the program, which is not based upon financial need. An applicant must submit an autobiographical essay and complete a personal interview. For more information, write to the Ada Comstock Scholars Program, Smith College, Northampton, Massachusetts 01063.

Congressional Fellowships on Women and Public Policy

This program provides financial assistance for 1 year to women who are graduate and preprofessional students and who work for a member of Congress on issues affecting women. For further information, write to the Women's Research and Education Institute, 1700 18th Street, N.W., Suite 400, Washington, D.C. 20009.

Daughters of the American Revolution (DAR)

This organization sponsors financial assistance programs for qualified women students. Most of the scholarship funds are administered by individual state societies, which have their own requirements, deadlines, and application procedures. The American History Scholarship is awarded to high school seniors who plan to major in American history. The Enid Hall Griswald Memorial Scholarship is awarded to junior or senior college students who are majoring in political science, history, government, or economics. The Caroline E. Holt Educational Fund Scholarship is awarded to first-year nursing students. The Occupational Therapy Scholarship is awarded to first-year students pursuing degrees in occupational, physical, musical, or art therapy. The number and amounts of the awards vary. Contact your local DAR chapter, or write to the Office of Committees, 1776 D Street, N.W., Washington, D.C. 20006.

Daughters of the Cincinnati

This organization provides financial assistance to financially needy women students to complete their education. Only high school seniors may apply. Applicants must be the daughters of active duty or retired officers of the Army, Navy, Air Force, Coast Guard, or United States Marine Corps. Write to the Daughters of the Cincinnati, 122 E. 58th Street, New York, New York 10022, or call (212) 319-6915.

Fellowship on Women and Public Policy

Administered through the State University of New York at Albany, this program provides financial assistance to graduate women students to develop public policy affecting women. For further information, write to the Center for Women in Government, Draper 310, SUNY at Albany, Albany, New York 12222.

General Electric Scholarship Program

This financial assistance program provides scholarships for first-year college women majoring in engineering. Write to the Society of Women Engineers, 345 E. 47th Street, New York, New York 10017.

Gillette Hayden Memorial Foundation

This organization provides low-interest loans to eligible third- and fourth-year women dental students. Women enrolled in graduate dental programs are also eligible to apply for these loans. Write to Gillette Hayden Memorial Foundation, 95 W. Broadway, Salem, New Jersey 08079.

Sid Guber Memorial Award

Administered through the Foundation of American Women in Radio and Television, this award provides financial assistance to undergraduate and graduate women students in the performing arts. For further information, contact the Foundation of American Women in Radio and Television, Inc., 1101 Connecticut Avenue, Suite 700, Washington, D.C. 20036.

Georgia Harkness Scholarship Award

These scholarships are awarded to prepare women for the ordained ministry in the United Methodist church. An applicant must be over 35, have an undergraduate degree, be accepted to an accredited seminary, and be a certified candidate for the ordained ministry. Write to the Georgia Harkness Scholarship Award Program, Division of Ordained Ministry, The United Methodist Church, P.O. Box 871, Nashville, Tennessee 37202, for further information, or call (615) 327-2700.

International Business Machines (IBM) Fellowship Program for Women

IBM offers fellowships to women enrolled in graduate and postdoctoral programs at selected universities. For more information, write to the Manager, University and Scientific Relations, Thomas J. Watson Research Center, P.O. Box 218, Yorktown Heights, New York 10598.

Jewish Foundation for Education of Women

This organization provides scholarships and loans for women who are undergraduate, graduate, or professional school students. The awards are made on a nonsectarian basis. Applicants must live within 50 miles of the New York Metropolitan area and must have financial need. For further information call (212) 265-2565, or write to the Jewish Foundation for Education of Women, 330 W. 58th Street, New York, New York 10019.

Junior League of Northern Virginia

This organization provides financial assistance to women students who are 28 years old or older and who have financial need. Recipients must be U.S. citizens and live in northern Virginia. For further information, write to the Scholarship Chairman, Junior League of Northern Virginia, 7921 Jones Branch Drive, Suite 320, McLean, Virginia 22102.

Kappa Kappa Gamma Scholarship Program

This organization offers scholarships to women students who are juniors or seniors in college or are graduate students working toward degrees in rehabilitation. Applicants must be located on a campus where there is a chapter of Kappa Kappa Gamma. For further information on this program, write to the Kappa Kappa Gamma Fraternity Headquarters, P.O. Box 2079, Columbus, Ohio 43216.

Grace Legendre Fellowship Program

This program provides financial assistance to qualified women graduate students. Candidates must be both U.S. citizens and residents of New York State and must be enrolled in an advanced degree program at an approved school. Write to the Scholarship Chairperson, 414 Beach 136th Street, Belle Harbor, New York 11694.

152

Legislative Fellowships on Women and Public Policy This program, funded by the Revson Foundation and other organizations, is designed to develop specialists in policy issues of concern to women. The program is administered by the Center for Women in Government, Graduate School of Public Affairs, State University of New York at Albany. Applicants must be women graduate students in New York State. For further information, write Director, Legislative Fellowship on Women and Public Policy, Center for Women in Government, Room 302, Draper Hall, State University of New York at Albany, 1400 Washington Avenue, New York, New York 12222.

Helen Miller Malloch Scholarship This program provides scholarship assistance to women pursuing careers in journalism; applicants must be professional journalists or journalism students. Contact the National Federation of Press Women, Inc., 1105 Main Street, P.O. Box 99, Blue Springs, Missouri 64013, for further information.

Massachusetts Federation of Polish Women This organization provides financial assistance to women of Polish ancestry who are interested in pursuing careers in medicine. For more information, write to the Massachusetts Federation of Polish Women, 300 Sunnymeade Avenue, Chicapee, Massachusetts 01013.

National Education Foundation Administered through Zeta Phi Beta sorority, this organization provides financial assistance to both graduate and undergraduate students. Eligibility requirements vary according to academic program. For further information, contact Zeta Phi Beta Sorority, Inc., 1734 New Hampshire Avenue, N.W., Washington, D.C. 20009.

National Home Fashions League, Inc. This organization provides financial assistance to encourage women students in the fields of arts, crafts, or design. Annual competitions are held, and winners are judged on creativity, versatility, and presentation. Contact the National Home Fashions League, Inc., 107 World Trade Center, P.O. Box 58045, Dallas, Texas 75258.

National Society of Professional Engineers This organization provides scholarship assistance to women students who are engineering majors. Applicants must graduate in the top 25% of their high school class. Contact the National Society of Professional Engineers, 2029 K Street, N.W., Washington, D.C. 20006, for additional information and application forms.

Polish Women's Alliance Scholarship Program This organization provides financial assistance to members enrolled in undergraduate degree programs. For further information, write to the Polish Women's Alliance of America, 205 S. Northwest Highway, Park Ridge, Illinois 60068.

Program for Continuing Education Grant Women students who are U.S. citizens and who have had at least a 1-year interruption in their formal education are eligible to apply for this grant. A recipient must be sponsored by a local PEO chapter. For further information, write to the International PEO Sisterhood, PEO Executive, 3700 Grand Avenue, Des Moines, Iowa 50312.

Project Ahead The University of Kentucky offers scholarships and internships to prepare women for the transition from school to job market and to better prepare women to obtain employment in business, government, or community service. To be eligible a student must be at least 25 years old and a second-, third-, or fourth-year undergraduate at the University of Kentucky. For more information, write to the Continuing Education for Women/Project Ahead, University of Kentucky, 106 Frazee Hall, Lexington, Kentucky 40506-0031.

Jeannette Rankin Foundation This organization provides financial assistance to women over the age of 35 who are enrolled either in undergraduate degree programs or in vocational/technical programs. For further information, write to the Jeannette Rankin Foundation, P.O. Box 6653, Athens, Georgia 30604.

Jean Arnot Reid Scholarship Program This organization provides scholarships to women who are pursuing careers in banking and finance and are members of the National Association of Bank Women. Contact the National Association of Bank Women, Inc., 500 N. Michigan Avenue, Suite 1400, Chicago, Illinois 60611 for more information.

Olive Lynn Salembier Scholarship This program offers scholarships to women pursuing careers in engineering. Applicants must be out of the job market for at least 2 years and must be enrolled in undergraduate or graduate engineering programs. For further information, write to the Society of Women Engineers, United Engineering Center, Room 305, 345 E. 47th Street, New York, New York 10017.

Sigma Delta Epsilon This organization provides fellowships to women for both predoctoral and postdoctoral research. An applicant must have a doctoral or medical degree in biological, physical, or mathematical sciences, and must demonstrate research ability. Contact Graduate Women in Science, Inc., P.O. Box 4748, Ithaca, New York 14850.

Soroptimist International of the Americas This organization provides financial assistance, based upon need, academic merit, and service to the community, to women who are high school seniors. Aid is also given to women who are entering vocational or technical training programs or completing undergraduate degree programs. Applications are distributed by the local Soroptimist Club. For further information, contact the Scholarship Committee, Soroptimist International of the Americas, 1616 Walnut Street, Philadelphia, Pennsylvania 19103.

The Irene Stambler Vocational Opportunities Grant Program This program provides grants to Jewish women who are displaced homemakers in the Washington, D.C., area to finance their education or vocational training. The awards are based upon financial need. For more information and application forms, write to the Jewish Social Service Agency, 6123 Montrose Road, Rockville, Maryland 20852-4880.

Veterans Administration (VA) Dependents' Programs The VA offers a number of financial assistance programs to the widows and dependent children of deceased or disabled veterans. The wives and children of POWs or MIAs are also eligible to apply to the Veterans Administration for financial assistance. Recipients receive a monthly stipend based upon student enrollment status. For information on all VA programs, write to the Veterans Administration, 810 Vermont Avenue, N.W., Washington, D.C. 20420, or call (202) 393-4120.

Clara Weir/Soraria Alumnae Scholarship Fund This fund provides scholarships to women students who are residents of Washington State and are resuming studies at the University of Washington. Preference is given to junior, senior, or graduate students. For further information, contact the University of Washington, Financial Aid Office, 1400 NE Campus Parkway, Room 105, Seattle, Washington 98105, or call (206) 545-1985.

Women's Job Center This agency provides counseling and job placement without a fee to residents of Middlesex County, New Jersey. Preference is given to single parents, displaced homemakers, and economically disadvantaged women. Call (201) 247-9304, or write to the Women's Job Center, 256 Easton Avenue, New Brunswick, New Jersey 08901, for further information.

Women Working Technical This program trains and places economically disadvantaged women in electronics and mechanics jobs. Applicants must be residents of Bergen County, New Jersey, and must be at least 18 years old. Women who are economically disadvantaged, dislocated workers, or displaced homemakers are eligible for tuition sponsorship under the Job Training Partnership Act. Contact the Bergen County Technical Institute, 280 Hackensack Avenue, Hackensack, New Jersey 07601, for further information, or call (201) 343-6000.

Woodrow Wilson Women's Studies Research Grants This program provides financial assistance to women doctoral students who are conducting research on some aspect of women's role in society. For specific information on program requirements, write to the Woodrow Wilson National Fellowship Foundation, Box 642, Princeton, New Jersey 08542.

Margaret Yardley Fellowship Program This program provides fellowship assistance to women enrolled in postgraduate programs. Preference is given to New Jersey residents. An applicant must be enrolled full-time in an approved program and must have financial need. Contact the Margaret Yardley Fellowship, New Jersey State Federation of Women's Clubs, 55 Clifton Avenue, New Brunswick, New Jersey 08901, for further information.

YWCA of New York City This organization provides financial assistance to separated, divorced, or widowed women to help them to reenter the job market. A wide variety of counseling services is provided. The program is funded by the New York State Department of Labor. For further information, write to the YWCA Department of ReEntry Employment, 610 Lexington Avenue, New York, New York 10022, or call (212) 735-9726.

Zonta International This organization awards Amelia Earhart Fellowships to women students pursuing careers in aerospace. The awards are available only to graduate students. Contact Zonta International, 557 W. Randolph Street, Chicago, Illinois 60601.

Publications That Provide Information on Funding Sources for Women

Better Late Than Never: Financial Aid for Re-Entry Older Women Seeking Education and Training Women's Equity Action League, 1250 I Street, N.W., Suite 905, Washington, D.C. 20005.

Displaced Homemaker's Network Directory Displaced Homemaker's Network Directory, 1010 Vermont Avenue, N.W., Washington, D.C. 20005.

Directory of Financial Aids for Women Dr. Gail Ann Schlachter, Reference Service Press, 1100 Industrial Road, Suite 9, San Carlos, California 94070.

Directory of Special Opportunities for Women Martha Merrill Doss, Garrett Park Press, P.O. Box 190, Garrett Park, Maryland 20896.

Federal Financial Aid for Men and Women Resuming Their Education or Training Consumer Information Center, Department DD, Pueblo, Colorado 81009. Free.

Financial Aid: A Partial List of Resources for Women Association of American Colleges, 1818 R Street, N.W., Washington, D.C. 20009.

Happier By Degrees: A College Re-Entry Guide for Women Pam Mendelsohn, Box 7123, Berkeley, California 94705.

Higher Education Opportunities for Minorities and Women U.S. Department of Education, U.S. Government Printing Office, Washington, D.C. 20402.

How to Get Money for Research Mary Rubin, The Feminist Press, P.O. Box 1645, Hagerstown, Maryland 21741.

Professional Women's Groups American Association of University Women, 2401 Virginia Avenue, N.W., Washington, D.C. 20007.

Resources for Women in Science Association for Women in Science, 1346 Connecticut Avenue, N.W., Washington, D.C. 20036. Free.

Women's Organizations: A National Directory Garrett Park Press, P.O. Box 190, Garrett Park, Maryland 20896.

Women's Sports Foundation College Scholarship Guide Women's Sports Foundation, 342 Madison Avenue, Suite 728, New York, New York 10173.

Organizations That Can Provide Information on Specific Women's Programs

American Association of University Women
Educational Foundation
2401 Virginia Avenue, N.W.
Washington, D.C. 20037

Business and Professional Women's Foundation
2012 Massachusetts Avenue, N.W.
Washington, D.C. 20036

General Federation of Women's Clubs
1734 N Street, N.W.
Washington, D.C. 20036

Jewish Foundation for the Education of Women
330 W. 58th Street
New York, New York 10019

National Society of the Daughters of the American Revolution
Office of the Committees
1776 D Street, N.W.
Washington, D.C. 20006

Society of Women Engineers
United Engineering Center
345 E. 47th Street, Room 305
New York, New York 10017

Some Final Notes About Financial Assistance Programs for Women

1. Because women can expect to earn less than their male colleagues in some job positions, be careful when borrowing. You will probably have less money to repay your student loans than will male borrowers.

2. Be certain to check all federal, state, and institutional programs specifically funded for women.

3. Check with your college or university for available day-care facilities.

4. Don't let age or lack of education or of training prevent you from enrolling in some program of higher education. It's never too late! Help is available from the offices of admission and financial aid at colleges and universities.

15 PROGRAMS FOR THE HANDICAPPED

For handicapped students there are financial assistance programs offered by both the federal government and individual states. Federal legislation forbids discrimination on the basis of handicap and encourages enrollment in postsecondary institutions by handicapped persons. Colleges and universities must meet the needs of their handicapped students or risk losing their federal financial aid funds. The U.S. Department of Education Rehabilitation Services Administration administers the Rehabilitation Act, which determines financial eligibility for handicapped persons. However, each state has its own programs for the handicapped; check the chapter on State Programs.

Handicapped students have expenses not usually incurred by other students that should be considered when calculating financial need. These costs include special equipment needs, transportation, interpreters, notetakers, and personal attendants. The student's financial aid director should be informed of any additional expenses, and information should be coordinated with the institution's director for handicapped or disabled persons.

Programs That Provide Financial Assistance to Handicapped Students

American Council of the Blind This organization offers scholarships to legally blind students who are enrolled in vocational or technical programs at the undergraduate or graduate school level. Contact the American Council of the Blind, 1010 Vermont Avenue N.W., Washington, D.C. 20005, for additional information and application materials.

American Foundation for the Blind This organization offers scholarship assistance to blind women. Awards range from $1000 to $3000 per academic year. Contact the American Foundation for the Blind, 15 W. 16th Street, New York, New York 10011, for additional information and application forms.

Alexander Graham Bell Association for the Deaf This organization offers scholarships ranging from $500 to $1000 for deaf students. Write to the Alexander Graham Bell Association for the Deaf, 3417 Volta Place, N.W., Washington, D.C., for additional information and application forms.

Developmental Disabilities Program This program makes use of existing services in health, education, welfare, and rehabilitation to provide services to people with developmental disabilities. Included in the services offered are job training and education. Each state has a designated agency to administer the developmental disabilities program. For further information, write to the Administration on Developmental Disabilities, Department of Health and Human Services, Room 351D, Humphrey Building, Washington, D.C. 20201.

Disabled American Veterans Auxiliary National Education Loan Fund This loan program is supported by the auxiliaries of the Disabled American Veterans. The fund provides interest-free loans to qualified disabled students. Fully paid members of the Disabled American Veterans Auxiliary, the children of fully paid life members, and the children of deceased fully paid life members are eligible to apply. The amount of each loan is determined by a committee, and repayment begins 90 days after graduation or withdrawal from school. For further information, write to the National Education Loan Fund Director, National Headquarters, Disabled American Veterans Auxiliary, 3725 Alexandria Pike, Cold Spring, Kentucky 41076.

Gallaudet University This federally funded university provides a liberal arts education for deaf persons. Gallaudet offers both undergraduate and graduate programs. For further information contact the Office of Admissions, Gallaudet University, 800 Florida Avenue, N.E., Washington, D.C. 20002.

Gore Family Memorial This program provides scholarship assistance for undergraduate and graduate handicapped students in any field of study. The amount of the award is based upon financial need. For further information, write to the Gore Family Memorial Foundation Trust, 230 S.E. First Avenue, Fort Lauderdale, Florida, 33301.

Kappa Kappa Gamma   This organization provides scholarship assistance to undergraduate and graduate students who have completed at least 2 years of study in physical, speech, occupational, hearing, rehabilitation, or mental health therapy. Membership in the organization is not required. For further information, write to Kappa Kappa Gamma, c/o Mrs. L. Williams, 4720 Pickett Road, Fairfax, Virginia 22032.

National Association of American Business Clubs
This association provides financial assistance to both undergraduate and graduate students who plan to major in physical therapy, clinical therapy, music therapy, speech-language pathology, hearing therapy, and related fields. For further information, write to the National Association of American Business Clubs, P.O. Box 5127, High Point, North Carolina 27262.

National Federation of the Blind   This organization offers scholarship assistance to legally blind students, both undergraduate and graduate. Write to the National Federation of the Blind, 814 Fourth Avenue, Grinnell, Iowa 50112.

Quota International Fellowship Fund   Awards from this fund provide fellowships to graduate and undergraduate students who are deaf or hearing impaired or to hearing students who plan to work with the deaf. For further information, write to Quota International Fellowship Fund, 1420 21st Street, N.W., Washington, D.C. 20036.

Social Security Benefits   This federal program provides financial assistance to handicapped workers and eligible dependents. For further information, contact your local Social Security Administration office.

Supplemental Security Income   This federal assistance program is designed to provide financial assistance to needy people who are disabled, blind, and aged. The amount of assistance is determined by need and resources. For further information, contact your local Social Security Administration office.

Talent Search, Educational Opportunity Centers, and Special Services for Disadvantaged Students Programs   These federally funded programs, located throughout the United States, provide counseling and other services to disadvantaged students and students with disabilities. For more information, write to the Chief, Special Services Branch, Division of Student Services Programs, Box 23772, L'Enfant Plaza Station, Washington, D.C. 20026-3772, or call (202) 732-4804.

Vocational Rehabilitation   All states have coordinated programs of vocational rehabilitation to help people with handicaps become employable and independent. Assistance includes educational opportunities,

such as payment of college tuition and fees and other college expenses. Contact your state's Office of Vocational Rehabilitation for further information.

It is a federal requirement that persons receiving assistance from a vocational rehabilitation agency file for federal financial aid programs. Handicapped persons are advised to coordinate information between the school's financial aid director and the vocational rehabilitation administrator.

State Vocational Rehabilitation Agencies That Provide Information on Services Offered for the Handicapped

Alabama
Division of Rehabilitation and Crippled Children Service
P.O. Box 11586
Montgomery, Alabama 36111
(205) 281-8780

Alaska
Division of Vocational Rehabilitation
Box F, MS 0581
Juneau, Alaska 99881
(907) 465-2814

Arizona
Rehabilitation Services Administration
Department of Economic Security
1300 W. Washington Street
Phoenix, Arizona 85007
(602) 255-3332

Arkansas
Division of Rehabilitation Services
Arkansas Department of Human Services
Little Rock, Arkansas 72203
(501) 371-2571

Division of Services for the Blind
Department of Human Services
P.O. Box 3237
411 Victory Street
Little Rock, Arkansas 72203
(501) 371-2587

California
Department of Rehabilitation
830 K Street Mall
Sacramento, California 95814
(916) 445-3971

Colorado
Division of Rehabilitation
Department of Social Services
1575 Sherman Street, Fourth Floor
Denver, Colorado 80203-1714
(303) 294-2804

Connecticut

Division of Rehabilitation Services
State Board of Education
600 Asylum Avenue
Hartford, Connecticut 06105
(203) 566-4440

Board of Education and Services for the Blind
Department of Human Resources
170 Ridge Road
Wethersfield, Connecticut 06109
(203) 566-5800

Delaware

Division of Vocational Rehabilitation
Department of Labor
Elwyn Building
321 E. 11th Street
Wilmington, Delaware 19801
(302) 571-2850

Division for the Visually Impaired
Department of Health and Social Services
305 W. Eighth Street
Wilmington, Delaware 19801
(302) 571-3333

Florida

Division of Vocational Rehabilitation
Department of Labor and Employment Security
1709-A Mahan Drive
Tallahassee, Florida 32399-0696
(904) 488-6210

Division of Blind Services
Department of Education
2540 Executive Center Circle, West
Douglas Building
Tallahassee, Florida 32301
(904) 488-1330

Georgia

Division of Rehabilitation Services
Department of Human Services
878 Peachtree Street, N.E., Room 706
Atlanta, Georgia 30309
(404) 894-6670

Hawaii

Division of Vocational Rehabilitation and Services for
the Blind
Department of Human Services
P.O. Box 339
Honolulu, Hawaii 96809
(808) 548-4769

Idaho

Division of Vocational Rehabilitation
Len B. Jirdon Building, Room 150
650 W. State
Boise, Idaho 83720
(208) 334-3390

Idaho Commission for the Blind
341 W. Washington Street
Boise, Idaho 83702
(208) 334-3220

Illinois

Illinois Department of Rehabilitation Services
623 E. Adams Street
P.O. Box 19429
Springfield, Illinois 62794-9429
(217) 782-2093

Indiana

Indiana Department of Human Services
Capital Center, 251 N. Illinois Street
P.O. Box 7083
Indianapolis, Indiana 46207-7083
(317) 232-1139

Iowa

Iowa Division of Vocational Rehabilitation Services
Department of Education
510 E. 12th Street
Des Moines, Iowa 50319
(515) 281-4311

Department for the Blind
524 Fourth Street
Des Moines, Iowa 50309
(515) 281-7986

Kansas

Department of Social and Rehabilitation Services
2700 W. Sixth
Biddle Building, Second Floor
Topeka, Kansas 66606
(913) 296-3911

Kentucky

Office of Vocational Rehabilitation
930 Capital Plaza Tower
Frankfort, Kentucky 40601
(502) 564-4566

Department for Blind Services
Education and Arts Cabinet
427 Vercailles Road
Frankfort, Kentucky 40601
(502) 564-4754

Louisiana

Division of Rehabilitation Services
Office of Community Services
Department of Health and Hospitals
P.O. Box 94371
1755 Florida Street
Baton Rouge, Louisiana 70821
(504) 342-2285

Division of Blind Services
Office of Human Development
Department of Health and Human Resources
P.O. Box 28
1755 Florida Street
Baton Rouge, Louisiana 70821
(504) 432-5284

Maine

Bureau of Rehabilitation
Department of Human Services
32 Winthrop Street
Augusta, Maine 04330
(207) 289-2266

Maryland

Division of Vocational Rehabilitation
State Department of Education
200 W. Baltimore Street
Baltimore, Maryland 21201-2595
(301) 333-2270

Massachusetts

Commission for the Blind
110 Tremont Street, Sixth Floor
Boston, Massachusetts 02108
(617) 727-5550

Rehabilitation Commission
Statler Office Building, 11th Floor
20 Park Plaza
Boston, Massachusetts 02116
(617) 727-2172

Michigan

Michigan Rehabilitation Services
Department of Education
P.O. Box 30010
Lansing, Michigan 48909
(517) 373-3390

Commission for the Blind
Department of Labor
309 N. Washington Square
Lansing, Michigan 48909
(517) 373-2062

Minnesota

Vocational Rehabilitation Division
Departments of Jobs and Training
390 N. Robert Street, Fifth Floor
St. Paul, Minnesota 55101
(612) 296-9154

State Services for the Blind
Division of Rehabilitation Services
Department of Jobs and Training
1745 University Avenue
St. Paul, Minnesota 55104
(612) 642-0500

Mississippi

Vocational Rehabilitation Services
P.O. Box 1698
Jackson, Mississippi 39205
(601) 354-6825

Vocational Rehabilitation for the Blind
P.O. Box 4872
Jackson, Mississippi 39215
(601) 354-6411

Missouri

State Department of Education
Division of Vocational Rehabilitation
2401 E. McCarty
Jefferson City, Missouri 65101
(314) 751-3251

Bureau for the Blind
Division of Family Services
619 E. Capitol
Jefferson City, Missouri 65101
(314) 751-4249

Montana

Department of Social and Rehabilitation Services
Rehabilitation Services Division
P.O. Box 4210, 111 Sanders
Helena, Montana 59604
(406) 444-2590

Nebraska

Division of Rehabilitative Services
State Department of Education
301 Centennial Mall, Sixth Floor
Lincoln, Nebraska 68509
(402) 471-2961

Services for the Visually Impaired
Department of Public Institutions
4600 Valley Road
Lincoln, Nebraska 68510-4844
(402) 471-2891

Nevada

Rehabilitation Division
Department of Human Resources
Kinkead Building, Fifth Floor
505 E. King Street
Carson City, Nevada 89710
(702) 885-4440

New Hampshire

Division of Vocational Rehabilitation
State Department of Education
78 Regional Drive
Concord, New Hampshire 03301
(603) 271-3471

New Jersey

Division of Vocational Rehabilitation Services
New Jersey Department of Labor and Industry
John Fitch Plaza
Trenton, New Jersey 08625
(609) 292-5987

Commission for the Blind and Visually Impaired
1100 Raymond Boulevard
Newark, New Jersey 07102
(201) 648-2324

New Mexico

Division of Vocational Rehabilitation
State Department of Education
604 W. San Mateo
Santa Fe, New Mexico 87503
(505) 827-3511

Commission for the Blind
Pera Building, Room 205
Santa Fe, New Mexico 87503
(505) 827-4479

New York

Commission for Vocational Rehabilitation
The New York State Education Department
Office of Vocational Rehabilitation
99 Washington Avenue, Room 1907
Albany, New York 12234
(518) 474-2714

State Department of Social Services
Commission for the Blind and Visually Handicapped
10 Eyck Office Building
40 N. Pearl Street
Albany, New York 12243
(518) 473-1801

North Carolina

Division of Vocational Rehabilitation Services
Department of Human Resources
State Office
P.O. Box 26053
Raleigh, North Carolina 27611
(919) 733-3364

Division of Services for the Blind
North Carolina Department of Human Resources
309 Ashe Avenue
Raleigh, North Carolina 27606
(919) 733-9822

North Dakota

Office of Vocational Rehabilitation
Department of Human Services
State Capitol
Bismarck, North Dakota 58505
(701) 224-2907

Ohio

Ohio Rehabilitation Services Commission
400 E. Campus View Boulevard
Columbus, Ohio 43235-4604
(614) 438-1210

Oklahoma

Division of Rehabilitation Services
Department of Human Services
P.O. Box 25352
2409 N. Kelly
Oklahoma City, Oklahoma 73125
(405) 424-6006

Oregon

Division Vocational Rehabilitation
Department of Human Resources
2045 Silverton Road, N.E.
Salem, Oregon 97310
(503) 378-3850

Commission for the Blind
535 S.E. 12th Avenue
Portland, Oregon 97214
(503) 238-8375

Pennsylvania

Office of Vocational Rehabilitation
Department of Labor and Industry Building
Seventh and Foster Streets
Harrisburg, Pennsylvania 17120
(717) 787-5244

Bureau of Blindness and Visual Services
Department of Public Welfare
Capital Association Building, Room 300
P.O. Box 2675
Harrisburg, Pennsylvania 17105
(717) 787-6176

Puerto Rico

Vocational Rehabilitation
Department of Social Services
P.O. Box 1118
Hato Rey, Puerto Rico 00919
(809) 725-1792

Rhode Island

Vocational Rehabilitation
Department of Human Services
40 Fountain Street
Providence, Rhode Island 02903
(401) 421-7005

South Carolina

South Carolina Vocational Rehabilitation Department
P.O. Box 15
1410 Boston Avenue
West Columbus, South Carolina 29171-0015
(803) 734-4300

Commission for the Blind
1430 Confederate Avenue
Columbia, South Carolina 29201
(803) 734-7520

South Dakota

Department of Vocational Rehabilitation
Richard F. Kneip Building
700 Governors Drive
Pierre, South Dakota 57501
(605) 773-3195

Tennessee

Division of Rehabilitation Services
Department of Human Services
Citizen Plaza Building, 15th Floor
400 Deaderick Street
Nashville, Tennessee 37219
(615) 741-2521

Texas

Texas Rehabilitation Commission
118 E. Riverside Drive
Austin, Texas 78704
(512) 445-8018

Texas Commission for the Blind
Administration Building
4800 N. Lamar Street
P.O. Box 12886, Capitol Station
Austin, Texas 78756
(512) 459-2600

Utah

Division of Rehabilitation Services
Utah State Office of Rehabilitation
250 E. South
Salt Lake City, Utah 84111
(801) 538-7530

Services for the Visually Handicapped
Utah State Office of Education
309 E. First South
Salt Lake City, Utah 84111
(801) 533-9393

Vermont

Vocational Rehabilitation Division
Agency of Human Services
Osgood Building, Waterbury Complex
103 S. Main Street
Waterbury, Vermont 05676
(802) 421-2189

Vermont Division for the Blind and Visually Impaired
Agency of Human Services
Osgood Building, Waterbury Complex
103 S. Main Street
Waterbury, Vermont 05676
(802) 241-2211

Virginia

Department of Rehabilitative Services
Commonwealth of Virginia
4901 Fitzhugh Avenue
P.O. Box 11045
Richmond, Virginia 23230-1045
(804) 367-0316

Virginia Department for the Visually Handicapped
397 Azalea Avenue
Richmond, Virginia 23227
(804) 371-3145

Washington

Division of Vocational Rehabilitation
Department of Social and Health Services
OB 21 C
Olympia, Washington 98504
(206) 753-2544

Department of Services for the Blind
521 E. Legon Way, MS: FD-11
Olympia, Washington 98504-1422
(206) 586-1224

West Virginia

Division of Rehabilitation Services
State Board of Rehabilitation
State Capitol Complex
Charleston, West Virginia 25305
(304) 766-4601

Wisconsin

Division of Vocational Rehabilitation
Department of Health and Social Services
One W. Wilson, Eighth Floor
P.O. Box 7852
Madison, Wisconsin 53707
(608) 266-2168

Wyoming

Division of Vocational Rehabilitation
Department of Health and Social Services
347 Hathaway Building
Cheyenne, Wyoming 82002
(307) 777-7385

American Samoa

Vocational Rehabilitation
Department of Manpower Resources
P.O. Box 3492
American Samoa Government
Pago Pago, American Samoa 96799
011 684 633-1805

Commonwealth of Northern Mariana Islands

Vocational Rehabilitation Division
Commonwealth of the Northern Mariana Islands
Saipan, Northern Mariana Islands 96950
011 670 734-6538

Guam

Department of Vocational Rehabilitation
Government of Guam
122 Harmon Plaza, Room B201
Harmon Industrial Park, Guam 96911
(671) 646-9468

Republic of the Marshall Islands

Health Services Department
P.O. Box 832
Marjuro, Marshall Islands 96960

Republic of Palau

Bureau of Education
P.O. Box 189
Koror, Palau
Western Carolina Islands 96940

Virgin Islands
Division of Disabilities and Rehabilitation Services
c/o Department of Human Services
Barbel Plaza
St. Thomas, Virgin Islands 00802
(809) 774-0930

Organizations That Provide Further Information on Financial Assistance Programs for Handicapped Students

American Council of the Blind
1010 Vermont Avenue
Washington, D.C. 20005

American Foundation for the Blind
15 W. 16th Street
New York, New York 10011

Alexander Graham Bell Association of the Deaf
3417 Volta Place, N.W.
Washington, D.C. 20007

Association on Handicapped Student Service Programs in Post-Secondary Education
P.O. Box 21192
Columbus, Ohio 43221

Council of Citizens with Low Vision
1400 Drake Road, #218
Kalamazoo, Michigan 49007

Deafness and Communicative Disorders Branch
Switzer Building, M/S 2312
Washington, D.C. 20202

Epilepsy Foundation
4251 Garden City Drive
Landover, Maryland 20785

Foundation for Science and the Handicapped
1141 Iroquois Drive #14
Napierville, Illinois 60540

Gallaudet University
800 Florida Avenue, N.E.
Washington, D.C. 20002

Health Resources Center
One Dupont Circle, N.W.
Washington, D.C. 20036-1193

Immune Deficiency Foundation
P.O. Box 586
Columbia, Maryland 21045

Helen Keller National Center
111 Middle Neck Road
Sands Point, New York 11050

Learning Disability Association
4156 Library Road
Pittsburgh, Pennsylvania 15234

Lifecare Scholarship for Respiratory Dependent
505 Central Avenue
Boulder, Colorado 80301

Ronnie Milsap Foundation
600 Renaissance Center
Detroit, Michigan 48234

National Association of the Deaf
814 Thayer Avenue
Silver Spring, Maryland 20910

National Federation of the Blind
1800 Johnson Street
Baltimore, Maryland 21230

National Information Center for Children and Youths with Handicaps
1555 Wilson Boulevard, Suite 508
Rosslyn, Virginia 22209

Office of Career Opportunities
National Technical Institute for the Deaf
One Lomb Memorial Drive
Rochester, New York 14623

Office of Special Education Programs
U.S. Department of Education
Office of Special Programs
400 Maryland Avenue
Washington, D.C. 20202

Recording for the Blind
20 Rozelle Road
Princeton, New Jersey 08540

Spina Bifida Association of America
1700 Rockville Pike
Rockville, Maryland 20852

United Cerebral Palsy Association
66 East 34th Street
New York, New York 10016

Some Final Notes on Financial Assistance Programs for the Handicapped

1. To obtain information on specific financial assistance programs, contact federal, state, and local organizations that provide services for the handicapped.

2. For help in locating funds, consult your school's director of financial aid.

3. For information on employment opportunities for handicapped persons, write to the Handicapped Information Resources for Employment, 95 Chestnut Ridge Road, Montvale, New Jersey 07645.

4. For additional information on programs and resources available to disabled persons, consult the following publications:

Directory of Facilities and Services for the Learning Disabled Academic Therapy Publications, 20 Commercial Boulevard, Novato, California 94947-6191.

Financial Aid for the Disabled and Their Families Gail Ann Schlachter, Reference Service Press, 10 Twin Dolphin Drive, Redwood City, California 94068.

Transition Resources to Facilitate the Transition from School to Work of Learners with Special Needs Technical Assistance for Special Populations, University of Illinois, 345 Education Building, 1310 S. Sixth Street, Champaign, Illinois 61820.

Unlocking Potential: College and Other Choices for Learning Disabled People: A Step-By-Step Guide Barbara Scheiber and Jeanne Talpers, Woodbine House, 10400 Connecticut Avenue, Kensington, Maryland 20895.

16 PROGRAMS FOR GRADUATE STUDENTS

Students enrolled in postbaccalaureate programs are classified as graduate students. Need-based aid for graduate students consists of loan, grant, and work-study programs. Eligibility is determined by federal and state regulations, and the formula used is similar to the needs formula for undergraduate students. Need-based aid is administered by a school's financial aid office. Students are required to file either a Financial Aid Form (FAF) or a Graduate and Professional School Financial Aid Service (GAPSFAS) application form.

There are no programs like the Pell Grant or Supplemental Education Opportunity Grant Program for graduate students; loans are the primary funding sources. Graduate students can borrow from the following federal sources:

Carl D. Perkins Loan Program

Parent Loans for Undergraduate Students (PLUS) Program

Stafford Student Loan Program

Supplemental Loan for Students (SLS) Program

Graduate students should seek funding also from private sources, including foundations, corporations, and research centers. Many graduate schools provide financial assistance to their students in the form of fellowships and assistantships. These academic and financial arrangements require the graduate student to teach or conduct research in exchange for a tuition waiver and living stipend. Each school determines its own eligibility requirements for fellowships and assistantships, but generally academic merit and scholarly promise are considered when making the awards. During their senior year in college, interested students should investigate funding opportunities at each graduate school they are considering. Apply early and observe deadlines. Realize that you are on your own in locating the financial resources necessary to finance your graduate education.

Funding Available to Graduate and Postdoctoral Students

American Association of School Administrators
This organization awards scholarships to full-time graduate students who are planning careers in school administration. Recipients must be recommended by the dean of their school. For further information, write to the Executive Director, AASA, 1801 N. Moore Street, Arlington, Virginia 22209.

American Association of University Women
This organization awards fellowships to women who are U.S. citizens or permanent residents and who are at the dissertation or postdoctoral level of graduate study. For further information, contact the American Association of University Women, 2401 Virginia Avenue, N.W., Washington, D.C. 20037, or call (202) 728-7603.

American Council of Learned Societies
This organization usually supports postdoctoral research in the humanities, including philosophy, literature, linguistics, history, and anthropology. Grants-in-aid provide stipends to assist graduate scholars with research projects. Grants for traveling to international meetings are also included in the organization's funding programs. There are also specific grants for graduate students engaged in the study of China and the Chinese language, as well as grants for students studying some aspect of East European countries. For further information, write to the American Council of Learned Societies, 228 E. 45th Street, New York, New York 10017-3398.

American Mensa Education and Research Foundation Scholarship Program
This organization provides financial assistance to graduate students. Applicants are required to submit essays stating their career objectives. Write to the American Mensa Scholarship Committee, 1701 W. Third Street, Brooklyn, New York, 11223, for additional information and application forms.

American Museum of Natural History   This organization sponsors several programs for graduate students. The Lerner Fund for Marine Research awards grants to graduate and postdoctoral students for marine biology research. The Frank M. Chapman Fund provides grants for ornithological research, and the Theodore Roosevelt Memorial Fund provides financial assistance to graduate students engaged in some aspect of wildlife conservation or natural history. For further information and application forms, write to the American Museum of Natural History, Central Park West at 79th Street, New York, New York 10024.

Amoco Foundation   This foundation provides financial assistance to encourage students to obtain doctorates in engineering. Awards are made for 1 to 3 years. For further information, write to Ph.D. Fellowship Program, Amoco Foundation, Inc., 200 E. Randolph Drive, Chicago, Illinois 60601-6404.

Assistantships   These arrangements allow graduate students to assist professors in classroom instruction in return for a reduction in tuition costs and/or a living stipend. Eligibility varies from school to school. Some assistantships are based upon financial need; others, upon academic merit. Check with the dean of your school or your school's financial aid director for further information and eligibility requirements.

California State University Loan Forgiveness   The state of California has initiated a program for women and minorities who are pursuing doctoral degrees and who plan to teach for at least 5 years in one of the California State schools. If hired after graduation, the recipient will have the loan canceled at the rate of 20% a year for up to 5 years. For further information, contact the California Student Aid Commission at (916) 445-0880.

Council of Logistics Management Graduate Scholarship Program   This program, managed by Citizens' Scholarship Foundation of America, Inc., is available to college seniors who plan to enroll in a graduate logistics management program, as well as to students enrolled in the first year of a graduate logistics management program. The application deadline is April 1. For applications, write to the Citizens' Scholarship Foundation of America, Inc., 1505 Riverview Road, P.O. Box 297, St. Peter, Minnesota 56082, or call (507) 931-1682.

Fellowships   These programs provide financial assistance to graduate students to help them continue with their studies. Financial assistance is given in exchange for teaching or clerical work. Eligibility varies from school to school. Check with your dean or financial aid director for further details.

Graduate Assistance in Areas of National Need
This program awards funds to academic departments to assist graduate students who are interested in teaching or conducting research in areas of national need. The Secretary of Education selects the areas of national need, which currently are considered to be mathematics, chemistry, physics, and engineering. For further information, contact your school's academic advisor.

Graduate and Professional Opportunities Program
This program awards fellowships to students enrolled in graduate or professional degree programs. The Secretary of Education allocates fellowships to selected institutions with approved programs of study. Institutions receiving the fellowships award them to eligible students. Write to the Office of Postsecondary Education, U.S. Department of Education, Room 3514, 400 Maryland Avenue, S.W., Washington, D.C. 20202, for further information and list of approved institutions.

Graduate Women in Science Fellowship Program
This program awards fellowships to women students conducting research in the sciences. The awards are based upon need and merit. For further information, write to Sigma Delta Epsilon, Graduate Women in Science, P.O. Box 4748, Ithaca, New York 14850.

Bishop Greco Graduate Fellowship Program   This program provides financial assistance to graduate students who are enrolled in programs that educate teachers of the mentally retarded. The fellowships are administered by the Knights of Columbus. Priority will be given to applicants who select Catholic schools. For applications, write to the Committee on Fellowships, Knights of Columbus, P.O. Drawer 1670, New Haven, Connecticut 06507.

John Simon Guggenheim Memorial Foundation Fellowship Program   This program awards fellowships to distinguished scholars who have made exceptional contributions to scholarship and the arts, promoting research and improving the quality of education and the practice of the arts. Write to the President, John Simon Guggenheim Memorial Foundation Fellowship Program, 90 Park Avenue, New York, New York 10016, for further information.

Patricia Roberts Harris Public Service Education Fellowship Program   This program provides financial assistance to students enrolled in public administration master's and doctoral programs. Recipients are selected by participating institutions. Write to the Department of Education, Graduate Programs Branch, 400 Maryland Avenue, S.W., Washington, D.C. 20202-5172 for further information.

Fannie and John Hertz Foundation Fellowships
These fellowships are offered to outstanding students in the physical sciences. Awards are made to both undergraduate and graduate students and can be renewed. The foundation supports fellowships only at select colleges and universities. For a list of schools and for further information, write to the Hertz Foundation, P.O. Box 5032, Livermore, California 94551.

Institute for Advanced Study   This organization provides financial assistance to post-doctoral students engaged in a variety of disciplines. For specific details, write to the Office of the Director, Institute for Advanced Study, Olden Lane, Princeton, New Jersey 08540.

International Business Machines (IBM) Fellowships
IBM sponsors a 1-year fellowship program for students who are enrolled full-time in doctoral programs at selected universities. The awards cover all tuition and fee charges and provide a living stipend. Fields of study include physics, chemistry, electrical engineering, mathematics, computer or information science, mechanical engineering, and materials science. For further information, write to the Manager, University and Scientific Relations, Thomas J. Watson Research Center, P.O. Box 218, Yorktown Heights, New York 10598.

Jacob Javits Fellowship Program
This program provides fellowships to graduate students enrolled in humanities, social sciences, or arts programs. For further information, contact the Department of Education, Graduate Programs Branch, 400 Maryland Avenue, S.W., Washington, D.C. 20202.

W. K. Kellogg Foundation
This organization awards fellowships to graduate students to develop leadership skills and broaden perspectives on the national and international problems facing the world today. For specific details, write to W. K. Kellogg National Fellowship Program, W. K. Kellogg Foundation, 400 North Avenue, Battle Creek, Michigan 49017-3398.

Kosciuszko Foundation
This organization provides financial assistance to full-time graduate and postgraduate students. Recipients must be U.S. citizens or permanent residents and must be of Polish descent. Americans who are not Polish but are studying Polish subjects are also eligible to apply. For further information, write to the Assistant Grants Officer, Kosciuszko Foundation, 15 E. 65th Street, New York, New York 10021-6595.

Law School Assured Access Program
This loan program provides loans to qualified law school students. For further information, write to the Law School Assured Access Program, Law School Admission Services, P.O. Box 2500, Newtown, Pennsylvania 18940-0990.

Masters in Business Administration Loans
This loan program is designed to assist students in MBA programs. Loan components include features of the Stafford Student Loan Program, the Supplemental Loans for Students Program, and the Tuition Loan Program. To qualify for this loan, students must be enrolled at least part-time and must have financial need. Loan consolidation options are available. For further information, write to MBA Loans, Processing Center, P.O. Box 64722, St. Paul, Minnesota 55164-0772, or call 1-800-366-6227.

Mellon Fellowships
These awards are granted to graduate students to encourage teaching and scholarship in the humanities. The fellowships cover all tuition costs and provide a living stipend. Several disciplines are included in award consideration. For further information and application forms, write to the Mellon Fellowship Program, Woodrow Wilson National Fellowship Foundation, 330 Alexander Street, Princeton, New Jersey 08542.

National Collegiate Athletic Association
This association awards scholarships to full-time graduate students who plan careers in athletics or in the administration of intercollegiate athletics. For further information, write to the National Collegiate Athletic Association, P.O. Box 1906, Mission, Kansas 66201.

National Endowment for the Humanities
This organization provides a number of fellowship and financial assistance programs for qualified teachers, scholars, and students. Write to the National Endowment for the Humanities, Division of Fellowships and Seminars, 1100 Pennsylvania Avenue, N.W., Washington, D.C. 20506, for a description of all programs and for application forms.

National Science Foundation
This organization awards fellowships to students enrolled in graduate schools and studying mathematics, engineering, social sciences, and the history and philosophy of science. Write to the Fellowship Office, National Research Council, 1800 G Street, N.W., Washington, D.C. 20550, for further information.

Office of Naval Research
The U.S. Navy offers awards to U.S. citizens or nationals who are studying engineering or one of the sciences. Write to ONR Graduate Fellowships, American Society for Engineering, 11 Dupont Circle, Suite 200, Washington, D.C. 20036.

Charlotte W. Newcomb Doctoral Dissertation Fellowship Program
This program provides financial assistance to students who are conducting research and completing their dissertations on some aspect of ethical or religious values in the humanities and social sciences. For further information, write to the Newcomb Fellowship Foundation, 330 Alexander Street, Princeton, New Jersey 08542.

Professional Education Plan
This program makes loans to students enrolled in graduate and professional schools. A variable interest rate is charged, and aggregate borrowing depends on the type of program. Deferments are available, and borrowers have up to 20 years to repay their loans. For further information, contact The Education Resources Institute (TERI), 330 Stuart Street, Suite 500, Boston, Massachusetts 02116.

Annie Ryder Memorial Scholarship Fund
This fund makes one scholarship award to a graduate student who plans a career in teaching. For further

information, write to the Education Chairman, Annie Ryder Memorial Fellowship Fund, 360 Woodland Road, Chestnut Hill, Massachusetts 02167.

United States Department of Education The Department of Education sponsors a number of financial assistance programs for graduate students and faculty. Write to U.S. Department of Education, Washington, D.C. 20202, for descriptions of all available programs and for application forms.

United States Department of Justice Law Enforcement Assistance Administration This organization provides financial support to doctoral students engaged in crime-related fields of study. Write to the Graduate Research Fellowship Program, National Criminal Justice Reference Service, Box 6000, Rockville, Maryland 20850.

Woodrow Wilson National Fellowship Foundation
This organization provides financial support for graduate students enrolled in humanities programs. The fellowship includes tuition costs and a living stipend. For further information, write to the Woodrow Wilson National Fellowship Foundation, P.O. Box 642, Princeton, New Jersey 08542.

State Financial Assistance Programs Offered to Graduate and Postdoctoral Students

The following are examples of the types of financial assistance programs offered by individual states to graduate and professional school students. Check the chapter on State Programs for further details.

Alaska

Jeane Kline Memorial Scholarship Program

A.W. "Winn" Brindle Memorial Scholarship Program

California

California Student Aid Commission Competitive State Graduate Fellowship Program

Colorado

Graduate Grant and Fellowship Program

Delaware

Delaware Postsecondary Scholarship Fund

Professional and Graduate Financial Assistance Programs

District of Columbia

Consern Loan Program

Florida

Critical Teacher Shortage Loan Forgiveness Program

Florida Graduate Scholars' Fund Program

Florida Teacher Scholarship Loan Program

Florida Teacher Tuition Reimbursement Program

Master's Fellowship Loan Program for Teachers

Georgia

Regents Scholarship Program

State Direct Student Loan Program

State-sponsored Loan Program

Hawaii

State Higher Education Loan Program (SHEL)

Kansas

James B. Pearson Fellowship Program

Kansas Rhodes Scholarship Program

Maine

Blain House Scholars Loan Program

Student Incentive Scholarship Program

Maryland

Child Care Provider Program

Ed Conroy Grant Program

House of Delegates Scholarship Program

Christa McAuliffe Critical Shortage Teacher Program

Christa McAuliffe Fellowship Program

Professional Scholarship Program

Resident Loan Program

Senatorial Scholarship Program

Massachusetts

EXCEL and GradEXCEL Loan Programs

Family Education Loan Program

Graduate Grant Program

Professional Education Loan Program

Security Education Loan Program

SHARE and GradSHARE Loan Programs

TERI Supplemental Loan

Minnesota

Graduated Repayment Income Protection Program

Student Educational Loan Fund

Mississippi

Graduate and Professional Degree Scholarship Program

Public Management Graduate Internship Program

New Jersey

Educational Opportunity Fund Graduate Grant

New Mexico

Graduate Fellowship Program

Professional Student Exchange Program

Three Percent Scholarship Program

New York

Empire State Fellowships

Jacob Javits Fellowship Program

SUNY Graduate Opportunity Tuition Scholarships

SUNY Graduate and Professional Tuition Scholarship Program

SUNY Minority Graduate Fellowships

Supplemental Higher Education Loan Financing Program (SHELF)

North Carolina

Minority Presence Grant Program

North Carolina Bar Association Scholarship Program

Oregon

Oregon Teacher Corps Program

Rhode Island

Knights Templar Educational Foundation

South Carolina

South Carolina Graduate Incentive Fellowship Program

Texas

Hinson-Hazelwood College Student Loan Program

Texas Teacher Education Loan Program

Vermont

EXTRA Loan Program

Washington

Western Interstate Commission for Higher Education

Western Interstate Commission for Higher Education Regional Graduate Program

West Virginia

Underwood-Smith Teacher Scholarship Program

Organizations That Provide Further Information on Financial Assistance Programs for Graduate and Postdoctoral Students

American Council of Learned Societies
228 E. 45th Street
New York, New York 10017-3398
(212) 697-1505

Association of American Law Schools
One Dupont Circle, Suite 370
Washington, D.C. 20036
(202) 296-8851

Council of Graduate Schools
One Dupont Circle, Suite 430
Washington, D.C. 20036
(202) 223-3791

Graduate Management Admission Council
1299 Ocean Avenue, Suite 313
Santa Monica, California 90401
(213) 478-1433

Law School Admission Council/Law School Admission Services
1707 N Street, N.W.
Washington, D.C. 20036
(202) 293-3140

Publications That Provide Information on Financial Assistance Programs for Graduate Students

Fellowships and Grants American Council of Learned Societies, 228 E. 45th Street, New York, New York 10017-3398.

Fellowships: United States of America and Canada John Simon Guggenheim Memorial Foundation, 90 Park Avenue, New York, New York 10026.

Financial Aid for Graduate and Professional Education Peterson's, P.O. Box 2123, Princeton, New Jersey 08543-2123.

Fulbright and Other Grants for Graduate Study Abroad Institute of International Education, 809 United Nations Plaza, New York, New York 10027.

Graduate Assistantship Directory in the Computer Sciences Association for Computing Machinery, Inc., 11 W. 42nd Street, New York, New York 10036.

The Graduate Scholarship Book: The Complete Guide to Scholarships, Fellowships, Grants, and Loans for Graduate and Professional Study Prentice-Hall, 200 Old Tappan Road, Old Tappan, New Jersey 07675.

Graduate School and You: A Guide for Prospective Graduate Students Council of Graduate Schools, One Dupont Circle, N.W., Suite 430, Washington, D.C. 20036.

Graduate Study in Psychology and Associated Fields American Psychological Association, Educational Affairs Office, 1200 17th Street, N.W., Washington, D.C. 20036.

Grant Guidelines New York Council for the Humanities, 33 W. 42nd Street, New York, New York 10036.

Grants, Fellowships, and Prizes of Interest to Historians American Historical Association, 400 A Street, S.E., Washington, D.C. 20003.

The Grants Register St. Martin's Press, 175 Fifth Avenue, New York, New York 10010.

Guide to Graduate Study in Economics and Agricultural Economics in the United States and Canada Richard D. Irwin, 1818 Ridge Road, Homewood, Illinois 60430.

Guide to Graduate Study in Political Science American Political Science Association, 1527 New Hampshire Avenue, N.W., Washington, D.C. 20036.

Guide to Grants and Fellowships in Languages and Linguistics LSA Secretariat, 1325 18th Street, N.W., Suite 211, Washington, D.C. 20036-6501.

Overview of Endowment Programs National Endowment for the Humanities, 1100 Pennsylvania Avenue, N.W., Washington, D.C. 20506.

Social Science Research Council Fellowship and Grants for Research Social Science Research Council, 605 Third Avenue, New York, New York 10158.

Some Final Notes on Financial Assistance Programs for Graduate Students

1. Students who are interested in continuing their education after undergraduate school should remember that financial aid funding for graduate students is different. There are few federal direct subsidies and no federal grant programs. However, funding is available; it is up to the graduate student to locate specific sources.

2. Recent federal legislation allows a tax exemption of $5250 in education benefits paid to employees by their employer. This tax break applies to non-job-related graduate study. There is no dollar limit on job-related graduate courses. These courses are tax-free as well.

17 HEALTH PROFESSIONS STUDENTS

Health professions programs include the following disciplines:

Medicine

Dentistry

Nursing—Associate, Diploma, Baccalaureate, Graduate

Osteopathic Medicine

Veterinary Medicine

Pharmacy

Optometry

Podiatric Medicine

Chiropractic Educaion

Clinical Psychology

Public Health Administration

Occupational Safety

Occupational Therapy

Physical Therapy

Rehabilitation Therapy

Nutrition

Social Work

Allied Health

Health professions students can be either undergraduate or graduate students. Pharmacy and nursing students are generally classified as undergraduates and therefore are eligible to apply for all of the federal programs listed in the chapter on Federal Programs, which include:

Pell Grant Program

Supplemental Educational Opportunity Grant (SEOG) Program

Stafford Student Loan Program

Carl D. Perkins Loan Program

College Work-Study Program (CWSP)

Students enrolled in other health professions disciplines are generally classified as graduate and professional school students and are eligible for the following federal financial assistance programs:

Health Education Assistance Loan Program

Health Professions Student Loan Program

Stafford Student Loan Program

Carl D. Perkins Loan Program

College Work-Study Program (CWSP)

Parent Loans for Undergraduate Students (PLUS) Program

Supplemental Loan for Students (SLS) Program

Federal Programs for Undergraduate and Graduate Health Professions Students

Health professions students have specific and separate federal funding sources. These sources are listed below for both undergraduate and graduate health professions students.

Financial Assistance for Disadvantaged Health Professions Students Program (FADS)
This program provides financial assistance to students enrolled in schools of medicine, dentistry, and osteopathy. Recipients must demonstrate exceptional financial need and must come from a disadvantaged background as defined by the U.S. Department of Health and Human Services. Recipients must be enrolled or accepted for enrollment in an approved health professions school as full-time students and must be U.S. citizens or permanent residents. These scholarships pay for the cost of tuition, fees, and educational and living expenses and may be awarded for any year of study. Continued funding depends upon future federal allocations. Contact your school's director of financial aid, or write to the Division of Student

Assistance, Bureau of Health Professions, Health Resources and Services Administration, Parklawn Building, Room 8-48, 5600 Fishers Lane, Rockville, Maryland 20857.

Health Education Assistance Loan Program (HEAL)

This loan program provides financial assistance to qualified health professions students. Applicants must be U.S. citizens or permanent residents and must be enrolled or accepted for enrollment in an approved health professions school as full-time students. Students enrolled in schools of medicine, dentistry, veterinary medicine, osteopathy, optometry, and podiatry may borrow up to $20,000 per academic year, for a total of $80,000. Students in other health disciplines may borrow up to $12,500 a year, for a total of $50,000.

Loans may be used only for educational expenses, and recipients must demonstrate financial need. Creditworthiness is checked before the loan is granted. There is no federal interest subsidy for this loan. At the lender's option, the interest rate on a HEAL loan may be calculated on a fixed or a variable basis. Interest is calculated using the 91-day U.S. Treasury bill average plus 3.5%. Some lenders use 2.75% in their calculation of interest. Repayment begins 9 months after a borrower ceases to be a full-time student. Borrowers have up to 25 years to repay this loan. Deferments of the principal are granted while a student is enrolled full-time in a health professions program and for up to 4 years during internship and residency training periods. Deferments of principal are also granted for up to 3 years for serving in the Peace Corps, National Health Service Corps, Armed Services, or VISTA.

There is a separate application for HEAL loans, and it can be obtained from your school's financial aid office. Contact the Division of Student Assistance, HEAL Branch, 5600 Fishers Lane, Rockville, Maryland 20857 for more information.

Health Professions Student Loan Program (HPSL)

These loans are available through a revolving loan fund originally funded by the federal government and now financed with repayments of previous borrowers. This is a need-based program, and only students classified as having the greatest financial need qualify for loans. Applicants must be U.S. citizens or permanent residents. Recipients must be enrolled full-time in an approved health professions school and must maintain satisfactory academic progress as defined by their school.

Because there is no annual allocation from the federal government, the amount of the award can change from year to year. The maximum that can be borrowed annually is the amount equal to the cost of tuition and fees plus $2500. Students cannot apply directly to this program; awards are made by the school's financial aid director after reviewing the student's financial aid

application. Students usually file the Graduate and Professional School Financial Application Service (GAPSFAS) form to apply for this program. The interest rate is 9%. No interest accrues while the borrower is in school, and there is a 1-year grace period after graduation.

Deferments of principal and interest are granted for periods of advanced professional training, such as internship and residency, and for up to 3 years for serving in the Peace Corps, Armed Services, or U.S. Public Health Service. The maximum period for repayment is 10 years. Loan forgiveness options are available for borrowers who agree to practice in a federally designated shortage area after graduation. For more information on this program, contact your school's director of financial aid, or write to U.S. Department of Health and Human Services, Bureau of Health Personnel, Development and Service, Student and Institutional Assistance Branch, Parklawn Building, Room 9A-25, 5600 Fishers Lane, Rockville, Maryland 20857.

National Health Corps Loan Repayment Program

This program was created by the federal government to alleviate the shortages of health professionals by granting financial incentives to students to complete health professions degrees. Under this program, health professions students can have up to $20,000 a year of their educational loans paid for by the National Health Service Corps in return for practicing for at least 2 years in a federally designated health shortage area. Contact your school's director of financial aid, or write to the National Health Service Corps Repayment Program, Parklawn Building, Room 7-16, 5600 Fishers Lane, Rockville, Maryland 20857, for further information.

National Health Service Corps Scholarship Program

This program provides a limited number of awards to eligible students enrolled in medicine, dentistry, and osteopathy programs. The scholarship pays for all tuition, fees, books, and a monthly living stipend. Recipients are required to serve 1 year for each year of support, or a minimum of 2 years, in the National Health Service Corps in a federally designated health shortage area. For further information, contact the National Health Service Corps Scholarship Program, Room 7-16, Parklawn Building, 5600 Fishers Lane, Rockville, Maryland 20857.

Nursing Student Loan Program

This program provides low-interest loans to both full-time and half-time nursing students attending accredited schools. The Nursing Student Loan Program, although a federal loan program, does not receive new annual funding from the federal government; loans are made from moneys collected from previous borrowers. Recipients must be U.S. citizens, nationals, or permanent residents. A student enrolled in a program leading to a diploma, associate degree, bachelor's degree, or graduate nursing degree is eligible to apply. Students may borrow up to $2500 per year for a total of $10,000. The interest rate is 6%, and borrowers have 10 years to repay the loan, beginning 9 months after leaving school. Deferments are granted to borrowers who are enrolled in full-time graduate nursing degree programs who serve in the Armed Forces, U.S. Public Health Service, or Peace Corps. There is no separate application for this loan. Awards are made by the school's director of financial aid. For further information, write to the Health Services Administration, Division of Student Assistance, Room 8-44, 5600 Fishers Lane, Rockville, Maryland 20857.

Scholarship Program for Students with Exceptional Financial Need   This scholarship program is offered to students enrolled in schools of medicine, dentistry, osteopathy, optometry, pharmacy, podiatry, or veterinary medicine. Students must demonstrate exceptional financial need. Funds are allocated to each health professions school, and the director of financial aid selects the recipients. The scholarship can pay up to the cost of tuition, books, and instruments. There is no separate application. Contact your school's director of financial aid for more information. Although this scholarship covers only 1 year of study, recipients usually receive priority if they apply for National Health Service Corps Scholarships for their additional years of study.

Military Programs for Health Professions Students

Several military programs are available to health professions students; most of the programs are for students enrolled in professional schools. Examples of military programs for health professions students include:

Armed Forces Health Professions Scholarship Program   This program is available to qualified health professions students and pays for the student's tuition, fees, and books. A monthly living stipend is also part of the scholarship award. Recipients must agree to serve in one branch of the Armed Forces after graduation. Contact your school's director of financial aid for further information, or write to:

Air Force
Headquarters, USAF
Recruiting Service
Director of Health Professions Recruiting
Randolph Air Force Base
San Antonio, Texas 78150

Army
Commander, Army Medical Department Personnel
SGPE-PDM-S
1900 Half Street, S.W.
Washington, D.C. 20304-2000

Navy and Marine Corps
Navy Recruiting Command
4015 Wilson Boulevard
Arlington, Virginia 22203

Reserve Officer Training Corps (ROTC) Nursing Scholarship Program   The Army and Air Force offer scholarship programs to nursing students enrolled in approved colleges or universities with ROTC units. The scholarships cover all tuition and fees and offer a monthly stipend. Students must agree to serve as commissioned officers for 4 years after graduation. Write to the Air Force ROTC Scholarship Program, Office of Public Affairs, Maxwell Air Force Base, Alabama 36112, for information offered by the Air Force. Contact the Army ROTC Scholarship Program, Fort Monroe, Virginia 23651, for information offered by the Army. Contact the Navy ROTC Scholarship Program, Information Center, P.O. Box 5000, Clifton, New Jersey 07015-9939, for information offered by the Navy.

Uniformed Service University of the Health Sciences   This medical school, administered by the military, enrolls a limited number of students each year. There are no tuition or fee charges, and students receive a salary equal to that of a lieutenant. For further information, write to the Director of Admissions, Uniformed Service University of the Health Sciences, 4301 Jones Bridge Road, Bethesda, Maryland 20814.

Contact the following for further information on all military programs for health professions students:

Air Force
U.S. Air Force Health Professions Recruiting
Airman Memorial Building
5211 Auth Road, Suite 201
Suitland, Maryland 20746
(301) 238-2152

Army
AMEDD Personnel Counselor
Forest Glenn Section
Walter Reed Army Medical Center
Washington, D.C. 20012
(202) 576-1607

Navy
Navy Recruiting District
Naval Belcrest Road, Suite 301
Hyattsville, Maryland 20782
(202) 436-2072

State Financial Assistance Programs Offered to Health Professions Students

The following are examples of the types of programs offered by individual states to health professions students. Further information may be obtained by checking Chapter 9, State Programs.

Alabama

Dental Scholarship Awards

Medical Merit Scholarship Award Program

Medical Scholarship Award Program

Nursing Scholarship Program

State of Alabama Chiropractic Scholarship Program

Alaska

Alaska Student Loan Program

WAMI Medical Education Program

Arizona

State of Arizona Medical Student Loan Program

Arkansas

Arkansas Rural Medical Practice Loan and
Scholarship Program

California

California Loans to Assist Students

California Medical Education and Research
Foundation Loan Program

Health Careers Educational Assistance Grants

Colorado

Colorado Alternative Student Loan Program

Colorado Graduate Grant Program

Delaware

Delaware Academy of Medicine Loan Program

Delaware Nursing Incentive Scholarship Loan
Program

Professional and Graduate Financial Assistance
Program

District of Columbia

Consern Loan Program

Florida

Florida Dental Association Student Loan Fund

Georgia

Georgia Regents and Opportunity Grant for Graduate
and Professional Students

Georgia Regents Scholarship Program

Medical Scholarship Program

Osteopathic Medical Loan Program

Hawaii

Community Scholarship Program

State Higher Education Loan Program (SHEL)

Idaho

WAMI Medical Education Program

Illinois

Illinois Family Practice Scholarship Program

Kansas

Dentistry Assistance Program

Kansas Medical Scholarship Program

Kansas Nursing Scholarship Program

Kansas Osteopathic Scholarship Program

Optometry Scholarship Program

Kentucky

Rural Kentucky Medical Loan Fund Program

Maine

Maine Medical Loan Program

Maine Student Incentive Scholarship Program

Maryland

Edward Conroy Scholarship Program

Family Practice Scholarship Program

House of Delegates Scholarship Program

Maryland State Nursing Scholarship Program

Physical and Occupational Therapist and Assistants
Scholarship Program

Professional Scholarship Program

Senatorial Scholarship Program

Massachusetts

Medical, Dental, Veterinary Scholarship Program

Medical Student Loan Program

Professional Education Loan Program

Security Educational Loan Program

TERI Supplemental Loan Program

Minnesota

Graduated Repayment Income Protection Program
(GRIP)

Nursing Grant Program

Student Educational Loan Fund

Mississippi

Graduate and Professional Scholarship Program

Nursing Education Scholarship Grant Program

Nursing Education Scholarship for Study in
Baccalaureate Nursing Education Program

Special Medical Education Loan Program

State Medical/Dental Education Loan Program

New Hampshire

Nursing Education Grant Program

Tuition Loans for Veterinary Medicine Program

Nebraska

Nebraska Medical Student Loan Program

New Mexico

Minority Doctoral Assistance Program

New Mexico Nursing Student Loan Program

Osteopathic Medical Student Loan Program

Parent Alternative Loan Program (PAL)

Physician Student Loan Program

Professional Student Exchange Program

New York

Graduate and Professional Tuition Waiver Program for Economically Disadvantaged Students

New York State Health Service Corps Scholarship Program

Physician Loan Forgiveness Program

Regents Health Care Opportunity Scholarship Program

Regents Professional Opportunity Scholarship Program

Tuition Assistance Program (TAP)

North Carolina

Board of Governors Dental Scholarship Program

Board of Governors Medical Scholarship Program

North Carolina Student Loan Program for Health, Science, and Mathematics

Nurse Education Scholarship Program

Nursing Scholars Program

North Dakota

Loans for Medical and Dental Students Program

North Dakota Nursing Scholarship-Loan Program

Ohio

Regents Graduate/Professional Fellowship Program

Oklahoma

Chiropractic Education Assistance Program

Oklahoma Rural Medical Education Program

Oklahoma Tuition and Grant Program

Oregon

Medical and Dental Student Loan Program

Nursing Grant Program

Nursing Loan Program

Pennsylvania

State Grant Program

South Carolina

South Carolina Graduate Incentive Fellowship Program

Texas

College Access Loan Program

Hinson-Hazelwood College Student Loan Program

State Rural Medical Education Program

Texas Public Educational Grant Program

Vermont

Vermont EXTRA Loan Program

Vermont Incentive Grant Program

Virginia

General Assembly Nursing Scholarship Program

Rural Dental Scholarship Program

State Family Medicine Scholarship Program

Virginia Tuition Assistance Grant Program

Washington

Nurses Conditional Scholarship Program

West Virginia

Professional Degree Program

Teddi Bear Loan Program

West Virginia Board of Regents Medical Student Loan Fund

West Virginia Public Health Trust Scholarship Progam

Other Financial Assistance Programs for Health Professions Students

Several other financial assistance programs are available to health professions students. These include:

Alpha Epsilon Iota Scholarship Fund Female students who have been accepted to or are enrolled in accredited medical schools are eligible to apply for financial assistance from this fund. Awards are based upon academic merit and financial need. Contact the Trust Officer, Security Bank, P.O. Box 8612, Ann Arbor, Michigan 48107-8612 for additional information.

American Association for Dental Research
This organization provides financial assistance to dental students who are enrolled in accredited dental schools and are conducting research under the supervision of a faculty member. Contact the American Association for Dental Research, Central Office, 1111 14th Street, N.W., Suite 1000, Washington, D.C. 20005, for additional information.

American Association of University Women
This organization provides financial assistance to women in their final year of medicine. Recipients must be enrolled in accredited medical schools. The amount of the award varies. For further information and application materials, contact the American Association of University Women Educational Foundation Programs, 1111 16th Street, N.W., Washington, D.C. 20036.

American Fund for Dental Health
A number of financial assistance programs are offered to dental students and faculty. Contact the American Fund for Dental Health, 211 E. Chicago Avenue, Chicago, Illinois 60611, for additional information on all sponsored programs.

American Medical Student Association HEAL DEAL Loan
The American Medical Student Association offers loans to medical students who are association members. Recipients must meet the same criteria as those for Health Education Assistance Loans. The interest rate is variable and adjusted every quarter. For further information and application forms, contact the American Medical Student Association, 1980 Preston White Drive, Reston, Virginia 22091.

American Medical Technologists Scholarship Program
This program awards scholarships to qualified high school seniors who are planning careers in medical technology or medical assisting. Call American Medical Technologists, at (708) 823-5169, for additional information.

American Nurses Association Baccalaureate Scholarship Program
This program provides scholarship assistance to registered nurses who are pursuing baccalaureate degrees in nursing and who are members of a minority. Contact the Director, American Nurses Association, 1030 15th Street, N.W., Washington, D.C. 20005, for further information.

American Osteopathic Association
This organization awards scholarships to sophomore students attending osteopathic colleges. Applicants must complete an interview and must demonstrate academic ability and financial need. Contact the Executive Director, Auxiliary to the American Osteopathic Association, 142 E. Ontario, Chicago, Illinois 60611, for additional information and application forms.

American Podiatric Medical Association
This organization offers scholarship assistance to senior podiatry students who plan to continue with their studies. Write to the American Podiatric Medical Association, 9312 Old Georgetown Road, Bethesda, Maryland 20814-1621, for additional details.

Bureau of Health Manpower Health Training Grants
Allied Health Advanced Traineeship Programs provide full-time academic training to qualified health professions students enrolled in master's or doctoral degree programs in teaching, administration, or supervision in allied health fields. Contact the Education Employment Branch, Division of Associated Health Professions, Parklawn Building, 5600 Fishers Lane, Rockville, Maryland 20857, for further information.

Commissioned Officer Student Training and Extern Program (COSTEP)
This is a federally sponsored program coordinated by the U.S. Public Health Service. Students who have successfully completed at least 1 year of medical, dental, or veterinary school are eligible to apply. While students are participating in COSTEP, they are commissioned as reserve officers of the Public Health Service. Recipients work in Public Health Service facilities during school vacations and are paid at the rate of a lieutenant's salary. There are no service requirements after graduation. The program is competitive, and interested students should apply by February 1. For more information, write to the Chief, Employment Operations Branch, Division of Commissioned Personnel, Room 4-35, 5600 Fishers Lane, Rockville, Maryland 20857, or to COSTEP, PHS Recruitment, 8201 Greensboro Drive, Suite 600, McLean, Virginia 22102.

Dental Education Assistance Loan Program (DEAL)
This loan program provides financial assistance to dental students who are members of either the American Association of Dental Schools or the American Student Dental Association. The program is offered by Key Bank of central Maine and Knight Tuition Payment Plans, Inc. Using a single application form, a student can also apply for a Stafford Student Loan, Health Education Assistance Loan, Supplemental Loans for Students, and Private Loan Program. Interest rates are competitive. For further information, write to the American Association of Dental Schools, 1625 Massachusetts Avenue, N.W., Washington, D.C. 20036, or to the Key Bank, Dental Education Assistance Loan Program, 855 Boylston Street, Boston, Massachusetts 02116.

Dental General Practice Residency Program
General practice residency programs are offered by the Army, Navy, and Air Force to qualified dental graduates. The program is designed to broaden the techniques and skills of recent graduates and to provide them with the opportunity to practice dentistry and assume responsibility for total patient care under the supervision of a qualified staff. Selected applicants with no other service obligation are required to serve on active duty for a specific period

of time. Applications are made in the third year of dental school. Contact your school's director of financial aid, academic dean, or local Armed Forces recruiter for further information and application materials.

Foundation of the National Student Nurses Association Scholarship Programs   Several scholarship and financial assistance programs are offered for students who are enrolled or accepted for enrollment in nursing programs. Contact the Foundation of the National Student Nurses Association Inc., 555 W. 57th Street, New York, New York 10019, for additional information and application forms.

Geriatric Dentistry Fellowship Program   This 2-year training program funded by the Veterans Administration supports the training of dentists in the field of geriatrics and gerontology. The fellowships are for 2 years and award an annual stipend. For further information, contact your nearest Veterans Administration office.

Gillette Hayden Memorial Foundation   This foundation provides loan assistance to third- and fourth-year female dental students who are financially needy. Write to the Gillette Hayden Memorial Foundation, 95 W. Broadway, Salem, New Jersey 08079, for additional information and application forms.

Hillenbrand Fellowship   This program provides fellowships to recently graduated dentists who are interested in pursuing careers in dental administration. Fellowships include a living stipend and funds for traveling. Applications are available from the American Fund for Dental Health, 211 E. Chicago Avenue, P.O. Box 7740-A, Chicago, Illinois 60680.

Knights Templar Loan Fund   Loans are made to qualified health professions students. Contact the Knights Templar Foundation, 14 E. Jackson Boulevard, Suite 1700, Chicago, Illinois 60604-2293, for further information.

Massachusetts Federation of Polish Women   Women who are residents of Massachusetts and are of Polish origin, and who have been accepted to an accredited medical or dental school, may apply for financial assistance from this organization. Write to the Massachusetts Federation of Polish Women, 300 Sunnymeade Avenue, Chicopee, Massachusetts, 01013, for further information and application materials.

Medical School Loan Program (MEDLOANS)   This program provides funds to allopathic medical students to finance their medical school and residency training programs and is sponsored by the Association of American Medical Colleges. Students may also apply for a Stafford Student Loan, Supplemental Loans for Students, a Health Education Assistance Loan, and the Alternative Loan Program on the same application form. No interest is charged while the student is in medical school or in a residency program; a variable interest rate is charged once repayment begins. Graduated

repayment and loan consolidation options are available. Recipients must be enrolled or accepted for enrollment in an accredited Association of American Medical Colleges school in the United States. Candidates must be U.S. citizens, nationals, or permanent residents, and must continue to make satisfactory academic progress as determined by their school. For further information, contact your school's director of financial aid, or write to the Association of American Medical Colleges, 1776 Massachusetts Avenue, N.W., Suite 301, Washington, D.C. 20036-1989.

National Institute of Dental Research (NIDR)   This organization provides financial assistance to dental students who are pursuing careers in dental and biomedical research. Write to the National Institute of Dental Research, Westwood Building, Bethesda, Maryland 20892, for further information.

National Institutes of Health (NIH)   NIH offers several awards to support students' research activities. For further information, contact the Office of Grants Inquiries, Westwood Building, Room 449, National Institute of Health, Bethesda, Maryland 20892.

National Medical Fellowships   These fellowships are offered to minority students who are enrolled in the first or second year at an accredited medical school. For further information, contact the National Medical Fellowship Program, 254 W. 31st Street, New York, New York 10001.

National Research Service Awards   This program is administered by the National Institutes of Health and provides postdoctoral fellowships to medical and dental students. The awards are given for teaching or research for 2 or 3 years. There is a year for year payback commitment. Contact the Research Manpower Office, National Institutes of Health, Bethesda, Maryland 20014, for further information.

National Society, Daughters of the American Revolution Medical Scholarship Program   Under the Caroline E. Holt Education Fund, scholarships are awarded to students enrolled in accredited schools of nursing. Recipients are selected on the basis of financial need, academic grades, and letters of recommendation. The amounts of the award vary. For further information, write to the Office of Committees, NSDAR Administration Building, 1776 D Street, N.W., Washington, D.C. 20006-5392.

Nurses' Educational Funds   These funds provide scholarship assistance to registered nurses who are enrolled in advanced nursing degree programs. Contact the Nurses' Educational Funds, 555 W. 57th Street, New York, New York 10019 for further information.

William and Mary Shreve Foundation   This foundation provides financial assistance to students who have been accepted to accredited medical and dental schools. The amount of the award varies. Contact the

William and Mary Shreve Foundation, Box 240, 771 N. Penn Avenue, Morrisville, Pennsylvania, 19067, for further information and application forms.

Rock Sleyster Memorial Scholarship Program

This program provides financial assistance to fourth-year medical students who are planning to specialize in psychiatry. The awards are based upon academic merit, financial need, and interest in psychiatry. Contact the Department of Undergraduate Evaluation, American Medical Association, 535 N. Dearborn Street, Chicago, Illinois 60610, for further information.

Hattie M. Strong Foundation

This foundation provides interest-free loans of varying amounts to qualified fourth-year health professions students. For applications, write to the Hattie M. Strong Foundation, 1735 Eye Street, N.W., Washington, D.C. 20006.

Teamsters Union Scholarship Fund

Union members' children who have been accepted at approved health professions schools are eligible to apply. The amount of the award varies. Contact the local union for further information and application forms.

United States Department of Health and Human Services—Indian Health Service Health Professions Scholarship Program

This program is available to students enrolled in the following health professions programs: medicine, dentistry, nursing, public health administration. The scholarships provide full tuition assistance in addition to a monthly stipend. Recipients must agree to work for the Indian Health Service after graduation for 1 year for each year of assistance received. Contact the Indian Health Service Health Professions Scholarship Program, 1101 Kermit Drive, Oaks Tower #810, Nashville, Tennessee 37217, for additional information.

Veterans Administration Health Professions Scholarship Program

Federal law allows the Veterans Administration to award scholarships to nursing students who are enrolled full-time in an undergraduate or graduate school of nursing. Recipients receive funds to meet all tuition and fee costs as well as a living stipend. Students selected for this program are required to serve for 2 years in the Veterans Administration. For additional information, contact the Veterans Administration Professional Scholarship Program, Veterans Administration, Washington, D.C. 20420, or call 1-800-368-5896.

WICHE Professional Student Exchange Program

This program was created by the Western Interstate Commission for Higher Education, for the benefit of the western states and their citizens. Professional training programs in medicine, dentistry, veterinary medicine, dental hygiene, graduate nursing education, and public health are included in the exchange program. The states select from students in the available disiplines those they will support, and pay to the school the tuition costs and fees of these students. Contact your state's certifying officer for an application, or call (303) 492-5151. See the chapter on State Programs for a list of participating WICHE states.

Organizations That Provide Further Information on Financial Assistance Programs for Health Professions Students

The following organizations can provide specific information on scholarship and loan programs available to health professions students. Interested students should contact the organization of their specialty for further information.

American Association of Colleges of Nursing
One Dupont Circle, N.W., Suite 530
Washington, D.C. 20036
(202) 463-6930

American Association of Colleges of Osteopathic Medicine
6110 Executive Boulevard, Suite 405
Rockville, Maryland 20852
(301) 468-0990

American Association of Colleges of Pharmacy
1426 Prince Street
Alexandria, Virginia 22314
(703) 739-2330

American Association of Colleges of Podiatric Medicine
6110 Executive Boulevard, Suite 204
Rockville, Maryland 20852
(301) 984-9350

American Association of Dental Schools
1625 Massachusetts Avenue, N.W.
Washington, D.C. 20036
(202) 667-9433

American Nurses' Association
2420 Pershing Road
Kansas City, Missouri 64108
(816) 474-5720

American Public Health Association
1015 15th Street, N.W.
Washington, D.C. 20005
(202) 789-5600

American Veterinary Medical Association
1522 K Street, N.W., Suite 828
Washington, D.C. 20005
(202) 659-2040

Association of American Medical Colleges
One Dupont Circle, N.W., Suite 200
Washington, D.C. 20036
(202) 828-0400

Association of Schools and Colleges of Optometry
6110 Executive Boulevard, Suite 514
Rockville, Maryland 20852
(301) 231-5944

Association of Schools of Public Health
1015 15th Street, N.W.
Washington, D.C. 20005
(202) 842-4668

Association of University Programs in Health Administration
1911 N. Fort Meyer Drive, Suite 503
Arlington, Virginia 22209
(703) 524-0511

Bureau of Health Care Delivery and Assistance
Division of Health Services Scholarships
Parklawn Building
5600 Fishers Lane
Rockville, Maryland 20857

Bureau of Health Professions
Division of Student Assistance
Parklawn Building
5600 Fishers Lane
Rockville, Maryland 20857
(301) 443-4776

Council on Chiropractic Education
3209 Ingersoll Avenue
Des Moines, Iowa 50312
(515) 255-2184

National Association of Advisors for the Health Professions
P.O. Box 5017
Station A
Champaign, Illinois 61820
(217) 344-6013

National Health Service Corps Scholarship Program
Parklawn Building, Room 7-16
5600 Fishers Lane
Rockville, Maryland 20857
(301) 443-1600

National League for Nursing
10 Columbus Circle
New York, New York 10019
(212) 582-1022

National Medical Association
1012 Tenth Street, N.W.
Washington, D.C. 20001
(202) 347-1895

National Medical Fellowships, Inc.
254 W. 31st Street
New York, New York 10001
(212) 714-0033

National Student Nurses' Association
555 W. 57th Street, Suite 1325
New York, New York 10019
(212) 581-2211

United States Department of Health and Human Services
The following regional offices of the U.S. Department of Health and Human Services can provide information on all programs for health professions students.

Region I
(Connecticut, Maine, Massachusetts, New Hampshire, Rhode Island, Vermont)
Department of Health and Human Services
John F. Kennedy Federal Building
Government Center, Room 2411
Boston, Massachusetts 02203
(617) 565-1500

Region II
(New York, New Jersey, Puerto Rico, Virgin Islands)
Department of Health and Human Services
26 Federal Plaza, Room 3835
New York, New York 10278
(212) 264-4600

Region III
(Delaware, District of Columbia, Maryland, Pennsylvania, Virginia, West Virginia)
Department of Health and Human Services
P.O. Box 13716, Room 11480
Philadelphia, Pennsylvania 19101
(215) 596-6492

Region IV
(Alabama, Florida, Georgia, Kentucky, Mississippi, North Carolina, South Carolina, Tennessee)
Department of Health and Human Services
101 Marietta Tower, Suite 1515
Atlanta, Georgia 30323
(404) 331-2471

Region V
(Illinois, Indiana, Michigan, Minnesota, Ohio, Wisconsin)
Department of Health and Human Services
105 W. Adams
Chicago, Illinois 60603
(312) 353-5132

Region VI
(Arkansas, Louisiana, New Mexico, Oklahoma, Texas)
Department of Health and Human Services
1200 Main Tower Building, Room 1100
Dallas, Texas 75202
(214) 767-3301

Region VII
(Iowa, Kansas, Missouri, Nebraska)
Department of Health and Human Services
601 E. 12th Street, Room 210
Kansas City, Missouri 64106
(816) 426-2829

Region VIII
(Colorado, Montana, North Dakota, South Dakota, Utah, Wyoming)
Department of Health and Human Services
Federal Building, Room 1185
1961 Stout Street
Denver, Colorado 80294
(303) 844-3372

Region IX
(American Samoa, Arizona, California, Guam, Hawaii, Nevada, Northern Mariana Islands, Trust Territories of the Pacific Islands)
Department of Health and Human Services
Federal Office Building
50 United Nations Plaza, Room 431
San Francisco, California 94102
(415) 556-1961

Region X
(Alaska, Idaho, Oregon, Washington)
Department of Health and Human Services
2901 Third Avenue, MS-504
Seattle, Washington 98121
(206) 442-0420

United States Public Health Service

U.S. Department of Health and Human Services
Division of Commissioned Personnel
Parklawn Building, Room 4-35
5600 Fishers Lane
Rockville, Maryland 20857
(301) 443-3087

Publications That Provide Information on Financial Assistance Programs for Health Professions Students

The Directory of Biomedical and Health Care Grants Oryx Press, 2214 N. Central at Encanto, Phoenix, Arizona 85004.

Profiles of Financial Assistance Programs Public Health Service, 5600 Fishers Lane, Rockville, Maryland 20857.

Scholarships and Loans for Nursing Education National League for Nursing, Publications Order Unit, 10 Columbus Circle, New York, New York 10019.

A Selected List of Fellowship Opportunities and Aids to Advanced Education National Science Foundation, 1800 G Street, N.W., Washington, D.C. 20550.

Two Hundred Ways to Put Your Talent to Work in the Health Field National Health Council, Inc., 622 Third Avenue, 34th Floor, New York, New York 10017-6765.

Some Final Notes on Financing a Health Professions Education

1. Most health education programs will cost more than an undergraduate education. Be prepared to invest time and money.

2. Health professions students with high debt should investigate loan consolidation options.

3. There are ways to reduce the cost of a health professions education. Public Health Service and military programs will require a commitment after graduation but will allow you to obtain your health professions degree at a reduced cost or no cost at all.

4. Students interested in serving in a federally designated shortage area should contact the Bureau of Health Professions, Parklawn Building, Room 9A-25, 5600 Fishers Lane, Rockville, Maryland 20857, for a current listing of the approved areas. The list frequently changes so be certain you obtain the most recent information.

18 INTERNATIONAL PROGRAMS

Every year thousands of U.S. students travel abroad to study, and almost 400,000 foreign nationals come to the United States to continue their studies. The long-term benefit to both groups of students and to their countries cannot be measured in words or in dollars. International programs add a dimension to one's education—they are an investment in the future. Bringing people together from other countries and cultures results in a greater understanding and appreciation of everyone involved—students, faculty, and administrators. This chapter will serve as a guide to U.S. students seeking ways to fund their international experience and to foreign nationals looking for ways to finance their U.S. education.

Important Facts to Know

1. If you are a U.S. citizen and are planning to study abroad, you should check with your school's Office of International Programs for information and eligibility requirements of all available programs.

2. Most study-abroad programs allow students to receive financial assistance from federal and state sources. If you are interested in foreign study, you should check with your school's financial aid director for further information and eligibility requirements.

3. If you are a foreign national wishing to study in the United States, you should check with the nearest U.S. Embassy Office to determine visa eligibility and to obtain information on education in the United States.

4. If you want to study as a foreign student in the United States, you should investigate funding sources from private foundations, international organizations, and from your country of residence.

Important Terms to Know

F-1 Visa A visa, issued to foreign nationals who come to the United States as full-time students, that is granted for a specific period and reflects the expected time needed to complete educational requirements. The form I-20A, or Certificate of Eligibility, must be issued by the school the student will attend before a student can receive an F-1 visa. The I-20A indicates the length of the program for which the foreign student has applied and the way in which the student will meet expenses. A bank statement is necessary to confirm financial resources.

An international student with an F-1 visa who has completed 1 year of study at an American institution is permitted to work off-campus for up to 20 hours a week and to work full-time during vacation periods and between terms. A student must be in good academic standing in order to be eligible to work.

Foreign Student Advisor The authorized school official who administers all of the international programs for American students and international students.

I-94 A document issued to foreign nationals when they enter the United States. It indicates how long the person may stay in the country and serves as a record of any changes in status.

Immigration and Naturalization Service (INS) The federal agency that administers the rules and regulations regarding entry into and exit from the United States for immigrants, foreign nationals, international students, exchange scholars, and teachers.

J-1 Visa A visa issued to foreign nationals coming to the United States as full-time exchange students, research scholars, and teachers. Students with J-1 visas must maintain the approved academic course load. The form IAP-66, or Certificate of Eligibility, must be issued by the institution the student will attend. Exchange visitors must show proof of financial resources during study in the United States.

M-1 Visa A visa issued to foreign nationals who wish to pursue a course of study in a vocational school in the United States. International students must be accepted into an approved program and must show proof of financial resources in order to be granted this type of visa.

Q Visa A new visa category, designed principally for international exchange program participants. It allows international students up to 15 months of residency in the United States for the purposes of obtaining practical training, employment, and the sharing of the culture of the participant's home country.

Passport An official document issued by a country to allow its citizens to enter and leave other countries.

Test of English as a Foreign Language (TOEFL)

The examination given to international students to determine their level of English proficiency. The American Language Institute of Georgetown University (ALIGU) Test and the Michigan Test of English Language Proficiency (MTELP) are two other examinations that test for English proficiency. For information on these examinations, contact the following:

Test of English as a Foreign Language
Box 2882
Princeton, New Jersey 08541

American Language Institute of Georgetown
  University
3605 O Street, N.W.
Washington, D.C. 20057

University of Michigan
English Language Institute
Testing and Certification
North University Building
Ann Arbor, Michigan 48104

Visa An official document issued by a country indicating the amount of time a person may remain.

Applying Financial Aid for Study Abroad

Current federal law permits awarding federal financial aid to eligible students in approved study-abroad programs. Most colleges and universities allow their students to apply all types of financial aid, including federal and state aid, to finance their international educational experience. Interested students should contact their school's foreign student advisor or financial aid officer to have their school's policy and application procedures explained.

How American Students Can Finance Their International Educational Experience

Many American students would like to include an international educational experience as part of their college life. Most students, however, do not have the financial resources to do this on their own. There are ways to fund an international program. The two biggest sources of funding are as follows:

Fulbright Program Fulbright awards provide financial assistance to American and international students,

teachers, scholars, and administrators to study, teach, lecture, and conduct research. The awards are based upon academic merit and professional qualifications. The Fulbright Program is administered by the U.S. Information Agency and awards about 4500 grants each year. Fulbright awards include round-trip travel and a living stipend for the student and family. The American Scholar Program, the Predoctoral Fellowship Program, and the Fulbright Teacher Exchange Program all offer the opportunity for an international experience. Most schools have foreign student advisors who can provide information on the Fulbright Program. Interested students may also obtain information by writing to the Institute of International Education, U.S. Student Programs, 809 United Nations Plaza, New York, New York 10017, or to the U.S. Information Agency, 301 Fourth Street, S.W., Washington, D.C. 20547.

Institutional Programs Many colleges and universities offer student exchange or study-abroad programs to their students. The foreign student advisor at your school will have details and eligibility requirements for available programs and different options. Many federal and state financial aid programs may be used to finance a semester or a year abroad. After meeting with your foreign student advisor, you should meet with your financial aid counselor to discuss how you can apply your financial aid award to your international program.

There are also other ways that students can finance an international educational experience, and ingenuity, perseverance, and patience often lead to other funding sources. Funding from private foundations and corporations may be available. Rotary International, for example, provides scholarships and fellowships to both graduate and undergraduate students to study abroad. Some study-abroad offices may have specific funds set aside to assist students to study abroad. The University of Tennessee has compiled a resource directory listing all of the funding sources for study abroad. This publication, *Fellowships, Scholarships and Related Opportunities in International Education,* may be purchased from the university. Write to University of Tennessee, Division of International Education, Knoxville, Tennessee 37996-0230. Some colleges and universities have reciprocal exchange agreements with international schools, whereby students from one institution are allowed to attend the other at little or no cost. Your school's foreign student advisor or admission officer should be able to provide further information on this type of program.

Because of the increased interest in international experience and the realization that students have already inherited a world that is global, many colleges and universities are providing employment and internship opportunities abroad as a part of their programs. Many graduate management programs, for example, require students to have some experience working abroad. The Council on International Educational

Exchange offers a Work Abroad Program. Further information may be obtained by calling the Council at (212) 661-1414.

Other funding sources are also available to American students interested in studying abroad. The following is a list of organizations and agencies that provide financial assistance for international study. *Note:* Many of the programs are available only to graduate students.

Alliance Francaise de New York Scholarship Program

This program provides scholarships for graduate study and research in France. Recipients must have a knowledge of French. The application deadline is November 1. Contact the Institute of International Education, Division of Study Abroad Programs, 809 United Nations Plaza, New York, New York 10017, for application materials and further information.

American Council of Learned Societies

This organization provides financial assistance for graduate students enrolled in postdoctoral graduate research programs in the humanities. An applicant must be a U.S. citizen or permanent legal resident and must have a doctoral degree. Awards provide fellowships for 1 year. For further information and application materials, write to the Office of Fellowships and Grants, ACLS, 228 E. 45th Street, New York, New York 10017-3398.

Colombian Government Grants

These grants enable American college graduates to study in Colombia for up to 2 years. Preference is given to students with teaching and research experience. Recommended fields of study include agriculture, biology, business administration, chemistry, economics, education, engineering, geography, health services administration, history, Latin American literature, law, linguistics, physics, political science, and regional development. The grant covers the cost of tuition, fees, health insurance, living expenses, books, and travel costs. Contact your school's foreign student advisor for further information.

Denmark's International Study Program

This program allows American third- and fourth-year students in liberal arts and business to study at the University of Copenhagen for 1 semester or for 1 academic year and receive transfer credit. Student housing, as well as housing with a Danish family, is available. All courses are taught in English by Danish faculty. Admission to the program is based upon academic merit. For further information, contact the DIS Study Program, Vestergade 7, DK-1456 Copenhagen K, Denmark.

East-West Center

This organization provides financial assistance to qualified U.S. citizens to participate in programs concerned with Asian and Pacific-area countries. Awards are given to graduate students with interests in developing a greater understanding of economics, international relations, and education of the region. The center makes awards in the following categories: research fellowships, professional interns, professional associates, doctoral research interns, and graduate students. For further information and application materials, write to the Award Services, East-West Center, 1777 East-West Road, Honolulu, Hawaii 96848.

German Academic Exchange Service Grants

These grants provide financial assistance to graduate students, with preference given to those involved in doctoral research. An award includes funding for round-trip travel to Germany, book allowance, living stipend, and accident and sickness insurance. Contact the German Academic Exchange Office, 950 Third Avenue, New York, New York 10022 for further information.

International Business Machines (IBM) Fellowship Program

This program provides financial assistance, in the form of an annual stipend, to qualified U.S. citizens to pursue research in the following areas: chemistry, physics, mathematics, computer science, mechanical engineering, and electrical engineering. The 1-year awards are made to students who are pursuing or have just received their doctoral degrees. Applications from women and minority graduate students are welcomed. For further information and application materials, write to Manager, University and Scientific Relations, Thomas J. Watson Research Center, P.O. Box 218, Yorktown Heights, New York 10598.

International Student Exchange Program (ISEP)

This is a program of international student exchange for 1 year. Under the terms of agreement, an American student pays the usual tuition costs of his or her home institution and takes the place of a foreign student, who also pays the tuition and fee costs of a home college or university. The two students switch places, although not necessarily at the same schools. Participants are selected by their home institutions on the basis of academic merit and a personal interview. The students are responsible for their airfare and living costs, but there are no extra fees for participation. Contact your school's foreign student advisor, or write to the Office for International Student Exchange at Georgetown University, 1236 36th Street, N.W., Washington, D.C. 20057.

ITT International Fellowships

These awards, funded by the ITT Corporation, are based upon academic merit. Ten fellowships are awarded each year, and applications are accepted from students graduating from college in any discipline. The fellowships cover the cost of air travel, tuition, living expenses, books, and accident and health insurance. Write to the ITT Program, c/o Institute of International Education, 809 United Nations Plaza, New York, New York 10017.

Marshall Scholarship Program

Under the terms of agreement of this program, scholarships are awarded to qualified U.S. citizens by the British government. Recipients must be graduate students and must agree to study at one of the approved British institutions. The fields of study are unrestricted. Contact your school's foreign student advisor or the nearest British Consulate for further information.

National Program for Advanced Study and Research in China

This program is administered by the Committee on Scholarly Communication with the People's Republic of China, with funding from U.S. agencies. Recipients must be U.S. citizens or permanent residents and must be graduate students. Funding includes financial support for conducting research in China or taking courses at Chinese universities. Contact the Committee of Scholarly Communication, People's Republic of China, National Academy of Sciences, 2101 Constitution Avenue, Washington, D.C. 20418.

Rhodes Scholarships

These scholarships are offered to qualified U.S. citizens for study at Oxford University. Applicants must be single and between the ages of 18 and 23. The awards are based upon academic merit, scholarship, leadership, and physical ability. Contact your school's financial aid advisor, or write to the Rhodes Scholarship Office, Pomona College, Claremont, California 91711-6303 for further information.

Rotary Foundation Scholarships for International Understanding

This scholarship program, offered by Rotary Clubs throughout the world, provides funding to undergraduate students, graduate students, vocational students, journalists, and teachers of handicapped students. Recipients must be nominated by their local Rotary Club and must meet specific language requirements. For further information, contact the Rotary Foundation of Rotary International, 1600 Ridge Avenue, Evanston, Illinois 60201.

School for International Training—The Experiment in International Living

This program offers scholarship assistance to students who are enrolled in the school's graduate programs in language teaching and international management, and in the school's undergraduate programs in international studies. Contact the School for International Training, The Experiment in International Living, Brattleboro, Vermont 05301, for additional information.

United Nations Educational, Scientific, and Cultural Organization (UNESCO)

This organization provides funding to nationals of member states and associate members of UNESCO. The awards provide funding for up to 1 year. Applicants must meet specific language requirements. Areas of study include science, social science, education, and communications. The organization sponsors both individual and group fellowships. Contact your school's foreign student advisor for further information.

United States Department of Education

This branch of government provides a number of international scholarship programs to qualified U.S. citizens. Graduate students enrolled in language programs or area studies programs of Europe, Asia, Africa, Latin America, and the Middle East may apply for funding. Other grants are made to undergraduate students with financial need; the fields of study are unrestricted. Contact your school's foreign student advisor, or write to U.S. Department of Education, Division of International Education, 400 Maryland Avenue, S.W., Washington, D.C. 20202.

Woodrow Wilson International Center for Scholars

The center makes awards to qualified U.S. citizens for up to 1 year. Fields of study include law, humanities, social sciences, journalism, business, and the arts. Candidates should have doctoral degrees, and each recipient must conduct a project in Washington, D.C. Awards are based upon academic merit and originality of proposal. Write to the Woodrow Wilson International Center for Scholars, Smithsonian Building, Washington, D.C. 20560.

Publications

American students interested in finding adequate funding to support their international education will have no difficulty in locating reference sources. Publications that can be of assistance in locating funds for international study include the following:

Academic Year Abroad Communications Division, Institute of International Education, 809 United Nations Plaza, New York, New York 10017.

Aid to Individual Scholars American Council of Learned Societies, 228 E. 45th Street, New York, New York 10017.

Awards for Postgraduate Study in Australia The Graduate Careers Council of Australia, P.O. Box 28, Parkville, Victoria 2052, Australia.

Basic Facts on Foreign Study Communications Division, Institute of International Education, 809 United Nations Plaza, New York, New York 10017.

Canadian Directory of Awards for Graduate Study Association of Universities and Colleges of Canada, 151 Slater Street, Ottawa, Ontario, Canada K1P 5N1.

CISP International Studies Funding Book Learning Resources in International Studies, 777 United Nations Plaza, New York, New York 10017.

Commonwealth Universities Yearbook Gale Research Company, Book Tower, Detroit, Michigan 48226.

Directory of Financial Aid for American Undergraduates Interested in Overseas Study and Travel Adelphi University Press, Levermore Hall 201, Garden City, New York 11530.

Directory of Financial Aids for International Activities University of Minnesota, Office of International Programs, 201 Nolte West, 315 Pillsbury Drive, S.E., Minneapolis, Minnesota 55455.

Exchange Programs with Eastern Europe and the Soviet Union IREX, 655 Third Avenue, New York, New York 10017.

Fellowships, Scholarships and Related Opportunities in International Education University of Tennessee, Division of International Education, Knoxville, Tennessee 37996-0230.

Financial Aid for Study Abroad: A Handbook for Advisors and Administrators Stephen Cooper, William W. Cressey, and Nancy K. Stubbs, National Association of Foreign Student Administrators, 1860 19th Street, N.W., Washington, D.C. 20009.

Financial Resources for International Study: A Definitive Guide to Organizations Offering Awards for Overseas Study Institute of International Education and Peterson's Guides, P.O. Box 2123, Princeton, New Jersey 08543.

Fulbright Grants and Other Grants for Graduate Study Abroad Council for International Exchange of Scholars, 11 Dupont Circle, Washington, D.C. 20036. Free.

Global Guide to International Education Facts on File, 460 Park Avenue South, New York, New York 10016.

Grants and Fellowships in International Studies University of Pittsburgh, International Studies Association, Dept. A, 4G3L Forbes Quadrangle, Pittsburgh, Pennsylvania 15260.

The Grants Register St. Martin's Press, 175 Fifth Avenue, New York, New York 10010.

Guide to Graduate Study in Economics and Agricultural Economics in the United States of America and Canada Richard D. Irwin, 1818 Ridge Road, Homewood, Illinois 60430.

Guide to Graduate Study in Political Science American Political Science Association, 1527 New Hampshire Avenue, N.W., Washington, D.C. 20036.

Guide to Grants and Fellowships in Languages and Linguistics LSA Secretariat, 1325 18th Street, N.W., Suite 211, Washington, D.C. 20036-6501.

Higher Education in the United Kingdom Longman, Inc., 19 W. 44th Street, New York, New York 10036.

International Directory for Youth Internships Social Development Division, United Nations, NGO Youth Caucus, United Nations, New York, New York 10017.

National Directory of Summer Internships for Undergraduate College Students Haverford College, Career Planning Office, Haverford, Pennsylvania 19041.

Scholarships and Fellowships for Foreign Study—A Selected Bibliography Institute of International Education, 809 United Nations Plaza, New York, New York 10017.

A Stanford Student's Guide to Study, Work and Travel Abroad The Overseas Opportunity Center, Bechtel International Center, Stanford University, Stanford, California 94305.

Study Abroad UNESCO Press, Box 433, Murray Hill Station, New York, New York 10016.

Transitions Abroad: Guide to International Study, Work, and Travel Transitions Abroad, P.O. Box 344, Amherst, Massachusetts 01004.

Vacation Study Abroad Institute for International Education, 809 United Nations Plaza, New York, New York 10017.

Whole World Handbook: A Guide to Study, Work, and Travel Abroad Council on International Educational Exchange, 205 E. 42nd Street, New York, New York 10017.

Work-Study-Travel Abroad United States Information Agency, Office of Public Liaison, 301 Fourth Street, S.W., Washington, D.C. 20547.

How International Students Can Finance Their Education in the United States

For many international students, the prospect of coming to the United States to study may seem like an impossible dream. Different admission requirements, high costs, and limited funds all contribute to making enrollment in U.S. colleges and universities difficult for foreign students. However, careful planning and creative investigation can result in positive results.

Expenses Involved in Enrolling in U.S. Schools

Application Fees   Most U.S. schools charge a fee to review the credentials of all students applying for admission. These fees range from $20 to $50.

Tuition   U.S. colleges and universities charge tuition to all enrolled students. Tuition can be as little as $1000 a year at a community college or as expensive as $10,000 a year at a private university. Tuition and fees are usually paid twice a year, at the beginning of each semester.

Books and Supplies and Miscellaneous Fees
Depending on the program, these costs can range from $300 to $500 a year.

Room and Board Costs Depending on the type of housing arrangement, room and board (meal) costs can range from $2500 to $5000 per year.

Medical and Dental Insurance All international students are required to have insurance to meet any medical or dental expenses they may have while studying in the United States. There are insurance plans for both international students and American students studying abroad. One program is administered by Hinchcliff International, Inc. Payments range from $26 per month for single students to $100 per month for family coverage. For more information and application forms, write to Hinchcliff International, Inc., 11 Ascot Place, Ithaca, New York 14850, or call (607) 257-0100.

Travel Expenses International students must include the cost of at least one round-trip airline ticket to and from the United States in their expense budget. A student must also pay travel costs from a major airport to the school. International students are also advised to purchase travel insurance when planning their trips to the United States. Many colleges and universities make this a requirement for enrollment.

Miscellaneous Expenses Included in this category are all of the other expenses related to the international student's educational stay in the United States. Foreign students interested in pursuing an education in the United States should consult the publication of the Institute of International Education, *Costs at U.S. Educational Institutions,* which lists all of the colleges in the United States and the costs at each college. It is available at Fulbright Offices and U.S. Embassies and Consulates.

International students should be aware that the expenses listed above are for the academic year only and do not include, for example, the costs associated with attending summer school. Some schools may require their international students to attend an English as a Second Language (ESL) training session and orientation program before enrollment. Also, it is important for foreign students to know that tuition, fees, and room and board charges will increase each year.

International Students and Taxes

There are some basic regulations regarding international students and payment of income taxes. Foreign students should have basic knowledge of the following facts:

1. A working international student on a nonimmigrant visa is required to file a U.S. tax form. This regulation applies to all foreign students working either on-campus or off-campus.

2. How much money a student earns determines whether or not income tax must be paid.

3. In general, students with F-1 and J-1 visas are exempt from paying social security tax.

4. International students are subject to taxation only on funds received from American sources. Generally, an international student with a J-1 or F-1 visa files a nonresident alien income tax return, or Income Tax Form 1040NR. The filing deadline for federal and state income taxes is April 17.

5. International students may receive information and assistance regarding their tax situation by calling the Internal Revenue Service in their state of residence.

6. The U.S. federal government frequently changes the rules governing international students and taxation. Foreign students are advised to check with their school's foreign student advisor for the latest information.

International students should be familiar with IRS publication 515—*Withholding of Tax on Non-Resident Aliens and Foreign Corporations.*

Funding Sources for International Students

There are several ways foreign students can fund their international education. The majority of international students are financed by their families. The next largest category of funding is the student's home country, followed by the individual U.S. college or university and, finally, by the U.S. government. Other sources of funding include:

Private Organizations

Foundations

Corporations

International Agencies

Employment Programs/Cooperative Education

Exchange Programs

Let's examine some of the more important of these sources:

United States Colleges and Universities Funding for International Students Most of the financial support for international students from U.S. colleges and universities is reserved for graduate students. Funding includes scholarships, fellowships, and assistantships. This last type of funding reduces the student's tuition costs while requiring some instructional commitment on the part of the student. Stipends for living expenses are also included in the awards. International students should request information on funding from each school they are considering. Awards are competitive and are usually based upon academic merit.

Some colleges and universities do reserve a certain percentage of their internal scholarship and grant funds for international students. Awards include tuition waivers and partial travel grants. Some schools also provide employment opportunities for international students, which allow the students to meet a portion of their college expenses by working. International students should write to the specific schools they are considering for admission and request information on the schools' policies of funding international students.

Another way for international students to study in the United States is to participate in the International Student Exchange Program (ISEP) administered by Georgetown University. This program allows a foreign student to pay the usual costs of attending the home institution while taking the place of an American student who has also paid the tuition and fee costs at the home school. Interested students should contact their school's foreign student advisor or write to the Office for International Exchange at Georgetown University, Washington, D.C. 20057.

Employment   Another way for international students to finance their education in the United States is to work. Employment opportunities can be found both on-campus and off-campus. In fact, it may be to the student's advantage to work while going to school in the United States. Employment experience, especially if it is related to the student's major field of study, will strengthen the academic credentials of the student in his or her home country.

Employment regulations are determined by the Immigration and Naturalization Service (INS). International students should be aware of the following rules:

1. International students are not permitted to work off-campus during their first year of study in the United States. After the first year, foreign students with F-1 or J-1 visas are permitted to work off-campus but employment cannot exceed 20 hours per week.

2. If an international student works on-campus and that employment is part of a scholarship, assistantship, or fellowship award, approval from the INS is not required. International students with F-1 visas must receive permission from the INS to work off-campus. On-campus employment may be authorized by the school's international student advisor. Students with J-1 visas can receive authorization for off-campus employment usually from their college's international student advisor. Permission to work off-campus is generally based upon economic necessity.

3. Employment under the federally sponsored College Work-Study Program is not available to international students. On-campus employment is usually sponsored by the college or university.

4. International students seeking full-time employment during the summer months must obtain permission from the INS.

5. Students with F-1 visas seeking any type of practical training will be required to file an Employment Authorization Document. Students with F-1 or J-1 visas seeking authorization from the INS are also required to file an Employment Authorization Document. Applicants for this document must go in person to the INS and file Form I-765. The current processing fee is $35. Practical training programs must be related to a student's major field of study.

6. Cooperative education programs, integrating a student's academic and career interests, are available at some colleges and universities for international students. Currently, about 900 colleges and universities offer cooperative programs, and each year approximately 200,000 students participate. It is possible to earn about $7000 a year. Students on F-1 and J-1 visas who have completed at least 1 academic year and who meet specific academic requirements are eligible to participate in cooperative education programs. Permission to work under these programs must be obtained from the school's international student advisor. International students should obtain information about cooperative education programs at all schools they are considering at the time of application for admission. The earlier a student applies, the better the chances are for obtaining a cooperative employment arangement. Students should be advised that, if they participate in a cooperative education program, it usually takes 5, rather than 4, years to obtain a baccalaureate degree. However, the practical work experience and the financial benefits may make this program attractive for some international students.

United States Government Funding for International Students   Although not a major funding source for international students, the U.S. government does provide some assistance to foreign students. The following are examples of the type of assistance offered by the United States:

The Agency for International Development provides financial assistance to qualified students from developing countries. Recipients are selected by the agency and local government officials. Awards are based upon the future contribution the student can make to the developing country. Applicants must meet all of the admission requirements of the college or university and all of the specific requirements of the Agency for International Development. For further information, contact the Office of International Training, Washington, D.C. 20523, or the appropriate home government department.

The Council on International Educational Exchange provides information to international students seeking information on educational opportunities in the United States. Write to CIEE, 205 E. 42nd Street, New York, New York 10017.

Fulbright Program is funded by an annual appropriation by the Congress of the United States. Awards are made to qualified foreign graduate students wishing to continue with their education in the United States. Awards are based upon academic merit. The Predoctoral Fellowship Program and the Scholar-in-Residence Program allow foreign students to travel and study in the United States for up to 1 year. The Hubert Humphrey Fellowship Program makes awards to public service professionals from developing countries for a year of study and practical work. Fields of study include agriculture, public administration, and public health. Contact the U.S. Information Service, the Fulbright Commission, or the education officer at U.S. embassies and consulates for more information and application materials for this program.

The Institute of International Education administers several programs for international students. Funding is provided from private agencies and individual governments. Awards are made to both undergraduate and graduate students. For more information, contact the Institute of International Education, 809 United Nations Plaza, New York, New York 10017.

The United States International Communication Agency provides a variety of services to international students, including advising, counseling, and orientation programs and can be a valuable resource in helping students select U.S. colleges and universities. For further information, contact the education officer at the United States Embassy or Consulate.

Other funding sources for international students include:

Alliance Francaise de New York Scholarship Program allows French citizens to study in the United States. A knowledge of English is required. Contact the Commission Franco-Americaine d'Exchanges Universitaires et Culturels, 9, Rue Chardin, 75016 Paris, France.

American Association of University Women Educational Foundation Fellowships are provided to international students who are women with exceptional leadership abilities. Awards are made to students for graduate studies and advanced research. Knowledge of English is required. Contact the Educational Foundation Programs Office, AAUW, 2401 Virginia Avenue, N.W., Washington, D.C. 20037.

American/Scandinavian Foundation offers awards to Scandinavian students to study and conduct research in the United States. For further information, write to the American/Scandinavian Foundation, 127 E. 73 Street, New York, New York 10021.

Food and Agriculture Organization of the United Nations provides financial funding to students whose countries have signed agreements with the United Nations Development Program or Trust Fund. The fields of study include agriculture, economics, statistics, forestry, nutrition, and fisheries. Contact your United Nations representative or Minister of Education for further information.

John Simon Guggenheim Memorial Foundation sponsors two annual competitions—one for citizens of the United States and Canada; the other for citizens and permanent residents of 50 American states, the Caribbean, the Philippines, and the French, Dutch, and British possessions in the Western Hemisphere. The purpose of the award is to foster research and international understanding. Write to the President, John Simon Guggenheim Memorial Foundation, 90 Park Avenue, New York, New York 10016.

Harkness Fellowship of the Commonwealth Fund of New York provides funding to qualified students in the United Kingdom, Australia and New Zealand. The fields of study are unrestricted. Awards may be for 1 year or up to 21 months. British students should write to 28 Bedford Square, London WC1B 3EG, England. In Australia, the address is 46 Creswell Street, Campbell ACT 2601, Australia. New Zealand students should write to 15 City View Road, Harborview, Lower Hutt, New Zealand.

Hubert H. Humphrey North-South Fellowship Program provides financial assistance to professionals from developing countries who are engaged in careers in public service agriculture, health and nutrition, planning and resource management. The program is funded by the U.S. International Communication Agency and is part of the Fulbright Exchange Program. Candidates must be fluent in English and demonstrate leadership abilities. For additional information, write to the Hubert H. Humphrey Fellowship Program, 809 United Nations Plaza, New York, New York 10017.

Institute for Advanced Study provides for funding for postdoctoral scholars to study at Princeton University. The fields of study include history, mathematics, and the natural sciences. Contact the Director, Institute for Advanced Study, Olden Lane, Princeton, New Jersey 08540.

International Peace Scholarships, established to promote peace, are made to qualified students enrolled in colleges or universities in the United States or Canada. Write to the P.E.O. International Peace Fund, Executive Office, 3700 Grand Avenue, Des Moines, Iowa 50312.

International Student Exchange Program (ISEP) provides for a 1-year exchange program for international students. Under the terms of agreement, the ISEP international student pays the fees or tuition charges of his or her home institution and takes the place of an ISEP American student who also pays the tuition and fee charges of the home college or university. The two students switch places, although not necessarily at the same school. The students are responsible for their airfare and living costs, but there are no additional fees for participation in the program. Students are selected by their home institution on the basis of academic merit and a personal interview. Contact your school's foreign student advisor, or write to the Office for International Student Exchange at Georgetown University, 1236 36th Street, N.W., Washington, D.C. 20057.

Kennedy Scholarship Program provides funding to British citizens for study at Harvard University or the Massachusetts Institute of Technology. The fields of study are unrestricted. The awards cover tuition expenses, a living expense stipend, transportation, and health insurance fees. Write to the Secretary, Kennedy Memorial Trust, Association of Commonwealth Universities, 36 Gordon Square, London WC1H OPF, England.

Latin American Scholarship Program of American Universities (LASPAU) provides funding to qualified students in Latin America and the Caribbean. The fields of study are unrestricted, and awards are generally made for graduate-level study. Knowledge of English is not required. Write to LASPAU, 25 Mount Auburn Street, Cambridge, Massachusetts 02138.

Organization of American States (OAS) provides fellowships and special training programs to qualified citizens of OAS member countries. Contact the Chief, Trainee Selection, Organization of American States, 19th and Constitution, N.W., Washington, D.C. 20006, for further information and application forms.

Pan American Health Organization provides funding to qualified students of member countries. Preference is given for study in any health-related field. Contact your country's health department for further information on this program.

Leo S. Rowe Pan American Fund makes interest-free loans to students from Latin America who are studying in the United States or who want to pursue advanced study or research in this country. Loans must be repaid within 5 years after completion of studies. For more information, contact the Secretariat, Leo S. Rowe Pan American Fund, Department of Fellowships and Training, Organization of American States, 19th and Constitution, N.W., Washington, D.C. 20006.

Texas Good Neighbor Scholarship Program provides financial assistance to qualified undergraduate and graduate international students in the form of exempted state tuition. The fields of study are unrestricted. Only students from the American hemisphere are eligible for this program. For further information on this program contact the Texas Education Agency, 201 E. 11th Street, Austin, Texas 78701.

Publications

There are several publications that foreign students can use to locate funds for international study. These resources include:

Admissions Requirements for International Students at Colleges and Universities in the United States Intercultural Press, Inc., P.O. Box 768, Yarmouth, Maine 04096.

Barron's Profiles of American Colleges Barron's Educational Series, Inc., 250 Wireless Blvd., Hauppauge, New York 11788.

The Community, Technical and Junior College in the United States: A Guide for Foreign Students Communications Division, Box STA, Institute of International Education, 809 United Nations Plaza, New York, New York 10017.

Costs at U.S. Educational Institutions 1991/92 Communications Division, Box STA, Institute of International Education, 809 United Nations Plaza, New York, New York 10017.

A Directory of International Internships Michigan State University, Career Development and Placement Services, 113 Student Services Building, East Lansing, Michigan 48824.

Directory of Public Service Internships National Society for Internships and Experimental Education, 124 St. Mary's Street, Raleigh, North Carolina 27605.

English Language and Orientation Programs in the United States Communications Division, Box STA, Institute of International Education, 809 United Nations Plaza, New York, New York 10017.

Fellowship Guide for Western Europe Council for European Studies, 1509 International Affairs Building, Columbia University, New York, New York 10027.

Fields of Study in U.S. Colleges and Universities Communications Division, Box STA, Institute of International Education, 809 United Nations Plaza, New York, New York 10017.

Financial Planning for Study in the U.S.: A Guide for Students from Other Countries College Board Publication Orders, Box 2815, Princeton, New Jersey 08541.

Financial Resources for International Study: A Selected Bibliography Institute of International Education, 809 United Nations Plaza, New York, New York 10017.

A Foreign Student's Selected Guide to Financial Assistance for Study and Research in the United States Adelphi University Press, South Avenue, Garden City, New York 11530.

A Guide to Scholarships, Fellowships, and Grants: A Selected Bibliography Communications Division Box STA, Institute of International Education, 809 United Nations Plaza, New York, New York 10017.

A Handbook for Citizens Living Abroad Doubleday Books, P.O. Box 5017, Des Plaines, Illinois 60017.

Higher Education in the United States: Opportunities for Foreign Students American Jewish Committee, Institute of Human Relations, 165 E. 56 Street, New York, New York 10022.

The Insider's Guide to Colleges St. Martin's Press, 175 Fifth Avenue, New York, New York 10010.

International Foundation Directory Gale Research Company, Book Tower, Detroit, Michigan 48226.

International Research and Exchange Board Program Announcement International Research and Exchange Board, 655 Third Avenue, New York, New York 10017.

The International Student's Guide to the American University: From Choosing the Right School to Adjusting to Campus Life Gregory A. Barnes, National Textbook Company, Chicago.

International Studies Funding and Resource Book Education Interface, P.O. Box 3649, Princeton, New Jersey 08543-3649.

An International Visitor's Guide to U.S. Higher Education American Council on Education, Division of International Education, 11 Dupont Circle, Washington, D.C. 20036.

Open Doors: Report on International Education Exchange Communications Division, Box STA, Institute of International Education, 809 United Nations Plaza, New York, New York 10017.

Profiles: The Foreign Student in the U.S. Communications Division, Box STA, Institute of International Education, 809 United Nations Plaza, New York, New York 10017.

A Selected List of Fellowship Opportunities and Aids to Advanced Education for U.S. Citizens and Foreign Nationals The National Science Foundation, Publications Office, 1800 G Street, N.W., Washington, D.C. 20550.

Selected List of Major Fellowship Opportunities and Aids to Advanced Education for Foreign Nationals Fellowship Office, National Academy of Sciences, National Research Council, 2101 Constitution Avenue, N.W., Washington, D.C. 20418.

Social Science Research Council Fellowships and Grants for Research Social Science Research Council, 605 Third Avenue, New York, New York 10158.

Specialized Study Options Institute of International Education, 809 United Nations Plaza, New York, New York 10017.

Study in U.S. Colleges and Universities Communications Division, Box STA, Institute of International Education, 809 United Nations Plaza, New York, New York 10017.

Summer Learning Options U.S.A.: A Guide for Foreign Nationals Communications Division, Box STA, Institute of International Education, 809 United Nations Plaza, New York, New York 10017.

Organizations That Provide Information on International Education

The following organizations can provide information to American and international students on international educational opportunities:

African-American Institute
833 United Nations Plaza
New York, New York 10017
(212) 949-5666/5670

American Association of Collegiate Registrars and Admissions Officers
One Dupont Circle
Washington, D.C. 20036
(202) 293-9161

American Institute for Foreign Study
102 Greenwich Avenue
Greenwich, Connecticut 06830
(203) 869-9090 Telex: 965932

American-Mideast Educational and Testing Services, Inc. (AMIDEAST)
1100 17th Street, N.W.
Washington, D.C. 20036
(202) 797-7900

American-Scandinavian Foundation
725 Park Avenue
New York, New York 10021
(212) 879-9779

Asia Foundation
4655 California Street
San Francisco, California 94104
(415) 982-4640

Association for International Practical Training
10 Corporate Center
10400 Little Patuxent Parkway
Columbia, Maryland 21004
(410) 997-2200

Committee on Scholarly Communication with the People's Republic of China
2101 Constitution Avenue, N.W.
Washington, D.C. 20418
(202) 389-6795

Council of Graduate Schools
One Dupont Circle
Washington, D.C. 20036
(202) 223-3791

Council on International Educational Exchange
205 E. 42nd Street
New York, New York 10017
(212) 661-1414

Council for International Exchange of Scholars
3400 International Drive, N.W.
Washington, D.C. 20008-3017
(202) 686-4000

European Council of International Schools
21B Lavant Street
Petersfield, Hants
GU32 3EL
United Kingdom
34-20-252727

Experiment in International Living
Kipling Road
Brattleboro, Vermont 05301
(802) 257-4628

Ford Foundation
320 E. 43rd Street
New York, New York 10017
(212) 573-5000

Hariri Foundation
1020 19th Street, N.W.
Washington, D.C. 20036
(202) 659-9200

Institute of International Education
809 United Nations Plaza
New York, New York 10017
(212) 984-5331

International Student Service
236 E. 47th Street
New York, New York 10017
(212) 319-0606 Telex: ISS620675

Latin American Scholarship Program of American Universities (LASPAU)
125 Mount Auburn Street, Room 302
Cambridge, Massachusetts 02138
(617) 495-5255

National Association of International Educators
1875 Constitution Avenue, N.W.
Washington, D.C. 20009-5728
(202) 462-4811
Fax (202) 667-3419

Organization of American States
17th and Constitution Avenue, N.W.
Washington, D.C. 20006
(202) 458-3140

Overseas Placement Service for Educators
University of Northern Iowa
Cedar Falls, Iowa 50614-0390
(319) 273-2061

Partners in International Education and Training
1707 L Street, N.W.
Washington, D.C. 20038
(202) 429-0810

Rockefeller Foundation
1133 Avenue of the Americas
New York, New York 10036
(212) 869-8500

United States Agency for International Development
Division of Support Services
Washington, D.C. 20533
(202) 235-1984

United States Information Agency
301 Fourth Street, N.W.
Washington, D.C. 20547
(202) 619-4700

United States International Communication Agency
Office of Student and Academic Support Services
1750 Pennsylvania Avenue, N.W.
Washington, D.C. 20547
(202) 724-9943

Youth for Understanding
3501 Newark Street, N.W.
Washington, D.C. 20016
(202) 966-6800

Binational Educational Foundations and Commissions

The following offices can provide information on Fulbright-Hayes Scholarships:

Argentina
Commission for Education Exchange
United States of America and the Argentine Republic
Maipú 672
Buenos Aires, Argentina
Telephone - 392-4971

Australia
Australian-American Educational Foundation
Churchill House, Northbourne Avenue
Braddon, A.C.T., Australia 2601
Telephone - (062) 4793331

Austria
Austrian-American Educational Commission
Schmidgasse 14
Vienna, 1082, Austria
Telephone - 34-66-11

Belgium and Luxembourg
Commission for Educational Exchange
United States of America, Belgium, and Luxembourg
Rue du Marteau, 21
Hamerstraat 1040
Brussels, Belgium
Telephone - 2-218 4780

Brazil

Commission for Educational Exchange
United States of America and Brazil
Edificio Casa Thomas Jefferson
W-4 Sul, Entre Quadra 706/906
70390 Brasilia, D.F., Brazil
Telephone - 244-1080

Chile

Commission for Educational Interchange
United States of America and Chile
Casilla 2121
Santiago, Chile
Telephone - 380-580

Colombia

Commission for Educational Exchange
United States of America and Colombia
Apartado Aero 03420
Carrera 21 No. 39-70
Bogotá, Colombia
Telephone - 287-3995

Cyprus

Commission for Educational Exchange
United States of America and Cyprus
c/o American Embassy
Nicosia, Cyprus
Telephone - 49757

Denmark

Commission for Educational Exchange
United States of America and Denmark
Raddhosstraede 3, No. 1466
Copenhagen K., Denmark
Telephone - (01) 128223

Ecuador

Commission for Educational Exchange
United States of America and Ecuador
10 De Agasta 1832 y Roca
P.O. Box 826-A
Quito, Ecuador
Telephone - 230-119

Egypt

Commission for Educational and Cultural Exchange
United States of America and Arab Republic of Egypt
c/o American Embassy
Cairo, Egypt

Finland

United States Educational Foundation in Finland
Etelaesplanadi 22 A 15
00130 Helsinki 13, Finland
Telephone - 647-845

France

Franco-American Commission for Educational
   Exchange
9 Rue Chardin
Paris, France 75016
Telephone - 870-4654

Germany

Commission for Educational Exchange
United States of America and the Federal Republic of
   Germany
Theaterplatz 1A (Postfach 200-208)
5300 Bonn 2
Federal Republic of Germany

Greece

United States Educational Foundation in Greece
6 Vassilissis Sofis Avenue
Athens 138, Greece
Telephone - 741-811

Iceland

United States Educational Foundation in Iceland
Neshvegur 16
P.O. Box 7133
Reykjavik, Iceland
Telephone - 10860

India

United States Educational Foundation in India
12 Hailey Road
New Delhi, India 110001
Telephone - 388944

Ireland

Scholarship Exchange Board in Ireland
c/o Ministry of External Affairs
80 St. Stephen's Green
Dublin 2, Ireland
Telephone - 78022

Israel

United States-Israel Educational Foundation
71 Hayarkon Street
Post Office Box 26160
Tel Aviv, Israel

Italy

Commission for Educational and Cultural Exchange
United States of America and Italy
Via Boncompagni 16
Rome, Italy 00187
Telephone - (06) 4759742

Japan

United States Educational Commission in Japan
Sanno Grand Building 14-2, Second Floor
Nagata-cho, Chiyoka-ku
Tokyo 100, Japan
Telephone - 13-580-3231

Korea

Korean-American Educational Commission
No. 1801 Garden Tower
98-70 Wooninnidong Chongno-ku
Seoul 110, Korea
Telephone - 21-5502

Liberia

United States Educational and Cultural Foundation in
  Liberia
P.O. Box 1011
Monrovia, Liberia
Telephone - 222657

Malaysia

Commission for Educational Exchange
United States of America and Malaysia
198 Jalan Ampang
Kuala Lumpur 16-03, Malaysia
Telephone - 423-547

Morocco

Commission for Educational Exchange
United States of America and Morocco
3 Rue Tid d'as
Rabat, Morocco

Nepal

United States Educational Foundation in Nepal
P.O. Box 380
USIS Building
Kathmandu, Nepal
Telephone - 11698

Netherlands

Netherlands-America Commission for Educational
  Exchange
Nieuwe Spiegelstraat 26, 017, DG
Amsterdam, Netherlands
Telephone - 20-24235

New Zealand

New Zealand-United States Educational Foundation
Box 3465, Chief Post Office
Wellington, New Zealand
Telephone - 722-065

Norway

United States Educational Foundation in Norway
Nedre Vollgate 3
Oslo, Norway
Telephone - 41-42-55

Pakistan

United States Educational Foundation in Pakistan
P.O. Box 1128
Islamabad, Pakistan
Telephone - 21563

Peru

Commission for Educational Exchange
United States and Peru
Maximo Abril 599
Lima 11, Peru
Telephone - 24-5494

Philippines

Philippine-American Educational Foundation
12th Floor, Ramon Magsaysay Center
1680 Roxas Boulevard
Manila, Philippines, D-406
Telephone - 50-10-44

Portugal

Luso-American Educational Commission
Av. Elias Garcia 59-5
Lisbon 1, Portugal
Telephone - 767976

Spain

Commission for Educational Exchange
United States of America and Spain
Cartagena 83-85, 3rd Floor
Madrid 28, Spain
Telephone - 256-1658

Sri Lanka

United States Educational Foundation in Sri Lanka
39 Ernest de Silva Mawatha
Colombo 7, Sri Lanka
Telephone - 27405

Sweden

Commission for Educational Exchange
United States of America and Sweden
Norrmalmstorg 1, UPPG, B. IV, III, 46
Stockholm C., Sweden
Telephone - (08) 10-64-50

Taiwan

Foundation for Scholarly Exchange
1-A Chuan Chow Street
Taipei 107, Taiwan

Thailand

Thailand-United States Educational Foundation
125 South Sathorn Road
Bangkok 12, Thailand
Telephone - 281-0547

Turkey

Commission for Educational Exchange
United States and Turkey
Cinnah Caddesi 103/1
Cankaya
Ankara, Turkey
Telephone - 276423

United Kingdom

United States-United Kingdom Educational
  Commission
6 Porter Street
London W. 1M 2 HR, England
Telephone - 1-486-7697

Uruguay

Commission for Educational Exchange
United States of America and Uruguay
Paraguay 1217
Montevideo, Uruguay
Telephone - 91-41-60

Yugoslavia

Yugoslav-American Commission for Educational
  Exchange
Trg Marksa i Englesa 1
Belgrade, Yugoslavia 11000
Telephone - 338-183

The Institute of International Education

The Institute of International Education has offices throughout the United States with staff who can answer questions about international programs. Contact the office nearest you.

Main Office—East Coast Area

(Maine, Vermont, New Hampshire, Massachusetts, Connecticut, Rhode Island, New York, New Jersey, Pennsylvania, Delaware, Maryland, Washington, D.C.)
Institute of International Education
809 United Nations Plaza
New York, New York 10017-3580
(212) 984-5330

Midwest Area

(Illinois, Iowa, Kentucky, Michigan, Minnesota, Missouri, North Dakota, Ohio, South Dakota, Wisconsin)
Institute of International Education
401 N. Wabash Avenue, Suite 722
Chicago, Illinois 60611
(312) 644-1400

Rocky Mountain Area

(Arizona, Colorado, Idaho, Kansas, Montana, Nebraska, New Mexico, Utah, Wyoming)
Institute of International Education
700 Broadway, Suite 112
Denver, Colorado 80203
(303) 837-0788

Southeast Area

(Alabama, Florida, Georgia, North Carolina, Puerto Rico, South Carolina, Tennessee, Virginia, West Virginia)
Institute of International Education
133 Carnegie Way, N.W., Suite 500
Atlanta, Georgia 30303
(404) 523-7216

Southern Area

(Arkansas, Louisiana, Mississippi, Oklahoma, Texas)
Institute of International Education
World Trade Center, Suite 1-A
1520 Texas Avenue
Houston, Texas 77002
(713) 223-5454

West Coast Area

(Alaska, California, Hawaii, Nevada, Oregon, Washington)
Institute of International Education
312 Sutter Street, Suite 610
San Francisco, California 94108
(415) 362-6520

Some Final Notes on International Education

1. An international educational program can provide students with lifetime experiences. Learning about other people and cultures is necessary in the era of the global village. A student should try to find a way to finance this part of his or her education through creative and positive means.

2. Any student participating in an international educational experience should be prepared to meet the financial obligations associated with the program. This requires not only having the necessary financial resources to meet the listed educational expenses but also planning to have the funds to meet emergency financial situations.

3. Finding the resources to finance an international education requires careful planning and patient investigation. For an American student, the search should begin with his or her foreign student advisor, who can provide guidance and can save the student time in searching for funds. For an international student, the search should begin with the home institution and with the binational centers providing information on educational programs in the United States. United States foreign embassies can also provide information to foreign nationals seeking information about education in this country. Interested students should begin with these sources in their search for appropriate educational programs and financial funding.

4. Immigration laws change from time to time and can affect international student programs. Students should check the immigration rules and regulations before applying for any program.

5. International students studying in the United States should seek the advice of their school's foreign student advisor in all matters relating to their stay in this country.

19 CONSUMER RIGHTS AND OBLIGATIONS

Finding the money to attend college involves both rights and responsibilities. There are some financial assistance funds you are entitled to receive. Other programs require investigation on your part. In either case there are certain responsibilities that should guide your financial aid application process.

Important Facts to Know

1. Every school has a written institutional financial aid policy. You should know what this is before enrolling. Be certain that you understand the school's financial aid philosophy and packaging guidelines. Know the difference between need-based aid and merit scholarship assistance. Find out whether the school sponsors its own loan program and whether tuition can be paid in installments. Find out the rules regarding emergency loans and the awarding process.

2. Every school should have a written refund policy. Find out your institution's policies regarding financial refunds, and follow those regulations.

3. Every school has an appeal process, which allows a student to request additional financial aid funds. If you did not receive adequate funding or if circumstances have changed your financial situation, write a letter of appeal to your school's financial aid director. Be specific. Type your request, and keep it short. Directors of financial aid have neither the time nor the energy to read several pages of requests. Simply state *why* you need more money and *how much* you need. After writing your letter, schedule an appointment and discuss your situation with a financial aid counselor. If the school cannot provide additional funds, ask about alternative loan or work programs. REMEMBER: there is a solution to *every* aid problem.

Important Terms to Know

Packaging Philosophy A school's written statement on the guidelines it follows in awarding student aid.

Included in this statement is the school's philosophy on awarding need-based aid and merit scholarship assistance.

Professional Judgment The authority given to the school's financial aid director to make adjustments to a student's financial aid eligibility based on special circumstances that change that student's financial aid application.

The following is a list of your rights and responsibilities. Let this list serve as your guide as you begin your financial aid journey.

Students' Rights

1. Students have the right to know what financial aid programs are available at their schools.

2. Students have the right to know the deadlines for submitting applications.

3. Students have the right to know how their financial need was determined and what items were considered in their budget.

4. Students have the right to know how financial aid will be distributed.

5. Students have the right to know the school's institutional financial aid philosophy and packaging guidelines.

6. Students have the right to know what resources were used in the calculation of their financial aid eligibility.

7. Students have the right to know the school's appeal process.

8. Students have the right to know the school's refund policy.

9. Students have the right to know what portion of their aid package is a loan and must be repaid and what portion is a grant and does not have to be repaid.

10. Students have the right to know the school's definition and determination of satisfactory academic progress.

Students' Responsibilities

1. Students have an obligation to complete all application forms accurately and to submit them by the stated deadline.

2. Students have an obligation to tell the truth.

3. Students have an obligation to provide the financial aid office with any additional financial documentation, verification, corrections, or new information.

4. Students have an obligation to report any change in their family's financial status.

5. Students have an obligation to report any outside loans or scholarships.

6. Students have an obligation to read and understand all the terms and agreements of their award package.

7. Students have an obligation to repay all educational loans.

8. Students have an obligation to read, understand, and keep copies of all forms they sign.

9. Students have an obligation to perform satisfactorily the work agreed upon in a College Work-Study job.

10. Students have an obligation to notify their lender if they graduate or withdraw from school.

11. Students have an obligation to notify their lender if they transfer to another school.

12. Students have an obligation to notify their lender of any address changes.

13. Students have an obligation to notify their lender if they drop below half-time status.

14. Students have an obligation to notify their lender of anything that affects their ability to repay their loan or their eligibility for deferment or cancellation.

15. Students have an obligation to attend an exit interview before they leave school if they have borrowed from federal, state, or school loan sources.

Some Final Notes on Consumer Rights and Responsibilities

1. Always be honest in all of your financial aid transactions. Don't try to manipulate the system, and don't be dishonest in answering questions or completing forms.

2. Establish an honest relationship with your college's financial aid director. This person can be of great assistance in providing information to you and to your parents on the financial aid application process at your school.

3. Before signing any loan or financial aid award be certain you understand all of the terms and conditions.

20 THIRTY-FIVE WAYS TO REDUCE COLLEGE COSTS

Just as there are several different methods of financing a college education, so there are many ways to reduce college costs. The following are some suggestions on how students can lower their educational bills:

1. Most colleges and universities offer merit- or non-need-based scholarships to academically talented students. Students should check with each school they are considering to learn their criteria for merit scholarships.

2. The National Merit Scholarship Program awards scholarships to students based upon academic merit. The awards can be applied to any college or university to meet educational expenses at that school.

3. Many states offer scholarship assistance to academically talented students. Students should obtain the eligibility criteria from their state's education office.

4. Many schools offer scholarships to athletically talented students. Parents and students should be careful, however, to weigh the benefits of an athletic scholarship against the demands of this type of award.

5. Some colleges and universities offer special grants or scholarships to students with particular talents. Music, journalism, and drama are a few categories for which these awards are made.

6. A state college or university charges lower fees to state residents. Public institutions are subsidized by state revenues, and therefore tuition costs are lower than at private schools. The college selection process should include consideration of a state school. However, students should not base their choice of a school only on cost. Although cost should be *a* consideration, it should not be the *only* one.

7. Some students choose to attend a community college for 1 or 2 years, and then transfer to a 4-year school. Tuition costs are substantially lower at community colleges than at 4-year institutions.

8. Some parents may be financially able to purchase a house while their child is in school. If other students rent rooms in the house, the income may offset monthly mortgage payments. Families should make certain, however, that the property they purchase meets all of the requirements of rental property.

9. Commuting is another way for students to reduce college costs. A student living at home can save as much as $6000 per year.

10. Many schools provide lists of housing opportunities that provide free room and board to students in exchange for a certain number of hours of work each week.

11. Cooperative education programs allow students to alternate between working full time and studying full-time. This type of employment program is not based upon financial need, and students can earn as much as $7000 per year.

12. Another way to reduce college costs is to take fewer credits. Students should find out their school's policy regarding the Advanced Placement Program (APP), the College-Level Examination Program (CLEP), and the Proficiency Examination Program (PEP). Under these programs a student takes an examination in a particular subject and, if the score is high enough, receives college credit.

13. Some colleges give credit for life experiences, thereby reducing the number of credits needed for graduation. Students should check with the college for further information, or write to the National Home Study Council, 1601 18th Street, N.W., Washington, D.C. 20009.

14. Most schools charge one price for a specific number of credits taken in a semester. If academically possible, students should take the maximum number of credits allowed. This strategy reduces the amount of time needed to graduate.

15. In many cases a summer college course can be taken at a less expensive school and the credits transferred to the full-time school. Students should check with their academic advisor, however, to be certain that any course taken at another school is transferable.

16. Most schools have placement offices that help students find employment, and all schools have personnel offices that hire students to work on campus. These employment programs are not based upon financial need, and working is an excellent way to meet college expenses.

17. Most colleges and universities participate in the federal employment program, the College Work-Study Program. This program is based upon financial need and is administered by the school's financial aid director. Awards range from $1000 to $2500 per year.

18. Most colleges and universities offer their employees a tuition reduction plan or tuition waiver program. Under this type of arrangement, the school employee and family members can attend classes at a reduced cost or no cost at all. This type of program is based, not upon financial need, but rather on college employment.

19. Most colleges and universities sponsor resident advisor programs that offer financial assistance to students in the form of reduced tuition or reduced room and board costs in exchange for work in resident halls.

20. The Reserve Officers Training Corps (ROTC) Scholarship Program pays all tuition, fees, and textbook costs, as well as providing a monthly living stipend. Students should be certain, however, that they want this type of program before signing up because there is a service commitment after graduation.

21. Service Academy Scholarships are offered each year to qualified students to attend the U.S. Military Academy, the U.S. Air Force Academy, the U.S. Naval Academy, the U.S. Merchant Marine Academy, or the U.S. Coast Guard Academy. The scholarships are competitive and are based upon a number of factors, including high school grades, SAT or ACT scores, leadership qualities, and athletic ability. Students receive their undergraduate education at one of the service academies. They pay no tuition or fees, but there is a service commitment after graduation.

22. One of the most obvious ways of reducing college costs is to attend a low-cost school, either public or private. There are many colleges and universities with affordable tuition and generous financial assistance. Students should investigate all schools that meet their academic and financial needs.

23. Some schools offer combined degree programs or 3-year programs that allow students to take all of the courses needed for graduation in 3 years, instead of 4, thereby eliminating 1 year's educational expenses.

24. Partial tuition remission for the children of alumni is a common practice. Parents and students should investigate their "alma mater's" tuition discount policy for graduates.

25. Some colleges and universities offer special discounts if more than one child from the same family is enrolled.

26. Some colleges and universities offer discounts to enrolled students if they recruit another student.

27. Some schools offer a tuition discount to student government leaders or to the editors of college newspapers or yearbooks.

28. Some colleges offer bargain tuition rates to older students.

29. Some colleges and universities convert school loans into grants if the student remains in school and graduates.

30. Some schools will pay a student's loan origination fees.

31. Some schools offer reduced tuition rates to families if the major wage earner is unemployed.

32. Some colleges and universities have special funds set aside for families who do not qualify for federal or state funding.

33. Some private colleges will match the tuition of out-of-state institutions for certain groups of students.

34. Some companies offer tuition assistance to the children of employees. Parents and students should check with the personnel office for information.

35. Students should investigate buying used textbooks.

These are but a few of the ways to reduce college costs that should be incorporated into a family's overall college financial planning program.

21 SAMPLE PLANNING PROGRAM

This chapter summarizes the many tips offered in this book about how families can finance a college education. Read the letter that follows. Can you identify with these parents? Following the letter is the college financial planning program I offered to this family.

Dear Dean Dennis:

Help! My daughter is a senior in high school. She has been accepted to three colleges. Both my husband and I work, and our combined income is $50,000. When we filed for financial aid, we were told we made TOO MUCH MONEY to qualify for any federal or state financial aid programs. One college offered my daughter a financial aid package consisting of a $1000 grant, a $2500 loan, and a $1000 employment allotment. But are loans and work really financial aid?

What can we do? I want my daughter to attend the college of her choice, but I'm afraid we can't afford it. Please give us some advice.

Sincerely,

"Emotional" Middle-Class Parent

P.S. My son is a freshman in high school.

Dear "Emotional" Middle-Class Parent:

First, I want to tell you that I can offer some advice on how you can meet your daughter's college expenses. I think it was unwise, however, to wait until your daughter was a senior in high school to begin a college financing program. Finding the money for college doesn't just happen; it takes lots of planning to make the right choices. Think about how much time and effort we all put into buying a house or a car. Financing a college education should be considered as important as those major consumer purchases. But that's enough lecturing.

The suggestions that follow are applicable not only to your daughter but also to your son. In fact, they are more applicable to him since you have more time to plan to meet his future college financing needs. Ideally, a college financing program should begin in high school. My suggested program includes savings, employment, loans, and other aid.

I hope this information will be useful.

Optimistically,

Dean Dennis

Sample Program

Savings Program

Years Prior to College Enrollment:

If parents save $20 per week for 4 years at 6% interest, at the end of 4 years $4682 will be available to meet college costs.

If the high school student saves $10 per week for 4 years at 6% interest, at the end of 4 years $2341 will be available to meet college costs.

Enrollment Years:

If parents save $20 per week for the 4 years their child is enrolled in college, another $4682 will be available to meet college costs.

Savings Totals

Parents Prior to Enrollment	$ 4,682
Student Prior to Enrollment	$ 2,341
Parents During College Years	$ 4,682
Total	$11,705

Note: There are three times as many private colleges with tuition and fees of less than $5000 per year as there are schools charging more than $10,000. Public colleges and universities charge even less than private schools.

Employment Program

Years Prior to College Enrollment:

Summer and part-time jobs for 4 years at $500 per year	$2,000

College Years:

Summer and part-time jobs for 4 years at $1500 per year	$6,000
Employment Total	$8,000

Loan Programs

Stafford Loan, Perkins Loan, PLUS, SLS at $2500 per year	$10,000
Loan Total	$10,000

State, Institutional, or Private Organization Aid

$1,000 per year for 4 years	$4,000
Other aid total	$4,000

Fifteen Early Financial Planning Suggestions

1. "Baccalaureate" Bonds
2. Certificates of Deposit
3. Charitable Remainder Trust
4. Clifford Trust
5. Crummey Trust
6. Custodial Account
7. IRA, Keogh, and 401(K) Retirement Accounts
8. Life Insurance
9. Money Market Accounts
10. Money Market Funds
11. Stocks
12. Uniform Gift to Minors Act
13. United States EE Savings Bonds
14. Zero Coupon Bonds
15. Savings Accounts and Gifts

Note: Value cannot be estimated. This strategy would apply best to your son's situation.

Let's recap what could be available to finance their college educations:

SAVINGS	$11,705
STUDENT EMPLOYMENT	$ 8,000
LOANS	$10,000
OTHER AID	$ 4,000
GRAND TOTAL	$33,705

Each family must put together its own financing strategy, and the earlier the better. No one plan will work for all families. But remember: there is a strategy that will work for your family, and there is a school that you can afford.

22 QUESTIONS AND ANSWERS

The following are some of the questions most frequently asked by parents about the college financing process.

When should I begin planning for my child's college education?

Now. You can never begin too early to plan to meet future college expenses. In fact, some financial analysts recommend that, as soon as your child is born, you should initiate some college financial program. Early planning gives families options and can make the difference in the college selection process.

What is the best savings plan?

There is no one single savings or investment program that will work for all families. Each family must design and plan a financial strategy that will best meet its particular financial needs. The age of the child and the parents, and the financial resources of the family, will determine, to a great extent, the appropriate college savings program. The federal formula currently used to determine a family's ability to pay for college assesses greater weight to current income than to assets, so parents are not unjustly penalized for having made early financial arrangements to meet college costs. All families must assume the major responsibility for financing their children's educations, and that responsibility includes planning for college much earlier than has generally been the case with American families.

What about prepayment plans? Are they recommended?

Prepayment plans allow families to purchase a fixed, discounted tuition amount that represents the current 4-year cost of tuition. The money is then invested by the institution or the state to cover the future cost of tuition. Prepayment plans relieve families of the anxiety of escalating tuition bills. However, caution is urged. Prepayment programs are a new type of financing option. Before investing any money in a prepayment plan, find out whether the plan covers all college costs or just tuition expenses. Find out residency requirements and your tax liability. Know the maximum amount that can be invested, and determine what happens to your investment if your child decides not to attend that college or any college or drops out after the first year.

What about tuition stabilization plans?

This type of financing option is similar to prepayment plans, but the amount paid into the plan is generally less than 4 years of tuition. Most tuition stabilization plans require the family to pay a portion of the educational costs in advance. The advantage of this type of plan is that tuition is capped for all subsequent years that the student is enrolled at the school.

How will a family know whether they qualify for federal financial assistance?

No one can tell a family with certainty whether they will qualify for federal financial aid. For one thing, the federal government frequently changes the rules and regulations that determine eligibility. Some schools have a service that provides families with an estimate of what their aid will be if the student is accepted. Check with all schools you are considering for this service. If you know at the time of application what you can realistically expect to receive from all sources, you can determine whether you can afford to send your child to that particular school and what your financial contribution is expected to be.

I have twin sons. Should I give up on sending them to college?

No. Family contribution is divided by the number of family members enrolled in college at the same time. You may actually receive more money for having two children in college.

Is there an income cutoff for federal financial aid?

There is no income cutoff to receive federal financial aid. All families, regardless of income, should file the application for federal aid. REMEMBER: eligibility for funding from all sources is determined in part by costs. Attending an expensive school may actually mean that a family will qualify for more aid than if the student attended a lower cost institution. That is why it is so important for college selection to be based primarily on academic need and ability, and not on finances. Another good reason why all families should file for federal financial aid is that most colleges and universities will not consider a student for institutional aid unless a federal application form is on file.

Are some federal and state financial assistance programs easier than others to obtain?

In general, it is easier to obtain a loan than a grant. However, for a student to receive any financial aid, including federal and state loans, financial need criteria must be met. In most cases, a single financial aid form is used to determine eligibility for federal and state programs. Therefore, by applying for federal aid, a family is automatically considered for most other financial assistance programs.

Are there any alternatives if federal aid is denied?

Yes. There are many ways to finance a college education. Most schools and many states award scholarships based upon academic achievement. Many private organizations offer financial assistance to students who meet specific criteria. Many banks have college financing programs. Two federal loan programs, the PLUS and SLS programs, are awarded on the basis of creditworthiness, not financial need. Also, if a family has a savings plan and an investment program, and has been planning for several years to finance that college education, they have provided themselves with funding alternatives.

Isn't it true that the federal government has reduced the amount of money allocated for student financial assistance programs?

No. The federal government still provides about 75% of all aid awarded. While it is true that aid from the federal government has not kept pace with annual tuition increases, it is incorrect to state that the federal government no longer supports higher education. Financial assistance is still available. Funding sources have shifted from grants to loans, however, and at some schools employment allocations have decreased. Although deficit budgets will probably prevent the federal government from substantially increasing financial aid to college students, there are many other sources of funding, including state and institutional programs. It is the responsibility of the family to locate those sources.

The process is so complicated. Who can help me?

The first person who can help you is you. The process of finding the money for your child to attend college will seem complicated if you do not take the time to investigate, educate yourself, and explore all of your financial options. Find out as much as you can about financing a college education. As a purchaser of this book, you have already learned a great deal about financial aid. Compare college costs. Seek the advice of your accountant, banker, investment broker. Get to know a financial aid counselor at the local college or university. Save. Plan. Work. The more knowledge you have, the less complicated the process will be.

Should I pay someone to conduct a computerized scholarship search?

That's a personal choice. If you are willing to do the reading and research, and if you have access to a good library, you can locate many of the sources frequently listed by financial aid consultants. If you do use the services of a scholarship search firm, be prepared to spend from $40 to $70. I think you can and should be responsible for finding the financial resources necessary for your child to attend college.

Are there any "tricks" to applying for financial aid?

No. By the time your child is ready to enter college, the rules and regulations may be different from what they are today. For example, the federal government expects students to contribute 70% of their income and 35% of their assets toward meeting their college costs. Under the current federal formula, parents are expected to contribute 47% of their adjusted available income over $16,000 and 5.6% of their assets to meet college expenses. However, these percentages have frequently changed over the past several years, and there is reason to believe that they will change again before your child begins college. Don't try to "beat the system." Be honest on all of your applications for financial aid. Not only is this the right thing to do, but also there are severe penalties for dishonesty.

What about gifts from relatives and friends? How is that money treated in calculating student need?

Currently, federal financial aid regulations require that students contribute 35% of their assets to meeting their college costs. A $5000 gift from Aunt Marie means that the student is required to contribute $1750, or 35% of the $5000 asset. If, however, Aunt Marie gave the $5000 to you, the student's parents, the contribution would be $560, or 5.6% of $5000.

When should I cash in my stocks and bonds? Right before Junior begins college?

The federal aid formula used to determine a family's ability to contribute to a college education expects parents to hand over as much as 47% in profits realized from investments, such as stocks and bonds. It's unwise to do this right before your son begins college. Time your investments so that profits don't show up on your income tax return for the year preceding the one in which you apply for aid.

Why don't I just have my daughter declare herself independent from the family?

That's not so easy. Remember that the federal government has very specific criteria for determining who is independent and who is not. It isn't up to the family to establish the independent status of their children.

Will I receive the same amount of financial aid from each college?

Probably not. The amount of money you receive from one school could be very different from what you receive at another; many factors are used in calculating financial need and family contribution. An important factor for a family to consider is the cost of a college or university. Another factor to consider is the amount of institutional aid you are offered and the school's policy of awarding aid. These policies will differ from one college to another and will depend upon the amount of money a school allocates from its own budget for student financial aid.

How can I find out which colleges offer the best financial aid programs?

The first thing for a family to do is to select a college or university that meets the academic needs of the student. Visit as many schools as you can, and meet with both the admissions and the financial aid counselors. Get all of the available literature. Compare costs, financial aid policies, school financial assistance programs, and the average student indebtedness of recent graduates. Find out the percentage of first-, second-, third-, and fourth-year students receiving aid. Most families wait until a student is a junior in high school to conduct this type of comparative process. Don't procrastinate. The earlier you get this information, the easier it will be for you to plan your finances.

Will a student receive the same amount of money each year?

Probably not. The awarding of aid depends upon the family's financial circumstances and college expenses. It also depends upon the school's allocations of funds. Don't count on receiving the same dollar amount each year. Remember that a student must file for financial aid each year, and apply early. If all of the forms are on file, you will be notified sometime between April and June.

Can college students work without jeopardizing their academic success?

Yes. This may come as a surprise to many parents, but the majority of college students work while they are in school. Moreover, research indicates that in most cases the academic performance of employed students is not negatively affected. Working students learn how to manage their time. Also, they can acquire valuable skills that may translate into future jobs. Of course, there are limits; working 40 hours a week is not recommended. There are only so many hours in a day, and full-time students should not sacrifice study time to maximize income. However, working 20 hours per week has proved to be manageable for most college students.

There are so many different kinds of financing options and alternative sources of funding a college education. How do I know which one is best for my family's situation?

Only you, in collaboration with your financial consultant, can decide which college financial plan is best for your family. You should apply for all federal, state, and school aid before seeking alternative funding sources. Be certain you understand all of the terms

and conditions of all of the alternative programs you investigate, and compare programs. You don't want any surprises.

What about student debt? Is it really a problem?

Last year the federal government spent over $2 billion to cover student loan defaults. Currently, there are about 3 million defaulters. It is a fact that more students are borrowing more money to meet their college expenses. It is quite realistic to expect to have to borrow some money for college, but try to keep your child's borrowing under $10,000. Any amount over that may be unmanageable.

If my child must borrow, is there some way to structure the debt after graduation so that monthly payments will be reasonable?

Yes. There are loan consolidation programs for graduates with more than $5000 in student debt. The following loans can be consolidated: Stafford Student Loan, Perkins Student Loan, Health Professions Student Loan, and PLUS and SLS loans. Loan consolidation allows the borrower to extend the period of repayment and to make single, monthly loan payments. The interest rate, determined by federal law, is either 9% or the weighted average of all consolidated loans, rounded to the nearest whole percent, whichever is higher.

What should college graduates do if they cannot meet their monthly student loan bills?

The most important thing to do is not to fall into default status; this could affect a person's credit rating for years so come. Arrangements can be made with the lender if there are extenuating circumstances. Forbearance can be exercised. Students should never default on any student loan.

What should I do if my family's financial situation changes after my child enrolls in college?

The first thing to do is to meet with the school's financial aid director. If a family's financial circumstances change, adjustments can be made to the expected family contribution. The aid official can exercise professional judgment. This is another strong argument for filing a financial aid application, regardless of income. If this form is already on file, reconsideration can be given, even if aid was previously denied.

What are the most important things to remember in financing a college education?

First, plan early; second, begin to save regularly; third, don't borrow too much; fourth, get expert advice; fifth, diversify your college savings program; sixth, change your plan whenever necessary; and seventh, don't despair.

23 EDUCATIONAL COSTS

Throughout this book you have been asked to consider ways of reducing your college expenses and to contact your school's office of financial aid for information on financial aid programs. This chapter lists the educational expenses at schools throughout the United States and the phone numbers of the financial aid offices. The costs listed are for the 1991–92 academic year. It is safe to add 5–10% in estimating next year's expenses. Remember that costs differ for state residents and out-of-state students. Expenses will also be different for students living on campus and students who commute to school. The costs listed in this chapter are tuition and fees, room and board, and books and supplies. To obtain information on additional costs, contact all of the schools you are considering.

	Tuition and Fees	Room and Board	Books and Supplies	Financial Aid Office
Alabama				
Alabama Aviation and Technical College	$1,298	2,306	$500	(205) 774-5113
Alabama State Universtiy	1,268	1,910	570	(205) 293-4324
Athens State College	1,125	2,425	400	(205) 232-8122
Auburn University at Montgomery	1,428	-	600	(205) 244-3571
Auburn University	1,476	2,800	525	(205) 826-4723
Bessemer State Technical College	885	-	550	(205) 428-6391
Birmingham-Southern College	9,084	3,120	500	(205) 226-4688
Concordia College	3,176	2,796	550	(205) 874-5700 ext. 711
Enterprise State Junior College	645	-	300	(205) 347-2623
Faulkner University	4,635	2,800	300	(205) 272-5820
Gadsden State Community College	600	1,545	300	(205) 549-8266
Hobson State Technical College	1,035	-	450	(205) 636-9642
International Bible College	2,800	-	400	(205) 766-6610
Jackson State University	1,335	2,228	450	(205) 782-5006
James H. Faulkner State Junior College	795	1,875	450	(205) 937-9581
John C. Calhoun State Community College	798	-	500	(205) 353-3102
Livingston University	1,524	2,055	500	(205) 652-9661
Miles College	3,760	2,300	400	(205) 923-2771
Mobile College	4,710	2,980	400	(205) 675-5990
Northeast Alabama State Junior College	766	-	400	(205) 228-6001
Northwest Alabama State Junior College	1,000	-	400	(205) 993-5331
Northwest Alabama State Technical College	600	-	450	(205) 921-3177
Oakwood College	5,460	3,288	600	(205) 726-7208
Reid State Technical College	836	-	400	(205) 578-1313

	Tuition and Fees	Room and Board	Books and Supplies	Financial Aid Office
Samford University	6,540	3,354	450	(205) 870-2905
Snead State Junior College	774	1,900	450	(205) 593-5120
Southeast Bible College	3,790	2,623	300	(205) 969-0880
Southern Junior College	3,360	-	450	(205) 251-2821
Southern Union State Junior College	900	1,800	400	(205) 395-2211
Spring Hill College	10,153	4,158	500	(205) 460-2140
Stillman College	4,260	2,640	400	(205) 349-4240
Talladega College	4,373	2,050	500	(205) 362-0206
Troy State University	1,400	2,295	400	(205) 566-8112
Tuskegee University	6,250	3,000	550	(205) 727-8201
University of Alabama Birmingham	1,920	3,800	570	(205) 934-8132
University of Alabama Huntsville	2,019	3,240	450	(205) 895-6241
University of Alabama Tuscaloosa	1,900	3,400	525	(205) 348-6756
University of North Alabama	1,296	2,388	550	(205) 760-4278
University of South Alabama	1,797	2,595	470	(205) 460-6231
Walker College	2,028	1,978	500	(205) 387-0511
Walker State Technical College	614	-	600	(205) 648-3311
Wallace State Community College	603	-	400	(205) 352-6403

Alaska

	Tuition and Fees	Room and Board	Books and Supplies	Financial Aid Office
Alaska Pacific College	6,330	4,050	500	(907) 564-8248
Sheldon Jackson College	5,960	4,215	500	(907) 747-5241
University of Alaska Anchorage	1,270	-	440	(907) 786-1332
University of Alaska Fairbanks	1,660	2,690	500	(907) 474-7256
University of Alaska Juneau	1,226	-	300	(907) 789-2101

Arizona

	Tuition and Fees	Room and Board	Books and Supplies	Financial Aid Office
Arizona College of the Bible	4,370	-	400	(602) 995-2670
Arizona State University	1,590	4,150	500	(602) 965-4045
Arizona Western College	690	2,650	350	(602) 726-1000
Central Arizona College	570	2,420	400	(602) 426-4425
Eastern Arizona College	600	2,574	450	(602) 428-1133
Embry-Riddle Aeronautical University	6,310	3,540	490	(602) 778-4130
Gateway Community College	720	-	400	(602) 392-5136
Glendale Community College	720	-	500	(602) 435-3329
Grand Canyon College	6,330	2,800	570	(602) 589-2885
Mesa Community College	780	-	400	(602) 461-7441
Mohave Community College	490	-	500	(602) 757-0828
Northern Arizona University	1,540	2,534	650	(602) 523-4951
Northland Pioneer College	360	-	418	(602) 524-6111
Phoenix College	720	-	400	(602) 285-7501
Pima Community College	528	-	425	(602) 884-6950
Prescott College	7,905	-	700	(602) 778-2090
Rio Salado Community College	720	-	400	(602) 223-4060
Scottsdale Community College	780	-	320	(602) 423-6549

	Tuition and Fees	Room and Board	Books and Supplies	Financial Aid Office
South Mountain Community College	780	-	450	(602) 243-8300
University of Arizona	1,590	3,702	590	(602) 621-1643
University of Phoenix	5,328	-	600	(602) 921-8005
Western International University	3,300	-	500	(602) 943-2311
Yavapai College	590	2,440	475	(602) 776-2208

Arkansas

Arkansas Baptist College	1,670	2,200	600	(501) 374-0804
Arkansas College	6,400	2,810	430	(501) 793-9813
Arkansas State University	1,410	2,310	500	(501) 972-2310
Arkansas Tech University	1,260	2,080	450	(501) 968-0399
Capital City Junior College	5,760	-	-	(501) 562-0700
East Arkansas Community College	552	-	175	(501) 633-4480
Garland County Community College	624	-	400	(501) 767-9371
Henderson State University	1,220	1,900	400	(501) 246-3199
Hendrix College	7,253	2,775	400	(501) 450-1368
John Brown University	5,490	3,060	450	(501) 524-3131
Mississippi County Community College	648	-	250	(501) 762-1020
North Arkansas Community College	528	-	255	(501) 743-3000
Philander Smith College	2,350	2,300	400	(501) 375-9845
Phillips County Community College	600	-	450	(501) 338-6474
Rich Mountain Community College	580	-	300	(501) 394-5012
Shorter College	1,860	2,200	250	(501) 374-6305
Southern Arkansas University at El Dorado	720	-	400	(501) 862-8131
Southern Arkansas University at Magnolia	1,080	2,100	320	(501) 235-4023
Southern Baptist College	2,614	1,710	400	(501) 886-6741
University of Arkansas at Fayetteville	1,598	2,925	550	(501) 575-3806
University of Arkansas at Little Rock	1,570	-	500	(501) 569-3130
University of Arkansas at Monticello	1,410	1,880	400	(501) 460-1050
University of Arkansas at Pine Bluff	1,355	1,940	500	(501) 541-6632
University of Central Arkansas	1,290	2,156	300	(501) 450-3140
University of the Ozarks	3,420	2,310	500	(501) 754-3839
Westark Community College	672	-	400	(501) 785-7044

California

Allan Hancock College	118	-	360	(916) 484-6966
Antelope Valley College	100	-	384	(805) 943-3241
Azusa Pacific University	9,700	3,650	600	(213) 969-3434
Bakersfield College	120	3,415	400	(805) 395-4426
Barstow College	100	-	500	(619) 252-2411
Bay Valley Tech	4,605	-	350	(408) 727-1060
Bethany Bible College	6,210	3,000	550	(408) 438-3800

	Tuition and Fees	Room and Board	Books and Supplies	Financial Aid Office
Biola University	9,902	4,090	539	(213) 903-4742
Brooks College	5,710	3,580	1,000	(213) 597-6611
Butte College	155	-	450	(916) 895-2311
Cabrillo College	169	-	384	(408) 479-6415
California Baptist College	5,445	3,350	550	(714) 689-5771
California Institute of the Arts	12,250	5,100	800	(805) 253-7869
California Institute of Technology	14,310	4,630	630	(818) 356-8355
California Lutheran Technology	9,450	4,200	504	(805) 493-3115
California Maritime Academy	1,391	4,002	525	(707) 648-4227
California State Polytechnic University at Pomona	1,012	4,118	550	(805) 756-2927
California State Polytechnic University at San Luis Obispo	1,181	3,897	558	(805) 546-2927
California State University				
Bakersfield	1,067	3,476	500	(805) 664-3016
Chico	1,066	3,720	500	(916) 898-5017
Dominguez Hills	1,027	-	500	(213) 516-3691
Fresno	1,070	3,675	500	(209) 278-7044
Fullerton	1,108	-	500	(714) 773-3128
Haywood	1,051	-	500	(415) 881-3018
Long Beach	1,045	4,326	560	(213) 985-8410
Los Angeles	1,046	4,671	500	(213) 343-3247
Northridge	1,128	-	500	(818) 885-2085
Sacramento	1,048	4,713	500	(916) 278-7287
San Bernardino	1,068	-	500	(714) 880-5221
Stanislaus	1,072	3,795	500	(209) 667-3336
Cerritos Community College	100	-	420	(213) 860-2451
Chaffery College	100	-	450	(714) 941-2341
Chapman College	12,975	5,000	500	(714) 997-6741
Christ College Irvine	8,790	4,170	525	(714) 854-8002
Christian Heritage College	6,800	3,100	400	(619) 440-3043
Citrus Community College	115	-	450	(818) 914-8594
City College of San Francisco	100	-	460	(415) 239-3575
Claremont McKenna College	14,810	5,180	500	(714) 621-8356
Cogswell College	6,280	-	600	(408) 734-5610
College of Alameda	100	-	350	(415) 748-2203
College of the Desert	115	-	325	(619) 773-2532
College of Notre Dame	10,165	5,100	550	(415) 593-1601
College of the Redwoods	100	3,620	500	(707) 445-6782
College of the Sequoias	100	-	350	(209) 773-3748
Columbia College	125	-	500	(209) 533-5105
Columbia College at Hollywood	5,250	-	550	(213) 469-8321
Compton Community College	110	-	360	(213) 637-2660
Condie Junior College	2,720	-	125	(408) 866-6666
Cosumnes River College	100	-	450	(916) 688-7325
Cuesta Community College	150	-	360	(805) 546-3143
Cuyamaca College	125	-	433	(619) 670-1980
Cypress College	125	-	500	(714) 826-7311
De Anza College	165	-	560	(408) 996-4718
Dominican College of San Rafael	10,164	5,184	560	(415) 485-3220
El Camino Community College	100	-	400	(213) 715-3492
Evergreen Valley College	115	-	500	(408) 270-6460
Fashion Institute of Design and Merchandising	9,545	4,284	1,050	(213) 624-1200
Feather River College	125	-	600	(916) 283-0202

	Tuition and Fees	Room and Board	Books and Supplies	Financial Aid Office
Foothill College	150	-	500	(415) 949-7710
Fresno City College	115	-	500	(209) 442-4600
Fresno Pacific College	8,356	3,484	550	(209) 453-2041
Fullerton College	120	-	300	(714) 992-7050
Gavilan Community College	125	-	550	(408) 848-4727
Glendale Community College	125	:	350	(818) 240-1000
Golden Gate University	4,812	-	450.	(415) 442-7270
Golden West College	115	-	500	(714) 895-8707
Grossmont Community College	115	-	550	(619) 465-1700
Harvey Mudd College	14,900	5,890	450	(714) 621-8055
Holy Names College	8,510	4,150	500	(415) 436-1327
Kings River Community College	155	-	550	(209) 638-5040
Lake Tahoe Community College	100	-	525	(916) 541-1629
Laney Community College	100	-	430	(415) 464-3419
Loma Linda University	9,435	4,284	500	(714) 824-4509
Long Beach City College	120	-	450	(213) 420-4257
Los Angeles Valley College	100	-	450	(818) 781-1200
Los Medanos College	100	-	480	(415) 439-2181
Loyola Marymount University	11,376	5,671	560	(213) 338-2732
Marin Community College	106	-	400	(415) 485-9409
Marymount College	10,510	-	560	(213) 377-6950
Master's College	6,950	3,690	500	(805) 259-3540
Mendocino College	106	-	500	(707) 468-3110
Menlo College	12,390	6,030	525	(415) 323-6141
Merced College	116	-	450	(209) 384-6034
Merritt College	104	-	450	(415) 436-2467
Mills College	14,000	5,700	420	(415) 430-2134
Miracosta College	126	-	450	(619) 757-2601
Mission College	122	-	500	(408) 988-2200
Modesto Junior College	122	-	560	(209) 575-6040
Monterey Institute of International Studies	11,345	-	500	(408) 647-4119
Monterey Peninsula College	135	-	432	(408) 646-4031
Mount St. Mary's College	10,250	4,650	560	(213) 471-9505
Mount San Antonio College	129	-	450	(714) 594-5611
Mount San Jacinto College	102	-	450	(714) 654-9027
Napa Valley College	100	-	400	(707) 253-3021
National University	5,535	-	450	(619) 563-2570
New College of California	5,850	-	590	(415) 626-1694
Northrop University	10,700	3,980	800	(213) 337-4770
Occidental College	14,784	5,216	600	(213) 259-2548
Ohlone College	100	-	450	(415) 659-6150
Orange Coast College	151	-	500	(714) 432-5508
Pacific Christian College	5,600	5,000	500	(714) 879-3901
Pacific Oaks College	8,900	-	400	(818) 397-1346
Palomar College	115	-	500	(714) 774-1150
Pasadena City College	115	-	400	(818) 449-6372
Patten College	3,490	3,790	500	(415) 533-8300
Pepperdine University	15,230	6,070	800	(213) 456-4633
Pitzer College	16,282	5,002	650	(714) 621-8208
Point Loma Nazarene College	8,058	3,624	600	(619) 221-2579
Pomona College	14,030	5,700	550	(714) 621-8205
Rancho Santiago College	115	-	450	(714) 667-3080
Rio Hondo College	115	-	400	(213) 908-3411
Saddleback College	140	-	450	(714) 582-4860
Saint Mary's College	11,036	5,436	560	(415) 631-4370
Samuel Merritt College of Nursing	10,165	4,400	500	(415) 420-6131
San Diego State University	1,118	3,900	500	(619) 594-6323

	Tuition and Fees	Room and Board	Books and Supplies	Financial Aid Office
San Francisco State University	1,052	4,200	550	(415) 338-2437
San Joaquin Delta College	150	-	500	(209) 474-5114
San Jose City College	115	-	500	(408) 288-3740
San Jose State University	1,130	4,316	500	(408) 924-1515
Santa Clara University	10,485	5,007	500	(408) 554-4505
Santa Rosa Junior College	115	1,600	550	(707) 527-4478
Scripps College	14,800	6,350	500	(714) 621-8275
Shasta College	126	-	450	(916) 225-4830
Sierra College	115	3,241	500	(916) 624-3333
Simpson College	6,338	3,480	560	(415) 334-7400
Solano Community College	108	-	430	(707) 864-7000
Sonoma State University	1,074	4,332	500	(707) 664-2389
Southern California College	7,788	3,500	500	(714) 556-3610
Southern California Institute of Architecture	9,475	-	1,400	(213) 829-3489
Southwestern College	134	-	450	(619) 421-1149
Stanford University	15,102	6,159	750	(415) 723-1543
Taft College	100	1,870	250	(805) 763-4282
United States International University	9,810	4,725	500	(714) 693-4559
University of California				
Berkeley	2,020	5,580	500	(415) 642-0645
Davis	1,780	4,741	635	(916) 752-2396
Irvine	1,875	5,000	600	(714) 856-5337
Los Angeles	1,686	4,850	615	(213) 206-0404
Riverside	1,693	4,850	655	(714) 787-3669
San Diego	1,813	5,562	504	(619) 534-3800
San Francisco	2,019	4,455	949	(415) 476-4185
Santa Barbara	1,729	4,732	580	(805) 893-2697
Santa Cruz	1,829	4,787	550	(408) 459-4323
University of Judaism	8,260	5,800	700	(213) 476-9777
University of La Verne	11,165	4,500	504	(714) 593-0965
University of the Pacific	14,480	5,100	565	(209) 946-2421
University of Redlands	14,130	5,370	450	(714) 335-4047
University of San Diego	11,440	5,750	500	(619) 260-4514
University of San Francisco	11,040	5,214	500	(415) 666-6303
University of Southern California	15,306	6,260	600	(213) 743-8212
Ventura County Community College	115	-	430	(805) 654-6410
Vista College	100	-	400	(415) 841-8431
West Coast Christian College	3,560	2,904	500	(209) 299-7201
West Coast University	8,250	-	500	(213) 487-4433
Westmont College	12,070	4,650	450	(805) 565-6063
West Valley College	139	-	500	(408) 741-2024
Whittier College	14,532	4,966	500	(213) 907-4285
Woodbury University	10,236	5,200	615	(818) 767-0888
World College West	9,800	4,300	-	(707) 765-4500
Yuba Community College	115	3,400	400	(916) 741-6781

Colorado

Adams State College	1,440	2,612	500	(719) 589-7306
Aims Community College	663	-	270	(303) 330-8008
Arapahoe Community College	1,096	-	400	(303) 797-5661
Blair Junior College	4470	-	400	(303) 574-1082
Colorado Christian University	5,205	3,190	400	(303) 238-5386
Colorado College	13,665	3,645	400	(719) 389-6651
Colorado Institute of Art	7,150	-	1,000	(303) 837-0825

	Tuition and Fees	Room and Board	Books and Supplies	Financial Aid Office
Colorado Mountain College	1,600	3,200	400	(303) 945-8691
Colorado Northwestern Community College	210	2,690	500	(303) 675-3203
Colorado School of Mines	3,892	3,680	500	(303) 273-3301
Colorado State University	2,222	3,462	450	(303) 491-1089
Community College of Aurora	1,022	-	400	(303) 360-4761
Community College of Denver	1,098	-	415	(303) 556-2420
Denver Institute of Technology	9,295	-	500	(303) 650-5050
Denver Technical College	6,600	-	410	(303) 329-3000
Fort Lewis College	1,836	-	525	(303) 247-7142
Front Range Community College	1,092	-	365	(303) 466-8811
Lamar Community College	1,167	2,900	375	(303) 336-2248
Mesa College	1,432	2,932	425	(303) 248-1396
Metropolitan State College	1,321	-	420	(303) 556-3999
Naropa Institute	7,595	-	400	(303) 444-0202
Northeastern Junior College	604	3,300	300	(303) 522-6600
Otero Junior College	1,092	2,800	350	(303) 384-6834
Pikes Peak Community College	1,037	-	400	(303) 576-7711
Pueblo Community College	1,030	-	400	(303) 549-3326
Red Rocks Community College	1,024	-	450	(303) 988-6160
Regis College	9,860	4,800	435	(303) 458-4066
Trinidad State Junior College	1,204	3,340	430	(303) 846-5553
University of Colorado				
Boulder	2,256	3,340	400	(303) 492-7347
Colorado Springs	1,708	-	454	(719) 593-3460
Denver	1,458	-	450	(303) 556-2886
University of Denver	12,990	4,205	400	(303) 871-2331
University of Northern Colorado	1,942	3,450	500	(303) 351-2509
Western State College of Colorado	1,542	2,958	400	(303) 943-3085

Connecticut

	Tuition and Fees	Room and Board	Books and Supplies	Financial Aid Office
Albertus Magnus College	10,120	4,930	400	(203) 773-8508
Asnuntuck Community College	934	-	400	(203) 253-3030
Briarwood College	7,925	-	500	(203) 628-4751
Central Connecticut College	1,865	3,500	500	(203) 827-7330
Connecticut College	16,080	5,370	500	(203) 439-2057
Fairfield University	12,920	5,350	450	(203) 254-4125
Hartford College for Women	9,017	4,672	600	(203) 236-1215
Hartford State Technical College	1,230	-	500	(203) 527-4111
Holy Apostles College	3,000	4,320	600	(203) 632-3003
Manchester Community College	934	-	600	(203) 646-4900
Mattatuck Community College	934	-	400	(203) 575-8009
Norwalk Community College	934	-	450	(203) 853-2040
Norwalk State Technical College	1,230	-	1,000	(203) 855-6641
Post College	10,074	4,180	550	(203) 575-9691
Quinnipiac College	10,350	4,960	500	(203) 281-8761
Sacred Heart University	8,070	5,000	400	(203) 371-7980
St. Joseph College	10,400	4,050	500	(203) 232-4571
South Central Community College	934	-	425	(203) 789-7039
Southern Connecticut State University	1,690	3,478	600	(203) 397-4232
University of Connecticut	3,463	4,522	530	(203) 486-2819
University of Hartford	13,594	5,414	450	(203) 243-4296
University of New Haven	9,570	4,700	500	(203) 932-7315

	Tuition and Fees	Room and Board	Books and Supplies	Financial Aid Office
Waterbury State Technical College	1,230	-	600	(203) 575-8080
Wesleyan University	16,830	4,990	500	(203) 344-7901
Western Connecticut State University	1,855	3,090	600	(203) 797-4393
Yale University	16,300	5,900	500	(203) 432-4110

Delaware

Delaware Technical & Community College				
Wilmington Campus	1,011	-	450	(302) 571-5380
Southern Campus	1,011	-	450	(302) 856-5607
Terry Campus	1,011	-	450	(302) 739-5419
Goldey Beacom College	4,855	-	400	(302) 998-8814
University of Delaware	3,126	3,300	500	(302) 451-8761
Wesley College	8,055	3,800	500	(302) 736-2338
Wilmington College	4,690	-	600	(302) 328-9401

District of Columbia

American University	13,706	6,046	450	(202) 885-6100
Catholic University of America	11,876	5,685	500	(202) 319-5305
Gallaudet University	3,784	4,610	600	(202) 651-5290
Georgetown University	15,797	6,320	575	(202) 687-4547
George Washington University	15,027	6,350	600	(202) 994-6660
Howard University	6,405	3,500	560	(202) 806-2800
Mount Vernon College	12,510	6,090	500	(202) 331-3458
Trinity College	10,750	6,280	450	(202) 939-5047
University of the District of Columbia	800	-	475	(202) 282-3238

Florida

Art Institute of Fort Lauderdale	7,850	-	1,000	(305) 463-3000
Barry University	8,690	4,700	500	(305) 899-3660
Bethune Cookman College	4,835	3,172	600	(305) 255-1401
Broward Community College	750	-	485	(305) 475-6575
Central Florida Community College	840	-	350	(904) 237-2111
Chipola Junior College	668	1,950	375	(904) 526-2761
College of Boca Raton	12,200	4,700	400	(407) 994-0770
Daytona Beach Community College	802	-	470	(904) 255-8131
Eckerd College	13,040	3,210	550	(813) 864-8334
Edison Community College	750	-	350	(813) 489-9346
Edward Walters College	3,866	3,850	400	(305) 355-3030
Embry-Riddle Aeronatuical University	6,310	3,200	490	(904) 239-6299
Flagler College	4,550	2,840	500	(904) 829-6481
Florida Agricultural and Mechanical University	1,366	2,480	350	(904) 599-3730
Florida Atlantic University	1,403	3,345	500	(407) 367-2738
Florida College	3,700	2,400	450	(813) 988-5131
Florida Community College at Jacksonville	780	-	450	(904) 632-3132
Florida Institute of Technology	10,635	3,465	750	(305) 768-8070
Florida International University	1,358	3,810	800	(305) 348-2347

	Tuition and Fees	Room and Board	Books and Supplies	Financial Aid Office
Florida Keys Community College	690	-	350	(305) 296-9081
Florida Memorial College	4,350	2,752	400	(305) 625-4141
Florida Southern College	6,600	4,200	300	(813) 680-4140
Florida State University	1,308	3,418	400	(904) 644-5716
Gulf Coast Community College	660	-	500	(904) 872-3844
Hillsborough Community College	780	-	510	(813) 253-7017
Hobe Sound Bible College	3,380	2,315	450	(305) 546-5534
Indian River Community College	740	-	450	(305) 464-2000
Jacksonville University	7,960	3,580	600	(904) 774-3950
Jones College	3,600	-	650	(904) 743-1122
Lake City Community College	720	2,159	300	(904) 752-1822
Lake-Sumter Community College	750	-	400	(904) 365-3513
Manatee Community College	720	-	500	(813) 755-1511
Miami Christian College	4,930	-	500	(305) 953-1131
Miami-Dade Community College	803	-	600	(305) 347-2506
National Education Center: Tampa Campus	5,382	-	400	(813) 238-0455
North Florida Junior College	653	-	300	(904) 973-2288
Nova University	6,450	-	400	(305) 475-7519
Okaloosa-Walton Junior College	630	-	400	(904) 729-5370
Orlando College	3561	-	500	(407) 628-1344
Palm Beach Atlantic College	5,400	2,600	400	(407) 835-4320
Palm Beach Junior College	795	-	550	(305) 439-8061
Pasco-Hernando Community College	795	-	320	(813) 847-2727
Pensacola Junior College	795	-	375	(904) 476-1680
Polk Community College	810	-	300	(813) 297-1000
Ringling School of Art and Design	8,950	4,700	1,500	(813) 351-4614
Rollins College	13,900	4,295	600	(407) 646-2395
St. John's River Community College	630	-	375	(904) 328-1571
St. John's Vianney College	5,600	3,000	500	(305) 223-4561
St. Leo's College	7,870	2,290	400	(904) 588-8270
St. Petersburg Junior College	798	-	500	(813) 791-2601
Santa Fe Community College	720	-	700	(904) 395-5000
Seminole Community College	780	-	376	(407) 323-1450
Stetson University	10,020	4,070	500	(904) 734-4121
Tallahassee Community College	660	-	500	(904) 488-9200
University of Central Florida	1,373	3,620	400	(407) 823-2827
University of Florida	1,322	3,330	510	(904) 392-1271
University of Miami	14,080	5,575	525	(305) 284-2270
University of North Florida	1,325	-	450	(904) 646-2604
University of South Florida	1,401	2,750	450	(813) 974-3039
University of Tampa	10,920	4,500	550	(813) 253-6219
University of West Florida	1,321	3,450	450	(904) 474-2400
Valencia Community College	810	-	500	(305) 299-5000
Warner Southern College	5,375	3,140	425	(813) 638-1426

Georgia

	Tuition and Fees	Room and Board	Books and Supplies	Financial Aid Office
Abraham Baldwin Agricultural College	1,170	2,055	450	(912) 386-3235
Agnes Scott College	10,450	4,180	350	(404) 371-6395
Albany State College	1,599	2,355	520	(912) 430-4650
American College for the Applied Arts	6,900	-	800	(404) 231-9000
Andrew College	3,955	3,480	450	(912) 732-2171

	Tuition and Fees	Room and Board	Books and Supplies	Financial Aid Office
Armstrong State College	1,413	2,850	365	(912) 927-5272
Atlanta Christian College	3,620	2,600	400	(404) 761-8861
Atlanta Metropolitan College	969	-	450	(404) 756-4002
Augusta College	1,431	4,845	430	(404) 737-1431
Berry College	7,050	3,302	500	(404) 236-2244
Brenau College	7,242	5,658	450	(404) 534-6152
Brewton-Parker College	3,625	2,300	550	(912) 583-2241
Clark College	6,400	3,500	600	(404) 681-3088
Clayton State College	1,338	-	375	(404) 961-3511
Columbus College	1,413	3,519	600	(404) 568-2036
Crandall Junior College	4,560	-	250	(912) 745-6593
Darton College	970	-	375	(912) 888-8746
DeKalb College	1,005	-	350	(404) 299-4005
DeVry Institute of Technology	5,015	-	500	(404) 292-7900
Emmanuel College	3,501	2,610	600	(404) 245-7221
Emory University	14,780	4,532	600	(404) 727-6039
Floyd College	984	-	250	(404) 295-6311
Gainsville College	1,002	-	500	(404) 535-6263
Georgia College	1,476	2,205	490	(912) 453-5149
Georgia Institute of Technology	2,052	3,660	600	(404) 894-4582
Georgia Military College	3,270	3,650	450	(912) 453-3481
Georgia Southern College	1,563	2,730	450	(912) 681-5413
Georgia Southwestern College	1,527	2,220	600	(912) 928-1366
Georgia State University	1,812	-	700	(404) 651-3567
Gordon College	1,029	2,040	450	(404) 358-5059
Kennesaw College	1,344	-	450	(404) 423-6541
LaGrange College	5,537	3,175	600	(404) 882-2911
Macon College	1,000	-	400	(912) 471-2717
Mercer University				
Atlanta	6,547	-	400	(404) 451-0331
Macon	9,425	3,666	400	(912) 752-2650
Middle Georgia College	1,164	2,220	425	(912) 934-3084
Morehouse College	6,210	4,462	500	(404) 681-2800
Morris Brown College	6,140	3,250	500	(404) 525-7831
North Georgia College	1,494	2,190	550	(404) 864-1413
Oglethorpe University	10,250	4,000	450	(404) 261-1441
Oxford College of Emory University	11,000	4,040	500	(404) 784-8303
Paine College	5,256	2,660	400	(404) 722-4471
Phillips College	4,025	-	300	(404) 724-7719
Piedmont College	3,600	3,050	500	(404) 778-8814
Reinhardt College	3,915	3,375	500	(404) 479-1454
Savannah State College	1,564	2,085	450	(912) 356-2253
Shorter College	5,300	3,300	400	(404) 291-2121
South College	3,925	-	400	(912) 651-8107
South Georgia College	1,032	2,184	475	(912) 384-4285
Southern College of Technology	1,431	3,100	-	(404) 528-7290
Spelman College	6,707	4,770	450	(404) 681-3643
Toccoa Falls College	5,177	3,234	300	(404) 886-6831
Truett-McConnell College	3,723	2,400	450	(404) 865-2140
University of Georgia	2,010	2,950	400	(404) 542-8208
Valdosta State College	1,570	2,370	600	(912) 333-5935
Waycross College	1,024	-	500	(912) 285-6035
Wesleyan College	9,850	3,900	450	(912) 477-1110
West Georgia College	1,587	2,305	450	(404) 836-6421
Young Harris College	4,140	3,105	450	(404) 379-3111

	Tuition and Fees	Room and Board	Books and Supplies	Financial Aid Office
Hawaii				
Chaminade University of Hawaii	7,850	3,900	500	(808) 739-4649
Hawaii Loa College	8,400	4,800	600	(808) 235-3641
Honolulu Community College	430	-	425	(808) 845-9116
Kapiolani Community College	430	-	425	(808) 734-9538
Kauai Community College	430	-	425	(808) 245-8260
Leeward Community College	430	-	425	(808) 455-0248
University of Hawaii				
Hilo	470	3,186	550	(808) 933-3324
Manoa	1,387	3,186	550	(808) 956-7251
West Oahu College	850	-	585	(808) 456-5921
Windward Community College	440	-	400	(808) 235-7449
Idaho				
Boise Bible College	2,856	2,450	400	(208) 376-7731
Boise State University	1,350	2,750	400	(208) 385-1540
College of Idaho	9,985	2,710	450	(208) 459-5308
College of Southern Idaho	800	2,070	400	(208) 734-0307
Idaho State University	1,160	2,628	450	(208) 236-2756
Lewis Clark State College	1,120	2,720	450	(208) 746-2341
Northwest Nazarene College	7,260	2,510	450	(208) 467-8422
Ricks College	1,480	2,710	500	(208) 356-1015
University of Idaho	1,166	2,620	500	(208) 885-6312
Illinois				
Augustana College	11,175	3,600	450	(309) 794-7341
Aurora University	8,770	3,405	600	(312) 892-6431
Barat College	8,719	3,300	450	(312) 234-3000
Belleville Area College	850	-	448	(618) 235-2700
Black Hawk College				
East Campus	1,245	-	450	(309) 852-5671
Moline	1,245	-	450	(309) 796-1311
Blackburn College	7,750	3,130	500	(217) 854-3231
Bradley University	9,050	3,960	440	(309) 677-3089
Carl Sandberg College	880	-	425	(309) 344-2518
City Colleges of Chicago	820	-	400	(312) 855-8118
College of DuPage	945	-	750	(312) 858-2800
College of Lake County	993	-	330	(708) 223-3610
College of St. Francis	7,980	3,580	400	(815) 740-3403
Columbia College	5,828	-	500	(312) 663-1600
Concordia College	7,328	3,603	400	(708) 209-3113
Danville Area Community College	930	-	700	(217) 443-8760
De Paul University	9,342	4,703	450	(312) 362-8350
DeVry Institute of Technology/Chicago	5,015	-	500	(312) 929-8500
DeVry Institute of Technology/Lombard	5,015	-	500	(708) 953-1300
Eastern Illinois University	2,114	2,476	150	(217) 581-5034
Elgin Community College	990	-	550	(708) 697-1000
Elmhurst College	8,460	3,442	500	(708) 617-3079
Eureka College	8675	2,985	400	(309) 467-6301
Governors State University	1,646	-	450	(312) 534-5000

	Tuition and Fees	Room and Board	Books and Supplies	Financial Aid Office
Greenville College	8,750	3,880	400	(618) 664-1840
Highland Community College	660	-	450	(815) 235-6121
Illinois Benedictine College	8,900	3,690	550	(708) 960-1500
Illinois Central College	960	2,600	450	(309) 694-5311
Illinois College	6,600	3,250	500	(217) 245-3035
Illinois Eastern Community Colleges	605	-	400	(618) 395-4351
Illinois Institute of Technology	12,690	4,350	800	(312) 567-3303
Illinois State University	2,272	2,560	450	(309) 438-2231
Illinois Wesleyan University	11,115	3,700	400	(309) 556-3096
John A. Logan College	642	-	350	(618) 985-3741
John Wood Community College	990	-	400	(217) 224-6500
Joliet Junior College	910	-	400	(815) 729-9020
Judson College	8,090	4,090	450	(312) 695-2500
Kankakee Community College	825	-	450	(815) 933-0237
Kaskaskia College	848	-	400	(618) 532-1981
Kendall College	7,005	4,475	400	(312) 866-1349
Kishwaukee College	925	-	400	(815) 825-2086
Knox College	12,675	3,675	350	(309) 343-0112
Lake Forest College	13,895	3,155	475	(708) 234-3100
Lake Land College	1,096	-	250	(217) 235-3131
Lewis and Clark Community College	798	-	400	(618) 466-3411
Lewis College	8,505	3,990	450	(815) 838-0500
Lincoln Christian College	3,600	2,470	400	(217) 732-3168
Lincoln College	7,260	3,400	350	(217) 732-3155
Lincoln Land Community College	913	-	400	(217) 786-2237
Loyola University of Chicago	9,270	4,900	550	(312) 508-3164
MacCormac Junior College	5,925	-	500	(312) 922-1884
MacMurry College	7,650	3,170	400	(217) 245-6151
McHenry County College	906	-	450	(815) 455-3700
Midstate College	4,035	4,170	500	(309) 673-6365
Millikin University	10,061	3,784	450	(217) 424-6343
Monmouth College	12,450	3,350	400	(309) 457-2129
Morrison Institute of Technology	4,700	-	500	(815) 772-7218
Morton College	1,080	-	400	(312) 656-8000
Mundelein College	8,235	3,839	400	(312) 989-5439
North Central College	9,960	3,735	450	(708) 420-3420
Northeastern Illinois University	1,967	-	450	(312) 583-4050
Northern Illinois University	2,547	2,700	450	(815) 753-1300
North Park College	10,665	4,035	475	(312) 583-2700
Northwestern University	14,370	4,827	650	(708) 491-8555
Oakton Community College	628	-	400	(312) 635-1708
Olivet Nazarene University	6,472	3,510	450	(815) 939-5249
Parkland College	975	-	400	(217) 351-2443
Parks College of St. Louis University	7,100	3,400	450	(618) 337-7500
Prairie State College	1,230	-	550	(708) 709-3501
Principia College	11,100	4,590	450	(618) 374-2131
Quincy College	8,605	3,440	400	(217) 222-8020

	Tuition and Fees	Room and Board	Books and Supplies	Financial Aid Office
Rend Lake College	690	-	350	(618) 437-5321
Richland Community College	899	-	350	(217) 875-7200
Robert Morris College Carthage	7,350	3,120	400	(312) 836-4888
Rockford College	9,400	3,400	450	(815) 226-4052
Rock Valley College	1,020	-	400	(815) 654-4352
Roosevelt University	7,470	4,800	600	(312) 341-3565
Rosary College	9,225	4,035	450	(312) 366-2490
Rush University	8,125	-	615	(312) 942-6256
St. Xavier College	8,150	3,500	520	(312) 779-3330
Sangamon State University	1,825	-	500	(217) 786-6724
Shawnee College	710	-	300	(618) 634-2242
Shimer College	9,000	-	650	(312) 623-8400
Southeastern Illinois College	630	-	500	(618) 252-6376
Southern Illinois University at Carbondale	2,332	2,780	450	(618) 453-4334
Southern Illinois University at Edwardsville	1,821	3,250	400	(618) 692-3885
Spoon River College	1,050	-	500	(309) 647-4645
Springfield College in Illinois	4,925	-	500	(217) 525-1420
State Community College	924	-	350	(618) 583-2500
Trinity Christian College	7,785	3,360	450	(708) 597-3000
Trinity College	8,610	3,850	600	(312) 948-8980
Triton College	1,010	-	450	(312) 456-0300
University of Chicago	16,212	5,685	625	(312) 702-8666
University of Illinois at Chicago	2,790	4,272	600	(312) 996-5563
University of Illinois at Urbana-Champaign	2,846	3,650	450	(217) 333-0100
Western Illinios University	2,515	2,735	500	(309) 298-2446
Wheaton College	9,548	3,800	450	(312) 260-5021

Indiana

	Tuition and Fees	Room and Board	Books and Supplies	Financial Aid Office
Anderson University	8,060	2,870	500	(317) 641-4180
Ball State University	2,110	2,790	500	(317) 285-8924
Bethel College	7,500	2,800	450	(219) 259-8511
Butler University	10,500	3,850	400	(317) 283-9278
Calumet College	3,585	-	400	(219) 473-4216
DePauw University	12,288	4,450	450	(317) 658-4030
Earlham College	13,479	3,726	550	(317) 983-1267
Goshen College	7,720	3,275	500	(219) 535-7525
Grace College	7,302	3,318	400	(219) 372-5243
Hanover College	6,700	2,880	450	(812) 866-7030
Holy Cross Junior College	3,650	-	450	(219) 233-6813
Huntington College	7,890	3,100	450	(219) 356-6000
Indiana Institute of Technology	6,750	3,050	400	(219) 422-5561
Indiana State University	2,105	2,960	400	(812) 237-2223
Indiana University Bloomington	2,310	3,160	450	(812) 855-5439
East	1,826	-	500	(317) 973-8206
Kokomo	1,812	-	500	(317) 455-9216
Northeast	1,826	-	500	(812) 237-2223
South Bend	1,826	-	500	(219) 237-6241
Southeast	1,826	-	500	(812) 941-2246

	Tuition and Fees	Room and Board	Books and Supplies	Financial Aid Office
Indiana University—Purdue University at Fort Wayne	1,835	-	400	(219) 481-6820
Indiana University—Purdue University at Indianapolis	2,105	-	500	(317) 274-4162
Indiana Vocational Technical College	1,505	-	450	(317) 921-4730
Lockyear College	3,375	3,395	600	(812) 425-8157
Manchester College	8,270	3,250	400	(219) 982-5066
Marian College	7,585	3,150	450	(317) 929-0234
Martin Center College	4,830	-	400	(317) 543-3237
Oakland City College	6,425	3,150	450	(812) 749-1224
Purdue University				
Calumet	1,950	-	450	(219) 989-2660
North Central Campus	1,910	-	400	(219) 785-5279
West Lafayette	2,150	3,320	450	(317) 494-5090
Rose-Hulman Institute of Technology	10,935	3,625	500	(812) 877-8259
St. Francis College	6,600	3,300	500	(219) 434-3283
St. Joseph's College	9,410	3,570	. 450	(219) 866-6163
Saint Mary-of-the-Woods College	9,110	3,610	700	(812) 535-5108
St. Mary's College	10,010	4,200	500	(219) 284-4557
St. Meinrad College	5,450	4,065	600	(812) 357-6572
Taylor University	9,350	3,540	400	(317) 998-5358
Tri-State University	8,298	3,600	450	(219) 665-4174
University of Evansville	9,150	3,600	400	(812) 479-2364
University of Indianapolis	9,020	3,470	450	(317) 788-3349
University of Notre Dame	13,505	3,590	550	(219) 239-6436
University of Southern Indiana	1,688	-	450	(812) 464-1767
Valparaiso University	9,990	2,740	500	(219) 464-5011
Vincennes University	1,640	2,940	450	(812) 885-3350
Wabash College	10,700	3,650	500	(317) 364-4415

Iowa

	Tuition and Fees	Room and Board	Books and Supplies	Financial Aid Office
American Institute of Business	4,525	2,700	600	(515) 244-4221
Briar Cliff College	8,760	3,150	450	(712) 279-5440
Buena Vista College	10,900	3,120	450	(712) 749-2164
Central College	9,295	3,410	550	(515) 628-5268
Clarke College	8,190	2,850	350	(319) 588-6327
Coe College	10,380	3,840	450	(319) 399-8540
Cornell College	12,350	3,970	550	(319) 895-4216
Des Moines Area Community College	1,262	-	650	(515) 964-6514
Divine Word College	5,235	1,200	400	(319) 876-3353
Dordt College	7,900	2,250	650	(712) 722-6080
Drake University	11,040	4,210	500	(515) 271-2905
Emmaus Bible College	2,100	3,590	400	(319) 588-8000
Graceland College	7,850	2,650	550	(515) 784-5136
Grand View College	7,750	2,900	400	(515) 263-2819
Grinnell College	13,742	3,868	400	(515) 269-3250
Hawkeye Institute of Technology	1,383	-	700	(319) 296-2320
Indian Hills Community College	1,208	1,609	425	(515) 683-5151
Iowa Lakes Community College	1,280	2,369	425	(712) 852-3554

	Tuition and Fees	Room and Board	Books and Supplies	Financial Aid Office
Iowa State University	1,880	2,720	600	(515) 294-2223
Iowa Wesleyan College	8,200	3,000	500	(319) 385-8021
Iowa Western Community College	1,470	-	450	(712) 325-3287
Kirkwood Community College	1,344	2,178	400	(319) 398-5490
Loras College	9,115	3,200	400	(319) 588-7166
Luther College	10,600	3,300	600	(319) 387-1018
Marshalltown Community College	1,510	-	400	(515) 752-7106
Morningside College	9,205	2,980	350	(712) 274-5159
Mount St. Clare College	7,335	3,225	450	(319) 242-4023
North Iowa Area Community College	1,375	2,160	500	(515) 421-4246
Northwest Iowa Technical College	1,395	-	600	(712) 324-5061
Northwestern College	8,050	2,800	400	(712) 737-4821
St. Ambrose University	8,530	3,430	500	(319) 383-8885
Southeastern Community College	1,136	-	350	(319) 752-2731
Southwestern Community College	1,140	2,230	450	(515) 782-7081
University of Dubuque	9,205	3,100	450	(319) 589-3396
University of Iowa	1,952	2,775	550	(319) 335-1449
University of Northern Iowa	1,880	2,325	450	(319) 273-2701
Upper Iowa University	8,450	2,860	500	(319) 425-5280
Vennard College	4,395	2,300	425	(515) 582-8120
Waldorf College	7,090	2,850	450	(515) 352-8262
Wartburg College	9,640	3,080	350	(319) 352-8262
Western Iowa Technical Community College	1,182	-	425	(712) 274-6240
William Penn College	9,190	2,720	400	(515) 673-1060

Kansas

Allen County Community College	800	2,300	300	(316) 365-5516
Baker University	6,410	3,200	400	(913) 594-6451
Barton County Community College	690	2,000	400	(316) 792-2701
Benedictine College	7,270	3,060	350	(913) 367-5340
Bethany College	7,030	3,130	450	(913) 227-3311
Bethel College	7,460	2,800	450	(316) 283-2500
Brown Mackie College	5,885	1,500	550	(913) 827-1261
Bulter County Community College	885	2,142	400	(316) 321-5083
Central College	6,050	2,900	350	(316) 241-0723
Cloud County Community College	810	2,500	300	(913) 243-1435
Coffeyville Community College	680	2,100	325	(316) 251-7700
Colby Community College	832	2,300	300	(913) 462-3984
Cowley County Community College	750	2,290	500	(316) 442-0430
Dodge City Community College	930	2,600	350	(316) 225-1321
Donnelly College	2,300	-	300	(913) 621-6070
Emporia State University	1,382	2,480	400	(316) 343-5457

	Tuition and Fees	Room and Board	Books and Supplies	Financial Aid Office
Fort Hays State University	1,456	2,500	415	(913) 628-4408
Fort Scott Community College	660	2,200	400	(316) 223-2700
Friends University	7,155	2,630	550	(316) 261-5850
Garden City Community College	750	2,300	400	(316) 276-9598
Hesston College	6,000	3,150	500	(316) 327-4221
Highland Community College	810	2,600	300	(913) 442-3236
Hutchinson Community College	720	1,995	450	(913) 665-3569
Johnson County Community College	840	-	400	(913) 469-8000
Kansas City Kansas Community College	690	-	350	(913) 334-1000
Kansas Newman College	6,805	3,150	550	(316) 942-4291
Kansas State University	1,575	3,750	600	(913) 532-7077
Kansas Wesleyan	6,700	3,000	500	(913) 827-5541
Labette Community College	630	2,100	350	(316) 421-6700
Manhattan Christian College	3,300	2,444	650	(913) 539-3571
McPherson College	7,220	3,280	550	(316) 241-0731
Mid-American Nazarene College	5,552	3,158	600	(913) 782-3750
Neosho County Community College	550	2,085	300	(316) 431-6222
Ottawa University	5,990	2,898	400	(913) 242-5200
Pittsburg State University	1,358	2,562	450	(316) 235-7515
Pratt Community College	800	2,490	500	(316) 672-5641
St. Mary College	6,450	3,250	500	(913) 682-5151
St. Mary of the Plains College	6,420	3,000	400	(316) 225-4171
Southwestern College	5,050	2,810	400	(316) 221-4150
Sterling College	6,800	3,000	450	(316) 278-2173
Tabor College	6,800	3,000	550	(316) 947-3121
University of Kansas	1,564	2,496	500	(913) 864-4700
Washburn University of Topeka	2,492	2,895	450	(913) 295-6451
Wichita State University	1,608	2,727	500	(316) 689-3430

Kentucky

Alice Lloyd College	270	2,364	400	(606) 368-2101
Asbury College	7,372	2,491	500	(606) 858-3511
Bellarmine College	7,260	2,450	600	(502) 452-8131
Berea College	177	2,331	400	(606) 986-9341
Brescia College	5,500	3,220	450	(502) 686-4290
Campbellsville College	4,900	2,780	500	(502) 465-8158
Centre College	10,100	3,930	500	(606) 236-5211
Cumberland College	5,296	3,076	450	(606) 549-2200
Eastern Kentucky University	1,420	2,685	450	(606) 622-2220
Georgetown College	6,250	3,286	500	(502) 863-8027
Kentucky Christian College	3,250	2,950	600	(606) 474-6613
Kentucky College of Business	4,160	-	450	(703) 986-1800

	Tuition and Fees	Room and Board	Books and Supplies	Financial Aid Office
Kentucky State University	1,432	2,468	550	(502) 227-5960
Kentucky Wesleyan College	6,100	3,400	400	(502) 926-3111
Lees College	3,600	2,500	400	(606) 666-7521
Lindsey Wilson College	5,168	3,280	450	(502) 384-2126
Midway College	5,800	3,550	450	(606) 846-5410
Morehead State University	1,320	2,430	400	(606) 783-2011
Murry State University	1,410	2,395	500	(502) 762-2596
Northern Kentucky University	1,410	-	400	(606) 572-5144
Owensboro Junior College	3,525	-	450	(502) 926-4040
Paducah Community College	680	-	350	(502) 442-6131
Pikesville College	4,250	2,450	425	(606) 432-9382
Spalding University	6,695	2,760	300	(502) 585-9911
Thomas More College	7,430	3,440	400	(606) 344-3331
Transylvania University	9,619	4,048	400	(606) 233-8239
Union College	5,630	2,550	450	(606) 546-4151
University of Kentucky	1,830	3,055	425	(606) 257-3173
University of Louisville	1,620	2,994	500	(502) 588-5511
Western Kentucky University	1,440	2,900	400	(502) 745-2756

Louisiana

	Tuition and Fees	Room and Board	Books and Supplies	Financial Aid Office
Bossier Parish Community College	510	-	575	(318) 742-1081
Centenary College of Louisiana	7,210	3,060	550	(318) 869-5137
Delgado Community College	980	-	500	(504) 483-4013
Dillard University	5,500	3,250	500	(504) 286-4679
Grambling State University	1,778	2,636	500	(318) 274-2342
Louisiana College	4,160	2,650	520	(318) 487-7386
Louisiana State University				
Alexandria	924	-	500	(318) 473-6477
Eunice	888	-	500	(318) 457-7311
Shreveport	1,480	-	400	(318) 797-5363
Louisiana Tech University	1,841	2,160	500	(318) 257-2641
Loyola University	8,698	5,334	500	(504) 865-3231
NcNeese State University	1,626	2,100	500	(318) 475-5068
Nicholls State University	1,591	2,350	400	(504) 448-4077
Northeast Louisiana University	1,613	1,950	500	(318) 342-5321
Northwestern State University	1,749	2,024	550	(318) 357-5961
Our Lady of Holy Cross College	4,600	-	450	(504) 394-7744
Phillips Junior College	4,600	-	285	(504) 734-0123
Southeastern Louisiana University	1,700	2,280	500	(504) 549-2244
Southern University at				
New Orleans	1,450	-	400	(504) 286-5017
Shreveport	830	-	400	(318) 674-3331
Tulane University	16,980	5,505	400	(504) 865-5723
University of New Orleans	1,565	2,418	500	(504) 286-6603
University of Southwestern Louisiana	1,231	2,050	315	(318) 231-6497
Xavier University of Louisiana	5,905	3,200	500	(504) 483-7522

	Tuition and Fees	Room and Board	Books and Supplies	Financial Aid Office

Maine

Andover College	4,100	-	650	(207) 774-6126
Bates College	21,000	Incl.	600	(207) 786-6060
Beal College	3,610	2,300	650	(207) 947-4591
Bowdoin College	16,380	5,590	550	(207) 725-3273
Central Maine Vo-Tech Institute	1,475	2,400	500	(207) 784-2385
Colby College	16,460	5,350	600	(207) 872-3379
Eastern Maine Vo-Tech Institute	1,330	2,400	600	(207) 942-4625
Husson College	7,135	3,630	400	(207) 947-1121
Maine Maritime Academy	3,900	4,000	400	(207) 326-4311
Northern Maine Vo-Tech Institute	1,550	3,150	500	(207) 769-2461
Portland School of Art	9,145	4,212	1,550	(207) 775-3052
St. Joseph's College	8,500	4,300	550	(207) 892-6766
Southern Maine Vocational Technical Institute	1,380	2,500	680	(207) 799-7303
Thomas College	8,050	4,150	750	(207) 873-0771
Unity College	7,150	4,400	450	(207) 948-3131
University of Maine				
Augusta	1,965	-	500	(207) 622-7131
Farmington	2,070	3,388	450	(207) 778-3501
Fort Kent	2,025	3,395	450	(207) 834-3162
Machias	2,005	3,090	440	(207) 255-3313
Orono	2,470	3,945	450	(207) 581-1324
Presque Isle	2,000	3,284	400	(207) 764-0311
University of New England	9,770	4,525	500	(207) 283-0171
University of Southern Maine	2,214	3,844	500	(207) 780-5250
Westbrook College	9,800	4,650	600	(207) 797-7261

Maryland

Allegheny Community College	1,349	-	450	(301) 724-7700
Anne Arundel Community College	1,320	-	400	(301) 541-2538
Bowie State College	2,254	3,427	450	(301) 464-6546
Capitol College	6,965	-	550	(301) 953-0060
Catonsville Community College	1,022	-	500	(301) 455-4170
Cecile Community College	1,110	-	600	(301) 287-1000
Charles County Community College	1,422	-	350	(301) 934-2251
Chesapeake College	950	-	500	(301) 822-5400
College of Notre Dame of Maryland	9,500	4,800	450	(301) 532-5369
Columbia Union College	7,930	3,690	500	(301) 891-4005
Community College of Baltimore	1,040	-	400	(301) 396-0395
Coppin State College	2,241	-	600	(301) 333-5930
Dundalk Community College	1,082	-	500	(301) 285-9830
Essex Community College	1,082	-	500	(301) 522-1346
Frederick Community College	1,553	-	450	(301) 694-1247
Frostberg State University	2,068	3,910	500	(301) 689-4301
Garrett Community College	1,020	-	425	(301) 387-6666
Goucher College	12,885	5,700	400	(301) 337-6141
Hagerstown Junior College	1,764	-	550	(301) 790-2800
Harford Community College	1,230	-	600	(301) 836-4257
Hood College	12,208	5,675	400	(301) 663-3131

	Tuition and Fees	Room and Board	Books and Supplies	Financial Aid Office
Howard Community College	1,355	-	450	(301) 992-4859
Johns Hopkins University	16,000	6,120	450	(301) 338-8724
Loyola College	9,810	5,379	500	(301) 323-1010
Montgomery College	1,510	-	475	(301) 251-7320
Morgan State University	2,124	4,380	700	(301) 444-3178
Prince George's Community College	1,740	-	450	(301) 322-0824
St. John's College	14,262	4,696	300	(301) 263-2371
St. Mary's College of Maryland	2,760	4,100	500	(301) 863-0300
Salisbury State College	2,444	3,890	450	(301) 543-6165
Towson State University	2,409	4,510	530	(301) 830-2061
University of Baltimore	2,120	-	400	(301) 625-3363
University of Maryland				
Baltimore	2,152	-	550	(301) 328-7347
Baltimore County	2,390	3,784	450	(301) 455-2387
College Park	2,267	4,712	395	(301) 314-8279
Eastern Shore	2,114	3,534	500	(301) 651-2200
University College	3,540	-	810	(301) 985-7231
Villa Julie College	5,440	-	400	(301) 486-7001
Washington College	11,400	4,700	500	(301) 778-2800
Western Maryland College	12,500	4,740	400	(301) 848-7000

Massachusetts

	Tuition and Fees	Room and Board	Books and Supplies	Financial Aid Office
Amherst College	16,945	4,600	650	(413) 542-2296
Assumption College	9,210	4,700	400	(617) 752-5615
Atlantic Union College	9,996	3,250	450	(508) 368-2280
Babson College	13,853	5,476	500	(617) 239-4001
Bay Path Junior College	8,500	5,600	400	(413) 567-0621
Bay State College	6,825	5,700	500	(617) 236-8011
Becker Junior College	6,925	3,925	300	(617) 791-9241
Bentley College	11,390	4,768	450	(617) 891-3441
Berklee College of Music	9,040	6,190	550	(617) 266-1400
Boston College	14,084	6,150	450	(617) 552-3320
Boston University	16,190	6,320	410	(617) 353-4176
Bradford College	11,885	5,875	425	(617) 372-7161
Brandeis University	15,320	5,960	410	(617) 736-3700
Bridgewater State University	2,108	3,720	455	(508) 697-1341
Bristol Community College	1,604	-	400	(617) 678-2811
Bunker Hill Community College	1,226	-	400	(617) 241-8600
Cape Cod Community College	1,462	-	450	(508) 362-2131
Central New England College of Technology	7,100	-	400	(617) 755-4314
Clark University	14,380	4,500	450	(617) 793-7478
College of Holy Cross	15,530	5,700	400	(508) 793-2265
Curry College	11,470	5,250	600	(617) 333-0555
Dean Junior College	8,860	5,800	400	(617) 528-9100
Eastern Nazarene College	7,660	3,200	350	(617) 773-6350
Emerson College	13,072	7,121	500	(617) 578-8655
Emmanuel College	9,685	5,065	500	(617) 735-9725
Endicott College	9,640	5,310	400	(617) 927-0585
Fisher Junior College	8,590	5,800	400	(617) 236-8821
Fitchburg State College	2,058	3,104	450	(617) 345-2151
Framingham State College	2,879	3,300	450	(508) 626-4536
Franklin Institute of Boston	7,790	6,320	600	(617) 423-4630
Gordon College	11,400	3,630	400	(617) 927-2300
Greenfield Community College	1,765	-	500	(413) 774-3131

	Tuition and Fees	Room and Board	Books and Supplies	Financial Aid Office
Hampshire College	17,785	4,560	300	(413) 549-4600
Harvard University	15,530	5,125	400	(617) 495-9036
Hellenic College	5,845	3,620	450	(617) 731-3500
Holyoke Community College	1,390	-	400	(413) 538-7000
Labourne College	8,750	-	800	(617) 296-8300
Lasell Junior College	9,850	4,450	600	(617) 243-2227
Lesley College	10,710	4,770	450	(617) 868-9600
Marian Court Junior College	6,180	-	400	(617) 595-6768
Massachusetts Bay Community College	1,370	-	450	(617) 237-1100
Massachusetts College of Art	1,845	-	1,500	(617) 232-1555
Massachusetts College of Pharmacy	9,316	5,995	400	(617) 732-2864
Massachusetts Institute of Technology	16,900	5,330	600	(617) 253-4971
Massachusetts Maritime Academy	1,592	3,598	500	(617) 759-5761
Merrimack College	10,350	5,700	550	(508) 837-5103
Middlesex Community College	1,211	-	400	(617) 275-8910
Montserrat College of Art	7,700	-	800	(617) 922-8222
Mount Holyoke College	16,050	4,900	600	(413) 538-2291
Mount Ida College	9,140	6,245	650	(617) 969-7000
Mount Wachusett Community College	1,382	-	400	(508) 632-6600
New England Conservatory of Music	13,350	6,150	425	(617) 262-1120
Newbury College	8,200	5,260	350	(617) 730-7100
Nichols College	7,867	4,480	400	(508) 943-2055
North Adams State College	2,500	3,460	350	(413) 664-4511
North Shore Community College	1,404	-	600	(508) 922-6722
Northeastern University	9,968	6,375	500	(617) 437-3190
Northern Essex Community College	1,370	-	500	(617) 374-3650
Pine Manor College	14,000	5,700	400	(617) 731-7129
Quincy Junior College	1,890	-	400	(617) 984-1620
Quinsigamond Community College	1,212	-	500	(508) 853-2300
Regis College	10,550	5,200	400	(617) 893-1820
Roxbury Community College	1,423	-	500	(617) 541-5322
St. John's Seminary College	3,600	3,000	400	(617) 254-2610
Salem State College	1,980	3,425	420	(617) 741-6112
School of the Museum of Fine Arts	10,351	-	925	(617) 267-6100
Simmons College	14,074	6,000	400	(617) 738-2138
Smith College	15,770	6,100	400	(413) 585-2530
Springfield College	9,441	4,376	400	(413) 788-3108
Springfield Technical Community College	1,406	-	400	(413) 781-7822
Stonehill College	10,285	5,366	475	(508) 230-1347
Suffolk University	8,531	5,500	450	(617) 573-8470
Tufts University	15,917	5,170	625	(617) 381-3528
University of Lowell	2,711	3,900	400	(508) 934-4220
University of Massachusetts				
Amherst	3,476	3,694	500	(413) 545-3205
Boston	2,702	-	520	(617) 929-7210
Wellesley College	16,271	5,657	475	(617) 235-0320
Wentworth Institute of Technology	8,220	5,950	600	(617) 442-9010
Western New England College	7,967	4,900	450	(413) 782-3111
Westfield State College	1,940	3,600	400	(413) 568-3311
Wheaton College	15,760	5,480	550	(617) 285-7722

	Tuition and Fees	Room and Board	Books and Supplies	Financial Aid Office
Wheelock College	10,528	4,926	400	(617) 734-5200
Williams College	15,785	4,975	500	(413) 597-4181
Worcester State College	1,812	3,630	500	(508) 793-8110

Michigan

Adrian College	9,390	3,000	400	(517) 265-5161
Albion College	11,134	4,064	500	(517) 629-0440
Alma College	9,852	3,626	500	(517) 463-7347
Alpena Community College	1,220	-	300	(517) 356-9021
Andrews University	8,985	3,675	550	(616) 471-3334
Aquinas College	8,296	3,726	350	(616) 459-8281
Baker College	4,560	-	450	(313) 766-4202
Bay de Noc Community College	1,316	-	450	(906) 786-5802
Calvin College	8,100	3,350	375	(616) 957-6137
Central Michigan University	2,129	3,350	450	(517) 774-7424
Charles Stewart Mott Community College	1,240	-	500	(313) 762-0256
Cleary College	5,025	-	750	(313) 483-4400
Concordia College	7,102	3,456	400	(313) 995-7408
Davenport College of Business	7,236	-	600	(616) 451-3511
Delta College	1,300	3,072	425	(517) 686-9080
Detroit College of Business	5,300	-	500	(313) 581-4400
Eastern Michigan University	2,104	3,581	450	(313) 487-1333
Ferris State University	2,412	3,018	425	(616) 592-2110
Glen Oaks Community College	1,020	-	425	(616) 467-9945
Gogebic Community College	850	-	400	(906) 932-4231
Grace Bible College	3,860	2,750	250	(616) 538-2330
Grand Rapids Baptist College	5,386	3,460	400	(606) 949-5300
Grand Rapids Junior College	1,220	-	420	(616) 771-4031
Grand Valley State University	2,132	3,300	400	(616) 895-6611
Great Lakes Bible College	3,695	2,580	500	(517) 321-0242
Great Lakes Junior College of Business	4,080	-	450	(517) 755-3457
Henry Ford Community College	1,230	-	300	(313) 271-2910
Highland Park Community College	1,270	-	300	(313) 252-0475
Hillsdale College	9,610	4,000	500	(517) 437-7341
Hope College	9,426	3,610	450	(616) 394-7922
Jackson Community College	1,170	-	332	(517) 787-0800
Jordan College	5,280	-	600	(616) 696-1180
Kalamazoo College	12,669	4,053	450	(616) 383-8476
Kalamazoo Valley Community College	750	-	450	(616) 372-5340
Kellogg Community College	930	-	420	(616) 965-3931
Kendall College of Art & Design	8,250	-	900	(616) 451-2787
Kirtland Community College	1,320	-	375	(517) 275-5121
Lake Michigan College	1,080	-	425	(616) 927-3571
Lake Superior State University	2,040	3,454	425	(906) 635-2678
Lansing Community College	1,065	-	600	(517) 483-1304
Macomb Community College	1,208	-	400	(313) 445-7536
Madonna College	4,050	3,200	400	(313) 591-5036
Marygrove College	6,050	3,200	475	(313) 862-8000
Michigan Christian College	4,200	3,030	300	(313) 651-5800
Michigan State University	3,276	3,168	450	(517) 353-5940
Michigan Technological University	2,541	3,186	500	(906) 487-2622
Monroe County Community College	830	-	500	(313) 242-7300

	Tuition and Fees	Room and Board	Books and Supplies	Financial Aid Office
Montcalm Community College	984	-	400	(517) 328-2111
Muskegon Community College	1,000	-	350	(616) 777-0316
Nazareth College in Kalamazoo	7,724	3,174	300	(616) 349-5757
North Central Michigan College	1,110	3,300	400	(616) 347-3973
Northern Michigan University	2,120	3,326	400	(906) 227-2327
Northwestern Michigan College	1,461	3,020	450	(616) 946-5650
Northwood Institute	8,220	3,720	525	(517) 832-4230
Oakland Community College	1,160	-	400	(313) 471-7552
Oakland University	2,166	3,257	350	(313) 370-3370
Olivet College	7,890	2,860	500	(616) 749-7645
Reformed Bible College	5,236	2,960	375	(616) 363-2050
Saginaw Valley State University	2,131	3,212	475	(517) 790-4106
St. Clair County Community College	1,240	-	400	(313) 984-3881
Schoolcraft College	1,165	-	300	(313) 462-4433
Sienna Heights College	6,600	3,380	400	(517) 263-0731
Spring Arbor College	7,556	3,100	375	(517) 750-1200
Suomi College	8,300	3,200	400	(906) 482-5300
University of Detroit	8,890	3,466	400	(313) 927-1354
University of Michigan				
Ann Arbor	3,500	3,975	425	(313) 763-4119
Dearborn	2,526	-	400	(313) 593-5300
Flint	2,240	-	450	(313) 762-3444
Washtenaw Community College	1,035	-	450	(313) 973-3523
Wayne County Community College	1,014	-	400	(313) 496-2596
Wayne State University	2,405	-	500	(313) 577-6157
West Shore Community College	1,044	-	500	(616) 845-6211
Western Michigan University	2,275	3,375	400	(616) 387-6007
William Tyndale College	4,580	3,210	425	(313) 553-7200

Minnesota

	Tuition and Fees	Room and Board	Books and Supplies	Financial Aid Office
Alexandria Technical Institute	1,838	-	400	(612) 762-0221
Anoka-Ramsey Community College	1,474	-	450	(612) 427-1880
Augsburg College	10,245	3,832	400	(612) 330-1046
Bemidji State University	1,884	2,384	500	(218) 755-2034
Bethany Lutheran College	6,400	2,800	350	(507) 625-2977
Bethel College	9,950	3,590	450	(612) 638-6241
Carleton College	16,296	3,324	475	(507) 663-4254
College of St. Benedict	10,135	3,850	500	(612) 363-5388
College of St. Catherine	9,416	3,140	450	(612) 690-6540
College of St. Scholastica	9,192	3,018	425	(218) 723-6046
Concordia College				
Moorehead	8,690	2,985	400	(218) 299-3010
St. Paul	8,268	2,910	425	(612) 641-8204
Dakota County Area Vocational Technical Institute	1,727	-	550	(612) 423-8323
Gustavus Adolphus College	11,000	2,750	350	(507) 931-7527
Hamline University	11,500	3,631	375	(612) 641-2280
Inver Hills Community College	1,474	-	450	(612) 455-9621
Lakewood Community College	1,474	-	500	(612) 779-3307
Macalester College	12,471	3,714	375	(612) 696-6214
Mankato State University	1,868	2,388	425	(507) 389-1185
Metropolitian State University	1,654	-	450	(612) 296-6841
Minneapolis College of Art & Design	9,640	2,800	1,000	(612) 874-3783
Minneapolis Community College	1,476	-	450	(612) 341-7003

	Tuition and Fees	Room and Board	Books and Supplies	Financial Aid Office
Moorehead State University	1,975	2,350	450	(218) 236-2251
Normandale Community College	1,474	-	450	(612) 832-6313
North Central Bible College	4,690	2,912	450	(612) 343-4482
North Hennepin Community College	1,474	-	500	(612) 424-0728
Rochester Community College	1,474	-	450	(507) 285-7267
St. Cloud State University	1,868	2,379	500	(612) 255-2047
St. John's University	10,085	3,675	500	(612) 363-3664
St. Mary's College	9,225	3,150	450	(507) 457-1437
St. Olaf College	12,080	3,345	525	(507) 663-3019
St. Paul Bible College	6,390	3,160	450	(612) 446-4177
Southwest State University	1,680	2,030	500	(507) 537-6281
University of Minnesota				
Crookston	2,435	3,089	425	(218) 281-6510
Duluth	2,501	3,000	425	(218) 726-7500
Morris	2,412	2,835	500	(612) 589-2211
Twin Cities	2,587	3,132	525	(612) 624-5831
Waseca	2,416	2,430	450	(507) 835-1000
Wilmar Community College	1,572	-	475	(612) 231-5107
Winona State University	1,885	2,450	375	(507) 457-2049
Worthington Community College	1,474	-	400	(507) 372-2107

Mississippi

	Tuition and Fees	Room and Board	Books and Supplies	Financial Aid Office
Alcorn State University	1,750	1,925	400	(601) 877-6190
Belhaven College	6,030	2,100	350	(601) 968-5933
Blue Mountain College	3,248	2,030	500	(601) 685-4771
Clarke College	3,520	2,390	500	(601) 683-2063
Coahoma Junior College	700	2,512	450	(601) 627-2571
Copiah-Lincoln Junior College	850	1,800	400	(601) 643-5101
East Central Junior College	800	1,750	350	(601) 635-2111
Hinds Community College	740	1,554	400	(601) 857-3227
Holmes Junior College	810	1,400	400	(601) 472-2312
Itawamba Community College	800	1,710	350	(601) 862-3101
Jackson State University	1,786	2,488	450	(601) 968-2227
Jones County Junior College	610	1,670	350	(601) 477-4040
Mary Holmes College	4,100	3,800	500	(601) 494-6820
Millsaps College	9,170	3,280	600	(601) 974-1220
Mississippi College	5,010	2,550	600	(601) 925-3212
Mississippi Gulf Coast Community College	760	-	300	(601) 928-5211
Mississippi State University	2,061	2,785	400	(601) 325-2450
Mississippi State University for Women	1,840	2,095	500	(601) 329-7114
Mississippi Valley State University	1,725	1,925	450	(601) 254-9041
Northeast Mississippi Junior College	770	1,690	400	(601) 728-7751
Northwest Mississippi Community College	834	1,690	250	(601) 562-3270
Pearl River Junior College	710	1,750	250	(601) 795-4558
Phillips Junior College of Jackson	3,725	-	300	(601) 864-6096
Phillips Junior College of Gulf Coast	4,450	-	400	(601) 362-6341
Rust College	4,150	1,950	325	(601) 252-4661
Southwest Mississippi Junior College	750	1,700	500	(601) 684-0411
Tougaloo College	4,310	1,550	500	(601) 977-7766

	Tuition and Fees	Room and Board	Books and Supplies	Financial Aid Office
University of Mississippi	2,059	2,865	400	(601) 232-7175
University of Southern Mississippi	1,950	2,150	450	(601) 266-4774
Wood Junior College	2,400	2,500	400	(601) 263-5352

Missouri

Avila College	7,380	3,200	500	(816) 942-8400
Baptist Bible College	1,570	2,190	300	(417) 869-9811
Calvary Bible College	3,200	2,480	350	(816) 322-0110
Central Bible College	3,240	2,750	500	(417) 833-2551
Central Methodist College	6,710	3,270	400	(816) 248-3391
Central Missouri State University	1,680	2,616	250	(816) 429-4040
Columbia College	6,824	3,082	600	(314) 875-7362
Cottey College	4,500	2,600	400	(417) 667-8181
Culver-Stockton College	6,650	2,600	400	(314) 288-5221
Deaconess College of Nursing	5,110	2,400	400	(314) 768-3043
DeVry Institute of Technology: Kansas City	5,015	-	500	(816) 941-0430
Drury College	7,510	3,184	600	(417) 865-8731
East Central College	765	-	400	(314) 583-5193
Evangel College	6,178	2,880	600	(417) 865-2811
Fontbonne College	7,470	3,500	550	(314) 889-1414
Hannibal-LaGrange College	4,650	2,000	350	(314) 221-3675
Harris Stowe State College	1,490	-	600	(314) 533-3366
Jefferson College	720	-	350	(314) 789-3951
Kansas City Art Institute	10,315	4,050	800	(816) 561-4852
Kemper Military Junior College	7,600	2,200	1,800	(816) 882-5623
Lincoln University	1,340	2,728	480	(314) 681-6156
Lindenwood College	8,180	4,400	900	(314) 949-2000
Maple Woods Community College	1,050	-	500	(816) 436-6500
Maryville College: St. Louis	7,750	3,800	400	(314) 981-8100
Missouri Southern State College	1,532	2,340	400	(417) 625-9325
Missouri Valley College	7,479	4,356	990	(816) 886-6924
Missouri Western State College	1,446	2,050	500	(816) 271-4507
Northeast Missouri State University	1,800	2,584	400	(816) 785-4130
Northwest Missouri State University	1,590	2,645	350	(816) 562-1363
Park College	6,820	3,300	475	(816) 741-2000
Platt Junior College	4,750	-	250	(816) 364-5700
Research College of Nursing	7,700	3,500	400	(816) 276-9328
Rockhurst College	8,400	3,600	525	(816) 926-4100
St. Louis College of Pharmacy	5,375	3,500	300	(314) 367-8700
St. Louis Community College	1,020	-	500	(314) 644-9656
St. Louis University	9,160	4,250	500	(314) 658-2347
School of the Ozarks	100	1,600	400	(417) 334-6411
Southeast Missouri State University	1,786	2,825	250	(314) 651-2253
Southwest Baptist University	6,192	2,340	450	(417) 326-1820
Southwest Missouri State University	1,790	2,830	500	(417) 836-5262
State Fair Community College	720		350	(816) 826-7100
Stephens College	11,475	4,500	450	(314) 826-7106
Three Rivers Community College	750	-	250	(314) 686-4101

	Tuition and Fees	Room and Board	Books and Supplies	Financial Aid Office
University of Missouri				
Columbia	1,928	2,831	400	(314) 882-2751
Kansas City	2,277	3,065	500	(816) 235-1241
St. Louis	2,154	-	500	(314) 553-5527
Washington University	16,110	5,187	700	(314) 889-5900
Webster University	7,300	3,650	500	(314) 968-6992
Westminster College	8,400	3,350	500	(314) 642-3361
William Jewell College	7,450	2,560	450	(816) 781-7700
William Woods College	8,140	3,560	470	(314) 642-2251

Montana

	Tuition and Fees	Room and Board	Books and Supplies	Financial Aid Office
Blackfeet Community College	1,350	-	300	(406) 338-5421
Carroll College	6,570	3,230	400	(406) 442-3450
College of Great Falls	4,015	-	300	(406) 761-8210
Dawson Community College	774	-	450	(406) 365-3396
Eastern Montana College	1,389	3,300	525	(406) 657-2188
Flathead Valley Community College	936	-	500	(406) 756-3843
Miles Community College	864	-	500	(406) 232-3031
Montana College of Mineral Science and Technology	1,306	3,094	400	(406) 496-4213
Montana State University	1,390	3,276	450	(406) 994-2845
Northern Montana College	1,272	2,919	450	(406) 265-3787
Rocky Mountain College	7,212	3,250	500	(406) 657-1031
Univesity of Montana	1,474	3,212	350	(406) 243-5373
Western Montana College	1,274	2,770	400	(406) 683-7511

Nebraska

	Tuition and Fees	Room and Board	Books and Supplies	Financial Aid Office
Bellevue College	2,805	-	400	(402) 293-3763
Bishop Clarkson College of Nursing	3,080	-	400	(402) 559-2015
Central Community College	960	1,800	400	(308) 384-5220
Chadron State College	1,376	2,195	500	(308) 432-6230
College of St. Mary	7,250	2,960	400	(402) 399-2416
Concordia Teachers College	7,110	2,790	450	(402) 643-7274
Creighton University	8,995	3,795	550	(402) 280-2731
Dana College	7,370	2,770	450	(402) 426-7220
Doane College	7,830	2,465	300	(402) 826-8260
Hastings College	8,090	2,910	500	(402) 463-2402
Lincoln School of Commerce	5,250	-	425	(402) 474-5315
McCook Community College	764	1,700	350	(308) 345-6303
Metropolitan Technical Community College	875	-	450	(402) 449-8330
Midland Lutheran College	7,900	2,850	425	(402) 721-5480
Mid Plains Community College	760	-	400	(308) 532-8980
Nebraska Indian Community College	1,680	-	400	(402) 878-2414
Nebraska Wesleyan University	8,228	2,950	450	(402) 465-2166
Northeast Community College	846	-	300	(402) 644-0425
Peru State College	1,380	2,430	350	(402) 872-3815
Southeast Community College: Milford	1,004	1,710	475	(402) 761-2131
University of Nebraska				
Lincoln	1,915	2,625	400	(402) 472-2030
Omaha	1,530	-	600	(402) 554-3408

	Tuition and Fees	Room and Board	Books and Supplies	Financial Aid Office
Wayne State College	1,421	2,290	600	(402) 375-7230
Western Nebraska Community College	1,035	2,150	400	(308) 635-3606
York College	3,480	2,750	350	(402) 362-4441

Nevada

Clark County Community College	810	-	600	(702) 643-6060
Truckee Meadows Community College	780	-	400	(702) 673-7072
University of Nevada				
Las Vegas	1,470	4,438	500	(702) 739-3697
Reno	1,470	3,720	500	(702) 784-4666
Western Nevada Community College	720	-	550	(702) 887-3063

New Hampshire

Colby-Sawyer College	12,185	4,715	400	(603) 526-2010
Daniel Webster College	9,830	4,140	500	(603) 883-3556
Dartmouth College	16,335	5,160	1,100	(603) 646-2451
Franklin Pierce College	11,190	4,160	450	(603) 899-5111
Hesser College	5,600	3,500	500	(603) 668-6660
Keene State College	2,539	3,430	500	(603) 358-2280
New England College	10,570	4,420	400	(603) 428-2284
New Hampshire College	9,408	4,500	400	(603) 645-9645
New Hampshire Technical Institute	2,000	2,950	400	(603) 225-1871
New Hampshire Vocational/Technical College				
Berlin	1,900	-	500	(603) 752-1113
Claremont	1,930	-	450	(603) 542-7744
Laconia	1,925	-	500	(603) 524-3207
Manchester	1,920	-	500	(603) 668-6706
Notre Dame College	7,630	4,290	600	(603) 669-4298
Plymouth State College	2,574	3,860	500	(603) 535-2338
River College	8,750	4,310	400	(603) 888-1311
St. Anselm College	10,460	5,000	350	(603) 641-7110
University of New Hampshire				
Durham	3,558	3,456	500	(603) 862-3600
Manchester	2,570	-	400	(603) 668-0700

New Jersey

Atlantic Community College	1,224	-	500	(609) 343-5082
Bloomfield College	7,475	3,700	500	(201) 748-9000
Brookdale Community College	1,352	-	500	(201) 842-1900
Burlington County College	1,125	-	420	(609) 894-9311
Caldwell College	7,600	400	425	(201) 228-4424
Camden County College	1,280	-	500	(609) 227-7700
Centenary College	10,540	4,890	500	(201) 852-1400
College of St. Elizabeth	9,550	4,000	350	(201) 292-6344
Cumberland County College	1,205	-	450	(609) 691-8600
Drew University	14,926	4,475	480	(201) 408-3112
Essex County College	1,733	-	550	(201) 877-3468
Fairleigh Dickinson University	9,916	5,166	400	(201) 460-5230
Felician College	6,950	-	400	(201) 778-1190
Georgian Court College	7,300	3,750	600	(201) 364-2200
Glassboro State College	2,455	4,300	400	(609) 863-6141

	Tuition and Fees	Room and Board	Books and Supplies	Financial Aid Office
Gloucester County College	1,470	-	400	(609) 468-5000
Kean College of New Jersey	2,010	3,020	500	(201) 527-2050
Mercer County Community College	1,210	-	400	(609) 586-4800
Middlesex County College	1,484	-	600	(201) 548-6000
Monmouth College	10,700	4,330	480	(201) 571-3463
Monclair State College	2,255	4,132	500	(201) 893-7022
New Jersey Institute of Technology	4,000	4,300	700	(201) 596-3480
Ocean County College	1,226	-	500	(201) 255-0310
Passaic County Community College	1,643	-	700	(201) 684-6104
Princeton University	16,570	5,311	600	(609) 452-3330
Rabbinical College of America	5,500	4,500	500	(201) 370-1631
Raritan Valley Community College	1,242	-	550	(201) 526-1200
Rider College	10,120	4,330	600	(609) 896-5041
Rutgers University	3,432	3,829	500	(201) 932-7755
St. Peter's College	7,343	1,950	450	(201) 915-9308
Salem Community College	1,277	-	600	(609) 299-2100
Seton Hall University	10,450	5,520	500	(201) 761-9350
Stevens Institute of Technology	15,030	4,830	800	(201) 420-5201
Stockton State College	2,100	3,750	600	(609) 652-4201
Warren County Community College	1,150	-	500	(201) 689-1090
Westminster Choir College	10,600	4,550	500	(609) 921-7100

New Mexico

	Tuition and Fees	Room and Board	Books and Supplies	Financial Aid Office
Albuquerque Technical/ Vocational Insitute	834	-	350	(505) 768-0530
College of Santa Fe	7,656	2,510	450	(505) 473-6459
Eastern New Mexico University				
Portales	1,230	2,188	450	(505) 562-2194
Rosewell	550	3,250	500	(505) 624-7151
New Mexico Highlands University	1,270	3,160	375	(505) 454-3318
New Mexico Institute of Mining and Technology	1,392	3,027	500	(505) 835-5333
New Mexico Junior College	380	-	450	(505) 392-4510
New Mexico Military Institute	1,215	2,300	350	(505) 624-8065
New Mexico State University				
Alamogordo	600	-	350	(505) 434-3723
Carlsbad	660	-	450	(505) 885-8831
Grants	550	-	425	(505) 646-3212
Las Cruces	1,488	2,578	475	(505) 646-4105
Northern New Mexico Community College	468	2,728	450	(505) 753-7141
Parks College	4,320	-	350	(505) 843-7500
St. John's College	14,262	4,696	300	(505) 982-3691
San Juan College	360	-	340	(505) 326-3311
Santa Fe Community College	520	-	450	(505) 471-8200
University of New Mexico				
Albuquerque	1,453	2,990	420	(505) 277-5017
Gallup	630	-	500	(505) 722-7221
Western New Mexico University	1,034	2,200	400	(505) 538-6713

New York

	Tuition and Fees	Room and Board	Books and Supplies	Financial Aid Office
Adelphi University	10,380	5,450	475	(516) 877-3310
Adirondack Community College	1,415		450	(518) 793-4491

	Tuition and Fees	Room and Board	Books and Supplies	Financial Aid Office
Albany College of Pharmacy	7,375	4,000	425	(518) 445-7256
Alfred University	14,100	4,470	500	(607) 871-2159
American Academy of Dramatic Arts	7,175	-	500	(212) 689-9244
Bard College	15,710	5,160	450	(914) 758-6822
Barnard College	14,890	6,450	500	(212) 854-2154
Broome Community College	1,450	-	425	(607) 771-5028
Canisius College	8,902	4,650	400	(716) 888-2500
City University of New York				
Bronx Community College	1,550	-	350	(212) 220-6330
Brooklyn College	1,555	-	300	(718) 780-5044
Hostos Community College	1,524	-	300	(212) 960-1200
Hunter College	1,542	-	350	(212) 570-5416
Kingsborough Community College	1,540	-	300	(718) 934-5681
La Guardia Community College	1,551	-	300	(718) 482-7218
Manhattan Community College	1,530	-	300	(212) 618-1125
New York City Technical College	1,494	-	400	(718) 643-7204
Queens College	1,632	-	400	(718) 520-7233
Clarkson University	12,895	4,482	400	(315) 268-3839
Clinton Community College	1,403	-	400	(518) 561-6650
Colgate University	16,240	5,070	550	(315) 824-1000
College for Human Services	9,180	-	300	(212) 989-2002
College of Mount St. Vincent	8,940	4,550	400	(212) 549-8000
College of New Rochelle	9,750	4,640	500	(914) 632-5300
College of St. Rose	8,510	5,010	550	(518) 454-5168
Columbia University	15,858	6,122	650	(212) 854-4208
Concordia College	8,370	4,200	400	(914) 337-9300
Cornell University	16,214	5,336	450	(607) 256-5145
Daemen College	7,570	3,750	500	(716) 839-3600
Dowling College	7,310	-	450	(516) 244-3110
Dutchess Community College	1,445	-	450	(914) 471-4500
Empire State College	1,887	-	600	(518) 587-2100
Fashion Institute of Technology	1,860	4,555	1,000	(212) 760-7684
Five Towns College	5,600	-	475	(516) 783-8800
Fordham University	10,350	6,400	375	(212) 579-2155
Friends World College	9,000	-	400	(516) 549-5000
Hamilton College	16,650	4,550	300	(315) 859-4434
Hartwick College	13,450	4,350	450	(607) 431-4130
Hilbert College	5,810	4,110	400	(716) 649-7900
Hobart and William Smith Colleges	16,277	5,116	600	(315) 789-3560
Hofstra University	9,090	4,980	600	(516) 560-6680
Houghton College	8,676	3,134	500	(716) 567-2211
Interboro Institute, Inc.	4,828	-	450	(212) 399-0091
Iona College	6,270	5,600	450	(914) 633-2499
Ithaca College	11,946	5,104	500	(607) 274-3131
Julliard School	10,350	6,330	2,160	(212) 799-5000
Keuka College	8,120	3,850	500	(315) 536-4411
Le Moyne College	9,290	4,020	350	(315) 445-4400
Long Island University	9,170	4,360	450	(516) 299-2545
Manhattan College	11,100	5,760	500	(212) 920-0939
Manhattan School of Music	10,250	-	575	(212) 749-2802
Manhattanville College	11,660	5,250	400	(914) 694-2200
Maria College	3,960	-	500	(518) 438-3111
Marist College	8,835	5,100	500	(914) 575-3000

	Tuition and Fees	Room and Board	Books and Supplies	Financial Aid Office
Marymount College	10,200	5,750	500	(914) 332-8345
Marymount Manhattan College	8,800	-	350	(212) 517-0463
Medaille College	7,180	-	500	(716) 884-3281
Mercy College	6,600	-	500	(914) 693-4500
Mohawk Valley Community College	1,451	3,100	600	(315) 792-5415
Molloy College	8,200	-	600	(516) 678-5000
Monroe Community College	1,875	-	500	(716) 292-2050
Nassau Community College	1,440	-	600	(516) 222-7399
New York Institute of Technology	6,530	4,620	600	(516) 686-7680
New York University	14,520	6,880	375	(212) 998-4488
Niagara County Community College	1,340	-	350	(716) 731-3271
Niagra University	8,240	3,886	350	(716) 285-1212
Nyack College	7,430	3,440	500	(914) 358-1710
Onondaga Community College	1,414	-	350	(315) 469-7741
Orange County Community College	1,435	-	300	(914) 343-1121
Pace University	9,368	4,530	500	(914) 773-3751
Paul Smith's College	8,320	3,950	550	(518) 327-6227
Polytechnic University	14,100	-	450	(718) 260-3300
Pratt Institute	11,406	5,600	1,100	(718) 636-3599
Rensselaer Polytechnical Institute	15,625	5,150	475	(518) 276-6813
Rochester Institute of Technology	12,018	5,034	500	(716) 475-2186
Rockland Community College	1,651	-	450	(914) 356-4650
St. Bonaventure University	9,067	4,594	450	(716) 375-2528
St. Francis College	5,500	-	400	(212) 522-2300
St. John Fisher College	8,500	4,480	300	(716) 385-8042
St. John's University	7000	-	400	(718) 990-6043
St. Joseph's College	6,300	-	450	(718) 636-6800
St. Thomas Aquinas College	6,750	3,150	500	(914) 359-9500
Sarah Lawrence College	16,750	6,400	500	(914) 395-2570
Siena College	9,060	4,465	425	(518) 783-2427
Skidmore College	16,000	5,090	500	(518) 584-5000
State University of New York				
Albany	1,785	3,422	500	(518) 442-5480
Binghamton	1,853	4,152	500	(607) 777-2428
College at Brockport	1,911	3,795	480	(716) 395-2501
College at Buffalo	1,765	3,690	450	(716) 878-4901
College at Cortland	1,832	3,560	500	(607) 573-4717
College at Fredonia	1,893	3,840	500	(716) 673-3253
College at Geneseo	1,875	3,267	500	(716) 245-5731
College at New Paltz	1,831	3,720	500	(914) 257-3250
College at Old Westbury	1,825	3,578	600	(516) 876-3222
College at Oneonta	1,870	3,795	400	(607) 431-2461
College at Oswego	1,775	3,600	425	(315) 341-2248
College at Plattsburgh	1,785	3,416	500	(518) 564-2072
College at Potsdam	1,790	3,550	450	(315) 267-2162
College of Technology at Alfred	1,825	3,845	450	(607) 587-4253
College of Technology at Canton	1,830	3,610	550	(315) 386-7616
College of Technology at Delhi	1,785	3,710	450	(607) 746-4255
College of Technology at Farmingdale	1,907	3,750	475	(518) 420-2328

	Tuition and Fees	Room and Board	Books and Supplies	Financial Aid Office
College of Technology at Utica/Rome	1,809	-	475	(315) 386-7616
Maritime College	1,915	3,816	500	(212) 409-7268
Purchase	1,805	3,740	400	(914) 253-5174
Stony Brook	1,795	3,894	500	(516) 632-6847
Suffolk County Community College	1,500	-	400	(516) 451-4068
Sullivan County Community College	1,486	-	600	(914) 434-5750
Syracuse University	12,957	5,860	530	(315) 443-1039
Tompkins Cortland Community College	1,518	-	450	(607) 844-8211
Trociare College	4,850	-	600	(716) 826-1200
Ulster County Community College	1,749	-	500	(914) 687-7621
Union College	14,518	5,065	400	(518) 370-6123
University of Rochester	14,555	5,470	450	(716) 275-3226
Utica College of Syracuse University	10,446	4,549	450	(315) 792-3179
Vassar College	16,510	5,260	550	(914) 437-5320
Villa Maria College of Buffalo	4,860	-	450	(716) 896-0700
Wagner College	9,280	4,700	500	(718) 390-3183
Wells College	12,750	4,600	450	(315) 364-3289
Westchester Community College	1,564	-	400	(914) 285-6770
Wood School	8,035	-	700	(212) 686-9040

North Carolina

	Tuition and Fees	Room and Board	Books and Supplies	Financial Aid Office
Appalachian State University	460	2,450	300	(704) 262-2190
Asheville Buncombel Technical Community College	375	-	600	(704) 254-1921
Atlantic Christian College	5,762	2,596	500	(919) 237-3161
Beaufort County Community College	333	-	425	(919) 946-6194
Belmont Abbey College	7,870	3,804	500	(704) 825-6718
Bennett College	5,230	2,250	600	(919) 370-8677
Blanton's Junior College	4,025	-	600	(704) 252-7346
Blue Ridge Community College	336	-	425	(704) 692-3572
Brevard College	4,700	3,500	400	(704) 883-8292
Brunswick Community College	339	-	400	(919) 754-6900
Caldwell Community College	330	-	400	(704) 726-2246
Campbell University College	6,844	2,584	400	(919) 893-4111
Cape Fear Community College	342	-	500	(919) 343-0481
Carteret Community College	331	-	425	(919) 247-4142
Catawba College	7,300	3,500	350	(704) 637-4416
Central Piedmont Community College	323	-	500	(704) 342-6579
Chowan College	5,380	2,600	550	(919) 398-4101
College of Albemarle	345	-	400	(919) 335-0821
Craven Community College	342	-	500	(919) 638-4131
Davidson College	13,680	4,160	400	(704) 892-2000
Duke University	15,100	4,960	550	(919) 684-6225
East Carolina University	1,140	2,673	400	(919) 757-6610
Elizabeth City State University	1,077	2,464	300	(919) 335-0551
Elon College	7,150	3,350	400	(919) 584-2478
Fayetteville State University	981	2,150	425	(919) 486-6024

	Tuition and Fees	Room and Board	Books and Supplies	Financial Aid Office
Forsyth Technical Community College	445	-	500	(919) 723-0371
Gardner-Webb College	6,720	3,200	500	(704) 434-2361
Greensboro College	6,830	3,280	450	(919) 271-2217
Guilford College	9,450	3,929	450	(919) 292-5511
Guilford Technical Community College	338	-	600	(919) 334-4822
Halifax Community College	333	-	400	(919) 536-2551
Haywood Community College	335	-	425	(704) 627-2821
High Point College	6,710	3,200	550	(919) 841-9128
John Wesley College	3,569	-	300	(919) 889-2262
Johnson C. Smith University	5,671	2,186	400	(704) 378-1207
Johnston Community College	336	-	475	(919) 935-3051
Lees-McRae College	5,506	2,844	400	(704) 898-5241
Lenior Community College	342	-	450	(919) 527-6223
Lenoir-Rhyne College	8,584	3,326	500	(704) 328-7304
Louisburg College	5,639	2,840	450	(919) 496-2521
Mars Hill College	6,250	2,850	500	(704) 689-1123
Martin Community College	330	-	450	(919) 792-1521
Mayland Community College	330	-	550	(704) 765-7351
McDowell Technical College	330	-	450	(704) 652-6021
Meredith College	5,720	2,820	400	(919) 829-8565
Methodist College	7,700	3,100	500	(919) 488-7110
Mitchell Community College	342	-	400	(704) 878-3200
Montgomery Community College	330	-	500	(919) 572-3691
Montreat-Anderson College	5,832	3,118	500	(704) 669-8011
North Carolina Agricultural & Technical State University	1,113	2,344	500	(919) 334-7973
North Carolina Central University	1,054	2,764	350	(919) 560-5150
North Carolina School of the Arts	1,551	3,000	500	(919) 770-3297
North Carolina State University	1,109	3,030	500	(919) 737-2421
North Carolina Wesleyan College	6,730	3,250	400	(919) 977-7171
Pamlico Community College	330	-	500	(919) 249-1851
Peace College	4,545	3,875	500	(919) 832-2881
Pembroke State University	841	2,070	400	(919) 521-9868
Pfeiffer College	6,620	2,960	650	(704) 463-7343
Piedmont Community College	333	-	600	(919) 599-1181
Pitt Community College	333	-	400	(919) 355-4326
Queens College	9,300	4,400	450	(704) 337-2225
Randolph Community College	337	-	500	(919) 629-1471
Richmond Community College	333	-	400	(919) 582-7118
Roanoke-Chowan Community College	339	-	300	(919) 332-5921
Robeson Community College	333	-	350	(919) 738-7101
Rockingham Community College	342	-	350	(919) 342-4261
Rowan Cabarrus Community College	339	-	350	(704) 637-0760
St. Andrews Presbyterian College	8,150	3,670	400	(919) 276-3652
St. Augustine's College	4,950	3,200	600	(919) 828-4451
St. Mary's College	6,265	5,320	550	(919) 839-4006
Salem College	9,075	5,600	600	(919) 721-2808
Sampson Community College	345	-	500	(919) 592-8081
Sandhills Community College	339	-	400	(919) 692-6185
Shaw University	4,530	3,190	600	(919) 755-4853
Southeastern Community College	344	-	400	(919) 642-7141

	Tuition and Fees	Room and Board	Books and Supplies	Financial Aid Office
Stanly Community College	333	-	500	(704) 982-0121
Surry Community College	333	-	400	(919) 386-8121
University of North Carolina	843	2,450	350	
Asheville	1,043	2,900	350	(704) 251-6535
Chapel Hill	1,059	3,390	450	(919) 962-2193
Charlotte	1,032	2,592	375	(704) 597-2461
Greensboro	1,363	3,345	425	(919) 334-5702
Wilmington	1,187	3,034	450	(919) 395-3129
Vance-Granville Community College	342	-	477	(919) 492-2061
Wake Forest University	10,670	3,600	400	(919) 759-5176
Wake Technical College	324	-	450	(919) 772-7500
Warren Wilson College	8,810	2,852	400	(704) 298-3325
Wayne Community College	342	-	450	(919) 735-5151
Western Carolina University	1,114	2,300	250	(704) 227-7290
Western Piedmont Community College	337	-	450	(704) 438-6042
Wilkes Community College	335	-	350	(919) 667-8633
Wilson County Technical College	330	-	450	(919) 291-1195
Wingate College	6,120	2,750	500	(704) 233-8210
Winston-Salem State University	985	2,630	550	(919) 750-3280

North Dakota

Bismarck State College	1,596	1,928	450	(701) 223-4500
Dickinson State University	1,659	1,750	400	(701) 227-2371
Jamestown College	6,670	2,980	400	(701) 252-3467
Little Hoop Community College	1,130	-	200	(701) 766-4415
Mayville State University	1,684	2,029	400	(701) 786-2301
Minot State University	1,653	1,745	500	(701) 857-3375
North Dakota State University				
Bottineau	1,615	1,980	425	(701) 228-2277
Fargo	2,040	1,924	475	(701) 837-7533
Standing Rock College	1,720	-	300	(701) 854-3861
Trinity Bible College	4,010	3,128	400	(701) 349-3621
Turtle Mountain Community College	1,152	-	400	(701) 477-5605
University of Mary	5,650	2,400	500	(701) 255-7500
University of North Dakota				
Grand Forks	2,040	2,190	400	(701) 777-4463
Lake Region	1,632	2,010	550	(701) 662-8683
Willston	1,658	1,960	500	(701) 774-4244
Valley City State University	1,638	1,920	450	(701) 845-7412

Ohio

Antioch College	12,960	3,490	400	(513) 767-6367
Ashland College	9,966	4,119	450	(419) 289-5001
Baldwin-Wallace College	9,225	3,675	375	(216) 826-2108
Bluffton College	7,650	3,135	350	(419) 358-8015
Bowling Green State University	2,808	2,515	450	(419) 372-2651
Capital University	10,360	3,490	400	(614) 236-6511
Case Western Reserve University	13,710	4,930	500	(216) 368-3866
Central Ohio Technical College	1,822	-	550	(614) 366-9328
Central State University	2,247	3,753	400	(513) 376-6573
Circleville Bible College	3,122	3,500	400	(614) 474-8896
Clark Technical College	1,737	-	600	(513) 325-0691

	Tuition and Fees	Room and Board	Books and Supplies	Financial Aid Office
Cleveland Institute of Art	10,500	4,310	1,000	(216) 421-7425
Cleveland Institute of Music	11,005	4,735	600	(216) 791-5000
Cleveland State University	2,397	3,069	475	(216) 687-3766
College of Mount St. Joseph	8,170	3,810	400	(513) 244-4418
College of Wooster	13,410	4,240	450	(216) 263-2317
Columbus College of Art and Design	8,200	4,500	900	(614) 224-9101
Columbus State Community College	1,656	-	400	(614) 227-2648
Davis Junior College of Business	4,776	-	550	(419) 473-2700
Defiance College	8,690	3,160	400	(419) 784-4010
Denison University	14,700	3,980	450	(614) 587-6279
Dyke College	4,500	-	455	(216) 696-9000
Edison State Community College	1,575	-	475	(513) 778-8600
Heidelburg College	11,680	3,730	400	(419) 448-2293
Hiram College	12,165	3,780	400	(216) 569-5107
Jefferson Technical College	1,148	-	500	(614) 264-5591
John Carroll University	9,600	5,050	500	(216) 397-4248
Kent State University	3,006	3,188	450	(216) 672-2972
Lake Erie College	7,950	4,000	425	(216) 352-3361
Lakeland Community College	1,536	-	435	(216) 953-7071
Lorain County Community College	1,704	-	500	(216) 365-4191
Lourdes College	5,750	-	450	(419) 885-3211
Malone College	7,860	3,000	400	(216) 489-0800
Marietta College	11,800	3,460	425	(614) 374-4712
Miami University	3,388	3,100	450	(513) 529-5757
Mount Union College	10,680	3,100	450	(216) 823-2674
Mount Vernon Nazarene College	6,070	3,030	400	(614) 397-1244
Muskingum Area Technical College	1,965	-	450	(614) 454-2501
Muskingum College	11,855	3,510	450	(614) 826-8139
North Central Technical College	2,268	-	400	(419) 755-4899
Northwest Technical College	1,935	-	600	(419) 267-5511
Oberlin College	16,817	5,155	475	(216) 775-8142
Ohio Dominican College	6,660	3,680	400	(614) 251-4642
Ohio Northern University	10,845	3,195	600	(419) 772-2260
Ohio State University	2,345	3,726	450	(616) 292-1134
Ohio University	2,946	3,633	450	(614) 593-4141
Ohio Wesleyan University	13,610	4,884	450	(614) 368-3050
Otterbein College	10,800	3,912	350	(614) 898-1502
Owens Technical College	1,615	-	500	(419) 666-0580
Pontifical College Josephinum	4,270	2,800	400	(614) 885-5585
Rio Grande College	1,890	3,000	550	(614) 245-5353
Southern State Community College	1,869	-	450	(513) 393-3431
Stark Technical College	1,858	-	600	(216) 494-6170
Terra Technical College	1,596	-	500	(419) 334-8400
Tiffin University	6,100	3,380	500	(419) 447-6442
University of Akron	2,820	3,200	350	(216) 972-6343
University of Cincinnati	2,838	3,948	450	(513) 556-6982
University of Dayton	9,410	3,760	500	(513) 229-4311
University of Toledo	2,526	2,805	500	(419) 537-4066
Urbana University	7,476	3,880	500	(513) 652-1301
Ursuline University	6,600	3,380	400	(216) 449-4200
Walsh College	6,220	3,350	350	(216) 499-7090
Washington Technical College	1,944	-	500	(614) 374-8716

	Tuition and Fees	Room and Board	Books and Supplies	Financial Aid Office
West Side Institute of Technology	7,000	-	740	(216) 651-1656
Wilberforce University	5,816	3,200	500	(513) 376-2911
Wilmington College	8,680	3,200	500	(513) 382-6661
Wittenberg University	13,400	4,000	350	(513) 327-7321
Wright State University	2,649	3,630	475	(513) 873-2321
Xavier University	9,700	4,110	500	(513) 745-2990
Youngstown State University	2,305	3,410	475	(216) 742-3501

Oklahoma

	Tuition and Fees	Room and Board	Books and Supplies	Financial Aid Office
Bartlesville Wesleyan College	5,650	2,900	300	(918) 335-6219
Cameron University	1,270	2,200	500	(405) 581-2293
Carl Albert Junior College	864	-	450	(918) 647-8660
Central State University	1,160	1,992	450	(405) 341-2980
Connors State College	882	1,840	400	(918) 463-2931
East Central University	1,190	1,988	350	(405) 332-8000
Eastern Oklahoma State College	864	1,994	500	(918) 465-2361
Langston University	1,233	2,100	400	(405) 466-3282
Mid-America Bible College	3,875	3,475	400	(405) 691-3881
Murray State College	879	2,130	400	(405) 371-2371
Northeastern Oklahoma Agricultural and Mechanical College	819	1,900	400	(918) 542-8441
Northeastern State University	1,190	2,088	400	(918) 456-5511
Northern Oklahoma College	810	1,844	450	(405) 628-2581
Northwestern Oklahoma State University	1,187	1,648	450	(405) 327-1720
Oklahoma Baptist University	4,664	2,800	400	(405) 275-2014
Oklahoma Christian College	4,700	2,660	450	(405) 425-5190
Oklahoma City Community College	927	-	500	(405) 682-7566
Oklahoma City University	4,828	3,380	325	(405) 521-5239
Oklahoma Panhandle State University	1,261	1,800	400	(405) 349-2611
Oklahoma State University	1,133	2,744	500	(405) 744-6604
Oklahoma State University Technical Branch	1,103	1,950	550	(405) 947-4421
Oral Roberts University	6,025	3,495	450	(918) 495-6510
Phillips University	8,530	2,766	500	(405) 237-4433
Rogers State College	915	2,400	500	(918) 341-7510
Rose State College	786	-	600	(405) 733-7424
St. Gregory's College	3,700	2,660	425	(405) 273-9870
Seminole Junior College	895	1,880	400	(405) 382-9950
Southeastern Oklahoma State University	1,175	2,080	400	(405) 924-0121
Southern Nazarene University	5,070	3,092	400	(405) 491-6310
Southwestern College of Christian Ministries	2,960	2,070	450	(405) 789-7661
Southwestern Oklahoma State University	1,160	1,430	400	(405) 774-3022
Tulsa Junior College	864	-	400	(918) 587-6561
University of Oklahoma	1,527	3,127	550	(405) 325-5505
University of Tulsa	7,950	3,300	500	(918) 631-2526
Western Oklahoma State College	850	-	450	(405) 477-2000

Oregon

	Tuition and Fees	Room and Board	Books and Supplies	Financial Aid Office
Bassist College	8,400	2,700	500	(503) 288-6528
Blue Mountain Community College	792	-	375	(503) 276-1260

	Tuition and Fees	Room and Board	Books and Supplies	Financial Aid Office
Central Oregon Community College	780	2,996	600	(503) 385-5521
Chemeketa Community College	828	-	500	(503) 399-5018
Clackamas Community College	795	-	450	(503) 657-8400
Clatsop Community College	756	-	500	(503) 325-0910
Columbia Christian College	6,443	2,872	400	(503) 257-1209
Concordia College	8,070	2,550	400	(503) 280-8514
Eastern Oregon State College	1,764	2,910	400	(503) 963-1665
Eugene Bible College	3,307	2,250	600	(503) 485-1780
George Fox College	8,185	3,230	400	(503) 538-8383
Lane Community College	858	-	500	(503) 747-4501
Lewis and Clark College	12,588	4,386	350	(503) 768-7095
Linfield College	11,057	3,484	450	(503) 472-4121
Linn-Benton Community College	864	-	350	(503) 967-6104
Maryhurst College	6,780	-	500	(503) 636-8141
Mount Hood Community College	810	-	450	(503) 667-7265
Multnomah School of the Bible	4,950	2,900	360	(503) 251-5337
Oregon Health Sciences University	2,729	3,618	600	(503) 494-8249
Oregon Institute of Technology	1,890	3,180	500	(503) 885-1280
Oregon Polytechnic Institute	4,650	-	600	(503) 234-9333
Oregon State University	1,878	2,879	500	(503) 737-2241
Pacific Northwest University	6,690	-	700	(503) 226-4842
Pacific University of Art	10,477	3,145	400	(503) 357-6151
Portland Community College	972	-	500	(503) 452-4947
Portland State University	1,917	-	550	(503) 229-3461
Reed College	16,700	4,640	450	(503) 771-1112
Rogue Community College	968	-	450	(503) 479-5541
Southern Oregon State College	1,824	3,050	500	(503) 482-6161
Treasure Valley Community College	894	2,160	400	(503) 889-6493
Umpqua Community College	1,053	-	450	(503) 440-4602
University of Oregon	1,965	2,806	425	(503) 686-3205
University of Portland	9,080	3,500	450	(503) 283-7311
Warner Pacific College	7,511	3,228	400	(503) 775-4366
Western Baptist College	7,510	3,350	400	(503) 581-8600
Western Oregon State College	1,812	3,090	570	(503) 838-8475
Willamette University	11,480	3,950	375	(503) 370-6273

Pennsylvania

Albright College	13,560	4,015	500	(215) 921-7515
Allegheny College	14,850	4,120	450	(814) 332-4354
Alvernia College	6,958	3,630	450	(215) 777-5411
Baptist Bible College	4,979	2,971	450	(717) 587-1172
Beaver College	10,960	4,750	400	(215) 572-2956
Bloomsburg University	2,518	2,460	400	(717) 389-4279
Bryn Mawr College	15,600	5,850	450	(215) 526-5245
Bucknell University	15,650	3,825	550	(717) 524-1331
Bucks County Community College	1,524	-	300	(215) 968-8200
Cabrini College	7,740	4,790	575	(215) 971-8420
California University of Pennsylvania	2,648	2,680	400	(412) 938-4415
Carlow College	8,750	4,000	400	(412) 578-6058
Carnegie Mellon University	15,350	5,110	450	(412) 268-7581
Cedar Crest College	11,130	4,556	500	(215) 437-4471
Chatham College	10,160	4,490	400	(412) 365-1292
Chestnut Hill College	7,550	3,800	550	(215) 248-7101
Cheyney University	2,488	2,956	400	(215) 399-2000

	Tuition and Fees	Room and Board	Books and Supplies	Financial Aid Office
Clarion University	2,728	2,550	450	(814) 226-2315
College Misericordia	7,900	4,034	400	(717) 675-6280
Community College of Allegheny County	1,398	-	450	(412) 237-4606
Community College of Philadelphia	1,690	-	400	(215) 751-8275
Delaware County Community	1,120	-	300	(215) 359-5330
Dickinson College	15,550	4,530	650	(717) 245-1308
Drexel University	10,119	4,616	500	(215) 895-2537
Duquesne University	8,850	4,317	400	(412) 434-6607
Eastern College	8,925	3,470	400	(215) 341-5842
East Stroudsburg University	2,642	2,706	450	(717) 424-3340
Edinboro University of Pennsylvania	2,590	2,905	400	(814) 732-2821
Elizabethtown College	10,700	3,750	500	(717) 367-1151
Franklin and Marshall College	20,885	INC	450	(717) 291-3991
Gannon University	8,680	350	400	(814) 871-7337
Geneva College	7,184	3,480	450	(412) 847-6530
Gettysburg College	16,500	3,470	400	(717) 337-6611
Gwyneed-Mercy College	7,900	400	500	(215) 641-5570
Hahnemann University School of Health	7,150	-	500	(215) 448-4621
Harcum Junior College	6,008	3,900	400	(215) 525-6098
Harrisburg Area Community College	1,368	-	500	(717) 780-2330
Haverford College	16,150	5,400	550	(215) 896-1350
Holy Family College	700	-	500	(215) 637-7700
Hussian School of Art	5,635	-	700	(215) 238-9000
Indiana University of Pennsylvania	2,611	2,476	500	(412) 357-2218
Johnson Technical Institute	3,995	-	400	(717) 342-6404
Juniata College	12,470	3,690	500	(814) 643-4310
Keystone Junior College	7,410	4,440	500	(717) 945-5141
King's College	8,740	4,100	450	(717) 826 5868
Kutztown University	2,550	2,548	500	(215) 683-4077
Lackawanna Junior College	5,400	-	450	(717) 961-7863
La Roche College	6,711	3,590	600	(412) 367-9300
La Salle University	10,250	4,500	500	(215) 951-1070
Lebanon Valley College	10,650	4,240	425	(800) 445-6181
Lehigh County Community College	1,455	-	500	(215) 799-1133
Lehigh University	15,650	4,940	550	(215) 758-4504
Lincoln University	2,400	2,600	450	(215) 932-8300
Lock Haven University	2,588	2,676	400	(717) 893-2344
Luzerne County Community College	1,470	-	400	(717) 829-7395
Manor Junior College	5,860	3,000	400	(215) 885-2360
Mansfield University	2,628	2,490	500	(717) 662-4129
Marywood College	7,300	3,500	400	(717) 348-6225
Mercyhurst College	8,700	3,175	400	(814) 825-0287
Messiah College	8,700	4,380	450	(717) 766-2511
Millersville University	2,636	2,810	400	(717) 872-3026
Montgomery County Community College	1,580	-	350	(215) 641-6566
Moore College of Art	10,000	4,600	800	(215) 568-4515
Moravian College	11,600	3,780	400	(215) 861-1330
Mount Aloysius Junior College	6,400	2,990	500	(814) 886-4131
Muhlenberg College	15,115	4,260	450	(215) 433-3175
Neumann College	7,560	-	500	(215) 459-0905

	Tuition and Fees	Room and Board	Books and Supplies	Financial Aid Office
Northhampton County Area Community College	1,650	-	500	(215) 861-5510
Northeastern Christian Junior College	5,658	3,630	350	(215) 525-6780
Peirce Junior College	5,360	-	500	(215) 545-6400
Penn Technical Institute	6,250	-	600	(412) 355-0455
Pennsylvania State University				
Allentown Campus	3,922	-	400	(814) 865-6301
Altoona Campus	3,922	3,510	400	(814) 865-6301
Beaver Campus	3,922	3,510	400	(814) 865-6301
Berks Campus	3,922	-	400	(215) 320-4923
Delaware County Campus	3,922	-	400	(215) 565-3300
Du Bois Campus	3,922	-	400	(814) 371-2800
Erie Behrend College	4,048	3,510	400	(814) 898-6162
Fayette Campus	3,922	-	400	(412) 437-2801
Harrisburg Capital College	4,048	3,510	400	(717) 948-6307
Hazelton Campus	3,922	3,510	400	(717) 450-3163
McKeesport Campus	3,922	3,510	400	(412) 675-9160
Mont Alto Campus	3,922	3,510	400	(717) 749-3111
New Kensington Campus	3,922	-	400	(412) 339-7561
Ogontz Campus	3,922	-	400	(215) 886-9400
Schuylkill Campus	3,922	-	400	(717) 385-4500
Shenango Valley Campus	3,922	-	400	(412) 981-1640
University Park Campus	3,922	3,510	400	(814) 865-6301
Wilkes-Barre Campus	3,922	-	400	(717) 675-2171
Worthington-Scranton Campus	3,922	-	400	(717) 963-4781
York Campus	3,922	-	400	(717) 771-4555
Pennsylvania Institute of Technology	6,413	-	700	(215) 565-7900
Philadelphia College of Pharmacy and Science	8,580	4,375	400	(215) 596-8894
Philadelphia College of Textiles and Science	8,866	4,205	500	(215) 951-2940
Pinebrook Junior College	6,096	3,388	550	(215) 282-8216
Point Park College	7,122	3,950	400	(412) 392-3930
Robert Morris College	5,400	3,500	450	(412) 262-8209
Rosemont College	8,610	5,160	500	(215) 527-0200
St. Francis College	8,758	4,120	450	(814) 472-3010
St. Vincent College	8,990	3,520	400	(412) 537-4540
Seton Hill College	9,000	3,760	500	(412) 834-2200
Shippenburg University of Pennsylvania	2,694	2,594	400	(717) 532-1131
Slippery Rock University of Pennsylvania	2,668	2,794	400	(412) 738-2044
Spring Garden College	8,480	4,000	450	(215) 248-7905
Susquehanna University	13,950	4,030	400	(717) 372-4450
Swarthmore College	15,490	5,220	750	(215) 328-8358
Temple University	4,354	4,484	450	(215) 787-8760
Thaddeus Stevens State School of Technology	3,400	3,110	450	(717) 299-7772
Thomas Jefferson University	10,600	3,460	900	(215) 955-6531
Triangle Tech	5,705	-	900	(412) 359-1000
University of Pennsylvania	15,894	6,030	450	(215) 898-6784
University of Pittsburgh	4,314	3,514	400	(412) 624-7192
University of Scranton	8,756	4,088	400	(717) 961-7700
Ursinus College	11,520	4,250	400	(215) 489-4111
Valley Forge Christian College	4,498	2,640	350	(215) 935-0450
Villanova University	10,850	5,220	450	(215) 645-4010

	Tuition and Fees	Room and Board	Books and Supplies	Financial Aid Office
Washington and Jefferson College	12,850	3,290	300	(412) 223-6019
Waynesburg College	7,220	2,900	500	(412) 852-3227
West Chester University of Pennsylvania	2,528	3,194	450	(215) 436-2627
Westmoreland County Community College	1,193	-	450	(412) 925-4063
Widener University	10,500	4,610	500	(215) 499-4194
Wilkes College	9,275	4,250	500	(717) 824-4651
Williamsport Area Community College	1,693	-	400	(717) 326-3761
Wilson College	10,076	4,263	450	(717) 264-4141
York College of Pennsylvania	4,448	2,972	450	(717) 846-7788

Puerto Rico

	Tuition and Fees	Room and Board	Books and Supplies	Financial Aid Office
American University of Puerto Rico	2,100	-	400	(809) 786-0090
Bayamon Central University	2,200	-	400	(809) 786-3030
Catholic University of Puerto Rico	2,457	2,265	300	(809) 841-2000
Huertas Junior College	2,985	-	300	(809) 743-2156
ICPR Junior College	2,523	-	400	(809) 573-6335
Instituto Tecnico Comericial Junior College	2,380	-	400	(809) 767-4323
Inter American University of Puerto Rico	2,500	-	450	(809) 751-1324
Ramirez College of Business and Technology	620	-	720	(809) 763-3120
University of Puerto Rico	490	-	500	(809) 764-3710
University of the Sacred Heart	2,650	2,700	450	(809) 727-8500

Rhode Island

	Tuition and Fees	Room and Board	Books and Supplies	Financial Aid Office
Brown University	16,860	5,220	600	(401) 863-2721
Bryant College	10,993	5,935	450	(401) 232-6020
Community College of Rhode Island	1,100	-	450	(401) 825-2149
Johnson & Wales College	8,517	3,999	500	(401) 456-4649
New England Institute of Technology	7,980	-	600	(401) 467-7744
Providence College	12,065	5,300	500	(401) 865-2286
Rhode Island College	1,990	5,210	500	(401) 456-8234
Rhode Island School of Design	13,210	5,220	1,000	(401) 331-3511
Roger Williams College	9,765	4,750	500	(401) 253-1040
Salve Regina College	11,740	5,500	500	(401) 847-6650
University of Rhode Island	2,791	4,423	600	(401) 792-2314

South Carolina

	Tuition and Fees	Room and Board	Books and Supplies	Financial Aid Office
Aiken Technical College	600	-	600	(803) 593-9231
Anderson College	5,850	3,820	400	(803) 226-6181
Benedict College	4,571	2,418	600	(803) 253-5105
Central Wesleyan College	7,090	2,980	550	(803) 639-2453
The Citadel	2,513	2,276	630	(803) 792-5187
Clemson University	2,623	3,153	500	(803) 656-6431
Coker College	7,715	3,552	600	(803) 383-8055
College of Charleston	2,300	3,000	500	(803) 792-5540

	Tuition and Fees	Room and Board	Books and Supplies	Financial Aid Office
Columbia College	8,725	3,255	500	(803) 786-3644
Columbia Junior College of Business	2,585	-	300	(803) 799-9082
Converse College	10,368	3,240	500	(803) 596-9019
Erskine College	8,760	3,105	475	(803) 379-8832
Florence-Darlington Technical College	865	-	700	(803) 661-8086
Francis Marion College	1,800	3,010	400	(803) 661-1190
Furman University	10,566	3,771	425	(803) 294-2204
Horry-Georgetown Technical College	750	-	300	(803) 347-3186
Lander College	2,390	2,380	300	(803) 229-8340
Limestone College	6,464	3,100	400	(803) 489-7151
Midlands Technical College	750	-	300	(803) 738-7634
Morris College	3,717	2,255	600	(803) 775-9371
Newberry College	7,400	3,000	350	(803) 276-5010
North Greenville College	5,600	3,140	500	(803) 895-1410
Presbyterian College	10,326	3,098	500	(803) 833-2827
Spartanburg Methodist College	5,500	3,300	400	(803) 587-4000
Sumter Area Technical College	659	-	400	(800) 221-8711
Tri-County Technical College	675	-	450	(803) 646-8361
Trident Technical College	1,060	-	550	(803) 572-6108
University of South Carolina Columbia	2,560	2,928	400	(803) 777-3215
Williamsburg Technical College	800	-	400	(803) 354-7423
Winthrop College	2,326	2,124	350	(803) 323-2189
Wofford College	9,015	3,950	560	(803) 585-4821
York Technical College	495	-	375	(803) 327-8005

South Dakota

Augustana College	9,330	2,860	400	(605) 336-5216
Black Hills State College	1,712	2,200	400	(605) 642-0697
Dakota State College	1,866	2,020	400	(605) 256-5152
Dakota Wesleyan University	6,250	2,550	450	(605) 995-2654
Kilian Community College	3,185	-	400	(605) 336-1711
Mount Marty College	6,590	2,660	500	(605) 668-1589
National College	5,760	3,000	600	(605) 394-4880
Northern State College	1,700	2,544	450	(605) 622-2640
Oglala Lakota College	1,590	-	200	(605) 455-2321
Presentation College	5,740	2,466	600	(605) 229-8429
Sinte Gleska College	1,580	-	200	(605) 747-2263
Sioux Falls College	7,496	2,950	600	(605) 331-6623
Sisseton-Wahpeton Community College	2,070	-	360	(605) 698-3966
South Dakota School of Mines and Technology	1,899	2,100	450	(605) 394-2274
South Dakota State University	1,824	2,341	400	(605) 688-4703
University of South Dakota	1,869	2,116	500	(605) 677-5446

Tennessee

Aquinas Junior College	3,090	-	450	(615) 297-7545
Austin Peay State University	1,442	2,550	450	(615) 648-7907
Belmont College	5,900	3,150	450	(615) 383-7001
Bethel College	4,350	2,400	400	(901) 352-5321
Bristol University	5,450	2,500	550	(615) 968-1442
Carson-Newman College	6,000	2,560	350	(615) 475-9061

	Tuition and Fees	Room and Board	Books and Supplies	Financial · Aid Office
Chattanooga State Technical Community College	844	-	450	(615) 697-4402
Christian Brothers College	6,960	3,070	600	(901) 722-0307
Cleveland State Community College	848	-	450	(615) 472-7141
Columbia State Community College	844	-	425	(615) 388-8714
Cumberland University	4,400	2,720	450	(615) 444-2562
David Lipscomb College	5,670	3,020	500	(615) 269-1791
Draughon's Junior College of Business	4,196	-	400	(615) 584-8621
Dyersburg State Community College	850	-	400	(901) 286-3238
East Tennessee State University	1,396	2,640	400	(615) 929-4300
Fisk University	5,010	3,050	500	(615) 329-8738
Freed-Hardeman College	5,080	2,810	500	(901) 989-4611
Hiwassee College	3,800	2,600	300	(615) 442-3283
Jackson State Community College	850	-	400	(901) 424-2605
King College, Inc.	6,650	3,050	400	(615) 652-4726
Lambuth College	4,392	2,858	450	(901) 425-3330
Lane College	4,187	2,355	400	(901) 424-4600
Lee College	4,379	2,774	425	(615) 372-2111
Martin Methodist College	4,500	2,600	350	(615) 363-7456
Maryville College	7,750	3,550	450	(615) 981-8100
McKenzie College	4,000	-	350	(615) 756-7042
Memphis College of Art	8,180	4,500	800	(901) 726-4085
Memphis State University	1,564	2,000	600	(901) 678-2303
Middle Tennessee State University	1,384	1,822	400	(615) 898-2830
Milligan College	6,196	2,736	400	(615) 461-8713
Motlow State Community College	854	-	350	(615) 455-8511
Nashville State Technical Institute	848	-	400	(615) 353-3250
Rhodes College	12,958	4,516	500	(901) 726-3810
Roane State Community College	915	-	400	(615) 882-4545
Shelby State Community College	846	-	400	(901) 528-6727
Southern College of Seventh-Day Adventists	7,160	3,040	450	(615) 238-2834
State Technical Institute: Knoxville	842	-	380	(615) 584-6103
Tennessee State University	1,396	2,284	400	(615) 320-3340
Tennessee Technological University	1,430	2,900	600	(615) 372-3073
Tennessee Temple University	3,970	3,180	450	(615) 493-4209
Tennessee Wesleyan College	5,564	3,144	400	(615) 745-7504
Tomlinson College	3,640	2,700	300	(615) 476-3271
Trececca Nazarene College	5,136	2,580	450	(615) 248-1242
Tri-Cities State Technical Institute	884	-	625	(615) 323-3191
Tusculum College	6,000	3,100	550	(615) 636-7312
Union College	4,550	2,260	400	(901) 668-1818
University of the South	13,500	3,510	425	(615) 598-1312
University of Tennessee				
Chattanooga	1,488	-	500	(615) 755-4677
Knoxville	1,712	3,044	600	(615) 974-3131
Martin	1,546	2,670	500	(901) 587-7040
Memphis	1,486	3,780	600	(901) 528-5568
Vanderbilt University	15,234	5,420	600	(615) 322-3591

	Tuition and Fees	Room and Board	Books and Supplies	Financial Aid Office
Volunteer State Community College	850	-	400	(615) 452-8600
Walters State Community College	910	-	500	(615) 587-9722

Texas

	Tuition and Fees	Room and Board	Books and Supplies	Financial Aid Office
Abilene Christian University	6,480	3,050	425	(915) 674-2765
Alvin Community College	360	-	430	(713) 331-6111
Amarillo College	479	-	454	(806) 371-5310
American Technological University	3,020	2,500	400	(817) 526-1260
Angelina College	562	2,440	500	(409) 633-5291
Angelo State University	1,070	3,536	400	(915) 942-2246
Austin College	9,465	3,745	630	(214) 813-2389
Bauder Fashion College	5,690	3,780	850	(817) 277-6666
Baylor University	6,110	3,654	600	(817) 755-2611
Bee County College	356	2,110	400	(512) 358-3130
Blinn College	670	2,154	500	(409) 830-4144
Brazosport College	250	-	450	(409) 265-6131
Cisco Junior College	540	1,900	500	(817) 442-2567
Concordia Lutheran College	6,090	3,200	450	(512) 452-7661
Cooke County College	450	2,820	450	(817) 668-7731
Corpus Christi State University	910	3,042	400	(512) 994-2417
Dallas Baptist University	5,650	2,928	580	(214) 333-5460
Dallas Christian College	2,350	2,600	450	(214) 241-3371
Del Mar College	480	-	400	(512) 886-1599
DeVry Institute of Technology: Irving	5,015	-	500	(214) 258-6767
East Texas State University	980	3,090	600	(214) 886-5096
East Texas State University at Texarkana	930	-	600	(324) 838-6514
El Paso Community College	820	-	412	(915) 594-2561
Frank Phillips College	430	1,490	400	(806) 274-5311
Galveston College	522	-	400	(409) 763-6551
Hardin-Simmons University	5,432	2,612	425	(915) 670-1482
Howard County Junior College District	525	2,052	300	(915) 267-6311
Howard Payne University	4,162	2,470	350	(915) 643-7806
Huston-Tillotson College	4,440	3,290	500	(512) 476-7421
Incarnate Word College	7,000	3,230	500	(512) 829-6008
Jacksonville College	2,700	2,200	400	(214) 586-2518
Jarvis Christian College	3,720	2,999	400	(214) 769-2174
Kilgore College	380	2,000	450	(214) 983-8210
Lamar University	1,102	2,762	450	(409) 882-3342
Laredo Junior College	570	-	450	(512) 722-0521
Lee College	390	-	350	(713) 425-6389
Letourneau College	7,350	3,640	600	(214) 753-0231
Lon Morris College	4,004	3,186	450	(214) 586-2741
Lubbock Christian University	6,020	2,330	300	(806) 792-3221
McLennan Community College	460	-	350	(817) 756-6551
McMurry College	5,250	2,710	400	(915) 691-6211
Midland College	457	-	400	(915) 685-4507
Midwestern State University	1,110	2,918	600	(817) 696-6786
Navarro College	680	2,560	450	(214) 874-6501
North Harris County College	324	-	400	(713) 443-5464
Northeast Texas Community College	570	-	450	(214) 572-1911
Odessa College	460	2,875	450	(915) 335-6429

	Tuition and Fees	Room and Board	Books and Supplies	Financial Aid Office
Our Lady of the Lake University of San Antonio	5,992	2,860	650	(512) 434-6711
Panola Junior College	300	1,990	400	(214) 693-2039
Paris Junior College	2,070	2,584	400	(214) 784-9427
Paul Quinn College	3,635	2,975	400	(817) 753-6415
Prairie View A&M University	991	2,938	550	(713) 857-2423
St. Edward's University	7,750	3,450	450	(512) 448-8525
St. Mary's University	7,320	3,450	450	(512) 436-3141
St. Phillip's College	480	-	300	(512) 531-3274
Sam Houston State University	1,060	2,730	400	(409) 294-1770
San Antonio College	484	-	400	(512) 733-2974
San Jacinto College: Central Campus	310	-	350	(713) 476-1856
Schreiner College	7,425	4,990	400	(512) 896-5411
Southern Methodist University	11,768	4,832	550	(214) 692-2081
South Plains College	560	2,300	350	(806) 894-9611
Southwestern Adventist College	6,552	3,242	400	(817) 645-3921
Southwestern Assemblies of God College	3,540	2,750	400	(214) 937-4010
Southwestern Christian College	3,640	2,307	300	(214) 563-3341
Southwestern University	9,400	4,281	500	(512) 863-6511
Southwest Texas Junior College	650	2,360	400	(512) 278-4401
Southwest Texas State University	1,122	2,800	500	(512) 245-8011
Stephen F. Austin State University	850	2,994	500	(409) 568-2403
Sul Ross State University	985	2,860	450	(915) 837-8055
Tarleton State University	1,220	2,930	450	(817) 968-9070
Tarrant County Junior College	330	-	450	(817) 531-4564
Temple Junior College	568	3,000	500	(817) 773-9961
Texas A&M University				
College Station	1,324	3,884	550	(409) 845-8874
Galveston	1,225	3,124	400	(409) 740-4417
Texas Christian University	8,130	3,058	550	(817) 921-7858
Texas College	3,605	2,430	450	(214) 593-8311
Texas Lutheran College	5,870	2,820	450	(512) 372-8075
Texas Southern University	1,030	3,320	500	(713) 527-7600
Texas Southmost College	620	-	350	(512) 544-8277
Texas State Technical Institute				
Amarillo	816	2,780	875	(806) 335-2316
Harlingen	900	3,080	600	(512) 425-0670
Texas Tech University	1,198	3,348	500	(806) 742-3129
Texas Wesleyan College	5,600	3,080	400	(817) 531-4420
Texas Woman's University	1,064	2,882	400	(817) 898-3050
Trinity University	10,340	4,060	400	(512) 736-8315
Trinity Valley Community College	336	2,350	450	(214) 675-6233
Tyler Junior College	470	2,100	500	(214) 531-2385
University of Dallas	8,600	4,170	450	(214) 721-5384
University of Houston				
Clear Lake	1,030	-	550	(713) 488-9240
Houston	1,140	3,770	400	(713) 283-2489
University of Mary Hardin-Baylor	4,450	2,970	450	(817) 939-4518
University of St. Thomas	6,830	3,360	425	(713) 522-7911
University of Texas				
Arlington	1,000	3,564	450	(817) 273-3561
Austin	1,100	3,800	500	(512) 471-4001
Dallas	1,010	-	550	(214) 690-2341

	Tuition and Fees	Room and Board	Books and Supplies	Financial Aid Office
Vernon Regional Junior College	500	3,500	500	(817) 552-6291
Victoria College	390	-	400	(512) 572-6415
Wayland Baptist University	4,137	2,735	475	(806) 296-5521
Weatherford College	450	2,500	450	(817) 594-5471
Western Texas College	540	1,920	400	(915) 573-8511
West Texas State University	1,070	2,794	500	(806) 656-2055
Wharton County Junior College	990	1,900	500	(409) 532-4560

Utah

Brigham Young University	2,000	3,200	600	(801) 378-6433
College of Eastern Utah	1,005	2,400	600	(801) 637-2120
Dixie College	1,156	2,430	400	(801) 673-4811
Salt Lake Community College	1,239	-	500	(801) 967-4291
Snow College	1,005	2,500	400	(801) 283-4021
Stevens-Henager College of Business	7,500	-	500	(801) 394-7791
University of Utah	1,844	3,939	560	(801) 581-6211
Utah State University	1,596	2,590	600	(801) 750-1022
Utah Valley Community College	1,194	-	550	(801) 222-8000
Weber State College	1,398	3,100	450	(801) 626-6581
Westminster College of Salt Lake City	6,540	3,400	500	(801) 488-4106

Vermont

Bennington College	9,400	3,800	400	(802) 442-5401
Burlington College	6,030	-	500	(802) 862-9616
Castleton State College	3,319	4,300	600	(802) 468-5611
Champlain College	6,915	4,945	400	(802) 658-0800
College of St. Joseph in Vermont	6,520	3,840	450	(802) 773-5900
Community College of Vermont	2,010	-	350	(802) 241-3535
Goddard College	12,330	4,120	400	(802) 454-8311
Green Mountain College	7,890	4,880	400	(802) 287-9313
Johnson State College	3,060	4,086	400	(802) 635-2356
Lyndon State College	3,070	4,086	400	(802) 626-9371
Marlboro College	15,390	5,150	400	(802) 257-4333
Norwich University	11,800	4,500	450	(802) 485-2015
St. Michael's College	11,265	5,090	350	(802) 655-2000
School for International Training	9,820	3,585	400	(802) 257-7751
Southern Vermont College	7,430	3,820	500	(802) 442-5427
Sterling College	10,480	4,400	500	(802) 586-7711
Trinity College of Vermont	8,790	4,450	550	(802) 658-0337
University of Vermont	3,670	4,086	600	(802) 656-3156
Vermont Technical College	3,670	4,086	600	(802) 728-3391

Virginia

Averett College	8,750	4,200	350	(804) 791-5645
Bridgewater College	9,195	4,295	475	(703) 828-2501
Central Virginia Community College	858	-	400	(804) 386-4557
Christopher Newport College	2,010	-	350	(804) 594-7227
Clinch Valley College	2,356	3,050	450	(703) 328-0139
College of William and Mary	3,396	3,746	500	(804) 221-2420
Danville Community College	862	-	400	(804) 797-3553

	Tuition and Fees	Room and Board	Books and Supplies	Financial Aid Office
Eastern Mennonite College	7,900	3,300	500	(703) 432-4137
Eastern Shore Community College	873	-	400	(804) 787-3972
Emory and Henry College	7,270	3,956	600	(703) 944-3121
Ferrum College	7,400	3,400	400	(703) 365-4282
George Mason University	2,496	4,470	500	(703) 323-2178
Germanna Community College	867	-	300	(703) 399-1333
Hampton University	6,263	2,723	450	(804) 727-5332
Hollins College	10,810	4,350	400	(703) 362-6332
J. Sargent Reynolds Community College	858	-	400	(804) 371-3137
James Madison University	3,062	3,908	500	(703) 568-6644
John Tyler Community College	858	-	600	(804) 796-4160
Liberty University	5,850	3,700	500	(804) 582-2270
Lynchburg College	10,330	5,050	450	(804) 522-8228
Mary Baldwin College	9,165	6,175	450	(703) 887-7022
Mary Washington College	2,362	3,994	450	(703) 899-4684
Marymount University	9,707	4,650	450	(703) 284-1530
Mountain Empire Community College	875	-	400	(703) 523-2400
Norfolk State University	2,180	3,200	550	(804) 683-8158
Northern Virginia Community College	858	-	480	(703) 323-3199
Old Dominion University	2,510	4,164	400	(804) 683-4504
Patrick Henry Community College	864	-	400	(703) 638-8777
Paul D. Camp Community College	858	-	350	(804) 562-2171
Piedmont Virginia Community College	868	-	350	(804) 977-3900
Radford University	2,178	3,568	400	(703) 831-5408
Randolph-Macon College	10,810	4,600	350	(804) 752-7259
Randolph-Macon Women's College	11,680	5,140	350	(804) 846-9688
Richard Bland College	1,260	-	400	(804) 862-6223
Roanoke College	10,200	3,800	400	(703) 375-2270
St. Paul's College	4,556	3,010	400	(804) 848-3111
Shenandoah College and Conservatory	7,400	3,500	500	(703) 667-8714
Southern Seminary College	6,900	3,000	420	(703) 261-8419
Southside Virginia Community College	864	-	400	(804) 949-7111
Sweet Briar College	12,625	4,850	500	(804) 381-6156
Tidewater Community College	858	-	475	(804) 427-7293
University of Richmond	11,695	2,840	550	(804) 289-8438
University of Virginia	2,966	3,150	500	(804) 924-3725
Virginia Commonwealth University	2,719	3,532	500	(804) 367-9312
Virginia Highlands Community College	858	-	420	(703) 628-6094
Virginia Intermont College	6,570	3,930	400	(703) 669-6101
Virginia Military Institute	3,965	3,525	500	(703) 464-7208
Virginia Polytechnic Institute and State University	2,846	2,672	575	(703) 231-5179
Virginia State University	2,668	3,977	450	(804) 524-5990
Virginia Union University	5,840	3,010	300	(804) 257-5880
Virginia Wesleyan College	8,790	4,425	500	(804) 455-3208

	Tuition and Fees	Room and Board	Books and Supplies	Financial Aid Office
Virginia Western Community College	862	-	450	(703) 982-7331
Washington and Lee University	10,970	3,900	500	(703) 463-8716
Wytheville Community College	1,065	-	500	(703) 228-5541

Washington

Big Bend Community College	945	-	500	(509) 762-6218
Central Washington University	1,698	3,143	450	(509) 963-1611
Centralia College	945	-	425	(206) 736-9391
Clark College	945	-	500	(206) 699-0153
Columbia Basin College	945	-	500	(509) 547-0511
Cornish College of the Arts	7,479	-	1,100	(206) 323-1400
Eastern Washington University	1,698	3,150	500	(509) 359-2314
Edmonds Community College	945	-	550	(206) 771-7457
Everett Community College	945	-	500	(206) 388-9280
Evergreen State College	1,698	3,400	560	(206) 866-6000
Gonzaga University	10,335	3,700	550	(509) 328-4220
Grays Harbor College	945	-	500	(206) 532-9020
Green River Community College	945	-	480	(206) 833-9111
Griffin College	6,400	-	500	(206) 383-2263
Heritage College	4,450	-	500	(509) 865-2244
Highline Community College	945	-	500	(206) 878-3710
Lower Columbia College	945	-	500	(206) 577-2328
Lutheran Bible Institute of Seattle	2,440	3,240	500	(206) 392-0400
North Seattle Community College	945	-	500	(206) 527-3688
Northwest College	5,816	2,900	550	(206) 822-8266
Olympic College	945	-	500	(206) 478-4630
Pacific Lutheran University	11,075	3,890	550	(206) 535-7161
Peninsula College	945	3,050	500	(206) 452-9277
Pierce College	945	-	600	(206) 964-6620
Puget Sound Christian College	4,650	3,000	500	(206) 775-8686
St. Martin's College	9,070	3,500	500	(206) 438-4397
Seattle Central Community College	945	-	600	(206) 587-3888
Seattle Pacific University	10,581	3,699	525	(206) 281-2046
Seattle University	10,710	3,900	500	(206) 626-5841
Shoreline Community College	858	-	500	(206) 546-4762
Skagit Valley College	945	-	500	(206) 428-1191
South Puget Sound Community College	945	-	500	(206) 754-7711
South Seattle Community College	945	-	500	(206) 764-5317
Spokane Community College	945	-	550	(509) 536-8024
Spokane Falls Community College	945	-	550	(509) 459-3229
Tacoma Community College	945	-	530	(206) 756-5080
University of Puget Sound	11,420	3,800	500	(206) 756-3214
University of Washington	2,178	3,510	500	(206) 543-0128
Walla Walla College	9,083	2,955	550	(509) 527-2815
Walla Walla Community College	945	-	500	(509) 527-4301
Washington State University	2,178	3,300	600	(509) 335-9727
Wenatchee Valley College	945	3,400	500	(509) 664-2567
Western Washington University	1,698	3,143	550	(206) 676-3470
Whatcom Community College	945	-	550	(206) 647-3260
Whitman College	13,210	4,340	500	(509) 527-5178
Whitworth College	9,615	3,600	500	(509) 466-3215
Yakima Valley Community College	945	3,450	450	(509) 575-2368

	Tuition and Fees	Room and Board	Books and Supplies	Financial Aid Office
West Virginia				
Alderson-Broaddus College	7,950	2,665	550	(304) 457-1700
Beckley College	3,040	2,500	300	(304) 253-7351
Bethany College	11,650	4,022	400	(304) 829-7631
Bluefield State College	1,316	-	500	(304) 327-4020
Concord College	1,416	-	400	(304) 384-5359
Huntington Junior College of Business	3,600	-	400	(304) 697-7550
Marshall University	1,538	3,436	400	(304) 696-2280
Ohio Valley College	4,650	2,950	350	(304) 485-7384
Potomac State College of West Virginia University	1,256	2,650	400	(304) 788-3011
Salem College	6,740	3,760	400	(304) 782-5205
Shepard College	1,494	3,360	500	(304) 876-2511
Southern West Virginia Community College	844	-	400	(304) 752-4300
University of Charleston	7,950	3,500	400	(304) 357-4760
West Virginia Institute of Technology	1,422	3,250	450	(304) 442-3228
West Virginia State College	1,432	2,800	400	(304) 766-3131
West Virginia University	1,777	3,612	400	(304) 293-5242
West Virginia Wesleyan College	11,830	3,450	450	(304) 473-8080
Wheeling Jesuit College	7,970	3,730	600	(304) 243-2304
Wisconsin				
Alverno College	6,390	2,850	500	(414) 382-6046
Beloit College	13,050	3,300	400	(608) 363-2663
Berlin College of Nursing	5,622	-	500	(414) 433-3562
Blackhawk Technical Institute	1,186	-	400	(608) 757-7716
Cardinal Stritch College	6,960	3,260	500	(414) 352-5400
Carroll College	11,068	3,460	400	(414) 524-7298
Carthage College	10,640	3,350	500	(414) 551-6001
Chippewa Valley Technical College	1,230	-	400	(715) 833-6250
Concordia University Wisconsin	7,400	3,100	450	(414) 243-4347
Edgewood College	6,990	3,330	500	(608) 257-4861
Fox Valley Technical College	1,280	-	500	(414) 735-5720
Gateway Technical College	1,290	-	500	(414) 631-7367
Lakeland College	8,050	3,250	500	(414) 565-1297
Lawrence University	13,710	3,237	450	(414) 832-6583
Madison Area Technical College	1,150	-	550	(608) 266-6625
Marian College of Fond du Lac	7,550	3,500	400	(414) 923-7614
Marquette University	9,034	4,040	550	(414) 288-5261
Mid-State Technical College	1,315	-	600	(715) 422-5504
Milwaukee Area Technical College	1,375	-	600	(414) 278-6279
Milwaukee Institute of Art & Design	7,120	-	900	(414) 276-7889
Milwaukee School of Engineering	9,150	3,225	750	(414) 277-7224
Moraine Park Technical Institute	1,151	-	500	(414) 929-2123
Mount Mary College	6,950	2,460	400	(414) 258-4810
Mount Senario College	6,340	2,625	450	(715) 532-5511
Nicolet Area Technical College	1,390	-	450	(715) 369-4423
North Central Technical College	1,425	2,700	440	(715) 675-3331

	Tuition and Fees	Room and Board	Books and Supplies	Financial Aid Office
Northeast Wisconsin Technical College	1,167	-	540	(414) 498-5612
Northland College	8,380	3,450	400	(715) 682-1255
Northwestern College	3,174	1,770	275	(414) 261-4352
Ripon College	12,900	3,100	400	(414) 748-8101
St. Norbert College	10,225	3,995	450	(414) 337-3071
Silver Lake College	7,480	2,910	450	(414) 684-6418
Southwest Wisconsin Technical College	1,267	-	450	(608) 822-3262
Stratton College	5,470	-	450	(414) 276-5200
University of Wisconsin				
Eau Claire	1,760	2,420	350	(715) 836-3373
Green Bay	1,753	-	450	(414) 465-2075
La Crosse	1,984	2,180	350	(608) 785-8604
Madison	2,107	3,260	450	(608) 263-3202
Milwaukee	2,156	3,190	500	(414) 229-3751
Oshkosh	1,764	1,910	400	(414) 424-3377
Parkside	1,780	3,076	450	(414) 553-2577
Platteville	1,797	2,260	350	(608) 342-1836
River Falls	1,771	2,310	350	(715) 425-3141
Stevens Point	1,813	2,615	350	(715) 346-4771
Stout	1,793	2,300	350	(715) 232-1363
Superior	1,753	2,206	450	(715) 394-8201
Whitewater	1,810	2,150	450	(414) 473-1130
Waukesha County Technical College	1,256	-	600	(414) 691-5221
Western Wisconsin Technical College	1,375	3,300	550	(608) 785-9579
Wisconsin Indianhead Vocational/Technical College	1,239	-	500	(715) 468-2815
Wisconsin Lutheran College	7,578	3,200	500	(414) 774-8620

Wyoming

	Tuition and Fees	Room and Board	Books and Supplies	Financial Aid Office
Casper College	672	2,200	400	(307) 268-2596
Central Wyoming College	652	2,457	400	(307) 856-9291
Eastern Wyoming College	626	200	450	(307) 532-7111
Laramie County Community College	664	-	400	(307) 634-5853
Northwest Community College	808	2,464	500	(307) 754-6158
Sheridan College	688	2,250	420	(307) 674-6446
University of Wyoming	1,200	3,100	400	(307) 766-2118
Western Wyoming Community College	676	2,300	400	(307) 382-1642

INDEX